BRIDGING DIVIDES IN TRANSITIONAL JUSTICE

SERIES ON TRANSITIONAL JUSTICE

The Series on *Transitional Justice* offers a platform for high-quality research within the rapidly growing field of transitional justice. The research is, of necessity inter-disciplinary in nature, drawing from disciplines such as law, political science, history, sociology, criminology, anthropology and psychology, as well as from various specialised fields of study such as human rights, victimology and peace studies. Furthermore, the research is international in outlook, drawing on the knowledge and experience of academics and other specialists in many different regions of the world.

The series is aimed at a variety of audiences who are either working or interested in fields such as crime and justice; human rights; humanitarian law and human security; conflict resolution and peace building. These audiences include academics, researchers, students, policy makers, practitioners, non-governmental organisations and the media.

All books published within the series are subject to a double-blind peer review by recognised authorities in the field.

Published titles within this Series:

9. Edda Kristjánsdóttir, André Nollkaemper and Cedric Ryngaert (eds.), *International Law in Domestic Courts: Rule of Law Reform in Post-conflict States* (2012), 978-1-78068-041-5
10. Bas van Stokkom, Neelke Doorn and Paul van Tongeren (eds.), *Public Forgiveness in Post-Conflict Contexts* (2012), 978-1-78068-044-6
11. Ilse Derluyn, Cindy Mels, Stephan Parmentier and Wouter Vandenhole (eds.), *Re-Member. Rehabilitation, Reintegration and Reconciliation of War-Affected Children* (2012), 97894-000-0027-4
12. Anne-Marie de Brouwer, Charlotte Ku, Renée Römkens and Larissa van den Herik (eds.), *Sexual Violence as an International Crime: Interdisciplinary Approaches* (2012), 978-1-78068-002-6
13. Estelle Zinsstag and Martha Albertson Fineman (eds.), *Feminist Perspectives on Transitional Justice: From International and Criminal to Alternative Forms of Justice* (2013), 978-1-78068-142-9
14. Josep M. Tamarit Sumalla, *Historical Memory and Criminal Justice in Spain. A Case of Late Transitional Justice* (2013), 978-1-78068-143-6
15. Catherine Jenkins (ed.), Max du Plessis (ed.), *Law, Nation building and Transformation The South African experience in perspective* (2014), 978-1-78068-184-9
16. Susanne Buckley-Zistel and Stefanie Schäfer (eds.), *Memorials in Times of Transition* (2014), 978-1-78068-211-2
17. Nico Wouters (ed.), *Transitional Justice and Memory in Europe (1945–2013)*, 978-1-78068-214-3
18. Agata Fijalkowski and Raluca Grosescu (eds.), *Transitional Criminal Justice in Post-Dictatorial and Post-Conflict Societies*, 978-1-78068-260-0
19. S. Elizabeth Bird and Fraser M. Ottanelli (eds.), *The Performance of Memory as Transitional Justice* 978-1-78068-262-4
20. Bo Viktor Nylund, *Child Soldiers and Transitional Justice*, 978-1-78068-394-2
21. Peter Malcontent (ed.), *Facing the Past: Amending Historical Injustices through Instruments of Transitional Justice*, 978-1-78068-403-1
22. Francesca Capone, *Reparations for Child Victims of Armed Conflict: State of the Field and Current Challenges*, 978-1-78068-438-3

For previous volumes in the series, please visit http://tj.intersentia.com

Series on Transitional Justice, Volume 23

BRIDGING DIVIDES IN TRANSITIONAL JUSTICE

The Extraordinary Chambers in the Courts of Cambodia

Cheryl S. White

intersentia
Cambridge – Antwerp – Portland

Intersentia Ltd
Sheraton House | Castle Park
Cambridge | CB3 0AX | United Kingdom
Tel.: +44 1223 370 170 | Fax: +44 1223 370 169
Email: mail@intersentia.co.uk
www.intersentia.com | www.intersentia.co.uk

Distribution for the UK and Ireland:
NBN International
Airport Business Centre, 10 Thornbury Road
Plymouth, PL6 7 PP
United Kingdom
Tel.: +44 1752 202 301 | Fax: +44 1752 202 331
Email: orders@nbninternational.com

Distribution for Europe and all other countries:
Intersentia Publishing nv
Groenstraat 31
2640 Mortsel
Belgium
Tel.: +32 3 680 15 50 | Fax: +32 3 658 71 21
Email: mail@intersentia.be

Distribution for the USA and Canada:
International Specialized Book Services
920 NE 58th Ave. Suite 300
Portland, OR 97213
USA
Tel.: +1 800 944 6190 (toll free) | Fax: +1 503 280 8832
Email: info@isbs.com

Bridging Divides in Transitional Justice

Artwork on cover: Author Jan Jordaan, title 'Hurt', medium Linocut, 1999.
From the Universal Declaration of Human Rights – International Print Portfolio,
Article 5, published by Art for Humanity, South Africa, 1999.

ISBN 978-1-78068-440-6
D/2017/7849/29
NUR 828

GPRC
Guaranteed
Peer Reviewed
Content

British Library Cataloguing in Publication Data. A catalogue record for this book is available from the British Library.

ACKNOWLEDGEMENTS

This book is derived from a PhD thesis produced at the Australian National University from 2009 to 2014. I am indebted to my supervisor, Hilary Charlesworth, for her patient assistance during my candidature and advice upon completion. My examiners, Suzannah Linton, Kieran McEvoy and Sarah Williams were also the source of thoughtful scholarly guidance on the future directions of the work.

I am grateful to have been able to revise the manuscript at the ANU's School of Regulation and Global Governance (RegNet) and to enjoy the collegiality for which it is well known. Special thanks are due to Imelda Deinla and Emma Larking for their mentoring, insights and invaluable practical assistance as I undertook that task. Romina Paskotic and Julia Wee also provided essential administrative and moral support.

I would also like to acknowledge the help and encouragement of my teaching colleagues at the University of Newcastle, School of Law in Australia. I am grateful to those who listened to my initial ideas and encouraged me to take them further, especially Ted Wright, Neil Foster, Amy Maguire, Jeff McGee and Brendan Murphy.

The criminal trial as a transitional justice mechanism may be construed narrowly or broadly. In this book I take a broad approach to trial justice and try to address the various internal and external factors that may have an impact on the proceedings of an active internationalised court. To this end I have made extensive use of ECCC court documents including trial transcripts. Some of the English translations of the transcripts were poor, and for this reason the excerpts in the book were edited for the sake of clarity while retaining any cultural nuance as much as possible. Of course, all errors remain my own.

The editorial team at Intersentia gave wonderful support to this project. I thank Melanie Hamill and Tom Schiers in particular for their forbearance as I included new material at the final hour on the appeal judgment concluding the ECCC's second trial.

I also thank my family for quietly supporting me in the venture and dedicate the book to my late father James Henry White. Finally, in this work as in all the challenges of my life, God has given me strength and for that I am eternally grateful.

January 2017

CONTENTS

TABLE OF CASES

INTERNATIONAL COURTS

EUROPEAN COURT OF HUMAN RIGHTS

INTERNATIONAL COURT OF JUSTICE

INTERNATIONAL CRIMINAL COURT

INTERNATIONAL CRIMINAL TRIBUNAL FOR THE FORMER YUGOSLAVIA

INTERNATIONAL CRIMINAL TRIBUNAL FOR RWANDA

INTERNATIONAL MILITARY TRIBUNAL AT NUREMBURG

UNITED NATIONS HUMAN RIGHTS COMMITTEE

HYBRID AND INTERNATIONALISED COURTS

EXTRAORDINARY CHAMBERS IN THE COURTS OF CAMBODIA

SPECIAL COURT FOR SIERRA LEONE

SPECIAL TRIBUNAL FOR LEBANON

TABLE OF LEGISLATION

INTERNATIONAL

NATIONAL

CAMBODIA

SIERRA LEONE

KOSOVO

TABLE OF TREATIES

LIST OF ABBREVIATIONS

CGDK	Coalition Government of Democratic Kampuchea
CPK	Communist Party of Kampuchea
CPP	Cambodian People's Party
ECCC	Extraordinary Chambers in the Courts of Cambodia
FUNCINPEC	*Front uni national pour un Cambodge Indépendant, Neutre, Pacifique et Coopératif*
ICC	International Criminal Court
ICTR	International Criminal Tribunal for Rwanda
ICTY	International Criminal Tribunal for the Former Yugoslavia
ILM	International Legal Materials
IMT	International Military Tribunal
KPLNF	Khmer People's National Liberation Front
KPRP	Khmer People's Revolutionary Party
PDK	Party of Democratic Kampuchea
PRK	People's Republic of Kampuchea
PRT	The People's Revolutionary Tribunal
SCC	Supreme Court Chamber
SCSL	Special Court for Sierra Leone
SOC	State of Cambodia
STL	Special Tribunal for Lebanon
UNGA	United Nations General Assembly
UNSC	United Nations Security Council
UNTS	United Nations Treaty Series
UNTAC	United Nations Transitional Administration in Cambodia
UNMIK	United Nations Transitional Interim Administration in Kosovo
UNTAET	United Nations Transitional Administration in East Timor
VCLT	Vienna Convention on the Law of Treaties

CHAPTER 1
INTRODUCTION

1.1. EXPRESSIVISM AND COMMUNICATION IN TRANSITIONAL TRIALS

> Don't be afraid of death – just tell the truth! We reconstructed ourselves for the revolution, now we must change for humanitarian reasons – more than a million people died at the hand of the CPK.[1]

The appeal above by the accused to a witness in the first trial at the Extraordinary Chambers in the Courts of Cambodia (ECCC) in 2009 was communication of a kind rarely analysed in internationalised criminal justice literature. It captured the communicative nature of the trial proceedings, whereby witnesses or civil parties and accused persons were able to engage in mediated dialogue, leading to exchanges that produced greater understanding and meaning. Attention to the communicative dynamics of transitional trials contrasts with accounts of international proceedings as being concerned primarily with reflecting the development and enforcement of international norms, or demonstrating due process standards which promote the rule of law in societies recovering from atrocity crimes. In other words, the expressive value of transitional trials for the purposes of post-conflict nation building is usually highlighted rather than the communicative power of trials resonant with deeper social imperatives.

This book engages with the dissonance in transitional justice between the expressivism of internationalised criminal trials and their communicative value within the societies most affected by their operation. Using the proceedings of the Extraordinary Chambers in the Courts of Cambodia as a case study, it elucidates the limits of expressivism and proffers an alternative, or at least complimentary, theory of the transitional trial based on communication.

---

1 CPK refers to the Communist Party of Kampuchea, the organisation behind the Khmer Rouge regime in Cambodia from 17 April 1975 to 6 January 1979. Transcript of Trial Proceedings – *Kaing Guek Eav 'Duch'* (Case File No. 001/18-07-2007-ECCC/TC, Day 45, 15 July 2009) p. 64; See also LAURA MACDONALD, 'After Two Days of Questionable Witness Testimony, Duch Lectured his Former Subordinate – "Just Tell the Truth"', *Cambodia Tribunal Monitor* (15 July 2009).

In the Western criminal justice tradition, expressivism is concerned with the publicly constructed meaning of a trial.[2] Meaning derives from the authority of the prosecuting institution as it enforces norms and ritually engages the mechanism of sentencing or acquittal as the direct outcome of formal criminal procedure.[3] In the transitional justice context, the court's demonstration of due process standards is designed to reflect a model of justice for a society recovering from international crimes formerly perpetrated with impunity.[4] Within trials, the expressivism of the norm of accountability and the international rule of law has taken precedence over provision for the transitioning society's engagement with its history of large-scale violence within the sanctity of a court of justice. This is not to suggest that transitional justice can be confined to a courtroom, but rather that more can be contributed by trials to the long-term process of recovery from mass atrocity than has been recognised in the literature, or until recently, tested in transitional courts.

Moreover, the limits of expressivism suggest the need for a different conception of the transitional trial to aid deliberative recovery from past violence. In this, the work of theorists Mark Osiel and Frédéric Mégret provides some theoretical foundation for the communicative trial through emphasis on the value of discursive and more representative transitional trials.[5] Communicative theory is also grounded in developments in human rights law and the evolution of victim participation rights in international criminal justice.[6] In addition, this study of the modified inquisitorial trial procedure of the ECCC with its less restrictive approach to testimony reveals the feasibility of more discursive proceedings than we normally see at the international level.

Engaging a communicative theory of trials involves a change in emphasis from the direct outcomes of trials to the trial process. The word 'communicative' implies a readiness to impart ideas/information and willingness to engage with another. A communicative theory embraces a measure of discussion in trials under conditions of truth-telling within the criminal process not strictly limited to factual proof, but extending to causation and the consequences of crimes. Communicative trials adapt trial procedure to produce representative and

---

2 Elizabeth Anderson and Richard H. Pildes, 'Expressive Theories of Law: A General Restatement' (1999–2000) 148 *University of Pennsylvania Law Review* 1503, 1544.

3 Joel Feinberg, 'The Expressive Function of Punishment' (1965) 49 *The Monist* 397, 400; R.D. Sloan, 'The Expressive Capacity of International Punishment: The Limits of the National Law Analogy and the Potential of International Criminal Law' (2007) 43 *Stanford Journal of International Law* 39, 69, 71.

4 Ruti G. Teitel, *Transitional Justice* (Oxford University Press, 2000) p. 6.

5 Mark Osiel, *Mass Atrocity, Collective Memory and the Law* (Transaction Publishers, 1997); Frédéric Mégret, 'In Defence of Hybridity: Towards a Representational Theory of International Criminal Justice' (2005) 38 *Cornell International Law Journal* 725.

6 Göran Sluiter et al., *International Criminal Procedure: Principles and Rules* (Oxford University Press, 2013) pp. 1349–1350.

discursive proceedings that accommodate divergent views within the bounds of due process principles. Representation within trials is made possible by including the voices of members of constituencies with a legitimate interest in the subject-matter of the proceedings. This includes victims of crimes, as well as national and international trial actors. Discursive proceedings permit the airing of opposing views of the crimes with scope for deliberation on those views.

The justice forum is mediated by flexible rules of procedure applied by a judiciary imbued not only with retributive purpose, but also the court's reconciliatory role within the subject society. Accordingly, judges apply a broader procedural brush to facilitate discursive proceedings that find resonance in the wider community. While the expressivism of sentencing subsists in the communicative trial, discursive proceedings will have indirect outcomes which manifest themselves in both the immediate and longer term as the messages of the trial process resonate with live debates within the transitioning society and beyond.

A communicative theory of trials challenges the view within transitional justice scholarship that trials largely address the demand for accountability, and that non-judicial and restorative justice mechanisms tackle other significant justice issues in post-conflict contexts.[7] Uncovering patterns of criminality through factual or forensic truth provides some recognition of the past by individuals or groups in society.[8] However, as the South African Truth and Reconciliation Commission noted in its 1998 report, the complex, multi-faceted nature of truth includes 'the social or dialogic truth, established through interaction, discussion and debate.'[9] Expanding the theoretical framework of accountability to better understand the nature of atrocity crimes and their consequences through facilitated trial dialogue may connect trial processes with broader social needs. Perhaps unexpectedly, this is already occurring as international courts wrestle with the multiple goals assigned to them.

1.2. THE GOALS OF INTERNATIONAL TRIBUNALS

In a report in 2004, the UN Secretary-General canvassed the broad goals of international tribunals: criminal justice for those responsible for violations

---

7 Stephan Parmentier and Elmar G.M. Weitekamp, 'Political Crimes and Serious Violations of Human Rights: Towards a Criminology of International Crimes' in Stephan Parmentier and Elmar G.M Weitekamp (eds.), *Crime and Human Rights* (Elsevier Ltd, 2007) pp. 109, 130–132; Mark A. Drumbl, *Atrocity Punishment and International Law* (Cambridge University Press, 2007) pp. 3–5.

8 Ibid (Parmentier), p. 132.

9 *Truth and Reconciliation Commission of South Africa Report*, (1998) Vol. 1, p. 113, citing Albie Sachs, in Alex Boraine and Janet Levy (eds.), *The Healing of a Nation?* (Justice in Transition, 1995), p. 105.

of human rights and international humanitarian law; ending such violations and preventing their recurrence; securing justice and dignity for the victims; establishing a record of past events; promoting national reconciliation; re-establishing the rule of law and contributing to the restoration of peace in transitional contexts.[10] In practice, courts have narrowed their focus to four objectives summarised as follows:

1. Restoring international peace and security.
2. Strengthening human rights and international humanitarian law protections prospectively.
3. Punishing perpetrators of international crimes.
4. Creating a historical record of atrocities.[11]

While the shortened list represents judicial agreement as to the 'outer contours' of the goals, it does not reflect agreement as to the respective priority of individual goals within particular courts or the rationales underpinning them.[12] There is vigorous disagreement, for instance, over the goal of creating a historical record because giving priority or equal weight to the goal may overburden and significantly delay complex legal proceedings.[13] Establishing the historical context and record of crimes has involved courts in amassing and organising many volumes of evidence for use not only for trial purposes but for historians and the public alike. While broad contextual and historical evidence may be necessary in establishing the essential elements of crimes, the Court may also consider material well beyond that crucial to securing a conviction.[14] This may then conflict with the culture of procedural fairness that has become the cornerstone of international criminal justice.[15] However, fairness is difficult to measure in contexts where international courts must fulfil retributive aims of criminal justice and consider notions of justice recognising restorative concerns between victims, offenders and communities.[16]

Securing justice for victims of crimes and respecting their rights under human rights instruments has found expression in the statutes of a number of internationalised courts. The International Criminal Court (ICC), the Special Tribunal for Lebanon (STL) and the ECCC have introduced customised

10 *The Rule of Law and Transitional Justice in Conflict and Post-conflict Societies: Report of the Secretary General* UN Doc. S/2004/616 (23 August 2004) para. 38.

11 Sluiter, above n. 6, p. 56.

12 Ibid.

13 Ibid. p. 60.

14 Sluiter, above n. 6, p. 60.

15 Carsten Stahn, 'Between Faith and Facts: By What Standards Should We Assess International Criminal Justice?' (2012) 25 *Leiden Journal of International Criminal Justice* 252, 267.

16 Ibid.

victim participation schemes to give effect to such rights and take account of victims' justice interests. However, the schemes raised fair trial concerns, as the respective Courts confronted problems associated with their implementation. Some commentators argued that the rights of the accused as the historical bulwark of the criminal trial should not be diluted in international criminal proceedings by undue competition with the rights of victims as participants in or parties to trials.[17] Although noting the distinctive nature of criminal proceedings, others raised the social significance of victim inclusion in trial proceedings and highlighted the need for complementary linkages to restorative justice processes to serve the wider justice goal of building the peace within transitional societies.[18] Through comparative procedural analysis, other scholars examined the scope for transitional trials to be effectively both retributive and restorative.[19] In addition, some scholars argued for more direct restorative justice elements in international courts to both address the articulated goals of international criminal justice, and take proceedings beyond mere idealism and didactic function.[20]

Restorative justice processes involve structured settings for mediated engagement between wrongdoers, their victims and others harmed by the offences in question. Forms of restorative justice have been implemented with success, albeit on the fringes of domestic criminal process in various American States, Australia, Canada and New Zealand.[21] Bibas and Burke-White argued that more substantive integration of such mechanisms in international trial proceedings may enhance the quality of justice, and address the goals of international trials more explicitly. Giving voice to victims in trial proceedings empowers the formerly disempowered and 'takes their needs and views seriously.'[22] Engagements between victims and perpetrators may also take the parties constructively beyond the priority of retribution and tap into local culture and justice traditions more acutely, even precipitating movement towards

---

17 Salvatore Zappalà, 'The Rights of Victims v the Rights of the Accused' (2010) 8 *Journal of International Criminal Justice* 137, 143–145.

18 Donald Hafner and Elizabeth King, 'Beyond Traditional Notions of Transitional Justice: How Trials, Truth Commissions and other Tools for Accountability Can and Should Work Together' (2007) 30 *Boston College of International & Comparative Law Review* 91, 93–109; Jeremy Sarkin, 'Enhancing the Legitimacy, Status, and Role of the International Criminal Court Globally by Using Transitional Justice or Restorative Justice Strategies' (2012) *Interdisciplinary Journal of Human Rights Law* 84, 93–100.

19 Sluiter, above n, 6, pp. 1337–1371.

20 Stephanos Bibas and William A. Burke-White, 'International Idealism Meets Domestic Criminal Procedure Realism' (2010) 59 *Duke Law Journal* 637; M. Findlay and M. Henham, *Transforming International Criminal Justice: Retributive and Restorative Justice in the Trial Process* (Willan Publishing, Portland OR, 2005) pp. 273–359.

21 See Lawrence Sherman and Heather Strang, *Restorative Justice: The Evidence* (Smith Institute, London, 2007).

22 Bibas above n. 20, p. 689.

forgiveness, especially in cases of the assumption of guilt.[23] This emphasis aligns well with inter-disciplinary research which recognises that the participation of stakeholders through multi-dimensional restorative processes can result in deeper, more meaningful justice over the long durée of recovery from mass violence.[24]

In debate over the compatibility of the justice goals some theorists have argued that the aims of domestic criminal law transposed to the international context should operate unrestrained by other justice aims, with expeditious, cost-effective proceedings for a small number of defendants the chief priority.[25] However, in situations of mass atrocity 'uncertainty is the horrible norm' and the magnitude of crimes creates a pressing need to establish the truth about what happened and who is responsible.[26] Some scholarship highlights the fact that the aims of international criminal justice take account of the context-specific timeframes of transitional justice proceedings.[27] In the direct aftermath of conflict, swift, clinical trials of leading perpetrators of the former repressive regime may meet immediate accountability demands and promote the rule of law in the affected society. Where trials are held decades after the commission of atrocities and following uneasy transitions characterised by the prevalence of impunity for perpetrators, the historical record may carry as much weight as due process and retribution.[28] In the Cambodian situation, for instance, the impediments to a proper reckoning with the past, massive victim toll and wide-ranging social impacts of the Khmer Rouge regime, evident more than 30 years after the events meant that establishing an authoritative record of the crimes was as significant to the population as the convictions of a few high-level perpetrators.[29]

---

23 Ibid. pp. 688–689.

24 Ray Nickson and John Braithwaite, 'Deeper, Broader, Longer Transitional Justice' (2013) 11 *European Journal of Criminology* 445, 449–463.

25 Iain Bonomy, 'The Reality of Conducting War Crimes Trial' (2007) 5 *Journal of International Criminal Justice* 348, 353; O-Gon Kwon, 'The Challenge of an International Criminal Trial as seen from the Bench' (2007) 5 *Journal of International Criminal Justice* 360, 362.

26 Jean Galbraith, 'The Pace of International Criminal Justice' (2009) 31 *Michigan Journal of International Law* 79, 89.

27 Ibid. pp. 103–108; A. Whiting, 'International Criminal Prosecutions, Justice Delayed can be Justice Delivered' (2009) *Harvard International Law Journal* 323, 327–328 arguing that time and distance from the perpetration of crimes may improve justice outcomes; And see Susanne Karstedt, 'The Nuremburg Trial and German Society: International Justice and Local Judgement in Post-Conflict Reconstruction' in David A. Blumenthal and Timothy L.H. McCormack (eds.), *The Legacy of Nuremburg: Civilising Influence or Institutionalised Vengeance?* (Martinus Nijhoff Publishers, 2008) p. 13, pp. 33–34 noting the timing of the Auschwitz and Majdanak trials decades after the war as determining their positive reception.

28 Galbraith, above n. 26, pp. 104–109.

29 Suzannah Linton, *Reconciliation in Cambodia* (Documentation Center of Cambodia, 2004) pp. 60–61.

Tensions as to the appropriate aims and priorities of international criminal proceedings also arise as a result of their selectivity in prosecution, complexity, duration and financial cost.[30] Over time these factors may result in internal reviews of court operations and various modifications in trial procedure. The ECCC, for instance, restricted 'civil party' participation rights for its second trial in the interests of more expeditious trials, but at the same time expanded the reparations scheme. At the ICC, scepticism as to the viability of prosecutions in light of recurrent difficulties in securing the custody of indictees, problems in establishing accurate facts in cases, and the overall costs of running the Court for a select few threatened to undermine the value of the institution.[31] In light of this, Amoury Combs advocated the suspension of prosecutions and diversion of the Court's primary resources towards the restorative mandate of reparations.[32]

The growing demands on the particular Court and the context in which it operates will also result in certain adaptations. At the ICC (a permanent international justice mechanism operating at a distance from the societies suffering the effects of mass crimes) appropriate resourcing and prioritisation are imperative to ensure the continuance of the institution. In hybrid *in situ* transitional courts, different factors may impinge upon the effectiveness of the institution. The East Timorese Panels and the ECCC, for instance, have had to deal with opposition to some of their processes from local political authorities.

However, the tensions that arise as to the respective goals and factors impacting on the operations of international courts may detract from their achievements. These achievements are not limited to the increasing number of convictions for international crimes, but extend to their engagement initiatives with communities affected by the crimes prosecuted. International courts now have a growing track record of initiating projects designed to link affected local communities to the respective Courts which may also catalyse dialogue around the commission of the crimes.[33] Outreach programmes are integral units within

30 Payam Akhavan, 'The Rise, and Fall, and Rise, of International Criminal Justice' (2013) 11 *Journal of International Criminal Justice* 527, 534–535.

31 Nancy Amoury Combs, 'From Prosecutorial to Reparatory: A Valuable Post-Conflict Change of Focus' (2015) 36 *Michigan Journal of International Law* 219, 234–238.

32 Ibid. pp. 239–243, 262–275.

33 Peter Pham, 'A Viable Model for International Criminal Justice: The Special Court for Sierra Leone' (2006) 19 *New York International Law Review* 37, 104–107; International Federation for Human Rights (FIDH), *Five Myths about Victim Participation in ICC Proceedings* (FIDH, December 2014) pp. 14–18; Sarah Williams and Emma Palmer, 'Transformative Reparations for Women and Girls at the Extraordinary Chambers in the Courts of Cambodia' (2016) 10 *International Journal of Transitional Justice* 1, 18–19; Heather Ryan and Laura McGrew, *Performance and Perception: the Impact of the Extraordinary Chambers in the Courts of Cambodia* (Open Society Justice Initiative, 2016) pp. 33–34, 40–51; Human Rights Center, University of California, Berkeley, *The Victims' Court: A Study of 622 Victim Participants at the International Criminal Court*, (UC, Berkeley, 2015) pp. 32–33, 72–74.

international courts. Civil society groups monitor trial proceedings and use their social networks to connect victims of crimes to court processes. Where the Courts have instituted victim participation schemes, more people are brought into direct contact with the court. Victim participants become 'ambassadors' within their communities and extend knowledge on the work of the court.[34] Victim participation schemes produce more representative proceedings and some courts have adopted criminal procedure which has enhanced the communicative capacity of their trials.

1.3. COMMUNICATION AND TRIAL PROCEDURE

Creating space for dialogue within the transitional trial entails engaging with the concepts and principles underpinning criminal law procedure. The criminal trial adheres to rules respecting the norms of liberal legality, pursuant to which the defendant citizen is protected against the more powerful state through fair trial conventions.[35] The principles of procedural fairness and individual responsibility operate as conditions to criminal liability.[36]

The concept of due process derived from national criminal law and extended to international criminal proceedings has attained the status of universal principle.[37] Due process ensures procedural protections for defendants contained in binding customary and treaty-based international law, including the International Covenant on Civil and Political Rights (ICCPR).[38] Broadly, this law establishes minimum guarantees of fair trial to accused persons. The ICCPR for instance, provides, *inter alia*, for defendants to be promptly informed of any charges against them upon arrest; their right to trial within a reasonable time or to release; the right to adequate time and facilities to prepare their defence and communicate with counsel of their own choosing; their right to be presumed innocent and the right to trial without undue delay.[39]

While not enunciated specifically in human rights instruments, the principle of equality of arms observed in criminal proceedings is an important component of due process.[40] However, the operation of the principle to ensure procedural equality between the prosecution and the defence at the national level has required new interpretation in international proceedings. This is because

34 Ibid. (Ryan) p. 41.

35 Brianne McGonigle Leyh, *Procedural Justice? Victim Participation in International Criminal Proceedings* (Intersentia, 2011) p. 13.

36 Osiel, above n. 5, p. 69.

37 Sluiter, above n. 6, p. 63; *International Covenant on Civil and Political Rights*, opened for signature 16 December 1966, 999 UNTS 171 (entered into force 23 March 1976) [ICCPR].

38 Ibid.

39 Arts. 9, 14 ICCPR.

40 Sluiter, above n. 6, p. 64.

international proceedings have admitted new parties, or participants with rights which may conflict with those of the prosecution or defence.

As noted earlier, some international courts have established victim participation schemes which afford certain procedural rights to victims of crimes. Arguments on normative grounds have been raised over the capacity of courts to accommodate new voices in trial proceedings, despite the existence of substantive provisions on victims' rights in the ICC and STL Statutes, and the ECCC's constitutive instruments.[41] While the demand for victim participation in international proceedings may exceed a court's capacity to meet it, procedural adaptation to ensure representative participation does not necessarily conflict with liberal legality. Rather, expanded representation by inclusion of the victim voice may foster respect for basic individual rights, deliberative capacity and tolerance within fledgling democracies. It should be remembered, however, that complete coherence in legal process is neither expected nor fully achieved at the national level.[42] Given the larger purposes of international justice, to proceed with too much idealism may be to be to invite disappointment. A better view is that the procedural framework which already harnesses unselfconsciously the narrative tropes of the prosecution, defence and judiciary need not be undone by the equitable inclusion of another player in the drama of the trial.[43] Procedural adaptations will depend for their particulars on the form of the relevant court and take account of the specific transitional context it is addressing.

Consideration of a communicative theory of trials also involves investigating the procedural models conducive to the expansion of trial dialogue for the social purposes of transitional justice. International criminal trials have engaged predominantly adversarial criminal procedure. The adversarial model of procedure of common law systems features impartial adjudication, formal procedural rules and party control over the proceedings through partisan advocacy.[44] Adversarial trial proceedings take the form of a contest or dispute which unfolds as two adversaries present their cases and challenge their opponent's view of the case before a 'relatively passive decision maker whose principal duty is to reach a verdict.'[45] The structure of the trial is that of a clash between advocates – one prosecuting and the other defending the accused party.[46] The truth-finding process is also dualistic, but subject to judicial

41 McGonigle Leyh above n. 35, pp. 307–328; Christine Chung, 'Victims' Participation at the International Criminal Court: Are Concessions of the Court Clouding the Promise?' (2008) 6 *Northwestern Journal of International Human Rights* 459, 523–542.

42 Osiel, above n. 5, p. 67; And see Immi Tallgren, 'The Sense and Sensibility of International Criminal Law' (2002) 13 *European Journal of International Law* 561, 567.

43 Ibid. (Osiel) n. 5, p. 73.

44 David Luban, *Lawyers and Justice: An Ethical Study* (Princeton University Press, 1988) p. 58.

45 Mirjan Damaska, *The Faces of Justice and State Authority: A Comparative Approach to Legal Process* (Yale University Press, 1986) p. 3.

46 McGonigle Leyh, above n. 35, p. 74.

reasoning and the elimination of reasonable doubt.[47] The inclusion in the procedure of other parties not called for the purposes of either advocate poses normative and practical problems due to the construction of the trial as a battle between two sides only.[48]

Some internationalised transitional trials have engaged the inquisitorial criminal procedure of national civil law legal systems. Inquisitorial proceedings are not contests but judicially led investigative actions. Judicial officers, as state authorities, control the pre-trial investigation and trial proceedings to faithfully uncover the truth as to what happened.[49] Objectivity in the pursuit of the truth requires judicial investigation of inculpatory and exculpatory evidence.[50] There is an emphasis on narrative testimony which is unrehearsed and not rigidly constrained by inflexible procedural rules. Witnesses, victims and the accused may speak in narrative form and victims may have legal status beyond that of witness only. Narrative testimony and victim rights present fewer structural and normative challenges to proceedings controlled by inquisitorial judges and in which counsel for the prosecution, defence and victims have subordinate roles.[51]

Do either of these procedural models provide a sound theoretical basis for the transitional trial and a framework for wider trial discourse with constructive social impact? Engaging with this question, this book examines the international courts created since the end of the Second World War and evaluates them in terms of their communicative as opposed to expressive value. I note the legal distinction between international, internationalised and hybrid courts in Chapter three, but otherwise use both terms to refer to Courts composed of international elements created to address crimes of mass atrocity. The focus of the book narrows to a case study of the ECCC. Notwithstanding the politically vexed context in which the ECCC operates, I argue that the particular features of the ECCC's trial procedure and the Court's adaptation to its context have yielded more communicative trials with evident social benefits.

1.4. THE ECCC AS A CASE STUDY

Cambodia may be categorised as an uneasily transitioning society.[52] The context of creation of the ECCC and the ongoing political flux that surrounds the Court

---

47 Tom Decaigny and Paul de Hert, 'You Can Change Your Hair Colour, But Not Your Hair: Convergence in Inquisitorial and Adversarial Systems' in C. Kelk, F. Koenraadt and D. Siegel (eds.), *Veelzijdige gedachten. Liber amicorum Prof.Chrisje Brants*, Vol. 75 Willem Pompe Series (Willem Pompe Institute for Criminal Law, 2013) pp. 235, 239–240.

48 Jonathan Doak, 'Victims' Rights in Criminal Trials: Prospects for Participation' (2005) 32 *Journal of Law and Society* 294, 296.

49 Decaigny, above n. 47, p. 239.

50 McGonigle, above n. 35, p. 71.

51 Ibid. p. 73.

52 Galbraith, above n. 26, pp. 104–109.

are integral elements of the case study of this book. Cambodian independence in 1953 brought fierce political rivalry between national political parties and armed conflict in Cambodia for more than two decades. Amidst war to end colonialism in Indochina, the dissident Khmer Rouge, fearing Vietnamese territorial encroachment, broke with its former comrades in arms to bring radical communist revolution to Cambodia from 1975–1979. Their deconstruction of the society under the invisible, all-knowing organisation, Angkar, disconnected individuals, families and communities from their traditional social underpinnings. After the Khmer Rouge regime was ousted by the Vietnamese in 1979, a proxy war in Cambodia, instigated by foreign powers, from 1979–1989, inhibited any true reconciliation or open public discourse on the Khmer Rouge era. The Khmer Rouge was able to re-group during this time and for another decade influenced the Cambodian political agenda. The Khmer Rouge era was erased from school curricula and forgetting the past became the political mantra of reconciliation for a society deprived of voice, rights and memory.[53]

The longevity of the Khmer Rouge entrenched a culture of impunity in Cambodia and shaped the negotiations for the Agreement between the Royal Government of Cambodia and the United Nations to create the ECCC.[54] The Cambodian government insisted on locating the ECCC in Cambodia within the national court system, and majority control of the operations of the Court. The UN negotiators assumed a risk in agreeing to a reduction in international control of the ECCC under a Cambodian enabling law. Paradoxically, the timing of the trials three decades after the regime fell, the ECCC's *in situ* location and the Court's idiosyncratic features combined to produce an appropriate justice mechanism for Cambodia.

The fusion of Cambodian inquisitorial procedure with elements of international criminal procedure is a major feature of the controversial and unorthodox internationalised court. The case study highlights the communicative nature of the Court's procedure, including its specific hybrid nature and victim participation and reparations schemes. The study includes detailed examination of the proceedings of the ECCC's first trial, the *Duch* case, and its aftermath. The Duch trial material is drawn from witness and civil party testimony with subsequent examination by the Judges, the Co-Prosecution and Co-Defence counsel. There is also analysis of the *Duch* trial judgments. The coverage of Case 002 includes discussion of the nature of the proceedings in the severed trials (Case 002/01 and Case 002/02) following the overhaul of the civil party participation and reparations schemes. The analysis draws from trial transcripts of civil party 'statements of suffering' and the victim impact hearings convened

53 Linton, above n. 29, pp. 60–61.

54 *Agreement between the United Nations and the Royal Government of Cambodia Concerning the Prosecution under Cambodian Law of Crimes Committed During the Period of Democratic Kampuchea* signed 6 June 2003, ratified 19 October 2004.

by the Court. The Trial Chamber judgment and the defence appeals against the convictions of Nuon Chea and Khieu Samphân in Case 002/01 are also discussed in connection with the appeal judgment of the Supreme Court Chamber (SCC).

The study aimed to test the discursive capacity of the internationalised transitional trial. While the legitimacy of Courts and fairness in retributive proceedings are to be guarded, can activation of underlying communicative dynamics within trials reduce divides in transitional justice so as to more directly aid social recovery from international crimes? The methodology is interpretive analysis of trial transcripts, court decisions and constitutive documents, court monitor reports and other secondary source materials across the transitional justice field. It includes findings of various ECCC population perception surveys conducted before and after the trials, and surveys of civil party participants in Case 001 and Case 002/01.

1.5. CHAPTER OUTLINE

Chapter one discussed the assignment of multiple and arguably incompatible goals to the international tribunals that have been created in the post-Cold War era. While the new institutions brought the expressive value of the national criminal trial to the international arena to address impunity for mass crimes, their trial processes may be dissonant within affected societies. What can be learned from the procedural approaches of transitional courts that might bring local legitimacy?

Chapter two interrogates the notion of expressivism as the theoretical basis of the transitional trial. It highlights the ambiguous nature of expressivism through a review of criminal law and interdisciplinary literature. The limits of expressivism in international criminal justice are raised before an alternative theory of the transitional trial is proposed, utilising the lens of communication. From the work of theorists Mark Osiel and Frédéric Mégret two key elements of communicative trials emerge: discursivity and representation in trial proceedings. By discursivity, I mean dialogue in trial proceedings going to the social context and consequences of the crimes prosecuted.

In Chapter three the analysis of expressivism is extended to the political actions of creating international transitional courts. In the post-Cold War era the transitional trial exhibited expressive value as the two ad hoc Tribunals created by the UN Security Council prosecuted perpetrators of international crimes in the Balkans and Rwanda. However, the societies most affected by these crimes were largely remote from the processes of those trials. Later transitional trial models gradually incorporated features to enhance communication between the courts and the societies affected by the crimes, suggesting the possibility of evaluating trials from a communicative as well as an expressive basis.

Chapter four describes the political culture of Cambodia and the nature of the Khmer Rouge regime. The regime escaped international judicial scrutiny for more than two decades after the leadership was ousted by the Vietnamese invasion in January 1979. The chapter also discusses the deprivation of rights suffered by the Cambodian people in the decades following the regime, and the successor governments' policies of reconciliation by forgetting, to underscore the significance of the communicative trial in Cambodia. A politically tortuous road led to the negotiation of an agreement with the United Nations to create an internationalised transitional court in Cambodia to end the impunity of those most responsible for Khmer Rouge crimes. While the UN sought cost-effective, expeditious trials meeting minimum international standards of justice for the surviving key leaders and major perpertrators of atrocity crimes, the Cambodian government's insistence on majority control of the trials within the Cambodian court system brought forth an idiosyncratic Agreement for creation of the ECCC. An overview is provided of completed trials (Case 001, Case 002/01) and the current ECCC trial (Case 002/02), as well as the investigations for Cases 003 and 004.

In Chapter five, the features of the controversial Court which imbued it with communicative capacity are introduced. While the politics surrounding the Court continued to threaten its legitimacy, analysis of innovations in the ECCC procedural form reveals the potential for tipping the balance away from the expressivism of the Court's trials to their communicative value. The roles shared between international and national actors in the Court, the incorporation of the civil party action into the inquisitorial procedure and the added purpose of the Court of assisting reconciliation are identified as working together to produce a more representative and discursive trial procedure.

Chapter six investigates how the Trial Chamber judges, attentive to the retributive *and* reconciliatory purposes of the Court, examined the case against the accused, Kaing Guek Eav, alias Duch. The procedure engaged by the Court permitted trial dialogue beyond matters of strict culpability to the broader causes, context and consequences of the crimes in question. Causal understanding cannot be underestimated in a society where collective memory has been suppressed. In addition to profiling the life of the accused within a turbulent historical period in Cambodia, the proceedings included his confessions and commentary on the mechanics of the Khmer Rouge regime, as well as his engagement with witnesses. Expert witnesses provided factual data going to the guilt of the accused, but were also invited to give their opinion on broader matters such as the nature of the crimes in history, as well as the psychological dynamics of the accused during and after the regime. The open nature of the proceedings and their wide transmission in Cambodia and beyond allowed the public communication of facts behind the crimes to foster deeper reflection and enquiry about the regime. Through narrative testimony, experts also supported the civil parties' case for reparations and represented the specific nature of victimhood flowing from the Khmer Rouge era.

Chapter seven discusses the voice of the victim in transitional trials and engages with the fair trial debate around victim participation rights. The chapter explores how the ECCC judges managed disagreements between court actors over the role of civil parties in trial proceedings and discusses the procedural adaptations introduced after Case 001 which permitted their continued participation. Through analysis of trial transcripts of Cases 001, 002/01 and 002/02 the trial dialogue flowing from civil party story-telling in support of their reparations claims is examined. This includes discussion of exchanges between the civil parties and the accused, and other court actors under the ECCC's revised participation scheme. The discussion also illustrates how civil party statements of suffering following factual testimony, and their examination during victim impact hearings contributed to the truth-telling process, while also fostering discourse which resonated with social debates beyond the courtroom. However, the procedure demanded the Trial Chamber's regular mediation between the parties as it gave effect to the civil parties' rights to be heard in proceedings while respecting the rights of the accused to dignity and a fair trial.

The legal analysis of the case against Duch and the processes of judgment and appeal are dealt with in Chapter eight. The judgments of the Trial Chamber and Supreme Court Chamber are examined for their expressive and communicative value. The Trial Chamber's pursuit of a kind of ontological truth in determining the case, rather than the pluralistic approach to truth under adversarial procedure brought a holistic analysis of guilt, which communicated the causes and effects of Duch's crimes in the course of interpreting international norms in the Cambodian context.

The Supreme Court Chamber's (SCC) analysis of the grounds of appeal, while rich in expressivism, had communicative dimensions. A measure of dissent between the SCC judges communicated a diversity of views on the interpretation of standards of procedural fairness in transitional contexts. The judges remedied defects in the victim participation application process and overturned the Trial Chamber's revocation of the civil party status of a number of victims. The judgment of the SCC reflects a deliberately objective approach to sentencing that is firmly aligned with the expressivism of international criminal punishment. Overall, therefore, the process of judgment was both expressive and communicative.

Chapter nine completes the analysis by examining the viability and legacy of the ECCC. Operational impediments and fairness concerns occurring during the first two trials are discussed in the context of the ECCCs expressive legacy of norm development and the conviction of three Khmer Rouge leaders. The ECCC's communicative legacy is sketched through a discussion of the elements of communication in the Court's processes and as reflected in the recurrent themes of trauma and the victim/perpetrator equation in trial proceedings. The additional dynamic of active support of the ECCC by networks of civil society groups is also discussed as strengthening the communicative value of the Court.

The representative and dialogical proceedings offer a distinct alternative to the ambiguous social detachment of other international tribunals. Open and transparent justice process in the wake of the Khmer Rouge regime eluded Cambodians. A trial platform permitting discursive engagement with facts hidden from citizens for decades, and discourse that at least in part addressed their cries for truth and justice stands in contrast to the silence they have endured for so long. A growing number of impact studies point to the social significance of the unusually representative and discursive proceedings which have been transmitted throughout Cambodia.

CHAPTER 2

TRIALS IN TRANSITIONAL JUSTICE THEORY

2.1. INTRODUCTION

While the meaning of the term 'transitional justice' is not immediately apparent, there is consensus that transitional justice is concerned broadly with how post-conflict societies come to terms with their history of large-scale violence.[1] The notion of post-conflict justice, sometimes used interchangeably with the term transitional justice, is more narrowly focused on the norm of accountability for past human rights abuses, combatting impunity and restoring failed or weakened national justice systems following internal conflicts.[2] The two concepts converged in the notion of transitional justice articulated in the United Nations Secretary-General's 2004 report:

> The notion of 'transitional justice' ... comprises the full range of processes and mechanisms associated with a society's attempts to come to terms with a legacy of large scale past abuses, in order to ensure accountability, serve justice and achieve reconciliation.[3]

Multiple aims of transitional justice are identified in this formulation, and the significance of communication is implicit in the identification of a society's engagement with its past as the focal point of transitional justice work. Transitional justice is not limited to a single mechanism. According to the

1 Laurel E. Fletcher, 'Violence and Social Repair: Rethinking the Contribution of Justice to Reconciliation' (2002) 24 *Human Rights Quarterly* 573, 574; Ruti G. Teitel, *Transitional Justice* (Oxford University Press, 2000) p. 3; Mark Osiel, *Mass Atrocity, Collective Memory and the Law* (Transaction Publishers, 1997) p. 2.

2 M. Cherif Bassiouni, 'Introduction' in M. Cherif Bassiouni (ed.), *Post-Conflict Justice* (Transnational Publishers, 2002) p. xv.

3 *The Rule of Law and Transitional Justice in Conflict and Post-Conflict Societies: Report of the Secretary-General* UN Doc. S/2004/616 (23 August 2004) para. [8].

Secretary-General, the range of justice mechanisms or processes that may be engaged includes:

> Both judicial and non-judicial mechanisms, with differing levels of international involvement (or none at all) and individual prosecutions, reparations, truth seeking, institutional reform, vetting and dismissals, or a combination thereof.[4]

However, the form and philosophy of the respective mechanisms affect the nature and depth of engagement with the past that is possible within each as they operate. In other words, dialogue on the past will be shaped by the form that transitional justice assumes. Generally, truth-seeking mechanisms provide victims and perpetrators of crimes with a locally-based forum for dialogue on the crimes committed. Based on principles of restorative justice, the proceedings are victim-centred and operate to reintegrate offenders through relatively flexible procedure.[5] Criminal trials, on the other hand, follow rules of evidentiary procedure and fair trial conventions towards retributive outcomes.[6] Dialogue in trials is limited to evidentiary matters, unless flexibility in trial procedure permits broader discussion within the bounds of criminal law principles.

Evaluations in the transitional justice literature of the range of justice modalities highlight the scope for engagement with the past and the benefits of dialogue through restorative justice or non-judicial forms.[7] Trials, on the other hand, are described as 'top-down' mechanisms dominated by legal and political philosophy disconnected from the on-the-ground realities of transitioning societies.[8] Dialogically oriented processes, including truth commissions and more locally-based restorative justice mechanisms were found to more directly address key issues that recovering societies face both during and after political transitions. Parmentier has identified the key concerns of those societies as: the search for truth, ensuring accountability, provision of reparations, promotion of reconciliation, dealing with the trauma of victims, trust between individuals

---

4 Ibid.

5 Naomi Roht-Arriaza, 'The New Landscape of Transitional Justice' in Naomi Roht-Arriaza and Javier Mariezcurrena (eds.), *Transitional Justice in the Twenty-First Century: Beyond truth Versus Justice* (Cambridge University Press, 2006) p. 1, 4.

6 Mark A. Drumbl, 'Collective Violence and Individual Punishment: The Criminality of Mass Atrocity' (2004–2005) 99 *Northwestern University Law Review* 539, 577.

7 Lorna McDonald, 'International Law as a Tiered Process: Transitional Justice at the Local, National and International Level' in Kieran McEvoy and Lorna McGregor (eds.), *Transitional Justice from Below: Grassroots Activism and the Struggle for Change* (Hart Publishing, 2008) pp. 47, 56–58; Stephan Parmentier and Elmar G.M. Weitekamp, 'Political Crimes and Serious Violations of Human Rights: Towards a Criminology of International Crimes' in Stephan Parmentier and Elmar G.M Weitekamp (eds.), *Crime and Human Rights* (Elsevier Ltd, 2007) pp. 109, 130–132.

8 Stephan Parmentier, 'Dealing with International Crimes in Post-war Bosnia: A Look through the Lens of the Affected Population' (2012) 9 *European Journal of Criminology* 553, 554.

and groups in the post-conflict context, and dialogue between individuals and sectors of the society.[9]

However, the choice of which justice mechanism will be engaged in the aftermath of conflict is inevitably entwined with the dilemmas of transitional politics.[10] Teitel has argued that the choice boils down to the question of whether to punish or grant amnesty to former regime representatives responsible for atrocities.[11] The political transitions from authoritarian regimes to the fledgling democracies of the Americas in the 1980s illustrate how choices between transitional justice mechanisms may be made.[12] In those states the preference for truth commissions to demarcate the authoritarian past from the democratic present was conditioned by considerations around maintaining the fragile peace, as old political and military elites retained sufficient power to threaten political stability if they faced prosecution. Nevertheless, support groups for victims of crime pressed for trials of the perpetrators of atrocious crimes, and human rights organisations advocated an end to impunity for gross violations of human rights.[13]

In the following decade two international tribunals were created by UN Security Council Resolutions to address breaches of international criminal law in the Former Yugoslavia, and in Rwanda.[14] This marked the re-emergence of international criminal justice, absent since its first appearance after the Second World War at the International Military Tribunals of Nuremburg and Tokyo. The rationale informing the choice of trials as post-conflict justice mechanisms for the Balkans and Rwanda – and others that were subsequently created in Sierra Leone, Kosovo, East Timor and Cambodia – was that of accountability and deterrence of perpetrators. In 2002, the Rome Statute of the International Criminal Court (ICC) established a permanent justice mechanism, with jurisdiction over the most serious international crimes.[15] Ending impunity for such crimes and contributing to their prevention in the interests of world peace and security was the Court's stated purpose.[16]

From that time, institutions of this kind gained the ascendency among transitional justice mechanisms.[17] McEvoy argued that a strong positivistic

---

9 Ibid. pp. 555–557.

10 Diane Orentlicher, 'Settling Accounts Revisited: Reconciling Global Norms with Local Agency' (2007) 1 *The International Journal of Transitional Justice* 10, 12–13.

11 Teitel, above n. 1, p. 27.

12 Orentlicher, above n. 10, pp. 12–13.

13 Fletcher, above n. 1, p. 575.

14 UNSC Res. 827 (1993) UN Doc. S/RES/827 (25 May 1993); UNSC Res. 955 (1994) UN Doc. S/RES/955 (8 November 1994).

15 *Rome Statute of the International Criminal Court* 17 July 1998, opened for signature 17 July 1998, 2187 UNTS 90 (entered into force 1 July 2002) [ICC Statute].

16 ICC Statute, Preamble.

17 Mark A. Drumbl, *Atrocity Punishment and International Law* (Cambridge University Press, 2007) p. 5.

scholarship began to pervade transitional justice theory as generous resourcing of international and national tribunals brought legal formalism to the field.[18] Transitional justice was informally colonised by lawyers, and legalism, represented by retributive justice models, came to dominate the theoretical discourse of the field.[19]

Legal formalism or legalism harnesses what Bourdieu referred to as the force of law; the mysterious and pervasive influence of law in social, political and intellectual life.[20] The notion of the rule of law is far from solidified in societies subject to, or recovering from, repressive regimes.[21] Legal institutions, and legal instruments such as new constitutions, may not only symbolise a break with the past regime, but represent the legitimacy of the new path being forged toward a just and democratic future. However, legalism also operates to preserve law and legal convention from irrelevant considerations, and may demarcate legal considerations from social history, politics or morality.[22] Confining transitional justice to the importance of law in the new society and the legal analysis of crimes may also close off the prospect of deeper social engagement with the past, by keeping it within a limited frame where dialogue is largely excluded.[23]

Genocide, crimes against humanity and war crimes are not ordinary crimes. Since the exposure of the German concentration camps at the end of the Second World War and the decision of the victors to hold the perpetrators of evident extraordinary crimes accountable, international law scholars and policy-makers viewed criminal trials as the pre-eminent mode of justice for such crimes.[24] With this came the Nuremburg vision of careful trials that display the value of law and due process in establishing individual culpability. The suite of international criminal courts of the modern era quickly gained the ascendancy as the dominant transitional justice mechanism underpinned not only by retributivism, but also expressivism.

In the following sections I discuss the nature and complexity of expressivism as it operates in national and internationalised spheres of justice.[25] I begin with an outline of the nature of contemporary expressivist discourse. The trajectory of

---

18 Kieran McEvoy, 'Beyond Legalism: Towards a Thicker Understanding of Transitional Justice' (2007) 34 *Journal of Law and Society* 411, 415–416.

19 Ibid. p. 412.

20 Pierre Bourdieu, 'The Force of Law: Towards a Sociology of the Juridical Field' (1987) 38 *Hastings Law Journal* 805, 807.

21 Steven Ratner, 'New Democracies, Old Atrocities: an Inquiry in International Law' (1999) 87 *Georgetown Law Journal* 707, 719–720.

22 Judith Shklar, *Legalism: Law, Morals, and Political Trials* (Harvard University Press, 1964), p. 2.

23 McEvoy, above n. 18, p. 417.

24 Drumbl, above n. 17, p. 3.

25 'Internationalised' here is used in a general sense, but I discuss the legal distinction between 65 international and internationalised courts in Chapter three.

expressivism in criminal law from its origins in sociological theory to its modern application in internationalised spheres of criminal justice is then examined.

2.2. EXPRESSIVISM AND SOCIAL MEANING

Expressivist ideas derive from a range of disciplines including philosophy, sociology, semiotics, law and economics.[26] While not embodying a distinct moral, legal or linguistic theory, expressivist writings provide analyses of the social meaning of action – individual and collective.[27] Action is expressive and carries meaning, notwithstanding the intentions of actors.[28] Social meaning, distinguished from individual meaning, is contingent on the particular society within which the meanings of certain actions, inactions or statuses are interpreted.[29] Nevertheless, individual actions will often be informed by social norms, and governmental actions may reinforce or alter norms.[30] Expressivism is therefore concerned with how social meaning is constructed through political action and the techniques engaged to amplify, change or blur meaning.[31]

In international law, treaty-making and ratification by states are politically expressive acts that 'harness the pull of international society.'[32] However, compliance with international norms is contingent on factors shaping the particular society and enforcement policy at the local level. Human rights instruments, for instance, may be ratified by a state because it values membership of the international community, rather than the intrinsic significance of the norm within the domestic context.[33] The Cambodian government for example, ratified routinely the key Conventions but remained unwilling to comply substantively with treaty commitments or uphold human rights claims.[34]

---

26 Dianne Marie Amann, 'Group Mentality, Expressivism and Genocide' (2002) 2 *International Criminal Law Review* 93,118; Elizabeth Anderson and Richard H. Pildes, 'Expressive Theories of Law: A General Restatement' (1999–2000) 148 *University of Pennsylvania Law Review* 1503; Lawrence Lessig, 'The Regulation of Social Meaning' (1995) 62 *University of Chicago Law Review* 943, 951; Robert D. Cooter, 'The Theory of Market Modernisation of Law' (1996) 16 *International Review of Law and Economics* 141.

27 Cass R. Sunstein, 'On the Expressive Function of Law' (1995–1996) 144 *University of Pennsylvania Law Review* 2021.

28 Ibid. The expressivist approach to law attracted criticism for its focus on the identification of social meaning as opposed to linguistically framed moral intention. See Matthew D. Adler, 'Expressive Theories of Law: A Sceptical Overview' (2000) 148 *University of Pennsylvania Law Review* 1363, 1375.

29 Lessig, above n. 26, p. 951.

30 Sunstein, above n. 27, p. 2022.

31 Lessig, above n. 26, p. 951.

32 Alex Geisinger and Michael Ashley Stein, 'A Theory of Expressive International Law' (2007) 60 *Vanderbilt Law Review* 77, 77–79.

33 Ibid. pp. 97–99.

34 Hilary Charlesworth, 'Swimming to Cambodia: Justice and Ritual in Human Rights after Conflict' (2010) 29 *Australian Yearbook of International Law* 1, 11–13.

Legal instruments establishing a norm may carry both intrinsic and expressive value. In the face of widespread impunity for international crimes, during the Cold War of 1948–1991, the expressivism of the Genocide Convention signalled a prohibition on acts constituting genocide to the world.[35] However, the Convention definition of genocide was limited to acts directed only against national, ethnic, racial or religious groups, with intent to destroy the group either in whole or in part.[36] State-sponsored repression of political, social or economic sectors of populations fell outside the definition. Thus, the instrument created the norm, but was expressive in a negative sense by virtue of what it excluded from the realm of prosecution.

Similarly, the creation of international institutions may be expressive in both positive and negative ways. An example is the collective action taken by the Security Council in establishing international tribunals to prosecute violations of international humanitarian law in the Former Yugoslavia and Rwanda in the 1990s.[37] While the political actions were expressive of international will to deter future criminal enterprises and enforce practically dormant norms, the Tribunals struggled to secure the support of the communities they served through more representative procedure.[38] Thus, the instrumental value of the international messages sent by the institutions was diminished by a loss of legitimacy in the eyes of the directly affected societies.

2.2.1. EXPRESSIVISM AND NATIONAL LEGAL ACTION

Areas of law which have been the subject of expressivist analysis include United States constitutional and environmental law, and criminal law more broadly.[39] Expressivist critiques of law have generally focused on actions that express particular moral responses to certain substantive values.[40] Endangered species legislation, for example, may symbolise a certain ideal relationship between humans and the environment.[41] Emissions trading scheme legislation, on the other hand, may reflect an economic approach to environmental protection rather a broader normative principle.[42] Thus, expressivist analysis of a law's

---

35 *Convention on the Prevention and Punishment of the Crime of Genocide* opened for signature 9 December 1948, 78 UNTS 277 (entered into force 12 January 1951) [Genocide Convention].

36 Genocide Convention art. II.

37 UNSC Res. 827 UN Doc. S/RES/827 (25 May 1993); UNSC Res. 955 UN Doc. S/RES/955 (8 November 1994).

38 Laura A. Dickinson, 'The Promise of Hybrid Courts' (2003) 93 *American Journal of International Law* 295, 302–303; Jaya Ramji-Nogales, 'Designing Bespoke Transitional Justice' (2010–2011) 32 *Michigan Journal of International Law* 26, 28.

39 Anderson, above n. 26, pp. 1531–1556.

40 Ibid. p. 1504.

41 Sunstein, above n. 27, p. 2024.

42 Ibid.

content may reveal that it has more to do with the general statement it makes than its consequences, for instance, in the form of behavioural change.

Expressivism is also concerned with the regulation of social meaning. Legislation that is contrary to law or results in social harm is judicially evaluated through both doctrinal and expressive structures. Doctrinal analysis highlights certain values as objectively significant within the legitimate state; for example, the constitutional value of the equality of citizens of the United States.[43] An expressivist judicial analysis will examine attitudes towards that value and elucidate their social meaning. Thus, a judicial finding that racially segregated schools promote inequality because they embody a message of inferiority, or attitudes of disrespect, highlights the constitutional value through an expressive interpretation structure.[44] In summary, modern expressivist conceptions of legal actions focus on the expressive content of law and the public construction of social meaning through legal process.[45]

2.2.2. EXPRESSIVISM AND CRIMINAL LAW

The criminal law of national criminal justice systems is inherently expressive.[46] The moral condemnatory message of the criminal law towards criminal conduct is backed by the coercive power of the state to protect core values.[47] The state's power was justified in moral and political philosophy on the basis of either retribution or crime control.[48] Retribution carries the notion of 'just desert' for past criminal wrongdoing.[49] By contrast crime control or consequentialist theories of punishment are forward-looking and aim to achieve individual and general deterrence.[50] Punishment deters the offender from repeating the crime and its institutionalisation prevents wider offending.[51]

Expressivism in criminal law circumvents both approaches to the notion of punishment by emphasising its expressive and symbolic purpose. Contemporary

---

43 Anderson, above n. 26, p. 1544.

44 Ibid.

45 Ibid.

46 Jenia Iontcheva Turner, 'The Expressive Dimension of EU Criminal Law' (2012) 60 *American Journal of Comparative Law* 555, 557.

47 Henry M. Hart Jr., 'The Aims of the Criminal Law' (1958) 23 *Law and Contemporary Problems* 401, 402–406.

48 Robert D. Sloan, 'The Expressive Capacity of International Punishment: The Limits of the National Law Analogy and the Potential of International Criminal Law' (2007) 43 *Stanford Journal of International Law* 39, 69.

49 Ibid; Drumbl above n. 6, p. 577. And see M. Cherif Bassouni, *Introduction to International Criminal Law* (Transnational Publishers, 2003) pp. 691ff.

50 Matt Matravers, 'Introduction' in Matt Matravers (ed.), *Punishment and Political Theory* (Hart Publishing, 1999) pp. 1, 1–2.

51 Simon Bronitt and Bernadette McSherry, *The Principles of Criminal Law*, 3rd ed. (Thomson Reuters, 2010) p. 21.

theories of expressive punishment derive from the work of Emile Durkheim.[52] Writing in the context of social crisis due to the perceived moral decline of late-nineteenth-century France, Durkheim's theory of criminal punishment stemmed from his conception of crime as acts that offend 'strong and defined states of the collective conscience.'[53] Punishment avenged outrage to the collective conscience or the morality of society.[54]

> Although it proceeds from a quite mechanical reaction, from movements which are passionate and in great part unreflective, [punishment] does play a useful role. Only this role is not where we ordinarily look for it. It does not serve, or else only serves quite secondarily, in correcting the culpable or in intimidating possible followers. From this point of view, its efficacy is justly doubtful and in any case, mediocre. Its true function is to maintain social cohesion intact, while maintaining all its vitality in the common conscience.[55]

Punishment is collective action through an authorised intermediary, acting in the interests of justice and social solidarity.[56] Implicitly, Durkheim assumed a pre-existing solidarity which he categorised as of two types: mechanical and organic.[57] Mechanical solidarity is associated with 'likenesses' which attach the individual to the social group. Norms are well defined and there is common observance of sacred rituals.[58] Organic solidarity arises from the complex division of labour in society, where social cohesion is based on bonds created by networks of interdependence, economic reciprocities and the autonomy of the individual person.[59] Rather than the conformity required within mechanical societies, the organic solidarity of modern societies embraces difference, diversity and disagreement under a morality of individualism.[60]

Durkheim conceived of the division of labour positively but warned of its possible pathological manifestations where rules establishing relationships between social actors are threatened. This could produce a state of 'anomie' or breakdown in the social fabric.[61] He saw the potential for anomie in the rampant individualism of the new Industrial Age, and read attacks on an individual's

---

52 David Garland, 'Punishment and Social Solidarity' in Jonathon Simon and Richard Sparks (eds.), *The Sage Handbook of Punishment and Society* (Sage Publishers, 2013) pp. 21, 23.

53 Emile Durkheim, *The Division of Labor in Society*, George Simpson transl., (Free Press, 1933) p. 80 [transl. of *De la division du travail social* (first published 1893)].

54 Ibid. p. 88.

55 Ibid. p. 108.

56 Ibid. p. 96.

57 Ibid. p. 25.

58 Ibid. pp. 105–106, 30.

59 Ibid. p. 131.

60 Garland, above n. 52, p. 27.

61 Durkheim, above n. 53, p. 353.

constitutional rights as a threat to the moral order.[62] His public support of the wrongly convicted Captain Dreyfus in 1894, a French officer and a Jew, was based not on sympathy for the victim or protection of others' rights in the future, but the preservation of the moral life of the Third Republic of France.[63]

Durkheim charted an intellectual course between the opposing philosophical schools of liberalism and communitarianism. Along with other theorists including Weber and Marx, Durkheim criticised the narrow categorisation of Western societies in terms of economics and the self-interest characteristic of the laissez-faire liberalism of his day. He claimed that liberalism so conceived left little space for the shared belief systems and conventions advocated by communitarians as necessary to society. Analysing France's historical traditions, ideals and structural elements, Durkheim drew from key features of each school of thought to arrive at a mediating idea: the common good of society and the freedom of the individual meet in the central moral ideals of the society and the institutions which represent and protect them.[64] Thus, whether within mechanical or organic societies, only authoritative action to publicly enforce moral rules will prevent social disintegration.[65]

Joel Feinberg's modern formulation of the expressive value of punishment rejected the notion of punishment as the infliction of hard treatment of a convicted individual by the state. Feinberg asserted:

> Punishment is a conventional device for the expression of attitudes of resentment and indignation, and of judgments of disapproval and reprobation, either on the part of the punishing authority or of those 'in whose name' the punishment is inflicted. Punishment, in short, has a *symbolic significance* largely missing from other kinds of penalties.[66]

Punishment's expressive cast reflects its instrumental purpose.[67] Punishment expresses the community's condemnation of the criminal offence, and from it certain symbolic functions are derived.[68] These include authoritative disavowal of the criminal practice;[69] symbolic non-acquiescence in the crime;[70] vindication of the law in practice to encourage citizenry;[71] and the absolution of others by

---

62 Mark S. Cladis, *A Communitarian Defence of Liberalism: Emile Durkheim and Contemporary Social Theory* (Stanford University Press, 1992) p. 8.
63 Ibid. p. 24.
64 Ibid. pp. 9, 27–28.
65 Durkheim, above n. 53, p. 397.
66 Joel Feinberg, 'The Expressive Function of Punishment' (1965) 49 *The Monist* 397, 400.
67 Bronitt, above n. 51, p. 30.
68 Feinberg, above n. 66, p. 401.
69 Ibid. p. 404.
70 Ibid. p. 405.
71 Ibid. pp. 406–407.

punishing the guilty, thus relieving the innocent from suspicion particularly when there are few suspects.[72]

Beyond its instrumental value, punishment is expressive from a sociological perspective.[73] Garland described criminal punishment as both a discrete legal mechanism for dealing with criminal wrongdoing through public condemnation, and a social institution embodying multiple symbolic meanings which capture the social ethos, identity and emotion of the relevant community.[74] Bronitt and McSherry also concluded that punishment may have more symbolic than instrumental value, particularly in light of its failure to deter crimes.[75]

From either an instrumentalist or a sociological standpoint, the common denominator of the expressivism of punishment is the moral condemnation conveyed. However, modern expressivist analysis demonstrates how the meaning of moral denunciation is constructed. Kahan's expressivist analysis of the punishment of shaming compared to imprisonment, posits that the expressive value of punishment does not turn only on whether, or to what extent, a mode of punishment expresses moral condemnation. Rather, it is the way in which the moral condemnation accords with more fundamental and various cultural worldviews that makes a particular form of punishment more socially acceptable and consequently, politically economical.[76] Kahan's work engaged the four cultural indicators of hierocracy, individualism, egalitarianism and communitarianism, to evaluate shaming and incarceration in terms of their acceptability as moral condemnation.[77]

Kahan found that citizens wanted punishments to not only express condemnation but also 'to express it in way that coheres with, rather than assaults, their more basic cultural commitments.'[78] Shaming as a form of moral condemnation was unacceptable to some social groups because, like corporal punishment, shaming summoned the symbols of hierarchy or the collective which conflicted with their strong social commitments to egalitarianism and individualism.[79] Incarceration, on the other hand, condemns in multiple registers with meaning acceptable to all four cultural sectors:

> Hierarchists can see [incarceration] as supplying a delicious form of debasement for those who resist their proper place in the social order; communitarians, a fitting gesture

---

72 Ibid. p. 408.

73 Bronitt, above n. 51, p. 30.

74 David Garland, *Punishment in Modern Society* (University of Chicago Press, 1990) p. 287.

75 Bronitt and McSherry, above n. 51, p. 30.

76 Dan M. Kahan, 'What's Really Wrong with Shaming Sanctions?' (2006) 84 *Texas Law Review* 2075, 2086.

77 Kahan drew from the work of Aaron Wildavsky, 'Choosing Preferences by Constructing Institutions: A Cultural Theory of Preference Formation' (1987) 81 *American Political Science Review* 1; See also Mary Douglas, *Natural Symbols: Exploration in Cosmology* (Barrie & Rockliff, 1970) pp. 54–68.

78 Kahan, above n. 76, p. 2086.

79 Ibid. p. 2087.

> of banishment for those who wrongfully renounce social obligation; individualists, a reciprocal deprivation of liberty for those who fail to respect the liberty of others; and egalitarians, a uniquely democratic metric of punishment for persons who enjoy value by virtue of their capacity for autonomy.[80]

Kahan concluded that political actors seeking the allegiance of multiple cultural groups engaged the ambiguity of the social meaning of incarceration to entrench the prison as an enduring symbol of moral condemnation.[81] So constructed, the expressivism of imprisonment outweighs its social and economic costs.

2.2.3. THE EUROPEAN UNION AND EXPRESSIVE CRIMINAL LAW

The expressive value of criminal law may also be engaged regionally or internationally. The European Union's (EU) power to pass criminal laws is limited to serious crimes with cross-border dimensions.[82] The EU decision to harmonise the definitions of racism and xenophobic crime within all Member States has been the subject of expressivist analysis.[83] Arguments justifying the laws were based on factors outside any cross-border dimension to the racist and xenophobic crime. These included: the prevalence of race-based crimes, the lack of uniformity in national laws on the subject, problems in securing cooperation between jurisdictions and the difficulty of fighting crimes in Member States where prosecution originates from a complaint by a victim.[84] However, such reasons might equally apply to other crimes, but not necessarily ground any EU-wide legal action.[85]

The criminal law's expressive value provided sufficient justification for the new legislation.[86] Since the legislation promoted two of the EU's main priorities – human rights and the battle against racism within member countries, it supported an evolving EU mission.[87] By harnessing the criminal law's expressive

---

80 Ibid. p. 2089.

81 Ibid. p. 2090.

82 Consolidated Version of the Treaty for the Functioning of the Exercise of the European Union, 9 May 2008, [2008] OJ C115, art. 83(1).

83 TURNER, above n. 46, pp. 555–583.

84 Ibid. p. 569.

85 Ibid.

86 Ibid.

87 Ibid. p. 571 citing European Parliament, *Report on the Proposal for a Council Framework Decision on Combating Certain Forms and Expressions of Racism and Xenophobia by Means of Criminal Law* A6-0444/2007 (14 November 2005) 14; And see *European Parliament Recommendation to the Council of 21 June 2007 Concerning Progress of the Negotiations on the Framework Decision on Action to Combat Racism and Xenophobia*, [2008] OJ C146 E/361 (urging finalisation of the text in terms that 'send out a strong political message in support of a citizens' Europe.')

purposes in defence of common values and the punishment of those who treat them with contempt, the legislative action reinforced the political power and identity of the EU beyond the limits of its essentially economic mandate.[88] This attracted criticism of the EU for 'moral posturing' and use of its legislative power for making value statements only.[89] That the final form of the laws does not require full harmonisation, and national authorities remain responsible for enforcement also leads to the conclusion that their expressive value exceeds any practical use.[90] The action also demonstrates how the traditional expressive capital of criminal law may be transferred to the international law context with or without enforcement.

2.3. CRIMINAL LAW AND TRANSITIONAL SOCIETIES

Years of conflict and suppression of populations by violent regimes involving crimes of mass atrocity may threaten or destroy the social fabric of those societies, rendering them amply susceptible to the 'anomie' feared by Durkheim in relation to modern industrial societies. Given the fragile nature of transitional societies, how well does criminal justice drawn largely from stable Western polities transfer to such societies?

2.3.1. CRIMINAL LAW PRINCIPLES AND ATROCITY CRIMES

Pursuant to the legal instruments creating them, transitional courts impose punishments on the individuals they convict of national and/or international crimes within their jurisdiction.[91] The core international crimes that are prosecuted – genocide, crimes against humanity and war crimes – have a collective character in terms of perpetration and mass victimisation. International crimes carry elements of systemic criminality which distinguish them from national crimes. This has led international criminal courts to craft legal responsibility doctrines that help establish the liability of individuals who designed or planned a common criminal plan yet without directly engaging in criminal acts.[92]

Judicial developments in international criminal procedure of this kind attracted criticism for their perceived deviation from traditional criminal law

---

88 Turner, above n. 46, p. 571.

89 Maria Fletcher, Robin Lööf and Bill Gilmore, *EU Criminal Law and Justice* (Edward Elgar Publishing, 2008) pp. 194–202.

90 Turner above n. 46, p. 571.

91 Drumbl, above n. 6, pp. 577–578.

92 Mirjan Damaska, 'What is the Point of International Criminal Justice?' (2008) 83 *Chicago-Kent Law Review* 329, 353–355.

principles of individual culpability. The doctrine of joint criminal enterprise in particular, developed by the ICTY, was criticised for distorting criminal procedural standards by removing the requirement of proof of a direct causal link between the commission of crimes and the actual perpetrator.[93] One strand of the doctrine permits conviction of individuals based on the foreseeability of the criminal acts committed pursuant to the common criminal plan. Since the doctrine fails to admit the pressures and confusion affecting conduct within conflicts, as well as legitimate grounds for policy decisions, it seemed to stretch the stigma of conviction beyond socially acceptable bounds.[94] Tinkering with traditional doctrines may also produce negative responses to the work of the Court as the net of prosecution may appear to not discriminate sufficiently and so catch individuals too loosely connected with the plan.[95] Adaptation of criminal law concepts to the context of mass atrocity may therefore produce the perception, if not the actuality, of unfair justice processes.

2.3.2. JUSTIFYING PUNISHMENT IN TRANSITIONAL SOCIETIES

The transposition of the national criminal law analogy to the transitional justice sphere brought with it the traditional justifications of punishment: retribution and deterrence, as well as the rehabilitation of offenders. Post-conflict justice literature recorded apparent incongruities or at least equivocal operation of those justifications.[96]

The adequacy of retribution in grounding international criminal punishment was challenged on numerous fronts. The creation of transitional courts and tribunals is made possible by the selective exercise of political will, usually in the face of humanitarian crises and violation of human rights and international humanitarian law.[97] In the case of political action to create international criminal tribunals, hybrid and national courts with international elements, the international community may in fact carry some responsibility for the occurrence

93 Alison Marsten Danner and Jenny S. Martinez, 'Guilty Associations: Joint Criminal Enterprise, Command Responsibility and the Development of International Criminal Law' (2005) 93 *California Law Review* 75, 103–120.

94 Damaska, above n. 92, p. 353.

95 Ibid.

96 For example, Immi Tallgren, 'The Sense and Sensibility of International Criminal Law' (2002) 13 *European Journal of International Law* 561; Drumbl, above n. 6, p. 559; And see also Martti Koskenniemi, 'Between Impunity and Show Trials' (2002) 6 *Max Planck Yearbook of United Nations Law* 1; Sloan, above n. 48, p. 39; Margaret M. Deguzman, 'Giving Priority to Sex Crime Prosecutions: The Philosophical Foundations of a Feminist Agenda' (2011) 11 *International Criminal Law Review* 515, 522–523.

97 Sloan, above n. 48, p. 50.

of atrocities.[98] The delayed responses of the international community to the Balkan, Rwandan and Cambodian crises are cases in point.[99] Transitional trials typically target for prosecution the leaders and primary architects of criminal regimes.[100] While selectivity in prosecutions has the effect of not condemning whole or large swathes of populations for mass violence, it may also be the result of political concerns, often on the part of successor regimes and creators of the court, around wider accountability. Thus, selectivity in prosecutions means that retribution operates in a very limited sense.[101]

In addition, and apart from the conspicuous disproportion between maximum sentences and crimes of mass atrocity, retribution may also operate in a discriminatory way in the transitional context.[102] DeGuzman argued that, although communal harm caused by gender-based crimes may be greater in mass atrocity contexts than that resulting from killing crimes, the latter were given priority by international prosecutors.[103] This was either because of the prosecutorial policies of international courts or the inappropriate transfer of national crime selection priorities to transitional contexts.[104]

Furthermore, the selectivity in prosecutions belies the social complexity and group dynamics surrounding the commission of mass atrocity crimes.[105] Characterising most national crimes as ordinary crime resulting from individual deviation from accepted social norms, Drumbl noted that international crimes have a collective character distinct from the social deviance targeted by national criminal justice systems.[106] In the context of the Rwandan genocide, the population disengaged from the existing normative framework. This facilitated a form of ethnic cleansing on a massive scale with broad societal participation.[107]

In national criminal justice systems, the logic of the deterrent effect of punishment relies on an assumption of the inherent rationality of the perpetrator of crime.[108] In those contexts, both specific deterrence of the perpetrator and general deterrence by demonstration effect operate with a great degree of

---

98 The legal distinctions in the categorisation of transitional courts and tribunals are discussed in Chapter three.

99 Sloan, above n. 48, p. 47.

100 Ibid. p. 50.

101 Drumbl, above n. 17, p. 151; Dianne Marie Amann, 'Assessing International Adjudication of Human Rights Atrocities' (2003) 16 *Third World Legal Studies* 169, 173–174; See also Nancy Amoury Coombs, *Guilty Pleas in International Criminal Law* (Stanford University Press, 2007) pp. 46–47, 224–225.

102 Margaret M. DeGuzman, 'Choosing to Prosecute: Expressive Selection at the International Criminal Court' (2011–2012) 33 *Michigan Journal of International Law* 265, 301.

103 DeGuzman, above n. 96, pp. 522–523.

104 Ibid.

105 Drumbl, above n. 6, p. 567.

106 Ibid.

107 Ibid. p. 570.

108 Bronitt, above n. 51, p. 23.

uncertainty.[109] Deterrence is even more equivocal in the transitional justice context where trials address crimes of mass atrocity often perpetrated pursuant to a collective pathology or amorality.[110] Nevertheless, scholars argued that international criminal courts may, by virtue of their very existence, disempower perpetrators who manipulate conflict situations to ensure their political survival.[111] Akhavan argued that suspected international crime perpetrators in Uganda engaged in cost-benefit calculations in response to the issuance of warrants by the ICC even in the absence of convictions at that point.[112] In the same vein, Sloan suggested that we ought not to underestimate the reputational injury to powerful elites in contexts of conflict by the threat of prosecution for killing crimes.[113] And DeGuzman advocated leveraging the greater reputational damage arising from indictments for sex crimes.[114] Empirically, Bass found evidence that a number of ICTY indictments, or fear of indictment, averted some war crimes but not wider extermination programmes in the Balkans.[115]

As to general deterrence, Sloan suggested that the moral educative role of punishment over the longer term may encourage aversions to criminal behaviour more than the immediate cost-benefit analyses that may be undertaken by perpetrators of international crimes. However, many individuals involved in mass violence will not have complete control over their conduct in the face of social cataclysm orchestrated by agents of governments, military units or other entities.[116] Individual liability for crime that generally assumes a perpetrator's voluntary participation in extraordinary crime therefore strikes a very dissonant note.[117]

Rehabilitation of the offender as justification in the theory of punishment dates to the eighteenth century.[118] International human rights law made the social rehabilitation and restoration of criminal offenders a primary objective

109 Carsten Stahn, 'Between Faith and Facts: By What Standards Should We Assess International Criminal Justice?' (2012) 25 *Leiden Journal of International Criminal Justice* 252, 265.

110 Sloan, above n. 48, p. 58; Drumbl, above n. 6, p. 590.

111 Rosa Ehrenreich Brooks, 'The New Imperialism: Violence, Norms, and the Rule of Law' (2003) 101 *Michigan Law Review* 2275, 2302.

112 Payam Akhavan, 'Are International Criminal Tribunals a Disincentive to Peace? Reconciling Judicial Romanticism with Political Realism' (2009) 31 *Human Rights Quarterly* 624, 652.

113 Sloan, above n. 48, p. 74.

114 DeGuzman, above n. 96, p. 524.

115 Gary Bass, *Stay the Hand of Vengeance: The Politics of War Crimes Tribunals* (Princeton University Press, 2000) p. 294.

116 Drumbl, above n. 6, p. 571.

117 Ibid. p. 572.

118 Robert Cryer, Håkan Friman, Darryl Robinson and Elizabeth Wilmshurst, *An Introduction to International Criminal Law and Procedure* (Cambridge University Press, 2010) p. 28.

of imprisonment.[119] However, in practice, at the ad hoc Tribunals rehabilitation considerations only arose in cases where defendants pleaded guilty to at least some of the charges laid against them.[120]

2.4. THE EXPRESSIVISM OF INTERNATIONAL TRIALS

As international criminal justice was given form from the 1990s through the creation of a suite of transitional courts, Tallgren noted its representation as an ideal system of criminal justice based on a national model which could not in fact, be identified in any local context.[121] Notwithstanding the shortcomings of the national analogy of criminal law transposed to transitional societies, expressivism pervaded international criminal justice theory. International criminal proceedings were conceived as having didactic value in their narrations of the particulars of mass violence and documentation of atrocities, followed by the stigmatisation and punishment of perpetrators. Communication and expressivism were conflated as Drumbl described the 'dramaturgy' of trials in terms of moral education with transformative potential through the repudiation of collective criminality.[122]

Judicial statements enforcing international norms are another source from which the expressive value of international trials derives.[123] Such statements construct the meaning of international norms in general and specific ways. In *Prosecutor v. Aleksovski*, the ICTY declared that retribution in international criminal law in a general sense, 'is not to be understood as fulfilling a desire for revenge but as duly expressing the outrage of the international community at these crimes'.[124] Other statements conveyed more specific social meaning of norms with the authority of the international court.[125] As for the norm against genocide pursuant to the 1948 Genocide Convention for instance, Amann argued that international judges must take care in expressing the social meaning of the norm.[126] Too loosely construing the Convention definition of genocide could undermine the understanding that genocide is unique.[127] On the other

119 *International Covenant on Civil and Political Rights*, opened for signature 16 December 1966, 999 UNTS 171 (entered into force 23 March 1976), art. 10(3).

120 Frederik Harhoff, 'Sense and Sensibility in Sentencing: Taking Stock of International Criminal Punishment' in Ola Engdahl and Pal Wrange (eds.), *Law at War: The Law as it Was and the Law as it Should Be* (Martinus Nijhoff Publishers, 2008) pp. 121, 130.

121 Tallgren, above n. 96, p. 567.

122 Drumbl, above n. 17, pp. 174–175.

123 Amann, above n. 26, p. 142.

124 *Prosecutor v. Aleksovski (Judgment)* (International Criminal Tribunal for the Former Yugoslavia, Appeals Chamber, Case No. IT-95-14/1, 24 March 2000) para. [185].

125 Amann, above n. 26, pp. 142–143.

126 Ibid. p. 95.

127 Ibid. p. 142.

hand, 'too rigidly withholding protection from deserving groups could give rise to perceptions that the law is unfairly selective, or that it fails to comprehend the true nature of today's tragedies.'[128] Amann added that judicially construing the elements of the Convention definition in accordance with recognised subjective *and* objective criteria in relation to the context at hand, with careful exposition 'will convey condemnation in a manner rife with expressive meaning.' This will in turn, not only nurture the norm but also enhance the legitimacy of the system of international criminal justice.[129]

Scholars pointed to the expressivism of other aspects of international criminal trials. Paraphrasing Feinberg, Sloan highlighted the expressive dimensions of international punishment:

> By punishing perpetrators of serious international crimes, the international community attempts authoritatively to disavow that conduct, to indicate symbolically its refusal to acquiesce in the crimes, to vindicate international human rights norms and the laws of war, and to absolve ethnic or national communities, as collectives, of guilt by punishing individual perpetrators.[130]

Recognising the diversity of the international community and what may be construed as the immediate incompatibility of its norms within some transitional contexts, he argued that appropriate sentencing practice will ultimately help produce international social solidarity as to norms:

> Over time, punishment by international criminal tribunals can shape as well as express social norms. And the international sentencing process can reinforce and vindicate those norms even if it cannot, alone, realistically be expected to deter or fulfil retributive aspirations held by each affected local constituency.[131]

While sentencing conveys the distinctive symbolic significance of punishment by its expressive power, the legitimacy and authority of sentences requires careful calibration of crime and punishment. The latter must carry the right degree of international condemnation relative to other defendants before the particular tribunal, and fit the circumstances of the offender.[132]

Separate and public sentencing hearings where the process includes taking account of the different normative universes in which perpetrators operate, their status, role and background, will enhance the legitimacy of sentencing decisions.[133] Echoing Durkheim, Sloan emphasised the moral significance of the

---

128 Ibid. pp. 142–143.
129 Ibid. p. 143.
130 Sloan, above n. 48, p. 71.
131 Ibid. p. 85.
132 Ibid. pp. 82–83.
133 Ibid. pp. 90–91.

ritual of sentencing as approaching the sacred in its significance.[134] Moreover, it is the process of punishment that constitutes the appropriate ritual.[135] Sentences issued only in writing and attached to lengthy judgments without ritual performance will not have the necessary expressive effect.[136]

An expanding range of transitional courts with international elements was assigned multiple goals by their creators, which broadened their expressive value.[137] Those courts and tribunals were to transpose human rights and international criminal norms to transitional societies; conduct exemplary proceedings which promote respect for due process and foster the rule of law in the affected communities; provide space for the voice of victims of the international crimes; and produce an authoritative historical record of the context of the relevant crimes.[138] The Special Court for Sierra Leone was also to contribute to the process of national reconciliation and build the legal capacity of personnel, local and international.[139] The Extraordinary Chambers in the Courts of Cambodia were to be a model of justice within a society where the independence of the judiciary was compromised by executive interference.[140]

However, Damaska, drawing largely on analyses of the ad hoc Tribunals, concluded that operationally, the multiplicity of goals had negative implications for courts in terms of their expressive value at large and within their subject communities.[141] To sharpen the expressive purpose of transitional trials, Damaska advocated narrowing the priorities of international criminal justice to the global effects of human rights violations.[142] By this, 'judges are freer to follow impulses of disengaged reason and to concentrate on matters like the perfection of the normative content of international criminal law, or the expansion of its reach.'[143]

Damaska argued that it is more appropriate for international courts to make their priority the broad goal of accountability for international crimes and the stigmatisation of inhumane actions that prosecutions expose to the world.[144] He asserted that the central mission of international criminal justice should be the didactic one of strengthening the public sense of accountability for human

---

134 Ibid. p. 89.
135 Ibid. p. 90 citing MALCOLM M. FEELEY, *The Process is the Punishment* (Russell Sage Foundation, 1979).
136 Ibid.
137 FLETCHER, above n. 1, p. 578.
138 DAMASKA, above n. 92, p. 331.
139 UNSC Res. 1315, UN Doc. S/Res/1315 (14 August 2000) Preamble, para. [7].
140 *Report of the Secretary-General on the Khmer Rouge Trials* UN Doc. A/57/769 (2003) para. [11].
141 DAMASKA, above n. 92, pp. 331–335.
142 Ibid. p. 335.
143 Ibid.
144 Ibid. p. 345.

rights violations. From interdisciplinary literature on norm acceptance through persuasion, he argued that over the longer term, wider compliance with human rights norms may result from consistent denunciation of inhumane conduct and elevate the humanitarian principles implicit in such statements.[145] Damaska added that 'ideas are contagious, and may change perceptions of what is to one's own advantage, so that previously disinterested human rights concern may turn into an aspect of self-interest.'[146] His optimistic conception of trials orchestrated for maximum expressive effect suggested that ultimately a universal social solidarity may emerge over the longer term by consistent international adjudication. However, he noted that the didactic power of courts stems from their perceived legitimate authority. Legitimacy is a matter of considerable importance to international courts since they lack the coercive power of national courts. Much, therefore, turns on the quality of their decision-making and the procedure they adopt.[147]

The conception of individual criminal responsibility traditionally carried no notion of victims' justice.[148] However, McCarthy argued that victim redress may express ideas as forceful as that of denunciation of an individual's conduct as justification for punishment.[149] He also argued that the victim redress regime under the ICC Statute has an expressive dimension which goes some way towards ameliorating the limitations of the national criminal law analogy in transitional societies. An expressive function for victim redress can be identified in the recognition it gives not only to the harm the crime inflicted but the wrongfulness of the conduct:

> Redress represents an authoritative pronouncement that the conduct to which the victim was subjected was a specific, and particularly grave type of wrong, namely a crime under international law. When viewed in this light, the provision of victim redress arguably acquires an appreciable symbolic significance alongside the practical assistance it provides to victims of crimes under international law.[150]

McCarthy considered that the ICC victim reparations scheme had particular expressive value in that compensation may be awarded by the Court in specific cases, and victims of crimes within the jurisdiction of the Court and their families may also benefit in a general sense from the ICC's Victims Trust Fund.[151]

---

145 Ibid.
146 Ibid. p. 346.
147 Ibid.
148 Conor McCarthy, 'Victim Redress and International Criminal Justice: Competing Paradigms or Compatible Forms of Justice' (2012) 10 *Journal of International Criminal Justice* 351, 357.
149 Ibid. p. 366.
150 Ibid.
151 Ibid. p. 369.

Thus, the legal actions of prosecution, sentencing, victim redress, due process modelling and judicial statements constitute an armoury of expressivism in international criminal justice. These limit the expressivism of trials to authoritative messages delivered through a select group of courts. In the next section, I discuss literature which admits a conception of the criminal trial as communicative as distinct from expressive.

2.5. TOWARDS A COMMUNICATIVE THEORY OF THE TRANSITIONAL TRIAL

The moral and political philosophy of Jürgen Habermas provides a starting point for consideration of the role of communication in legal processes. Habermas' social theory of modernity challenged the classical tradition which gave pre-eminence to practical reason in shaping norms based on moral precepts for the purpose of creating reasonable social and political order.[152] Habermas argued that norm development was also subject to 'communicative reason.' Derived from the 'linguistic telos of mutual understanding', communicative rationality had guided the development of societies.[153] Drawing from anthropology and the work of Durkheim, Habermas saw language and linguistic understanding through communication as crucial in building social solidarity. He considered that Durkheim had neglected the significance of 'speech acts' in the formation of the collective conscience, and posited that communicative actions were the driving force of social solidarity.[154]

Habermas developed a theory of communicative action to guide social reconstruction. In this he departed from the dominant Weber-ian theory of action, which emphasised 'purposive activity and purposive rationality.'[155] While practical reason was received in the reconstructive social theory of Habermas, it did not provide the 'blueprint' for a normative theory of law and morality. Instead, practical reason was guided by the networks of social discourse which fuel and form the opinions that drive the democratic process, and ultimately confer legitimacy on legal institutions.[156]

In the area of moral philosophy, discourse theory had been influenced by the notion of will-formation in the Kantian sense and Aristotelian conceptions of ethics. Habermas advocated a break in legal theory from the framing of law from

---

152 Jürgen Habermas, *Between Facts and Norms: Contributions to a Discourse Theory of Law and Democracy* (Polity Press, 1996) pp. 3–4.

153 Ibid. pp. 4–5.

154 See Jürgen Habermas, *The Theory of Communicative Action: Volume 2 Lifeworld and System: A Critique of Functionalist Reason* (Beacon Press, 1987) pp. 57–76.

155 Ibid. p. 2.

156 Habermas, above n. 152, p. 5.

a purely normative perspective or political philosophy, and posited a discourse theory of law based on communicative action. He argued that in modern society there was often little connection between political theory and legal theory, and that normative approaches were constantly in danger of losing touch with social realities.[157] For this reason the 'production of legitimate law' required the mobilisation of the communicative freedom of citizens to permit the formation of political beliefs.[158]

Communicative freedom operates in the public sphere largely through civil society networks. From the perspective of liberal democratic theory, Habermas saw the social space for communications in the public sphere as signalling pressure points and thematising problems in society to be taken up by parliamentarians.[159] His theory highlighted the socially integrating impact of communicative and non-coercive processes.[160] For Habermas, law was the medium through which communicative action was transformed from the level of simple interactions to the abstract level of organised constitutional relationships.[161] Trials also operate in the public sphere. While trial dialogue is moderated by rules of procedure, courts are spaces where a degree of communicative freedom is permitted and where communicative reason may operate. Implicitly, Habermas saw a role for courts in reckoning with the social impact of mass crimes as trial actors engaged with the trauma of past violence and confronted the complexities of perpetration.[162]

Within criminal law philosophy, Antony Duff wrote of the communicative element of punishment and distinguished it from that of expression. Duff argued that punishment is communication rather than expression because:

> The idea of communication involves, as that of expression need not, the idea of a reciprocal and rational activity. Expression requires only one who expresses; if there is someone at whom it is directed, that person need figure only as its passive recipient; and if it aims (as it need not) to bring about any effect on its recipient, that intended effect could be entirely non-rational – it need not be mediated by the recipient's reason or understanding. By contrast, communication requires someone to, or with, whom we try to communicate; that person must (if communication is to be successful) be an active participant in the process, who receives and responds to the communication; and that reception and response must (or at least be intended to) be rational, in that communication appeals to the other's rational understanding.[163]

157 Ibid. pp. 5–6.
158 Ibid. pp. 146–147.
159 Ibid. p. 359.
160 Ibid. p. 6.
161 Ibid. p. 437.
162 Osiel above n. 1, p. 173.
163 Antony Duff, 'Punishment, Communication and Community' in Matt Matravers (ed.), *Punishment and Political Theory* (Hart Publishing, 1999) pp. 48, 49.

Conceiving punishment as a 'mode of rational communication (primarily with the offender)' to move him or her towards repentance reflected a kind of civic duty in the state, through the law, to treat all its citizens as 'as rational, responsible agents.'[164] Criticising Duff's theory, Ivison argued that while all criminal defendants are owed respect as rational and moral actors, Duff's formulation simply justified 'the murky ambiguities of punishment' in communicative terms. Ivison argued:

> [Punishment] is always in danger of being corrupted by the intrusion of desires for revenge or resentment, often fuelled and borne by cultural and social markers of race, gender, and class, and by historical contexts difficult to contain and transcend.[165]

Ivison highlighted the complexity of punishment's communicative value in multi-cultural societies, and in contexts where more than one source of law applies. Citing the Australian context, where the history of colonial relations with indigenous peoples continues to affect social attitudes towards appropriate criminal norms and punishment, he questioned the extent to which fundamental values are shared within a single polity. He concluded:

> This is critical for the communicative theory of punishment, for if we cannot show that a community of citizens share a set of fundamental norms and values, then it is not clear exactly what is being communicated to the offender via the 'communicative punishments' carried out in the name of the community.[166]

However, Duff maintained that the trial was a forum in which all members of a polity, by virtue of shared membership, call one another to account for public wrongs through fair legal process which is communicative and not merely expressive. Trials take this form because of a duty to both victims and perpetrators to establish the wrongfulness of crimes.[167] Bronitt and McSherry go further by arguing that trials are a site where social meaning is both contested and fleshed, thus raising the communicative potential of the dialogue and debates of criminal trial process.[168] In the next section I examine how transitional justice theorists have interpreted the criminal trial in transitional contexts beyond the goals of expressivism to reveal scope for a communicative theory of such trials.

---

164 Ibid.

165 Duncan Ivison, 'Justifying Punishment in Intercultural Contexts: Whose Norms?' in Matt Matravers (ed.) *Punishment and Political Theory* (Hart Publishing, 1999) pp. 88, 106.

166 Ibid. p. 100.

167 Antony Duff, 'Authority and Responsibility in International Law' in Samantha Beeson and John Tasioulas (eds), *The Philosophy of International Law* (Oxford University Press, 2010) pp. 589, 594–595.

168 Bronitt, above n. 51, p. 30.

2.5.1. TRIAL PROCESS AS DIALOGUE IN TRANSITIONAL JUSTICE THEORY

Mark Osiel took up the theme of dialogue or discursivity in the trial process in the context of transitional justice theory.[169] Osiel's conception of the transitional trial emphasised the conversations of the trial process rather than judicial suasion or the didactics of punishment. His theory located the communicative capacity of transitional trials in discursive procedure designed to foster public deliberation over past abuses by former regimes, to assist the society's transition to democracy.[170] Osiel's reference points were national post-conflict trials including the 1961 Eichmann trial and the 1985 Argentinian Military trials initiated by President Raul Alfonsín. He did not directly address the ad hoc Tribunals on which Damaska based his view of the expressive value of international criminal justice.

Osiel took as his analytic starting point the theory of Emile Durkheim on punishment and social solidarity. He regarded Durkheim's conception of the role of the criminal law and courts in organic (industrialised) societies as too limited.[171] Courts in particular operate not simply as 'interpreters of a society's collective conscience' whose essential unity is buttressed by moral values enshrined in the law.[172] Rather, courts have a creative function as well as capacity within the trial to accommodate disagreements within communities, including those deeply divided politically and where populations have been traumatised by state-sponsored violence.[173] Osiel argued that limiting courts to producing authoritative pronouncements that reinforce an illusory solidarity in such societies failed to recognise the benefits of discursive engagement with a society's past, which can be cultivated by the process of prosecution.[174] On his analysis, a discursive solidarity, not entertained by Durkheim, can be fostered by the internal dynamics of the trial, accompanied by public discussion of matters raised beyond the walls of the courtroom.[175]

Discursive solidarity admits of the reality and possible co-existence of conflicting interpretations of history, whereas the Durkheim-ian view assumed there was only one story to be told which evoked shared societal indignation at a breach of universally accepted moral principles.[176] Osiel conceived the transitional court as a site of civil dissension where parties to the trial express

---

169 Osiel, above n. 1, pp. 2–3, 37–55.
170 Ibid. p. 1.
171 Ibid. pp. 25–26.
172 Ibid. p. 32 citing Stephen Lukes and Andrew Scull (eds.), *Durkheim and the Law* (Robertson, 1983) p. 45.
173 Osiel, above n. 1, p. 35.
174 Ibid. p. 39.
175 Ibid.
176 Ibid. p. 140.

opposing views of justice and of the past events mediated by the ritual application of legal procedure.[177] A process of soul-searching by the affected community accompanies the trial and though painful, it is also poetic.[178] In describing the effect of the trial of Adolf Eichmann in Israel, Osiel cited a Jewish poet's metaphorical description of the trial as capturing 'the duality of our existence,' that is, of the Jews 'as a murdered people and the story of Israel as nation sitting in judgment.'[179]

Trials thus retain the element of social drama envisaged by Durkheim but, more importantly, according to Osiel:

> The judicial task … is to employ the law of evidence, procedure, and professional responsibility to recast the courtroom drama in terms of the 'theatre of ideas' where large questions of collective memory and even national identity are engaged.[180]

By putting such issues at the forefront of the proceedings, the court contributes to the emergence of a new social solidarity based not on consensus but engagement with difference.[181]

Osiel's approach means that the trial's concern with retribution, deterrence and broader expressivism will be reduced. While procedural rules will to some degree need to be modified, they must also constrain the public spectacle of the trial and stimulate public discussion 'in ways that foster the liberal virtues of toleration, moderation, and civil respect.'[182] The pedagogical purpose of trial proceedings then is to 'stimulate reflection' not only on past wrongdoing but on prospective norms.[183] While there is some correspondence here with Damaska's view of expressivism, Osiel's work harnesses the socio-political dynamics of the transitional trial for deeper localised purposes.

The significance of trials for mass atrocities calls for interpretation beyond the 'curative' or even symbolic meaning attached to punishment.[184] However, Osiel left open the question of whether transitional courts 'can entirely reconcile the traditional functions of criminal law: retribution and deterrence, with the dramaturgical demands of monumental didactics.'[185] This is because such trials play out a 'two-level game: legal and political, doctrinal and historiographical.'[186]

---

177 Ibid. p. 51.
178 Ibid. p. 16.
179 Ibid. citing Haim Gouri, 'Facing the Glass Booth' in Geoffrey H Hartman (ed.), *Holocaust Remembrance: The Shapes of Memory* (Wiley, 1993) p. 155.
180 Ibid. p. 3.
181 Ibid.
182 Ibid. p. 2.
183 Ibid.
184 Ibid. pp. 50–51.
185 Ibid. p. 293.
186 Ibid. p. 296.

Therefore, Osiel stressed that because the community's legal concepts and doctrines will typically 'have been severed from the underlying moral and political issues at stake', judges and court actors must apply a broad procedural brush. Crucially, the judiciary must allow all parties to the proceedings to 'widen the spatial and temporal frame of courtroom story-telling' to permit parties 'to flesh out their competing interpretations of history' and examine how the country was brought to a state where the crimes in question could happen. In this way debate within the court may resonate with public discourse beyond the courtroom.[187]

From discursive engagement with the historico-legal story told within the court, bolstered by freedoms of speech, press and assembly outside the court, a discursive solidarity emerges.[188] Discursive solidarity crystallises as common ground between differing perspectives on justice and the events of the past, which is settled on by means of engagement and cooperation to form the fabric of new collective memory.[189]

Damaska accepted Osiel's view of the communicative value of civil dissension in transitional trials insofar as debates at trial concern contextual issues surrounding the alleged crimes. However, Damaska cautioned against advancing the didactic role of transitional courts as entertaining anything in the 'theatre of ideas' that flouts moral fundamentals or agreements on basic protections.[190] Damaska suggested that any focus on narrow questions that stray from the universal moral minima of human rights law and its enforcement might lead to the suggestion that human rights are 'no more than an ethnic custom of the West' and as such incompatible with the ideals of international criminal justice.[191] Similarly, he concluded that the trial platform ought not to permit the accused 'freedom to advance his own account of events, unconstrained by legal relevancy' and from which may be 'propagated' views that international criminal justice would otherwise discourage.[192] While not opposed to adapting international criminal justice to local legal culture, Damaska sought to preserve its 'educational mission' within specific bounds and cautioned against providing space for enemies to represent international criminal justice as an 'alien imposition.'[193]

However, Osiel did not advocate the latitude in court proceedings suggested by Damaska. His emphasis is on the capacity of the liberal trial model (with some procedural modifications), to foster essential dialogue in transitional societies

187 Ibid.
188 Ibid. p. 50.
189 Ibid. p. 51.
190 Damaska, above n. 92, pp. 346–347.
191 Ibid.
192 Ibid. p. 359.
193 Ibid. p. 349.

from which local social solidarity destroyed by conflict may re-emerge. Legal procedure, adapted to provide public space for reflection on the past, mediates debate within the court. Although punishment of offenders forms part of the legal process, it is not the predominant ritual towards rebuilding solidarity. It is the process of engagement and deliberation that is the inherent value of the proceedings, as distinguished from the expressivism of due process modelling.

Osiel does not engage with the modifications to criminal procedure that international courts have made. In particular, he does not address the role of victims' voices in trial proceedings. His theory is a generic one based on the potential of legal process, sympathetically administered, to foster deliberative recovery in the transitional society. Damaska's view of the precedence of the expressive value of the transitional trial is also limited because his conclusions are based on the experience of the ad hoc Tribunals where the victim voice is absent, except as witness under adversarial procedure. Both theories have scope for deeper and richer interpretation if the victim is included through legal procedure which is more broadly dialogic and representational.

2.5.2. COMMUNICATION AND REPRESENTATION IN THE TRANSITIONAL TRIAL

The creation of a platform from which views of monumental past events may be openly communicated was significant in the Cambodian context. The long-term impunity of the Khmer Rouge imposed collective amnesia on the society either by the necessity of non-reflection during the period of rebuilding crushed lives after the Khmer Rouge revolution, or the insistence upon forgetting by successive governments for the purpose of political stability. This is discussed in historical context in Chapter four.

The Cambodian government's connections (past and current) with remnant Khmer Rouge cadres affected the negotiation of the Agreement for creation of the ECCC with the UN.[194] The government insisted that the court be located in Cambodia and comprised a majority of Cambodian judges. Of international concern was Cambodia's poor record of human rights enforcement, weak legal infrastructure and poorly trained judiciary, known to be subject to political interference.[195] These factors called for special measures within the Agreement to ensure that the Court functioned according to minimum international

194 Steven Ratner, 'Justice for the Khmer Rouge? Sir Ninian Stephen and the United Nations Group of Experts for Cambodia' in Timothy L.H. McCormack and Cheryl Saunders (eds.), *Sir Ninian Stephen: A Tribute* (Melbourne University Publishing, 2007) pp. 206, 219.

195 See *Report of the Secretary-General on the Khmer Rouge Trials* UN Doc. A/57/769 (31 March 2003), paras. [1], [11], [28]–[29].

standards of justice.[196] The ultimate form of the Court was a compromise to accommodate Cambodian sovereignty within an institution respecting human rights and due process of law.

Frédéric Mégret has pointed to the form of the ECCC in his analysis of hybridity in transitional trial forms.[197] I discuss hybrid courts in detail in Chapter three. The main elements of such courts are: their creation within the state where crimes were perpetrated; combined application of local and international law; and shared staffing of courts by national and international personnel.[198] Mégret saw in the hybrid transitional court the potential for greater representation of interests affected by the crimes it prosecutes.[199]

Mégret posited that the dual nature of certain international crimes provides a normative basis for the hybrid court form.[200] Even where there is political will and functional domestic courts to support local prosecutions, the magnitude of some international crimes may so threaten our sense of humanity that an international interest in accountability arises.[201] The ownership of such crimes by both national and international constituencies through the hybrid court form offered more representational justice by identifying and acknowledging the communities affected by them.[202]

Departiing from the dominant view of the expressive purpose of transtional trials, Megret described hybrid tribunals as 'sophisticated attempts at striking the best possible balance between the competing pulls of sovereignty and universalism in a way that maximizes the representational function of international criminal justice.'[203] While recognising that formation of the ECCC was 'probably above all a result of the pull and shove of international political negotiations,' he described the Tribunal as one for which the hybrid form was an appropriate fit.[204] Describing the infamous Cambodian killing fields as a product of 'domestic genocide ... borne of the nihilist folly of a totalitarian regime,' he concluded that a national court would not have done justice to what the world now views as clear breaches of humanity's most fundamental norms.[205] The

196 Ratner, above n. 194, p. 213. The special measures are discussed in Chapter four.

197 Frédéric Mégret, 'In Defence of Hybridity: Towards a Representational Theory of International Criminal Justice' (2005) 38 *Cornell International Law Journal* 725.

198 Dickinson, above n. 38, p. 295; David Cohen, 'Hybrid Justice in East Timor, Sierra Leone, and Cambodia: "Lessons Learned" and Prospects for the Future' (2007) 43 *Stanford Journal of International Law* 1; Sarah Williams, *Hybrid and Internationalised Criminal Tribunals: Selected Jurisdictional Issues* (Hart Publishing, 2012).

199 Mégret above n. 197, p. 742.

200 Ibid. p. 747.

201 Ibid. p. 737.

202 Ibid. pp. 740–743.

203 Ibid. p. 747.

204 Ibid. p. 747.

205 Ibid.

presence of international judges at the ECCC signals the international interest in the prosecution of the perpetrators, while an international court situated in The Hague would not do justice to the conspicuous national interest in judging the crimes.[206]

The representational function identified by Mégret is realised by a shift in focus from the outcomes of the transitional trial in the form of verdicts and sentences, to their process.[207] This, he wrote, invites recognition of the 'symbolic, aesthetic or communicative function' of such trials.[208] Referring to Durkheim, he suggested that transitional trials function to reconstitute the social through the theatre of hybrid court processes.[209] By focusing on the proceedings of the trial rather than their legal outcomes, the range of voices in trial processes expands the sociological meaning of the trial beyond the language of retribution and deterrence.[210]

Mégret did not examine the ECCC's form in detail. However, as I discuss in Chapter four, the application of inquisitorial criminal procedure under Cambodian law at the ECCC permitted inclusion of the victim's voice in proceedings to an unprecedented extent through the civil party action, which resulted in broader scope for representation of affected constituencies. This contrasts with the limited representational nature of proceedings in the ICTY, where the victim's role was restricted to that of witness under adversarial procedure. Moreover, the ICTY attracted criticism from Balkan communities because it was perceived as too remote from the affected communities and as such unrepresentative.[211]

2.5.3. COMMUNICATION, PROCEDURAL FAIRNESS AND JUSTICE

A communicative approach to transitional trials is also supported by studies on perceptions of fairness in judicial and arbitration processes.[212] This research indicates that the level of 'voice' afforded participants correlates with satisfaction

206 Ibid.
207 Ibid. p. 742.
208 Ibid.
209 Ibid.
210 Ibid. p. 741.
211 Dickenson, above n. 38, pp. 301–305.
212 See for example, J. Thibaut and L. Walker, *Procedural Justice: A Psychological Analysis* (Lawrence Erlbaum Associates Inc., Hillsdale NJ 1975); E. Lind and T. Tyler, *The Social Psychology of Procedural Justice* (Plenum, 1988); R. MacCoun, 'Voice, Control and Belonging: the Double Edged Sword of Procedural Fairness' (2005) 1 *Annual Review of Law and Social Science* 171–201.

that justice had been done.[213] The degree to which participants feel they are permitted to relate their experiences in a 'neutral and unbiased forum' becomes a criterion of fair process.[214] Even if participants had not secured their preferred outcomes, the research revealed that satisfaction with the justice process can be driven by opportunities to shape justice by being listened to in fair proceedings.[215] The research highlighted that trust in a court's authority may flow from inclusive, respectful proceedings.[216]

Other interdisciplinary research is applicable to the context of transitional justice and the issue of 'voice' in trials. Valerie Braithwaite's work on hope, power and governance theory, for instance, advocated making room within political and legal institutions for the doing of the extraordinary through the design of institutional structures that respect competing voices, but allow collective hopes to be articulated and engaged.[217] As discussed in Chapter nine, the ECCC's adaptive approach to reparations is one demonstration of the theory.

In addition, some peace and reconciliation studies inform the interpretation of the transitional trial in communicative terms. One example is Lederach's web analogy applied to peace building, wherein the 'critical yeast' is the network of relationships that connect multiple contributors to justice and reconciliation processes.[218] This may be applied to networks of civil society groups actively engaged with the work of Courts through education and victim support, thus facilitating greater justice dialogue within communities.

2.6. CONCLUSION

I suggest that the work of Osiel and Mégret taken together offers two markers of a communicative theory of trials: discursivity (or dialogue); and representation in trial process. Further indicators are recognition of victims' rights to redress and representation under human rights law, and the potential of inquisitorial trial procedure for broadening the ambit of trial discourse.[219] The trend towards

213 Eric Stover, Mychelle Balthazard and K. Alexa Koenig, 'Confronting Duch: Civil Party Participation in Case 001 at the Extraordinary Chambers in the Courts of Cambodia' (2011) 93 *International Review of the Red Cross* 503, 531–532.

214 T. Tyler, 'What is Procedural Justice? Criteria used by Citizens to Assess the Fairness of Legal Procedures' (1988) 22 *Law and Society Review* 103, 129.

215 Ray Nickson and John Braithwaite, 'Deeper, Broader, Longer Transitional Justice (2013) 11 *European Journal of Criminology* 445, 454.

216 Stover, above n. 213, p. 532.

217 Valerie Braithwaite, 'Collective Hope' in Valerie Braithwaite (ed), *Hope, Power, and Governance* (2004) 592 *The Annals of the American Academy of Political and Social Science* 6, 9.

218 John P. Lederach, *The Moral Imagination: The Art and Soul of Building Peace* (Oxford University Press, 2005) p. 91.

219 This is discussed in detail in Chapter five.

the greater inclusiveness of victims in trial processes and various procedural adaptations by Courts may also render transitional trials more amenable to a communication theory. In addition, interdisciplinary research offers important insights into how communicative trials might function constructively to aid societies in their recovery from gross violations of human rights.

After more than 20 years of experimentation in internationalised trial forms, it seems timely to both assess the viability of transitional trials based on the messages they send, and consider the possibility of an alternative or complementary theory of their operation. Juxtaposed with this is the expressivist approach to trials which is discussed further in the next chapter through examination of the political actions of instituting international criminal courts.

CHAPTER 3
THE DEVELOPMENT OF THE TRANSITIONAL TRIAL

3.1. INTRODUCTION

The nature of expressivism discussed in Chapter one is reflected in the political actions creating international transitional courts. The courts and tribunals created after the Cold War era (1948–1991) were vested with the expressive capital of the international community. This chapter explores the complexity of expressivism and its limitations as the theoretical basis of international transitional trials.

The chapter provides an overview of courts making up the modern international criminal justice system and identifies the general and specific expressivism underpinning constituent courts. The expressivism of international courts is traced to the International Military Tribunal at Nuremburg in 1945 which served in large part, as a model for the ad hoc Tribunals created in 1993 and 1994 to address international crimes in the Former Yugoslavia and the Balkans respectively. I argue that the later courts exhibited an expressive surplus in terms of their goals of ending impunity and deterring perpetration of international crimes. There was a corresponding deficit in their communicative value, through lack of resonance within the communities they served.

Evolution in institutional form brought hybrid transitional courts, which, due to their blend of national and international elements, promised more locally relevant justice processes. Some courts also began to integrate victim participation schemes which introduced new voices within retributive trial proceedings. This suggested the possibility of evaluating trials from a communicative as well as an expressive basis.

3.2. PROSECUTING INTERNATIONAL CRIMES

Until recently, when a state failed to criminalise conduct or prosecute individuals where it had an obligation to do so under international law, there were few prospects of accountability for international crimes.[1] The prosecution of individuals for criminal offences is a function of the state pursuant to national criminal law. Criminal jurisdiction stems from the notion of the sovereignty of states under international law.[2] Jurisdiction over crimes committed within states flows from the essential territoriality of sovereignty, while the principle of nationality gives states jurisdiction to prosecute nationals extraterritorially.[3] Under the Westphalian world order, this was easily interpreted by states as freedom of action within sovereign territory towards their citizens, with no guarantee of basic individual rights or international oversight of government actions. Internal sovereignty therefore, almost completely insulated governments and their representatives from criminal prosecution for abuse of their own citizens.[4] Furthermore, sovereignty safeguarded state actors under international law by the grant of immunity to representatives of sovereign states from the legal processes of other states.[5]

However, from the 1990s the international community endorsed the norm of accountability by instituting the first international criminal tribunals to enforce international human rights and humanitarian law. Those tribunals, and others that emerged to form the modern system of international criminal justice, prosecute individuals for crimes which are regarded as international due to their connection to international peace and security or their capacity to jolt the conscience of humanity.[6] At a minimum those crimes include genocide, crimes against humanity and potentially piracy and aggression.[7] It has also proved possible to prosecute terrorism under a national criminal code in at least one court brought into being by the United Nations Security Council.[8]

The path to vesting international courts with power to hold political leaders and others individually accountable for atrocity crimes began at the Nuremburg and Tokyo International Military Tribunals. Initiated by the Allied powers following the Second World War, the Tribunals were exercises in victors' justice by international trial. The broader authority of later international criminal tribunals reinforced the limits of state sovereignty. However, tension remained

---

1 Sarah Williams, *Hybrid and Internationalised Criminal Tribunals: Selected Jurisdictional Issues* (Hart Publishing, 2012) p. 1.

2 Ibid.

3 Ian Brownlie, *Principles of Public International Law*, 6th ed. (Oxford University Press, 2003) pp. 299, 301.

4 Steven R. Ratner, 'The Schizophrenias of International Criminal Law' (1998) 33 *Texas International Law Journal* 237, 242.

5 M. Cherif Bassiouni, *Introduction to International Criminal Law* (Transnational Publishers, 2003) p. 71.

6 Bruce Broomhall, *International Justice and the International Criminal Court: Between Sovereignty and the Rule of Law* (Oxford University Press, 2003) pp. 44–49.

7 Williams, above n. 1, p. 2.

8 See discussion of the applicable law of the Special Tribunal of Lebanon at section 3.6.2.2.

between the international interest of maintaining peace and security and enforcing international criminal law, and the enduring force of the sovereignty of states.[9] These factors were reflected in both political action and inaction towards creating international courts to prosecute international crimes. An overview of political actions with respect to the creation of international criminal justice institutions will illustrate the interplay of the factors.

3.2.1. THE INTERNATIONAL MILITARY TRIBUNAL AT NUREMBURG

Following Germany's seizure of Austria and Czechoslovakia in September 1939, Adolf Hitler's declared intention to invade Poland marked the beginning of the Second World War. In 1942, as reports of mass atrocities by German forces were received, the Allied Powers established the United Nations War Crimes Commission to investigate and gather evidence of war crimes.[10] In the Moscow Declaration of 1 November 1943, Britain, France and the Soviet Union expressed determination to prosecute Nazi operatives for war crimes.[11] The War Crimes Commission set the stage for creation of the first international trials at the end of the war by preparing a Draft Convention for the Establishment of a United Nations War Crimes Court.[12]

However, the form of the trials was not quickly agreed upon between the Allied Powers. Execution of the Nazi leadership of Germany was initially favoured among the Allies, but America ultimately pressed for trials, and triumphed.[13] Set against Stalin's initial preference for the mass shootings of Germans with some show trials, and the plan of US Treasury Secretary, Henry Morgenthau for harsh treatment of Germany with summary execution of many Germans, was Henry Stimson's opposition to summary executions. Stimson saw that option as vengeful, uncivilised and politically counter-productive in breeding more war.[14] The Stimson view, which ultimately prevailed, called for a display of due process in substantively American style.[15] Trials of Nazi war criminals were designed to expose to the German people the system of Nazi terror and demonstrate

9 Williams, above n. 1, p. 2.

10 Bassiouni, above n. 5, pp. 403–404.

11 William Schabas, *An Introduction to the International Criminal Court*, 3rd ed. (Cambridge University Press, 2007) p. 5.

12 *Draft Convention for the Establishment of a United Nations War Crimes Court*, UN War Crimes Commission, Doc. C.50(1), 30 September 1944.

13 Gary Bass, *Stay the Hand of Vengeance: the Politics of War Crimes Tribunals* (Princeton University Press, 2000) 147.

14 Ibid. p. 151.

15 Ibid.

American resolve to destroy any residue of it.[16] Trials rather than summary justice reflected the Stimson sense of the nobility of the American legal tradition, with criminal procedure consistent with the United States' *Bill of Rights* as its public expression.[17] The decision to hold trials seemed to establish a foundation for a new world order based on the rule of law.[18] Indeed, the Nuremburg trials did lay a foundation for the development of a body of international criminal law and the creation of a new generation of international courts which emerged nearly five decades later.[19]

At Nuremburg, Chief Prosecutor Robert Jackson, of the United States, knew that the legitimacy of the International Military Tribunal (IMT) proceedings turned on fair legal process in determining the guilt of the Nazi defendants. The notion of the fair trial is grounded in the epistemological basis of criminal law, and the justification for punishment premised on accurate and truthful fact-finding as to a defendant's guilt.[20] The expressive record of the proceedings would have had no credibility if the rights of the defendants to a fair trial were not respected.[21] Article 16 of the IMT Charter set down the defendants' minimum fair trial rights.[22] However, these were not the equivalent of those afforded defendants in the United States system where defence in trials is a constitutional right. The lean list of rights appears to have been in anticipation of 'obstructive' tactics by the defendants.[23]

In 1945, at the London International Assembly, a group of scholars and public officials developed the norms that emerged in the 1945 Charter of the International Military Tribunal of Nuremburg.[24] The United States advanced the argument that the future peace of the world would be served by an international judicial determination that aggressive war is a crime under international law, warranting individual criminal prosecution of those most responsible.[25] This

---

16 Ibid. p. 163, citing the *Stimson Diaries*, Vol. 48, pp. 36, 44.

17 Ibid. pp. 165, 173.

18 Leila Nadya Sadat, 'The Nuremburg Paradox' (2010) 58 *American Journal of Comparative Law* 151, 153.

19 Robert Cryer, *Prosecuting International Crimes: Selectivity and the International Criminal Law Regime* (Cambridge University Press, 2005) p. 40.

20 Salvatore Zappalà, 'The Rights of Victims v the Rights of the Accused' (2010) 8 *Journal of International Criminal Justice* 137, 145.

21 'United States: Report to the President from Justice Robert Jackson, Chief of Counsel for the United States in the Prosecution of the Axis War Criminal' (1945) 39:3 Supplement: Official Documents, *American Journal of International Law* 178, 182.

22 Göran Sluiter et al., *International Criminal Procedure: Principles and Rules* (Oxford University Press, 2013) p. 75; See *Agreement for the Prosecution and Punishment of the Major War Criminals of the European Axis Powers and Charter of the International Military Tribunal* 82 UNTS 279 [IMT Charter].

23 Ibid. p. 46, citing Justice Jackson's report to President Truman on 6 June 1945.

24 Bassiouni, above n. 5, p. 404.

25 Bass, above n. 13, p. 75.

appeared in the IMT Charter as crimes against peace as Article 6(a). However, the IMT had to determine whether the Charter's provisions on crimes against peace and crimes against humanity (Article 6(c)) constituted retroactive criminal law.[26]

In expressive judicial statements, the Tribunal construed the Article 6(a) crime as rooted in the larger principle of justice, in circumstances where treaties are defied and neighbouring states are attacked without warning.[27] Similarly, the prosecution of crimes against humanity under Article 6(c) was justified in terms of the offence to humanity that the crimes represented grounded in humanity itself, the law of nations and natural law.[28] As such the legal status of the charges transcended the precedence of national law pursuant to the principle of state sovereignty.[29] The perpetrators of such a crime were assumed to be enemies of mankind under international law and accordingly attracted universal jurisdiction.[30] Thus, the IMT's judgment of Nazi war criminals confronted the violent effects of extreme manifestations of state sovereignty and attendant unbridled disregard for human dignity.[31] Harnessing the expressive capital of criminal law with its condemnatory language and structures, the IMT declared certain limits to state power and sovereign immunity when it stated that 'individuals have international duties which transcend the national obligations of obedience imposed by the individual State.'[32]

While the IMT brought the first charges for crimes against humanity under Article 6(c) of its Charter, the crime was limited to the context of war or aggression towards other states.[33] This made possible the prosecution of Nazi officials for war crimes and large-scale, systematic persecution based on racial, religious, or political grounds against Jews during the war, but the requirement of a state of war prevented prosecutions for systematic persecution of Jews prior to the war. Accordingly, the IMT Charter's jurisdictional limits meant that the trials failed to fully comprehend the scope of the holocaust and the victimisation of European Jewry.[34]

---

26 Cryer, above n. 19, pp. 39–40, 248–249, 286.

27 'International Military Tribunal (Nuremburg), Judgment and Sentences, October 1 1946' (1947) 41 *American Journal of International Law* 172, 219 [IMT Judgment].

28 Diane Orentlicher, 'Settling Accounts' (1991) 100 *Yale Law Journal* 2537, 2556.

29 Ibid.

30 Ibid. p. 2557.

31 Antonio Cassese, *International Criminal Law*, 2nd ed. (Oxford University Press, 2008) p. 320.

32 IMT Judgment above n. 27, p. 221.

33 John Dugard, 'Reconciliation and Justice: the South African Experience' (1998) 9 *Transnational Law & Contemporary Problems* 277; *Charter of the United Nations* (1945) ATS 1 [UN Charter].

34 Yael Danieli, 'Reappraising the Nuremburg Trials and Their Legacy: The Role of Victims in International Law' (2005–2006) 27 *Cardozo Law Review* 1633, 1641.

The prosecution narrative aimed to express the depth of the defendants' culpability.[35] Amann argued that the expression of condemnation of the evils of Nazism received as much attention as the punishment of the indicted war criminals.[36] Indeed, Chief Prosecutor Jackson in his opening statement captured the essence of the trials when he spoke of the defendants not as individuals, but as 'symbols of an evil that had befallen Europe and that must never recur.'[37]

> What makes this inquest significant is that these prisoners represent influences that will lurk in the world long after their bodies have turned to dust. We will show them to be living symbols of racial hatreds, of terrorism and violence, and of the arrogance and cruelty of power. They are symbols of fierce nationalism and militarism, of intrigue and war-making which have embroiled Europeans generation after generation, crushing its manhood, destroying its homes, and impoverishing its life.[38]

Couched in these terms, the statement had specific expressive value in its condemnation of the Nazi authorities while not denouncing the nation as whole. Furthermore, the stigmatisation of acts of aggressive war and crimes against humanity illustrated the evils of totalitarianism and amplified the virtue of democratic governance.[39] In this, the IMT's use of the dual narratives of adversarial trial procedure arguably aided the prosecution's monumental didactics.

The public nature of the trials and the adversarial mode of evidence-testing probably enhanced the credibility of the proceedings over time, but there were departures from the Anglo-American model of procedure. The most notable was the Tribunal's reliance on a vast body of documentary evidence, more usually associated with inquisitorial proceedings.[40] The availability of ample documentary evidence from Germany's diplomatic and military records of the Nazi period, and large pools of financial assistance, primarily from the United States, to support legal teams made for expeditious trials.

However, the involvement of victims of crimes in IMT proceedings was minimal.[41] The failure to include more victim testimony or any substantive

---

35 Mark A. Drumbl, *Atrocity Punishment and International Law* (Cambridge University Press, 2007) p. 3.

36 Dianne Marie Amann, 'Group Mentality, Expressivism and Genocide' (2002) 2 *International Criminal Law Review* 93, 121.

37 Ibid.

38 Opening Statement of Supreme Court Justice, Robert H. Jackson, Chief Prosecutor for the International Military Tribunal, 21 November 1945, reprinted in *Trial of the Major War Criminals before the International Military Tribunal* (1948) Vol. 2, p. 99.

39 Sluiter, above n. 22, p. 46.

40 Ibid.

41 Brianne McGonigle Leyh, *Procedural Justice? Victim Participation in International Criminal Proceedings* (Intersentia, 2011) p. 136.

forum for victim communities kept the proceedings within narrow limits.[42] In this way, the carefully crafted messages of the IMT architects were not intercepted by voices of constituencies directly affected by the crimes before the Tribunal.

3.2.2. THE INTERNATIONAL MILITARY TRIBUNAL FOR THE FAR EAST IN TOKYO

The creation of the International Military Tribunal for the Far East (IMTFE) was by unilateral political action. Unlike the IMT, the drafting of the Tokyo Tribunal's Charter was by executive order, rather than an international conference.[43] Following the Potsdam Declaration on 14 August 1945, the United States Joint Chiefs of Staff commissioned General Douglas MacArthur to set up international courts for the investigation and arrest of Japanese war crimes suspects. On 19 January 1946, MacArthur ordered the creation of the IMTFE to implement the terms of the Japanese surrender to the Allied powers.[44] The Allies were consulted after the issuance of the order; a position purportedly justified by the greater military contribution of the United States against Japan and victory in the war.[45]

Like the IMT, the IMTFE had jurisdiction over war crimes, crimes against humanity, and crimes against peace. Participation in a common plan or conspiracy to commit crimes against peace, and crimes against humanity were also within the Tribunal's jurisdiction. Beyond this similarity, as Cryer wrote, 'it is almost as if the Nuremburg and Tokyo IMTs are related in the manner that Dorian Gray was to his painting.'[46]

Though the IMT was certainly criticised as representing victors' justice, it conducted trials in a manner generally perceived as fair. The IMTFE, on the other hand, has been assessed as fair in terms of its governing instruments, but substantively unfair in their application.[47] The nature of selectivity in the indictment process and unfairness towards the defendants at trial stand out as the reasons the Tokyo trials are now 'almost totally ignored.'[48] Several of the Tribunal judges were opposed to the exclusion of Japanese Emperor Hirohito from prosecution. Judge Bernard found the exclusion on grounds of expedience

---

42 Ibid.

43 Yves Beigbeder, International Criminal Tribunals: Justice and Politics (Hampshire, Palgrave Macmillan, 2011) pp. 37–38.

44 Cryer, above n. 19, 43–44.

45 Beigbeder, above n. 43, p. 38.

46 Cryer, above n. 19, p. 46.

47 Neil Boister and Robert Cryer, *The Tokyo International Military Tribunal: A Reappraisal* (Oxford University Press, 2008) pp. 324–325.

48 Cryer, above n. 19, p. 47.

for the Allied occupation in Japan to be unacceptable.[49] Tribunal President Webb also saw the emperor's immunity from prosecution as in the interests of the occupying power, and voted against the death penalty for the defendants on the grounds that Hirohito, who had the greatest authority over conduct of the war, had not been indicted.[50]

Judge Pal criticised the prosecution arguments and asserted that the legitimacy of the trial was tarnished by the hypocrisy of the Allies towards the defendants. After a history of Western colonial coercion, the Japanese defendants should not have been condemned for following European precedents in warfare. Moreover, no crime committed by the defendants approached the ubiquity of dropping nuclear bombs on Hiroshima and Nagasaki.[51]

West Germany initially rejected the Nuremburg precedents but following reunification they were widely accepted within the country. Moreover, in 1998, Germany was a strong supporter of the creation of the International Criminal Court.[52] However, the Tokyo trials failed to acquire legitimacy in Japan.[53] There was a corresponding lack of pedagogical value as an international trial model. Thus, Drumbl concluded that the didactic value of international proceedings is not guaranteed.[54] Unredeemed from the bias of victors' justice and unilateral political action, the IMTFE seems a model of the potential problems associated with prosecuting international crimes in such a mode. The IMTFE legacy therefore, is correspondingly expressive in a negative sense.

3.3. INTERNATIONAL CRIMES AND THE COLD WAR

While the International Military Tribunals established a jurisdictional foundation for the prosecution of international crimes, the period of the Cold War (1948–1991) was a one of expressive political inaction with respect to the creation of international transitional courts. However, the period saw the development of human rights and international criminal law, albeit constrained by state sovereignty concerns.

After the IMT trials, the United Nations General Assembly unanimously affirmed principles of law enshrined in the IMT Charter.[55] The United Nations

---

49 Ibid. p. 208; Richard H. Minear, *Victors' Justice: The Tokyo War Crimes Trial* (Princeton University Press, 1971) pp. 111–113.

50 Ibid.

51 Ibid. p. 207.

52 Christoph Burchard, 'The Nuremberg Trial and its Impact on Germany' (2006) 4 *Journal of International Criminal Justice* 800, 815–822.

53 Boister, above n. 47, pp. 316, 321.

54 Drumbl, above n. 35, p. 175.

55 UNGA Res. 95 (1) UN Doc. A/RES/1/95 (11 December 1946).

(UN) also commissioned a formulation of the Nuremburg principles by the International Law Commission.[56] A new legal framework for human rights law emerged but encountered opposition centred on sovereignty issues. In 1948, the Universal Declaration of Human Rights (UDHR) was adopted, proclaiming rights pursuant to Article 55 of the United Nations Charter. Article 55 called for 'universal respect for, and observance of, human rights and fundamental freedoms for all without distinction as to race, sex, language, or religion,' while Article 56 invoked members' commitment to cooperate in the achievement of that purpose.[57] That criminal sanction might attach to a state's failure to comply with human rights standards was not contemplated then, as states continued to view their dealings with their own citizens exclusively as a matter of national prerogative in line with Article 2(7) of the Charter, subject only to the UN Security Council enforcement power to maintain international peace and security pursuant to Chapter VII.[58]

In the same year, the Convention on the Prevention and Punishment of the Crime of Genocide established a duty on states to prosecute human rights violations amounting to genocide.[59] While it was envisaged that the Convention would include protection for social and political groups against genocidal acts, the negotiators of the Convention ultimately determined to exclude the possibility.[60] Article II of the Convention defines genocide by reference to five acts directed only against a 'national. ethnical, racial or religious group' 'with intent to destroy [the group] in whole or in part'.[61] Limiting the crime in this way was the result of drafting at the insistence of the Soviet Union to exclude alleged atrocities against political, social or economic groups.[62] Government-sponsored repression of political or social groups therefore falls outside the Convention definition.

The Genocide Convention also provided that genocidal acts would be 'tried by a competent tribunal of the State in the territory of which the act was committed, or by such international penal institution as may have jurisdiction' to do so.[63] In practice, both the limits of the definition of the crime and the absence of any international criminal tribunal until 1993 meant that individuals

---

56 'Principles of International Law Recognised in the Charter of the Nurnberg Tribunal and in the Judgment of the Tribunal, with Commentaries', *Yearbook of the International Law Commission* (1950) Vol. II, p. 195.

57 UN Charter arts. 55, 56.

58 Dugard, above n. 33, p. 277.

59 *Convention on the Prevention and Punishment of Genocide*, Opened for signature 9 December 1948, 78 UNTS 277 (entered into force 12 January 1951) [Genocide Convention].

60 Cryer, above n. 19, p. 176.

61 Genocide Convention Art. II.

62 Ratner, above n. 4, p. 246.

63 Genocide Convention Art. VI.

who committed acts against political groups with genocidal intent could evade prosecution. Orentlicher argued that opposition from states on the basis that members of governments might be subject to prosecution, and the fact that this could threaten conditions of international peace, effectively inverted the justification for the Nuremburg prosecutions of crimes against humanity.[64] Thus, the Convention was expressive for what it excluded from the realm of prosecution.

Added to the developing human rights framework were regional Conventions, such as the 1950 European Convention for the Protection of Human Rights and Fundamental Freedoms, as well as the International Covenant on Civil and Political Rights (ICCPR) in 1966. Both enhanced certain rights granted under the UDHR and provided machinery for gathering data on signatory states' compliance, while allowing a means for individual recourse to international monitoring bodies when rights were violated.[65] However, the instruments were similarly expressive in what they failed to include: for example, both were silent as to the culpability of state officials under international law for gross human rights violations against their own citizenry. Furthermore, the failure of the UN to create a permanent international criminal court seemed to indicate that prosecutions to enforce law against serious violations of human rights would not receive international support even as evidence of state-sponsored violence increased.[66]

During the years of the Cold War as international tensions between the Soviet Union and the United States mounted, the lack of political will within the UN Security Council on security matters hampered action to address impunity for international crimes occurring on a massive scale in numerous states.[67] In cases of civil war where egregious human rights violations occurred within the territory of a state, the international community did not intervene and justice mechanisms in the aftermath of conflict were decided upon by successor regimes based on national political imperatives.[68]

In some states, trials were chosen as the appropriate transitional justice mechanism; for example, the trials in 1975 of leaders of the military junta that ruled Greece from 1967–1974.[69] As the Soviet empire declined and former authoritarian regimes transitioned towards democracy, amnesty laws and truth commissions were engaged in the Americas to placate powerful military elites

---

64 Orentlicher, above n. 28, p. 2559.

65 Dugard, above n. 33, p. 277.

66 Ibid.

67 Michael P. Scharf, 'Tools for Enforcing International Criminal Justice in the New Millennium: Lessons from the Yugoslavia Tribunal' (1999–2000) 49 *DePaul Law Review* 925, 926.

68 Dugard, above n. 33, p. 278.

69 Naomi Roht-Arriaza, 'Overview' in Naomi Roht-Arriaza (ed.), *Impunity and Human Rights in International Law and Practice* (Oxford University Press, 1995) pp. 73, 78.

unwilling to cooperate if faced with prosecutions. The experience of Argentina in the 1980s exemplifies the nature of political transitions of the time: first, the former military dictatorship resisted national elections without amnesty laws; second, subsequent attempts by the elected president Raul Alfonsín to prosecute top military leaders for past abuses met with uprisings, leading to the making of an end date for trials and the creation of a truth commission as a substitute for the compromised trial process.[70]

Thus, in the several decades after the Nuremburg trials, accountability for grave human rights violations was captive to the '*realpolitik* of political settlements' often with impunity for state-sponsored atrocities.[71] In the background however, the UN-commissioned work by the International Law Commission on a draft code of offences against the peace and security of mankind continued, and a framework for international criminal law through an expanding body of treaty law was emerging.[72] The Geneva Conventions of 1949 and the 1977 Protocols thereto codified international humanitarian law and obligated states to extradite or prosecute individuals responsible for interstate crimes wherever they located them.[73] The 1984 Convention against Torture required States parties to criminalise and prosecute certain offences committed within their territory and established universal jurisdiction in the event of failure to prosecute.[74]

Incremental legal limits placed on sovereign prerogatives in this way also informed debates among human rights activists and international lawyers on the role international law could play in shaping the policies of new governments towards the crimes of former regimes, and in protecting fragile new democracies.[75] Simultaneously an international grassroots movement challenged international acquiescence to the pervasive state practice of impunity.[76]

Scholarly debate continued between transitional justice theorists on the dynamics, benefits and shortcomings of the various justice mechanisms that might be engaged to assist fragile societies.[77] However, as Cold War tensions subsided, the 1980s practice in transitional justice of granting amnesty, with or

70 Lisa Laplante, 'Outlawing Amnesty: The Return of Criminal Justice in Transitional Justice Schemes' (2009) 49 *Virginia journal of International Law* 915, 924.

71 M. Cherif Bassiouni, Accountability for Violations of International Humanitarian Law and Other Serious Violations of Human Rights *in* M. Cherif Bassiouni (ed.), *Post-Conflict Justice* (Transnational Publishers, 2002) 1.

72 UNGA Resolution 177 (II) UN Doc. A/RES/177(II) (21 November 1947).

73 *Geneva Convention IV Relative to the Prevention of Civilian Persons in Time of War*, opened for signature 12 August 1949, 75 UNTS 287, art. 146.

74 *Convention against Torture and Other Cruel, Inhumane or Degrading Treatment of Punishment*, opened for signature 4 February 1985, (1985) 23 ILM 1028 (entered into force 26 June 1987) art. 5(2).

75 Orentlicher, above n. 29, p. 2542.

76 Laplante, above n. 70, p. 934.

77 M. Cherif Bassiouni, 'Searching for Peace and Achieving Justice: The Need for Accountability' (1996) *Law & Contemporary Problems* 9, 13; Richard L. Siegel, 'Transitional

without truth commissions, to mark a new government's departure from an old regime was overtaken by new legal action at the geopolitical level.

3.4. CREATING INTERNATIONAL CRIMINAL COURTS

In 1992, the spectre of 'ethnic cleansing' in the Balkans, involving the forced removal of populations, brutality and inhumane acts against civilians, raised the prospect of another holocaust in Europe. World public opinion opposed inaction by the international community and threatened the credibility of the UN.[78] The UN Security Council, pursuant to Chapter VII of the UN Charter, took the unprecedented step of creating an international criminal tribunal to prosecute violations of international humanitarian law occurring on a massive scale in the territory of the Former Yugoslavia.[79]

The new tribunal was the International Criminal Tribunal for the Former Yugoslavia (ICTY). In 1994, by similar ad hoc process, the Security Council created the International Criminal Tribunal for Rwanda (ICTR).[80] The two international tribunals became known as the ad hoc Tribunals. Implicitly, both institutions gave effect to fair trial guarantees enshrined in the body of human rights instruments developed since the Nuremburg trials.[81] For example, Article 21 of the ICTY Statute and Article 20 of the ICTR Statute reflect protections for accused persons under Article 14 of the ICCPR. Such guarantees flowed as a matter of intrinsic justice. Although somewhat experimental initially, both Tribunals inaugurated international trials rich in expressivism.

Justice: A Decade of Debate and Experience' (1998) 20 *Human Rights Quarterly* 433; Miriam J. Aukerman, 'Extraordinary Evil, Ordinary Crime: A Framework for Understanding Transitional Justice' (2002) 15 *Harvard Human Rights Journal* 39; Charles P. Trumbull IV, 'Giving Amnesties a Second Chance' (2007) 25 *Berkeley Journal of International Law* 283; Lorna McDonald, 'International Law as a "Tiered Process": Transitional Justice at the Local, National and International Level' in Kieran McEvoy and Lorna McGregor (eds.), *Transitional Justice from Below: Grassroots Activism and the Struggle for Change* (Hart Publishing, 2008) p. 3.

78 Payam Akhavan, 'The Yugoslav Tribunal at the Crossroads: The Dayton Peace Agreement and Beyond' (1996) 18 *Human Rights Quarterly* 259, 263.

79 UNSC Res. 827 (1993) UN Doc. S/RES/827 (25 May 1993).

80 UNSC Res. 955 (1994) UN Doc. S/RES/955 (8 November 1994).

81 Sluiter, above n. 22, p. 75.

3.4.1. THE INTERNATIONAL CRIMINAL TRIBUNAL FOR THE FORMER YUGOSLAVIA

The establishment of the International Criminal Tribunal for the Former Yugoslavia (ICTY) in 1993 occurred during an armed conflict, as peace negotiations were not completed until several years after the Tribunal's creation. Akhavan noted that, while these circumstances were unique, the ICTY represented demand for institutionalised justice which 'perhaps inadvertently' became an integral part of the peace process.[82] Against the long-term practice of *realpolitik* overriding justice for the perpetrators of mass crimes, Scheffer argued that multiple reports made by the United States to the Security Council in early 1993, which substantiated the commission of atrocities in Bosnia and Croatia, made it untenable to dismiss the issue of accountability.[83] Following the Council's unanimous endorsement of an 'in principle' resolution to establish a criminal tribunal to address identified crimes within the Former Yugoslavia, the United States Secretary of State, Madeleine Albright, addressed the Council:

> There is an echo in this chamber today. The Nuremburg principles have been reaffirmed. We have preserved the long-neglected compact made by the community of civilised nations 48 years ago in San Francisco to create the United Nations and enforce the Nuremburg principles. The lesson that we are accountable to international law may have finally taken hold in our collective memory. This will be no victor's tribunal.[84]

Over the subsequent years, scholars claimed the expressive value of criminal punishment in deterring perpetrators of gross human rights violations and international crimes.[85] In time, the ICTY conveyed the 'moral propaganda of international criminal justice' against would-be aggressors at large.[86]

As the first international tribunal of its kind, the ICTY had functional difficulties in its early years. It took 14 months to appoint a prosecutor due to the opposition of Russia to any NATO country appointment, or any Muslim.[87] The ICTY struggled until after the negotiation of the Dayton Peace Accords to secure cooperation from states of the Former Yugoslavia and NATO forces in the investigation of cases and arrest of accused persons.[88] By 1997, however,

---

82 Akhavan, above n. 78, p. 259.

83 David Scheffer, *All the Missing Souls: A Personal History of the War Crimes Tribunals* (Princeton University Press, 2012) p. 22.

84 Ibid.

85 Payham Akhavan, 'Justice in the Hague, Peace in the Former Yugoslavia? A Commentary on the United Nations War Crimes Tribunal' (1998) 20 *Human Rights Quarterly* 737; And see Antonio Cassese, 'Reflections on International Criminal Justice' (1998) 61 *Modern Law Review* 1.

86 Ibid. p. 742.

87 Scheffer, above n. 83, p. 31.

88 Cryer, above n. 19, p. 108; See Scheffer, above n. 83, pp. 39–42 on bureaucratic delays in NATO intelligence sharing.

international forces were providing security for on-site investigations and were arresting higher-level ICTY indictees.[89] This gave impetus to efforts to deter 'conflict entrepreneurs' invested in the violent manipulation of social norms to consolidate their economic or political power.[90] The expressive potential of enforcement or even the prospect of it through issuance of warrants promised to dissuade existing or future perpetrators through loss of reputation and power.[91]

3.4.2. INTERNATIONAL CRIMINAL TRIBUNAL FOR RWANDA (ICTR)

In April 1994, a murderous rampage by Rwandan extremists attempted to expel the Tutsi people from Rwanda.[92] The Special Rapporteur of the United Nations Commission on Human Rights, Rene Degnui, reported on the unprecedented nature of the massacres in Africa, adding that they were systematic and incited by the media.[93] Referring to the definition of genocide in the Genocide Convention, he noted that evidence of the elements of the crime existed.[94] The UN Security Council established a commission of experts to investigate violations of international humanitarian law in Rwanda, while the idea of establishment of an international tribunal circulated in the media and in diplomatic circles.[95] By November 1994, the UN Security Council determined that 'genocide and other systematic, widespread and flagrant violations of international humanitarian law committed in Rwanda' constituted a threat to international peace and security.[96] The Security Council adopted UNSC Resolution 955 to authorise creation of the International Criminal Tribunal for Rwanda (ICTR) pursuant to Chapter VII of the Charter.[97]

The creation of this second tribunal seemed indicative of the determination to signal an end to impunity for international crimes.[98] Supporters of the new

---

89 Ibid.

90 Robert D. Sloan, 'The Expressive Capacity of International Punishment: The Limits of the National Law Analogy and the Potential of International Criminal Law' (2007) 43 *Stanford Journal of International Law* 39, 73.

91 Ibid. p. 74.

92 William A. Schabas, *The UN International Tribunals: The Former Yugoslavia, Rwanda and Sierra Leone* (Cambridge University Press, 2006) p. 22.

93 *The Situation of Human Rights in Rwanda*, UN Doc. A/49/508, S/1994/1157 (13 October 1994) [20], [42]–[59].

94 Ibid.

95 Schabas, above n. 92, p. 27.

96 *Report of the Secretary-General Pursuant to Paragraph 5 of Security Council Resolution 955 (1994)* UN Doc. S/1995/134 (13 February 1995) [1].

97 UNSC Res. 955 (1994) UN Doc. S/RES/955 (8 November 1994).

98 José E. Alvarez, 'Crimes of States/Crimes of Hate: Lessons from Rwanda' (1999) 24 *Yale Journal of International Law* 365, 372.

institutions, including international scholars, legal professionals and leaders of human rights organisations, rallied in support of the two ad hoc Tribunals as representing foundational steps towards the credible enforcement of international humanitarian law, and development of a body of jurisprudence to instil universal norms within fractured societies.[99]

3.4.3. NORM DEVELOPMENT BY THE AD HOC TRIBUNALS

While both institutions experienced operational problems in their early years, they nonetheless produced a body of expressive jurisprudence. Convictions for genocide were achieved and elements of the crime refined.[100] ICTY jurisprudence resolved a disparity in war crimes prosecutions by affirming that war crimes could be committed in both international and internal armed conflicts.[101]

The ad hoc Tribunals also contributed to development of international criminal law in the area of sexual violence. The ICTR's *Akayesu* decision established that sexual violence, including rape, constituted the enumerated act of serious bodily and mental harm under Article II(2)(b) of the Genocide Convention.[102] While the statute of the ICTY granted jurisdiction to prosecute rape as a crime against humanity, the ICTR reshaped formulations of the elements of the crime as physical invasion of a sexual nature in coercive circumstances.[103] In *Prosecutor v. Kunaric* the Tribunal held that the key criterion was lack of consent and violation of sexual autonomy.[104] Furthermore, in the Appeal Chamber, it was held that while force or threat of force may be relevant in providing evidence of the absence of consent, force is not an element *per se*.[105] The ICTY also found that rape can constitute torture where the elements of torture are satisfied, and secured convictions on that basis.[106]

Thus, from court chambers in The Hague and Arusha, Tanzania, international judges of the ad hoc Tribunals developed and expanded the normative content

99 Ibid.

100 See for example, *Prosecutor v. Kambanda (Judgment)* TC, ICTR-97-23-S (4 September 1998); *Prosecutor v. Akayesu (Judgment)* ICTR-96-4-T (2 September 1998); *Prosecutor v. Musema (Judgment)* TC, ICTR-96-13 (27 January 2000).

101 *Prosecutor v. Tadic*, Decision on the Defence Motion for Interlocutory Appeal on Jurisdiction TC, ICTY-94-1-AR72 (2 October 1995) paras. 97–137.

102 *Prosecutor v. Akayesu (Judgment)* TC, ICTR-96-4-T, (2 September 1998) paras. 706–707.

103 *Prosecutor v. Akayesu (Judgment)* TC, ICTR-96-4-T, (2 September 1998) paras. 597–598.

104 *Prosecutor v. Kunaric, Kovac & Vukovic (Judgment)* TC, ICTY IT-96-23 & IT-96-23/1 (22 November 2001) paras. 440–460.

105 *Prosecutor v. Kunaric, Kovac & Vukovic (Appeal Judgment)* AC, ICTY IT-96-23 & IT-96-23/1 (22 November 2002) para. 129.

106 *Prosecutor v. Delalić, Mucić, Delić & Landžo (Judgment)* TC, ICTY IT-96-21-T (22 November 1998) paras. 475–497.

of human rights and international humanitarian law jurisprudentially.[107] The international criminal justice paradigm emerged as the judges elucidated human rights norms and applied them to the two post-conflict contexts through formal due process of law.[108]

3.4.4. EXPRESSIVE SURPLUS AND COMMUNICATIVE DEFICIT AT THE AD HOC TRIBUNALS

Underpinning the emergent justice paradigm was the view that international criminal accountability is preferable to private vengeance, compromised national criminal justice, collective amnesia or amnesty regarding past crimes of atrocity.[109] International criminal trials were also espoused as mollifying victims' calls for justice, thereby fostering reconciliation, while promoting the national and international rule of law.[110] They were conceived as operating to end the impunity of those who violate human rights, while providing a mechanism for the transformation of social norms in developing democracies.[111]

Both ad hoc Tribunals were richly expressive in a positive sense in terms of their multiple goals, their achievements in securing convictions of high-level perpetrators, and the development of international norms.[112] However, their communicative value in the communities they served proved to be minimal. While the ICTY offered the perception of legitimacy, impartiality and efficacy attached to international trial proceedings, their remoteness from, and lack of connection with, local Balkans constituencies eroded their legitimacy.[113] An empirical study in 1999 indicated that perceptions of the ICTY held by a large sample of lawyers and judges of various ethnic backgrounds within Bosnian society were poorly informed about the work of the Tribunal and suspicious about its methods and trial outcomes.[114] Further studies revealed that negative local perceptions of the ICTY increased over time among Bosnians, Croats

---

107 Mirjan Damaska, 'What is the Point of International Criminal Justice?' (2008) 83 *Chicago-Kent Law Review* 329, 335, 345.

108 Alvarez, above n. 98, p. 374.

109 Cassese, above n. 85, pp. 1–8.

110 Alvarez, above n. 98, p. 374.

111 Ruti Teitel, 'Transitional Jurisprudence: The Role of the Law in Political Transformation' (1997) 106 *Yale Law Journal* 2009, 2036–2037.

112 Damaska, above n. 107, pp. 331–335.

113 Laura A. Dickinson, 'The Promise of Hybrid Courts' 2003) 93 *American journal of International Law* 295, 301, 303.

114 The Human Rights Center and International Human Rights Clinic, University of California, Berkeley and Center for Human Rights, University of Sarajevo, 'Justice Accountability and Social Reconstruction: An Interview Study of Bosnian Judges and Prosecutors' (2000) 18 *Berkeley Journal of International Law* 102, 136–140 [Justice Accountability Survey].

and Serbs alike.[115] The lack of perceived legitimacy stemmed from the lack of inclusion of the local population, even as observers, and the application of adversarial criminal procedure unfamiliar to local legal professionals trained in the inquisitorial procedure of the civil law tradition.[116]

Similarly, at the ICTR, survivor witnesses complained of being poorly treated by the Tribunal and felt estranged by the nature of the proceedings, which were alien to the communal justice system of Rwanda.[117] In both transitional contexts under the adversarial procedural model, the role of the victim in proceedings was limited to that of witness. This had the effect of excluding non-probative facts which local audiences might have viewed as relevant. In sentencing proceedings, each Tribunal allowed evidence of victim impact, but there was no right of victims to present victim impact statements.[118] Thus, any scope for victim story-telling was truncated and this, consequently, could distort the historical record.[119] Drumbl also observed that the international procedure of the ICTR failed to sufficiently address the structural dynamics of the Rwandan genocide and failed to provide a clear voice to key stakeholders in the justice process to support communal reconciliation.[120] Raub suggested that the primacy of ICTR jurisdiction deprived the local government of the right to try defendants under local law and of attendant legitimacy at a crucial time in the nation's recovery.[121]

In the former Yugoslavia, politicians capitalised on the ICTY's unpopularity with local populations and spread negative information about the work of the Tribunal to expand their political power.[122] The late incorporation of outreach programmes attempted to redress perceptions of bias and lack of information about the work of the Courts among local populations. The programmes revealed that the facilitation of dialogue among those involved in the conflict is crucial in altering perceptions of the past and has knock-on effects within recovering communities.[123] Thus, the ad hoc Tribunals exhibited an expressive surplus, with a corresponding communicative deficit due to the lack of resonance with the affected transitional societies.

---

115 Jaya Ramji-Nogales, 'Designing Bespoke Transitional Justice' (2010–2011) 32 *Michigan Journal of International Law* 26, 28.

116 Dickinson, above n. 113, pp. 302–303 citing Justice Accountability Survey above n. 107, pp. 144–147.

117 Alison Des Forges and Timothy Longman, 'Legal Responses to Genocide in Rwanda' in Eric Stover and Harvey M. Weinstein (eds.), *My Neighbour, Myself: Justice and Community in the Aftermath of Mass Atrocity* (Cambridge 2004) 49, 56.

118 Sluiter, above n. 22, p. 1328.

119 Drumbl, above n. 35, pp. 176–177.

120 Des Forges, above n. 117, p. 56; See also Maya Sosnov, 'The Adjudication of Genocide: Gacaca and the Road to Reconciliation in Rwanda' (2008) 36 *Denver Journal of International Law and Policy* 125, 129.

121 Lindsey Raub, 'Positioning Hybrid tribunals in International Criminal Justice' (2009) 41 *International Law and Politics* 1013, 1019.

122 Ramji-Nogales, above n. 115, p. 29.

123 Ibid. p. 30.

Against this background, massive case loads, delays and cost overruns precipitated operational strategies to implement completion plans for both Tribunals.[124] This involved the transfer of cases from the jurisdiction of the ad hoc Tribunals to national courts. This had the incidental expressive effect of nationalising the process of accountability.[125]

At the ICTY, the strategy resulted in a change in the Tribunal's jurisdictional relationship with national courts in Bosnia and coincided with demand at the national level for the establishment of a federal war crimes court in Bosnia Herzegovina.[126] By the end of 2004 a War Crimes Chamber in the State Court of Bosnia and Herzegovina not only facilitated implementation of the completion strategy, but made possible the exercise of domestic criminal jurisdiction over international humanitarian law violations.[127]

The War Crimes Chamber (WCC) was established by Bosnian law amending the Law on the State Court.[128] The Office of the Higher Commissioner interpreted its powers under the Dayton Peace Accords as including promulgation of laws with respect to the judiciary.[129] International and national judges were appointed to the WCC and under the revised Rule 11 *bis* of the ICTY Rules of Evidence and Procedure, both cases and investigative files were transferred from the Tribunal to the national court from 2005, albeit with the ICTY retaining a monitoring role over domestic prosecutions.[130] In the process the ICTY came to play a more direct role in local-capacity-building through processes of norm leadership and transfer of best practices.[131]

While the national War Crimes Chamber, assisted by the ICTY staff, ultimately engaged Bosnians in justice processes, the administrative action was precipitated by the need to wind up the work of the international court. The ICTY, although activating wider outreach in its later years, retained its communication-limiting adversarial process.

---

124 *Ninth Annual Report of the International Tribunal for the Former Yugoslavia for prosecution of Persons Responsible for Serious Violations of International Humanitarian Law Committed in the Territory of the Former Yugoslavia since 1991*, UN Doc. S/2002/985(4 September 2002) para. [6].

125 Dominic Raab, 'Evaluating the ICTY and Its Completion Strategy' (2005) 3 *International Criminal Law* 92.

126 William W. Burke-White, 'The Domestic Influence of International Criminal Tribunals: The International Criminal Tribunal for the Former Yugoslavia and the Creation of the State Court of Bosnia & Herzegovina' (2008) 46 *Columbia Journal of Transnational Law* 279, 329–331.

127 Ibid.

128 Williams, above n. 1, p. 106.

129 Ibid. p. 103.

130 Ibid.

131 Burke-White, above n. 126, pp. 335–339, 347.

3.5. THE INTERNATIONAL CRIMINAL COURT (ICC)

Despite their poor image at the local level, the expressive model of justice provided by the temporary ad hoc Tribunals as they tackled the complex task of prosecuting the perpetrators of international crimes galvanised many states towards creation of a permanent international justice mechanism.[132] Creation of an international court by treaty permitted states' input into an institution that potentially threatened sovereign interests through holding senior government officials internationally accountable for certain serious crimes.[133] This issue coloured negotiations between states and the drafters of the ICC Statute over a period of four years as a balance between state interests and a credible form of permanent international justice was sought.

The final form of the Statute was fleshed out at the United Nations Diplomatic Conference of Plenipotentiaries on the Establishment of an International Criminal Court in Rome from 15 June 1998 to 17 July 1998.[134] The complex and sometimes controversial negotiations involved navigating a path through conflicting conceptions of the Court held either by blocs of states, or individual states and refined by input from NGO Coalitions representing a wider constituency of interest within the international system.[135] Ultimately, the resultant instrument reflected a compromise to accommodate the particular interests of states, while expressing the international normative interest of repressing international crimes through the existence of a permanent institution.[136] The Statute of the Court came into force on 1 July 2002.[137]

3.5.1. THE MISSION OF THE ICC

Reflecting the hopes of the Court's founders, the Preamble of the ICC Statute situates the Court within the state-based international system as a permanent justice mechanism with jurisdiction over 'the most serious crimes of concern to the international community' for the purpose of ending impunity for such crimes and contributing to their prevention in the interest of world peace and security.[138]

---

132 Broomhall, above n. 6, p. 71.
133 Ibid.
134 Ibid.
135 Ibid. pp. 72–73.
136 Ibid.
137 *Rome Statute of the International Criminal Court*, opened for signature 17 July 1998, 2187 UNTS 90 (entered into force 1 July 2002) [ICC Statute].
138 ICC Statute, Preamble.

Achievement of the ICC mission is influenced by three factors: first, the ICC Statute reaffirms state sovereignty through recognition of the primacy of national prosecution over international crimes in the concept of 'complementarity';[139] second, there is a delicate interplay between the independence of the ICC in mounting international prosecutions and respect for the role of the Security Council under the UN Charter in the maintenance of international peace and security;[140] and third, a statutory regime of cooperation and support between States Parties in investigations and other prosecutorial processes.[141]

3.5.2. PRIMACY OF NATIONAL JURISDICTION AND COMPLEMENTARITY

Under the Rome Statute the exercise of ICC jurisdiction and admissibility are embedded in the joint operation of two fundamental elements of the international legal system: jurisdiction in criminal matters in accordance with state sovereignty based on the principles of territoriality and active personality (Article 12); and an admissibility regime based on the concept of complementarity (Article 17), whereby judicial proceedings may only be activated when states with jurisdiction are either unwilling or unable genuinely to exercise the right to prosecute.[142] State sovereignty therefore operates to make the ICC a court of last resort for cases where primary jurisdiction over perpetrators of international crimes will not or cannot be properly exercised through national criminal justice systems.[143]

Article 12 attaches specific preconditions to the exercise of jurisdiction by the Court. The ICC may exercise jurisdiction when either the state of the territory where the crime is committed or the state of nationality of the accused is party to the Statute.[144] The principles of territoriality and nationality thus preclude the exercise of jurisdiction by the state of custody of a suspect or the state of nationality of victims.[145] However, Article 12(3) allows non-States parties to give consent to the Court's jurisdiction by way of an ad hoc declaration filed with the Registrar.[146]

---

139 Hans-Peter Kaul, 'The International Criminal Court: Current Challenges and Perspectives' (2007) 6 *Washington University Global Studies Law Review* 575, 577.

140 Broomhall, above n. 6, p. 82.

141 Ibid. p. 83; Kaul, above n. 139, p. 578.

142 Kaul, above n. 139, p. 577.

143 Ibid.

144 ICC Statute art. 12(2)(a), (b).

145 Maria Carmen Colitti, 'Geographical and Jurisdictional Reach of the International Criminal Court: Gaps in the International Criminal Justice System and A Role for Internationalized Bodies' in Cesare P.R. Romano, Andre Nolkaemper and Jann K. Kleffner (eds.), *Internationalized Criminal Courts and Tribunals: Sierra Leone, East Timor, Kosovo, and Cambodia* (Oxford University Press, 2004) pp. 417, 420.

146 ICC Statute, article 12(3).

The regime of primacy and complementarity has an expressive dimension. Burke-White noted the positive expressive value of prosecuting a globally renowned despot in a model international court in The Hague.[147] On the other hand, it may be negatively expressive to extract the suspected perpetrator from the domestic context of the crimes and risk portrayal of the proceedings as 'an international abstraction rather than the prosecution of crimes rooted in particular societal causes.'[148]

3.5.3. VICTIMS' PARTICIPATION AND REDRESS

The ICC was the first international court with a statutory scheme which included active victim participation rights in trial proceedings.[149] The grant of victim participation rights by the Court marked a departure from the ad hoc Tribunals' approach to victims as witnesses only. It also recognised the evolving right to reparation for victims harmed through gross violation of international human rights law or serious violations of international humanitarian law.[150] The inclusion of victim participatory rights in trial proceedings, a reparations mandate and the creation of a victims' trust fund within the ICC's statutory framework suggested a shift in international criminal trials from a focus on purely retributive justice to a certain restorative justice emphasis. Victim participation rights at all stages of the proceedings introduced a more representative justice framework than any predecessor international Tribunal.

During the ICC Statute negotiations, France and some civil law countries argued for a participatory regime for victims of crimes along the lines of the French civil law system, which grants victims civil party status within the criminal proceedings.[151] Ultimately, the ICC embraced primarily adversarial trial procedure with a *sui generis* victim participation model. The ICC system recognised the victim of crimes before the Court as a 'third actor' in proceedings

---

147 William Burke-White, 'Proactive Complementarity: The International Criminal Court and National Courts in the Rome System of International Justice' (2008) 49 *Harvard International Law Journal* 53, 93..

148 Frédéric Mégret, 'In Defence of Hybridity: Towards a Representational Theory of International Criminal Justice' (2005) 38 *Cornell International Law Journal* 725, 749.

149 McGonigle Leyh, above n. 41, p. 225.

150 *Declaration of the Basic Principles for Victims of Crime and Abuse of Power*, Adopted by General Assembly Resolution 40/34, (29 November 1985), Principle 6(a); 2006 *Basic Principles and Guidelines on the Right to a remedy and Reparation for Victims of Gross Violations of International Human Rights Law and Serious Violations of International Humanitarian Law* (adopted by UN General Assembly Resolution 60/147, 16 December 2005), Principle 12.

151 Christine Van Den Wyngaert, 'Victims before International Criminal Courts: Some Views and Concerns of an ICC Trial Judge' (2011) 44 *Case Western Reserve University Law Review* 475, 478.

based on their 'personal interests' in the trial.[152] The 'personal interests' of the victim have been determined as including the victim's rights to truth, justice and reparation.[153] At the beginning of the *Katanga* trial, for instance, the victims' capacity to share their knowledge of the context of the alleged crimes was linked to their personal interest in establishing the truth about what had happened, thus grounding their right to participate in proceedings by testifying when it was deemed appropriate by the Court for them to do so.[154]

The ICC definition of victim includes 'natural persons who have suffered harm as a result of the commission of any crime within the jurisdiction of the Court' and, organisations and institutions that are similarly affected.[155] The key provision is Article 68 (3) of the ICC Statute. This provision permits the 'views and concerns' of victim participants to be raised 'at stages of the proceedings determined to be appropriate by the Court and in a manner which is not prejudicial to or inconsistent with the rights of the accused and a fair and impartial trial.'[156] In practice, victim requests to participate at various stages of proceedings have been judicially determined on a case-by-case basis taking account of the rights of the accused, the personal interests of the applicant and the need for expeditious and efficacious proceedings.[157]

Where victims are permitted to express their views and concerns at the trial stage it is usually through their legal representatives. Generally, the legal representatives may attend and participate in all proceedings in accordance with the ruling of the Chamber.[158] The legal representatives should be provided with the prosecutions' summary of presentation of evidence.[159] The Court has emphasised the neutrality of the representatives because they are not the equivalent of auxiliary prosecutors in civil law jurisdictions, but rather assistants to the judges in their work of determining the truth.[160] It is possible for victims to make opening and closing statements subject to Rule 89(1) of the Rules of

152 Sluiter, above n. 22, p. 1319.

153 *Prosecutor v. Al Bashir*, Decision on Applications a/0011/06 to/a/0013/06 and a/0443/09 to a/0450/09 for Participation in the Proceedings at the Pre-trial stage of the Case, PTC, No. ICC-02/05-01/09, (10 December 2009) para. 4.

154 *Prosecutor v. Katanga and Ngudjolo*, Decision on the Modalities of Victim Participation at Trial, TC, ICC-01-/04-01/07-1788-Teng (22 January 2010) paras. 60–61.

155 International Criminal Court, *Rules of Procedure Evidence* [ICC RPE] r. 85.

156 ICC Statute, Article 68(3).

157 *The Participation of Victims in International Criminal Court Proceedings: A Review of the Practice and Consideration of Options for the Future* (Redress Trust, London October 2012) p. 41 [Redress Report].

158 ICC RPE r. 91(2).

159 *Prosecutor v. Lubanga*, Decision on victims' participation, TC, No. ICC-01/04-01/06-1119 (18 January 2008) para. 38.

160 *Prosecutor v. Lubanga*, Decision on the Manner of Questioning Witnesses by the Legal Representatives of Victims, TC, No. ICC-01/04-01/06 (16 September 2009) paras. 25, 29.

Procedure and Evidence. Legal representatives have been permitted to question all types of witnesses, including defence witnesses.[161] The right of victims to challenge the admissibility of evidence has also been recognised.[162] However, the appropriate modalities of victim participation will not be replicated in every case and will turn on factors such as the nature of the charges and the number of participating victims.[163]

The victim participation scheme was scrutinised on a number of grounds. Normatively, the victim, as an additional participant in trial proceedings could be seen as creating a potential third protagonist in the ICC and thus disturbing the fair operation of the dual-party procedural model.[164] Fairness to the accused was the major concern within the adversarial proceedings. Zappalà argued that primacy of the rights of the accused was the bed-rock of modern criminal procedure from which judicial interpretation of the details and limits of victim participation at the ICC should proceed.[165] McGonigle Leyh doubted whether victims' participatory rights had been activated without impeding the Court's prosecution and sentencing priorities or threatening defendants' rights.[166]

In a minority judgment, Judge Pikis expressed the view that the victim's right to express views and concerns in proceedings was 'highly qualified' in participation in adversarial proceedings which are characterised by the equality of arms principle.[167] The majority of other judges sought to qualify the victim's

161 *Prosecutor v. Lubanga*, Decision on the Defence observation regarding the right of the legal representatives of victims to question defence witnesses and on the notion of personal interest on the defence application to exclude certain representatives of victims from the Chamber during the non-public evidence of various defence witnesses, TC, No. ICC-01/04-01/06-2340 (11 March 2010) paras. 37–40.

162 *Prosecutor v. Lubanga*, Judgment on the Appeals of The Prosecutor and the Defence against Trial Chamber 1's Decision on Victims' Participation of 18 January 2008, AC, No. ICC-01/04-01/06-1432 (11 July 2008) para. 101; *Prosecutor v. Katanga & Ngudjolo*, Decision on the Modalities of Victim Participation at Trial, TC, No. ICC-01-/04-01/07-1788-tENG (22 January 2010) para. 104.

163 *Prosecutor v. Katanga & Ngudjolo*, Decision on the Modalities of Victim Participation at Trial, TC, No. ICC-01-/04-01/07-1788-tENG (22 January 2010) para. 5; Sluiter, above n. 22, p. 1325.

164 Claude Jorda and Jérôme De Hemptinne, 'The Status and Role of the Victim' in Antonio Cassese, Paola Gaeta and John R.W.D. Jones (eds.), *The Rome Statute of the International Criminal Court: A Commentary* (Oxford University Press, 2002) pp. 1387, 1399; Christine Chung, 'Victims' Participation at the International Criminal Court: Are Concessions of the Court Clouding the Promise?' (2008) 6 *Northwestern Journal of International Human Rights* 459, 523–542.

165 Zappalà, above n. 20, pp. 143–145, 164.

166 McGonigle Leyh, above n. 41, p. 225.

167 *Prosecutor v. Jean-Pierre Bemba Gombo*, Fourth Decision on Victims' Participation, TC, No. ICC-01/05/08 (12 December 2008) paras. 15–19; *Prosecutor v. Lubanga*, Decision on the Manner of Questioning Witnesses by the Legal Representatives of Victims, TC, No. ICC-01/04-01/06 (16 September 2009) para. 24.

right to participate in relation to the defendant's right, and to differentiate victims to the proceedings from the prosecution by highlighting their lesser status as 'participants' as opposed to parties.[168] In the *Lubanga* case, the Court declared that the purpose of victims presenting their views and concerns was not the equivalent of giving evidence but may 'assist the court in its approach to the evidence in the case.'[169] This suggested a largely instrumental purpose to victim participation. Moffett argued that the Court took a progressively restrictive approach to victims' participation rights in trial proceedings and investigations, to protect the rights of defendants as well as the independence of the Prosecutor.[170]

Within the ICC Registry, the Victims Participation and Reparations Section (VPRS) enabled victims to access the ICC, assisted them in applying for participation and provided the initial processing point for applications. Applications are generally processed on an individual basis and are considered by the parties as well as the judges. This level of handling, combined with a burgeoning number of applications put increasing strain on the resources of the Court.[171] In 2011, Van den Wyngaert questioned whether the victim participation system was meaningful enough to justify the Court's considerable investment in it, and recommended a parallel forum for the exercise of victims' reparation rights severed completely from the criminal proceedings.[172] McCarthy also viewed the ICC as ill-equipped to support the restorative purposes of victim participation pursuant to reparative justice theory.[173]

However, criticism of the scheme should also take account of the views of the recipients of the Court's messages. A recent report of an independent study on victim participation at the ICC notes that completing an application to participate at the ICC was viewed as vital representation in itself for Ugandan

---

168 *Prosecutor v. Lubanga*, Decision of the Appeals Chamber on the Joint Application of Victims a/0001/06 to a/003/06 and a/015/06 concerning the 'Directions and Decision of the Appeals Chamber of 2 February 2007', AC, No ICC-01/04-01/06 (13 June 2007) paras. 15–19.

169 *Prosecutor v. Lubanga*, Decision on the request by victims a/0225/06, a/0229/06 and a/0270/07 to express their views and concerns in person and to present evidence during the trial, TC, No. ICC-01/04-01/06 (26 June 2009) para. 25.

170 Luke Moffett, *Justice for Victims before the International Criminal Court* (Routledge, London, 2014) p. 142; and see Redress Report, above n. 8, pp. 43–46, charting a steady dimunition of victims' rights at the investigation stage.

171 Redress Report, above n. 157, p. 10. The report notes a 300% increase in applications since 2010, drawn from the Court's, *Report on the Review of the System for Victims to Apply to Participate In Proceedings* (ICC, 24 September 2012) p. 2.

172 Van Den Wyngaert, above n, 151, p. 494.

173 Conor McCarthy, 'Victim Redress and International Criminal Justice: Competing Paradigms or Compatible Forms of Justice' (2012) 10 *Journal of International Criminal Justice* 351, 363–364. McCarthy identified restorative purposes as (*inter alia*) addressing harm between victims and perpetrators, affecting a measure of healing, and touching the brokenness of the transitional context.

victims and their communities.[174] One respondent put it this way: 'I feel that my voice should be heard throughout the world because it is not going to help only me, but the whole clan, the whole Acholi tribe.'[175] The report recommends reform of the existing programme, but in doing so underscores the importance of the link between communication with victims and trial justice. The report advocates that victims receive information more frequently about the progress of cases and that their legal representatives have more contact with them.[176]

Other grass-roots research revealed that the value of ICC dialogic processes at this level may have long-term significance aligned with the goal of international criminal justice in building peace and international security. Victims often fill out their application forms collectively with the help of their legal representatives. Realising their suffering is shared and being educated together about the justice process can foster a sense of solidarity as well as greater understanding of legal processes which may in turn assist post-conflict peace-building.[177]

3.5.4. EXPRESSIVE VS. COMMUNICATIVE DIMENSIONS OF THE ICC PROCEDURE

Certain aspects of ICC procedure suggest limitations to the expressive value of the ICC. First, the temporal jurisdiction of the Court is limited to crimes committed after the entry into force of the Statute (Article 11(1)). As a result, many cases of impunity for international crimes which pre-date the formation of the ICC and later cases occurring in non-signatory states fall outside the Court's jurisdiction. Even a Security Council referral of a situation involving crimes committed before entry into force of the Statute cannot be accepted by the Court because the ICC is a creature of Statute rather than the Security Council.[178] In addition, where ICC jurisdiction arises, the capacity of the Court to investigate and prosecute cases at any one time is limited to no more than a few senior figures of particular criminal regimes.[179] However, the Court's limited jurisdiction together with its necessary selectivity in prosecutions did

174 Human Rights Center, University of California, Berkeley, *The Victims' Court: A Study of 622 Victim Participants at the International Criminal Court* (University of California, Berkeley, 2015) pp. 32–33.

175 Ibid. p. 33.

176 Ibid. p. 5.

177 International Federation for Human Rights (FIDH), *Five Myths about Victim Participation in ICC Proceedings* (FIDH, December 2014) pp. 17–18.

178 Cryer, above n. 19, p. 138.

179 Estelle R. Higgonet, 'Restructuring Hybrid Courts: Local Empowerment and National Criminal Justice Reform' (2006) 23 *Arizona Journal of International & Comparative Law* 347, 349.

not rob the ICC of its positive expressive value as 'a new model of accountability' functioning at the global level.[180]

In addition, the Court's reparations mandate (Article 75), from which victim participation rights flow, had expressive value despite concerns about other elements of the participation scheme. The Court's capacity to award reparations combined with the Trust Fund for Victims, which may both implement judicial awards and assist victims in specific ways as individuals or collectives, had expressive value in displaying flexibility in the administration of international criminal justice.[181] Finally, despite her concerns over the viability of the victim participation scheme, Van den Wyngaert considered that a separate Victims' Reparations Commission would not conflict with the basic purpose and expressive ideal of the ICC 'which is to fight impunity.'[182]

Given the prominence of the ICC and the goals of international criminal justice it is important to recognise the communicative dynamics of victim participation as distinct from the general expressivism of reparations or accountability. ICC trials are held far from the relevant crime sites. In addition, the knowledge of the judges and the prosecution of the specific social contexts of the crimes may be very limited.[183] Additional information and discourse on significant local factors may expand their knowledge and appreciation of relevant issues. In the *Bemba* case, for example:

> [Victims'] legal representatives brought the attention of the Chamber to the local languages spoken in the Central African Republic (CAR). This was a matter contended by the Defence, and the Prosecution did not have sufficient information. Only the legal representatives who were from the CAR, could provide clarity on the issue.[184]

Here the Court's engagement with victims vindicated their personal interest in establishing the truth through the legal proceedings and informed the historical record being created by the Court without distortion of significant facts or 'procedural short-cuts.'[185]

Judges have acknowledged that victims have assisted their 'better understanding of contentious issues of the case in light of their local knowledge and socio-cultural background.'[186] Submissions made by victims and their

---

180 Kathryn Sikkink, *The Justice Cascade: How Human Rights Prosecutions are Changing the World* (W.W. Norton & Co., 2011) p. 18.

181 McCarthy, above n. 173, pp. 369–372.

182 Ibid.

183 Mariana Pena and Gaelle Carayon, 'Is the ICC Making the Most of Victim Participation?' (2013) 10 *Journal of International Criminal Justice* 1, 7.

184 FIDH Report, above n. 177, p. 15, citing *Prosecutor v. Bemba* Transcript of the Confirmation of Charges Hearing Doc. No. ICC-01/05-01/08-T-12-ENG (15 January 2009) pp. 97–98.

185 Zappalà, above n. 20, p. 161.

186 Directions for the Conduct of the Proceedings and testimony in accordance with rule 140, *Prosecutor v. Katanga & Ngudjolo* TC, No. ICC-01-/04-01/07-1665-Corr, (9 December 2009) para. 82;

legal representatives have also clarified crime contexts and pinpointed possible criminal methods.[187] Interviews conducted by victims' rights reseachers with former ICC judges revealed that in the *Lubanga* proceedings, there was significant participation by victims and their legal representatives.[188] This was 'not in any sense tokenistic' and included information that 'supplemented' material presented to the Chamber by the prosecution and the defence.[189] A few victims gave evidence in person, and victim representatives made brief, focused submissions on many legal issues before the Court which were not repetitive. Overall their participation did not delay the proceedings.[190] In addition, victim participation did not jeopardise the rights of the accused to a fair trial or the proceedings themselves.[191]

Nevertheless, despite concerted efforts, victim representatives' failed to have the scope of the charges in *Lubanga* reframed to encompass sexual slavery and gendered violence. The victim representatives submitted evidence of such crimes at the trial, but the Trial Chamber, by a majority, made no findings against the defendant in the absence of charges; rather, all judges determined to hear submissions on the matter in relation to sentencing and reparations.[192] At the sentencing stage the prosecutor argued that the evidence supported the conclusion that sexual violence and rape had been routinely committed and that this should be treated as an aggravating factor as to sentence. However, the two judges in the majority found that the link between Mr. Lubanga and the sexual violence had not been established beyond reasonable doubt. In a dissenting judgment, Judge Elizabeth Odio Benito, found that the evidence of harsh punishments and sexual violence suffered by child victims and their families should be considered in sentencing because it touched on the gravity of the crimes and harm caused. She disagreed with the majority's disregard for the damage caused to the child victims and their families as a relevant factor under Rule 145(1)(c), and sought a longer sentence.[193]

On the issue of reparations the Trial Chamber considered the submissions from victim representatives, the defence and numerous non-governmental organisations. Also drawing from international reparations frameworks, the Court clearly recognised the needs and vulnerabilities of victims of sexual

187 Pena, above n, 183, p. 7.

188 See reports of interviews with former ICC judges in (2014–2015) 25 *Access: Victims' Rights Working Group Bulletin* (www.vrwg.org/ACCESS/141201englishfinal.pdf) p. 4.

189 Ibid.

190 Ibid.

191 Ibid. p. 3.

192 *Prosecutor v. Lubango (Judgment)* TC, No. ICC-01/04/06-2842 (14 March 2012) para. 896.

193 *Prosecutor v. Lubango (Sentencing Judgment)* TC, No. ICC-01/04/06-2901 (10 July 2012) paras. 6, 22, 24.

violence.[194] The Chamber laid down a 'gender sensitive approach' to reparations strategies and principles that might contribute to the prevention of future conflict through measures that address 'underlying injustices.'[195]

Notwithstanding the lack of sexual violence charges against Thomas Lubanga Dyilo himself, charges were subsequently added to the arrest warrant of his co-accused Bosco Ntaganda.[196] In sum, victim submissions, whether initially successful or not, may raise significant facts, as well as highlight matters going to the truth in justice processes.

While the logistics of victim inclusion and accommodation of their voice in proceedings present challenges for the Court, the contributions of victim participants expand the communicative value of ICC proceedings as distinct from their expressivism. As to evident practical concerns over the Court's capacity to support victim participation, reform might be guided by the principle of equitable representation and informed by the experience of internationalised courts that have also wrestled with the mechanics of giving effect creatively to victim rights.

3.6. HYBRID AND INTERNATIONALISED COURTS

While the limited jurisdiction of the ICC did not preclude the creation of new ad hoc Tribunals, the spiralling costs of running the ICTY and ICTR became a disincentive to create new courts based on that model. In addition, varying political positions within the Security Council with respect to some national contexts made the consensus that characterised action with respect to the Bosnian and Rwandan conflicts impossible.[197] In the case of a proposal for justice for Khmer Rouge crimes in Cambodia, for instance, old Cold War alignments and past colonial action militated against support for an ad hoc Tribunal by permanent Security Council members, China, Russia and France.[198] In addition, perceptions of the existing ad hoc Tribunals as disconnected from on-the-ground realities of the communities they served prompted experimentation in new justice forms.[199]

---

194 *Prosecutor v. Lubango*, Decision establishing the Principles and Procedures to be applied to reparations, TC, No. ICC-01/04/06-2904 (7 August 2012) paras. 207–208, 200.

195 *Prosecutor v. Lubango*, Decision establishing the Principles and Procedures to be applied to reparations, TC, No. ICC-01/04/06-2904 (7 August 2012) paras. 192, 222, 240; See Andrea Burdach and Louise Chappell, 'Leaving Behind the Age of Impunity' (2014) 16 *International Feminist Journal of Politics* 543, 550.

196 Pena, above n. 183, p. 9.

197 Schabas, above n. 92, p. 32.

198 Ibid.

199 Higgonet, above n. 179, p. 349.

The hybrid court emerged as a new model of post-conflict justice. This type of court combined the expertise and credibility of international justice with a degree of ownership of the justice process from within the national contexts of relevant atrocities. Hybridity in each tribunal arises from their mixed jurisdiction in terms of applicable law, and composition as a blend of national with international judicial and administrative personnel.[200]

Locating the hybrid court within the territory where crimes were perpetrated offered the prospect of greater legitimacy of proceedings in the eyes of local communities than the ad hoc Tribunals had achieved.[201] Locally-based justice mechanisms also increased the prospect of international norm penetration, while punishment of high-profile individual offenders promoted the rule of law in transitioning societies. National location and the blending of international with national elements also offered capacity-building and infrastructure development potential in states where national criminal justice systems were too weak or corrupt to conduct a fair and efficacious legal process independently.[202] Hybrid courts were therefore imbued with expressive value beyond the traditional ambit of criminal law.

The hybrid court, which gives voice to both international and domestic concerns was justified on the grounds of the duality of international crimes.[203] Mégret argued that in a case where crimes of a certain magnitude are committed within a single state, the nature of those crimes has both national and international dimensions, giving rise to dual jurisdiction over the crimes.[204] Moreover, the participation of international and national actors in hybrid trial proceedings provides more representative transitional justice.[205]

Greater representation was also made possible by the grant of participation rights to victims in some hybrid courts and sometimes with remedies for harm suffered by them under international law. While states may fail in their primary obligation through their national legal systems to enforce human rights and international humanitarian law, hybrid tribunals activate both accountability for violations and a right to reparations for victims.[206]

The preceding discussion of hybridity emphasised the blending of national and international elements in courts designed to render transitional justice *in*

200 Dickenson, above n. 113, p. 295.

201 Ibid. p. 296.

202 Ibid. pp. 307–308.

203 Mégret, above n. 148, p. 741.

204 Ibid.

205 Ibid. p. 747.

206 Bassiouni, above n. 5, p. 720; See *Basic Principles and Guidelines on the Right to a remedy and Reparation for Victims of Gross Violations of International Human Rights Law and Serious Violations of International Humanitarian Law* (adopted by UN General Assembly Resolution 60/147, 16 December 2005) (2006) 13 IHRR 90.

situ. Scholars of international criminal justice initially wrote of the hybrid court form in similarly generic terms. The UN noted that the particular hybridity or degree of internationality of individual transitional courts was dictated by the on-the-ground political realities of the relevant national context and the extent of local legal capacity to hold fair trials.[207]

Williams made a distinction between the hybrid and internationalised court based on each court's mode of creation and jurisdictional basis.[208] She argued that to date, hybrid courts were created by either treaty or UN Security Council resolution; examples are the Special Court for Sierra Leone (SCSL), by treaty, and the Special Tribunal for Lebanon (STL), by Security Council resolution. However, Williams suggested that practice does not indicate that an internationalised court can be established by either treaty or SC resolution. Rather, internationalised courts are established under national law but carry international elements. The War Crimes Chamber of the State Court of Bosnia and Herzegovina, discussed earlier, is an example of one form of internationalised court. Another is the Iraqi High Tribunal (IHT), which was created as a national court by the occupying powers applying international humanitarian law. A third form of internationalised court is one authorised by a United Nations transitional administration; the mixed judicial panels created for Kosovo and East Timor are examples.[209]

There is a fourth internationalised court form; one that is created under national law as a result of negotiations with the UN and pursuant to which an Agreement may exist to regulate UN participation in, and international elements of, the court. Williams cited the Extraordinary Chambers in the Courts of Cambodia (ECCC) as an example.[210]

I accept William's categorisation of the ECCC as an internationalised court for reasons I will discuss in Chapter five. However, in the following section I discuss the expressive and communicative dimensions of courts belonging to the post-ad hoc Tribunal generation, some of which were referred to generically as 'hybrids' in the literature.

3.6.1. COURTS UNDER UN TRANSITIONAL AUTHORITY

In the wake of mass atrocities, internationalised courts were created under the mandates of UN Transitional Authorities in Kosovo and East Timor. In both

---

207 *Rule-of-Law Tools for Post-Conflict States: Maximising the Legacy of Hybrid Courts* (Office of the United Nations High Commissioner for Human Rights, 2008) pp. 3–4.

208 Williams, above n. 1, 249–300.

209 Ibid. pp. 249–250, 282.

210 Ibid. p. 250.

cases the capacity of each state to fairly and credibly prosecute international crimes and other crimes was severely limited or proved impossible due to overwhelming violence within the respective communities, and the destruction or corruption of their justice systems.[211]

3.6.1.1. *East Timor*

On 20 May 2002, East Timor secured independence after 24 years of Indonesian occupation preceded by Portuguese colonisation for 500 years. In the weeks after the UN assisted referendum on independence, held on 30 August 1999, there were outbreaks of extreme violence against the civilian population and extensive destruction of infrastructure.[212] The UN sent a security force to restore peace and the Security Council established a United Nations Transitional Administration in East Timor (UNTAET) with a wide mandate to exercise 'overall authority' in the territory.[213] This included exercise of 'all legislative and executive authority, including administration of the judiciary.'[214] However, Indonesia asserted jurisdiction over the serious violations of human rights and international humanitarian law committed by the state's armed forces and police in the months prior to and after the referendum.

Indonesia created an ad hoc Human Rights Court where 18 indictees were prosecuted for international crimes in 13 trials, resulting in six convictions. Throughout the trials, observers perceived a lack of commitment on the part of the prosecutors, who consistently failed to present adequate evidence and pursue an appropriate trial strategy.[215] Linton noted that while Article 34 of Indonesia's Law on Human Rights Courts contained specific provisions on victims and witnesses' rights to bodily security and protection from threats, harassment and violence throughout trial proceedings, the ad hoc Human Rights Court trials were frequently conducted in an atmosphere of hostility and intimidation. It appeared as though 'victims were on trial for their audacity in taking on the military as an organ of State.'[216] Overall, the trials were criticised for not being

---

211 Higgonet, above n. 179, pp. 372–384; Dickenson, above n. 113, p. 296.

212 Suzannah Linton and Caitlin Reiger, 'The Evolving Jurisprudence and Practice of East Timor's Special Panels for Serious Crimes on Admissions of Guilt, Duress and Superior Orders' (2001) 4 *Yearbook of International Humanitarian Law* 167, 167.

213 UNSC Res. 1272 (1999) UN Doc. S/RES/1272, (25 October 1999) para. 1.

214 UNSC Res. 1272 (1999) UN Doc. S/RES/1272, (25 October 1999) para. 5.

215 Megan Hirst and Howard Varney, 'Justice Abandoned: an Assessment of the Serious Crimes Process in East Timor' (Occasional Paper Series, International Center for Transitional Justice June, 2005) pp. 11–12.

216 Suzannah Linton, 'Putting Things into Perspective: The Realities of Accountability in East Timor, Indonesia and Cambodia' (2005) 3 *Maryland Series in Contemporary Asian Studies* 1, 71–72; And see Suzannah Linton, 'Unravelling the First Three Trials at Indonesia's Ad Hoc

conducted in good faith, attributable to a lack of political will on part of the government.[217]

In March and June 2000, UNTAET passed regulations enabling the prosecution of individuals accused of committing 'serious crimes' through dedicated judicial panels within the Dili District Court, constituted formally as the Special Panels for Serious Crimes (SPSC).[218] The panels had exclusive jurisdiction to prosecute the crimes of genocide, crimes against humanity, war crimes, murder, sexual offences and torture committed within international and non-international armed conflicts during the period 1 January 1999 to 25 October 1999.[219] The SPSC also had universal jurisdiction in respect of the core international crimes, although no indictments were raised on this basis.[220] The definitions of the international crimes closely followed the subject-matter jurisdiction of the ICC Statute. Furthermore, a framework for victim participation was instituted based on the ICC model.[221]

The panels were of mixed composition, consisting of two international judges and one East Timorese. The Serious Crimes Unit (SCU) was responsible for investigating processes and strategy.[222] Hybrid judicial panels to deal with appeals were also established in the Court of Appeal in Dili.[223] A truth and reconciliation commission operated in tandem with the SPSC to address less serious crimes.[224]

The SPSC applied a blend of the law of East Timor as amended or replaced by UNTAET, together with applicable international law. A uniform code of procedure, the Transitional Rules of Criminal Procedure (TRCP) regulated the conduct of trial proceedings.[225] The TRCP made provision for a range of victim participation rights, including the right to request the prosecutor to conduct specific investigations (section 12.6); to submit a right to be heard at any stage of the proceedings (excluding review hearings) (section 12.5); and to be notified of review hearings (section 12.3). However, Sluiter noted the lack of evidence of the

---

Court for Human Rights Violations in East Timor' (2004) 17 *Leiden Journal of International Law* 303, 324–327.

217 Sylvia de Bertondo, 'Current Developments in Internationalised Courts: East Timor Justice Denied' (2004) 2 *Journal of International Criminal Justice* 910, 925; Hirst, above n. 215, p. 12.

218 UNTAET Regulation 2000/11 *On the Organisation of Courts East Timor* (6 March 2000); UNTAET Regulation 2000/15, *On the Establishment of Panels with Exclusive Jurisdiction Over serious Criminal Offences* (6 June 2000).

219 UNTAET Reg. 2000/15, ss. 2.3, 2.4, 4–7.

220 UNTAET Reg. 2000/15, ss. 2.1, 2.2; See Williams, above n. 1, p. 96 fn. 296.

221 Linton, above n. 212, p. 168.

222 UNTAET Regulation 2000/16 On the Organization of the Public prosecution Service in East Timor (6 June 2000) s. 3.1.

223 UNTAET Regulation 2000/11 ss. 14–15.

224 UNTAET Regulation 2000/15 s. 2.5.

225 UNTAET Regulation 2000/30, *Transitional Rules of Criminal Procedure* (25 September 2000).

extent of exercise of such rights in practice or 'accommodation by authorities.'[226] The TRCP allowed victims to be legally represented, but in practice, victims only appeared in proceedings as witnesses.[227] UNTAET Regulation 15 provided expressly for witness protection measures to be implemented through appropriate measures, but the SPSC's initiatives in the area were considered by commentators to be less than adequate.[228]

The TRCP envisaged the possibility for victims to receive compensation or reparations by order of the SPSC, and section 25 of UNTAET Regulation 15 provided for creation of a Trust Fund for the benefit of victims of crimes and their families. However, it appears that no compensation orders were made and no such fund was established.[229]

In terms of the number of prosecutions, the SPSC record is impressive compared to other international criminal tribunals. When the work of the SPSC was suspended in May 2005, 55 trials involving 87 defendants had been held, resulting in 85 convictions.[230] However, analyses of the trial proceedings and SPSC decisions suggested that the quantitative record was not matched by qualitative justice. Most of the trials involved lower-level perpetrators with many charged with single offences unrelated to systematic violence.[231] Although the SCU adjusted its strategy to prioritise indictments and then shifted focus to the organisers of crimes, their efforts to apprehend indictees were thwarted.[232] Indictees in their hundreds belonging to the Indonesian military, including high-level commanders, did not face trial because the Indonesian government refused to extradite them.[233] The lack of ownership and cooperation between the UN, Indonesia and the East Timorese government in securing the arrest of high-level accused persons undermined the legitimacy of the SPSC.[234] The historical record produced by the SPSC was also distorted. Kent argued:

> Without evidence or statements from members of the Indonesian military with command responsibility, trials could not explore the relationship between East Timorese

226 Sluiter, above n. 22, pp. 1316–1317, 1321–1322.

227 TRCP s. 12; Ibid. p. 1310.

228 Sluiter, above n. 22, p. 1335 citing David Cohen, 'Indifference and Accountability: the United Nations and the Politics of International Justice in East Timor' East-West Center Reports No. 9 (East-West Center, Honolulu, 2006) pp. 38–39.

229 Ibid. Sluiter, p. 1362.

230 *Report of the Secretary-General on Justice and Reconciliation for Timor-Leste* UN Doc. S2006/580 (26 July 2006) para. 9. Following an acquittal by the Court of Appeal the number of convictions was reduced to 84. Lia Kent, *The Dynamics of Transitional Justice: International Models and Local Realities in East Timor* (Routledge, 2012) p. 78.

231 Williams, above n. 1, p. 97.

232 Hirst, above n. 215, p. 8.

233 David Cohen, 'Hybrid Justice in East Timor, Sierra Leone, and Cambodia: "Lessons Learned" and Prospects for the Future' (2007) 43 *Stanford Journal of International Law* 1, 14.

234 Ibid.

> militia and the Indonesian military in detail, including, the command structure and funding. This often resulted in a distorted picture of events that was unable to shed light on the military orchestrated nature of the 1999 violence.[235]

The lack of evidence may also have led to erroneous fact-finding and ad hoc approaches to substantive issues. Linton and Reiger's analysis of the SPSC's interpretation of the principles applied to the defence of superior orders, for instance, revealed that the Special Panels had adopted an approach that did not rely on recognised tests under international and other relevant law.[236] In addition, the panels had not taken into account the realities of everyday life and strong social norms in respect to the concept of authority in East Timor when ruling on the defences of superior orders and duress.[237]

Limiting investigations to 1999 also had negative effects on the truth-finding process. Kent argued that the narrowly-focused proceedings did not address the reasons why individuals assumed different roles, including joining the militias, under a coercive regime predating the 1999 atrocities by more than two decades. Such limited engagement with the social context of the crimes was unlikely to resonate with East-Timorese understanding of the events or build trust among victim communities in the legal proceedings.[238]

It seems the final blow for the serious crimes regime came in 2004 when the East Timorese President would not support the arrest warrant for former Indonesian military leader General Wiranto, who had been indicted for crimes against humanity based on command responsibility.[239] Thereafter, the general prosecutor refused to submit the warrant to Interpol and stopped submitting other SPSC warrants.[240] The work of the Panels was suspended on 20 May 2005 following the closure of the second UN mission.[241]

Thus, the primary goal of accountability through internationally assisted trials was largely unrealised in the serious crimes proceedings and their work was expressive in the negative for the UN and the East Timorese community. In addition, the prospect of more communicative trials through greater victim representation under the SPSC legal framework proved to be illusory.

The proceedings for less serious crimes through the Commission for Truth, Reception and Reconciliation (CAVR) provided greater scope for justice at the local level. Here a wider range of East Timorese could relate their experiences

---

235 Kent, above n. 230, p. 78.

236 Linton, above n. 212, p. 210.

237 Ibid. p. 209.

238 Kent, above n. 230, p. 83.

239 Hirst, above n. 215, p. 10.

240 Sluiter, above n. 22, p. 150.

241 The United Nations Mission in Support of East Timor (UNMISET) replaced UNTAET after independence.

of crimes and participate in community dispute resolution processes pertaining to incidents preceding 1999.[242] However, these truth-finding proceedings were not intended as an alternative to retributive justice but rather to facilitate accountability for the more serious crimes.[243]

Following the recurrence of political violence in East Timor in April and May 2006 the Security Council authorised a further UN assistance mission to the fledgling state. A Serious Crimes Investigation Team (SCIT) was established to assist the national investigation authorities with outstanding cases of human rights violations committed in East Timor in 1999.[244] Other assistance to strengthen East Timor's judicial capacity came through United Nations Development Program funded projects. This included a project involving international judges and prosecutors working within the national justice system, including within the District Court of Dili. In 2010, a special mixed judicial panel reactivated a number of cases opened by the SPCS, and some convictions have been achieved.[245]

Meanwhile, in 2008, under a bilateral agreement between the governments of Indonesia and East Timor (renamed Timor-Leste) a Commission of Truth and Friendship (CTF) was established as an alternative to prosecutions.[246] The final report of the Commission emphasised the institutional responsibility of the Indonesian military, police and government.[247] Thereafter, in expressive tones, the Indonesian government declared the commitments of both Indonesia and Timor-Leste to 'collective reparation, institutional reformation and reinforcing the culture of human rights.'[248] Here the public messages echo commitments made by continuing authoritarian states to ratify human rights treaties, while refusing to prosecute violations domestically or cooperate in trials conducted internationally.

3.6.1.2. Kosovo

In 1999, Kosovo was placed under UN transitional administration following civil war between Serbia and the majority Kosovo Albanian population. The

242 Kent, above n. 230, p. 91.
243 Ibid. p. 90.
244 Williams, above n. 1, p. 99.
245 Ibid. p. 100.
246 Ibid.
247 Commission of Truth and Friendship, *Final Report of the Commission of Truth and Friendship (CTF) Indonesia-Timor Leste* (CTF, 2008).
248 Williams, above n. 1, p. 100, citing Republic of Indonesia, Ministry Foreign Affairs, 'Commission of Truth and Friendship (CTF) *Indonesia–Timor Leste*' (7 July 2010). www.deplu.go.id/Pages/IIssueDisplay.aspx?IDP+4&l+en.

Security Council passed Resolution 1244 mandating the United Nations Interim Administration Mission in Kosovo (UNMIK) under which the people of Kosovo were to 'enjoy substantial autonomy in the Federal Republic of Yugoslavia'.[249] UNMIK was vested with 'all legislative and executive authority' with respect to Kosovo, including the administration of the judiciary.[250]

As the displaced population began to return to Kosovo, the North Atlantic Treaty Kosovo Force (KFOR) stationed in Kosovo detained individuals suspected of violations of human rights and international humanitarian law. UNMIK established an emergency justice system before establishing a permanent judicial system. However, newly appointed national judges seemed unable to remain impartial and independent, and lacked the necessary skills to adjudicate in such complex trials. Moreover, Serbian legal professionals and judges refused to participate, which created the perception of bias towards Serb defendants.[251]

The ICTY had jurisdiction to try perpetrators of crimes during the Kosovo conflict but at that stage, under its completion strategy, the Tribunal was only trying those who had committed the worst crimes on a widespread basis.[252] UNMIK therefore instituted specially constituted hybrid judicial panels within Kosovar courts by a series of Regulations.[253]

The judicial panels developed out of the International Judges and Prosecutors Programme (IJPP), which provided for the appointment of international officers on a case-by-case basis and without creation of a permanent internationalised court.[254] The allocation of cases under the IJPP was within the discretion of the international administration for the purpose of ensuring the independence and impartiality of the judiciary and broader administration of justice.[255]

In their early years, the judicial panels were the answer to legitimacy crises following serious missteps in implementing the justice mandate.[256] The initial UNMIK decision was to apply the law proclaimed by the Serbs after their revocation of Kosovo Albanian autonomy. However, this was rejected by local lawyers and judges, who refused to apply that law on the grounds that it was unlawful and discriminatory. UNMIK Regulation 24 overturned the decision and decreed the applicable law as that of 22 March 1989, the day prior to the Serbian revocation. Subsequent failure to explain the rationale for the judicial panels to the local population added to the tainted perceptions of the neutrality of the foreign initiative.[257]

---

[249] UNSC Res. 1244 (1999) UN Doc. S/RES/1244 (10 June 1999) para. [10].

[250] UNMIK Regulation 1999/1, s. 1.1.

[251] Williams, above n. 1, p. 83.

[252] Cryer, above n. 19, p. 155.

[253] UNMIK Regulations 2000/6, 2000/34, 2000/64.

[254] Williams, above n. 1, p. 84.

[255] Ibid. p. 85.

[256] Higgonet, above n. 179, p. 383.

[257] Ramji-Nogales, above n. 115, p. 35.

The panels were an awkward experiment in internationalised justice in a volatile context. Their subject-matter jurisdiction was not limited to the core international crimes of genocide, crimes against humanity and war crimes. Nor was the temporal jurisdiction restricted to the period of the conflict.[258] This meant that contemporary crimes were adjudicated on, including those involving inter-ethnic violence in March 2004.[259] As organised crime is a particular problem in the region, terrorism and human trafficking cases were similarly brought before the panels.[260] However, support for the work of the panels increased over time, despite misgivings about their capacity to make sufficient progress towards ending the impunity of known perpetrators in Kosovo.[261]

By 2003, the Provisional Criminal Code and Provisional Criminal Procedure Code of Kosovo were promulgated by the Special Representative of the Secretary-General for Kosovo.[262] The Code of Criminal Procedure reflects the civil law approach to criminal process, affording participatory rights to victims beyond that of witnesses.[263] Victims may participate as civil parties, referred to as 'injured parties' with respect to serious crimes.[264] An injured party enjoys rights under the Code including the right to: raise facts and propose evidence bearing on the offence or establishment of her property claim;[265] apply to the prosecutor to collect pre-trial evidence and exercise appeal rights thereto;[266] propose evidence at trial; question the defendant and witnesses; access the case file; and make written submissions.[267] An injured party is entitled to legal representation and such representative has a duty to safeguard her rights and integrity during proceedings.[268]

Despite the existing procedural framework, McGonigle Leyh noted that available records in 2008 suggested that 'the number of victims as injured parties participating in war crimes or related cases, was relatively low.'[269] However, the Humanitarian Law Center, a non-governmental human rights organisation based

258 Williams, above n. 1, p. 87.

259 Ibid., citing Human Rights Watch, *Not on the Agenda: the Continuing Failure to Address Accountability in Kosovo Post-March 2004* (May 2006).

260 Williams, above n. 1, p. 87; See also Jean-Christian Cady and Nicholas Booth, 'Internationalized Courts in Kosovo: An UNMIK Perspective' in C. Romano, A. Nolkaemper and J. Kleffner (eds.), *Internationalized Criminal: Sierra Leone, East Timor and Cambodia* (Oxford University Press, 2004) pp. 59, 67.

261 Higonnet, above n. 179, p. 383.

262 Williams, above n. 1, p. 87.

263 McGonigle Leyh, above n. 41, p. 157.

264 Provisional Kosovo Criminal Code, art. 78 [PCPCK].

265 PCPCK, art. 80.

266 PCPCK art. 239.

267 PCPCK arts. 61, 80 (3), (4).

268 PCPCK art. 81(4).

269 McGonigle Leyh, above n. 41, p. 158.

in Belgrade and Kosovo, is actively monitoring trials and filing compensation lawsuits for victims.[270] The Center's website provides the details of successful recent actions for compensation in the national courts, suggesting there is increasing participation and representation of victims in those courts.[271]

The latest chapter in the life of the judicial panels flows from Kosovo's declaration of independence from Serbia on 17 February 2008.[272] Kosovo's move to self-determination is supervised by the international community pursuant to the Comprehensive Proposal for the Kosovo Status Settlement prepared by the Secretary-General's Special Envoy in 2007. The Settlement Plan includes a European Union Rule of Law Mission (EULEX) to Kosovo and continued NATO force deployment. Russia questioned the legality of the mission in the Security Council and Serbia refused to recognise EULEX authority in Serb-controlled territories.[273] Other EU Member States, such as Spain, were reluctant to support EULEX in light of the uncertainties regarding the legality of its mandate.[274] In July 2010, an advisory opinion of the International Court of Justice (ICJ) confirmed Kosovo's declaration of independence to be 'in accordance with international law.'[275]

Reporting to the UN Security Council, EULEX is an expressive regional commitment under European foreign and defence policy, with strong backing from the United States.[276] The role of EULEX is to monitor and mentor Kosovo authorities in rule of law implementation, specifically with respect to policing, the judiciary and customs.[277] Responsibility for the judicial panels also now falls to EULEX, with UNMIK transferring its judicial functions and caseload to the new mission. In 2010, the European Union established a Human Rights Review Panel as an independent body to review complaints of victims of human rights violations by EULEX itself in Kosovo as it conducts its mandate.[278] The Panel was designed to safeguard the promise of EULEX to maintain overall operational and social accountability.[279]

270 Ibid.

271 See, for example, *Compensation to Five Kosovar Albanians for Torture and Unlawful Detention* Humanitarian Law Center (30 April 2013): http://hlc-rd.org/?=22889&lang=de.

272 'Kosovo Declaration of Independence', 17 February 2008, (2008) 47 ILM 467.

273 Erika de Wet, 'The Governance of Kosovo: Security Council Resolution 1244 and the Establishment and Functioning of EULEX' (2009) 103 *American Journal of International Law* 83, 85.

274 Ibid.

275 *Accordance with International Law of the Declaration of Independence in Respect of Kosovo (Advisory Opinion)* ICJ Reports 2010 p. 403.

276 de Wet, above n. 273, p. 83.

277 Council of the European Union [EU Council], Council Joint Action 2008/124/CFSP on the Rule of law Mission in Kosovo [2008] OJ L42/92, 16.02.2008.

278 Guglielmo Verdirome, *The UN and Human Rights: Who Guards the Guardian?* (Cambridge, Cambridge University Press, 2011) p. 266.

279 EULEX, 'Accountability': http://www.eulex-kosovo.eu/?page+2,23.

Analysis of the UN Missions in Kosovo and East Timor demonstrates a surplus of expressive values. In Kosovo, the judicial panels brought the criminal law's traditional moral condemnatory messages with internationality, heralding the guarantee of fair trial procedure. Subsumed within EULEX, the Panels develop local judicial capacity under the banner of regional state-building.[280] In East Timor, UN acquiescence towards an unrepentant Indonesia produced ad hoc and unrepresentative expressive justice, with little scope for communicative proceedings without mechanisms enabling the exercise of victims' rights under the applicable civil law procedure. Did Courts unconstrained by wide-ranging UN mandates exhibit more communicative dynamics as they operated?

3.6.2. HYBRID COURTS

The trend towards nationalising the prosecution of violations of international humanitarian law gained momentum through the creation of alternative court forms generically described as 'hybrid courts'. These were the Special Court for Sierra Leone (SCSL), the Extraordinary Chambers in the Courts of Cambodia, and the Special Tribunal for Lebanon (STL). Hybridity had expressive dimensions, as the following discussion of the SCSL and the SLT illustrates. The formation of the ECCC is discussed in Chapter four.

3.6.2.1. *The Special Court for Sierra Leone*

The creation of the Special Court for Sierra Leone was informed by negotiations underway at the time for a hybrid international tribunal for Cambodia.[281] The two national contexts have parallels in terms of the complexities arising from situations of intractable civil war and long periods of impunity for political leaders.[282] However, the negotiations for creation of the SCSL can be distinguished from those of the ECCC by strong domestic political will in favour of such a tribunal and support from key Security Council Members in the formation and operation of the Court.[283]

280 Higgonet, above n. 179, p. 381.
281 Craig Etcheson, *After the Killing Fields: Lessons from the Cambodian Genocide* (????, 2005) p. 181.
282 Ibid.
283 Cohen, above n. 233, p. 25.

Political Action Creating the SCSL

In June 2000, the President of Sierra Leone sent a request to the Security Council seeking creation of an international tribunal to prosecute members of the insurgent Revolutionary United Front (RUF) for commission of crimes against the Sierra Leonean people, and for taking United Nations peacekeepers as hostages.[284] This followed the resumption of hostilities in Sierra Leone despite a UN negotiated peace agreement, the 1999 Lome Accord.[285] The Security Council adopted Resolution 1315, pursuant to which the Secretary-General negotiated an agreement with the government of Sierra Leone to establish a special court with jurisdiction over the international crimes of genocide, crimes against humanity and other serious violations of international humanitarian law, and to which no amnesty would apply.[286] The resolution recognised the importance of a credible system of justice and accountability for international crimes committed, 'to end impunity … and [to] contribute to the process of national reconciliation and the maintenance and restoration of peace.'[287] The Security Council's broad statement of purpose reflected the Court's concurrent operation with the Truth and Reconciliation Commission provided for under the Lome Accord.[288]

An agreement between the United Nations and the Government of Sierra Leone provided the framework for a treaty-based hybrid court.[289] National legislation gave effect to the Court's statute and enabled the creation of the Court within Sierra Leone.[290] Though the SCSL was located in Freetown, Sierra Leone, it operated independently of the national court system.[291] The Court had concurrent jurisdiction with the national courts but had primacy over crimes in its jurisdiction and could issue binding orders to the national government.[292]

---

284 'Letter dated 9 August 2000 from the Permanent Representative of Sierra Leone to the United Nations addressed to the President of the Security Council' UN Doc. S/2000/786, annex cited in Schabas, above n. 85, p. 35.

285 *Peace Agreement between the Government of the Republic of Sierra Leone and the Revolutionary United Front of Sierra Leone*. UN Doc. S/1999/777 (7 July 1999) Annex, (*Lome Accord*).

286 Schabas, above n. 92, p. 36; See *Lome Accord*, art. xxvi.

287 UNSC Res. 1315 (2000) UN Doc. S/Res/1315 (14 August 2000) Preamble, para. [5].

288 Schabas, above n. 92, p. 36. The TRC was established in July 2002.

289 *Agreement between the United Nations and the Government of Sierra Leone on the Establishment of the Special Court for Sierra Leone* (16 January 2002).

290 *Statute of the Special Court of Sierra Leone* annexed to the *Agreement between the United Nations and the Government of Sierra Leone on the Establishment of the Special Court for Sierra Leone* UN Doc. S/2002/246, appendix II (2002); *Special Court Agreement (Ratification) Act 2002* Supplement to the *Sierra Leone Gazette* vol. CXXX. No. II (7 March 2002).

291 Article 2 establishes separate legal personality; Article 8 provides for inviolability of premises; Article 9 affords immunity as to funds, assets and property; Article 13 provides for immunity of international and national staff.

292 SCSL Statute art. 8(2).

The judiciary was composed of national and international judges, with a majority of international judges.[293] Other units of the Court were staffed by both international and national personnel.[294]

The applicable law of the SCSL combined national and international law. The Court was guided by the jurisprudence and procedure of the ICTY and ICTR, as well as decisions of the Supreme Court of Sierra Leone.[295] The SCSL had narrower jurisdiction than that of the ICTY or ICTR. Article 1(1) of the SCSL Statute grants jurisdiction over persons 'who bear the greatest responsibility for serious violations of international humanitarian law and Sierra Leonean law' committed in Sierra Leone from 30 November 1996, thus eliminating the pursuit of low- or mid-level perpetrators.[296]

With a narrower jurisdiction and a temporary mandate, the new hybrid court represented a more cost- and time-effective justice mechanism than the ad hoc Tribunals.[297] The SCSL budget was made up of voluntary contributions from supporting states rather than being drawn from general UN funds.[298] This amounted to approximately one-quarter of the budget for the ICTY.[299] Nevertheless, the SCSL was provided with purpose-built modern infrastructure, including court chambers with state of the art facilities, and a detention centre.[300] While the SCSL was not created by Chapter VII power, it was clear that some members of the Security Council wanted the Tribunal to succeed.[301] Actions by the United Kingdom and the United States in putting in place the necessary management committee structures, funding arrangements and experienced personnel ensured that the institution operated viably and efficiently.[302] Certain administrative innovations, including creation of a defence support unit, also enhanced the operations of the Court.[303]

---

293 SCSL Statute art. 12.

294 Article 1 of the SCSL Statute grants jurisdiction over crimes against humanity, violations of Common Article 3 of the Geneva Conventions and other violations of international humanitarian law, including intentional attacks on civilians or humanitarian personnel, and the abduction and forced recruitment of children under the age of 15.

295 SCSL Statute art. 20.

296 SCSL Statute art. 1 (1).

297 Cohen, above n. 233, p. 12.

298 Schabas, above n. 92, p. 37.

299 Based on two-year budgets for 2008–2009 for the ICTY at US$310,952,100 and the ICTR at US$267,356,200, cited in Sean Morrison, 'Extraordinary Language in the Courts of Cambodia: Interpreting the Limiting Language and Personal Jurisdiction of the Cambodian Tribunal' (2008–2009) 37 *Capital University Law Review* 583, 587.

300 Cohen, above n. 233, pp. 10–11.

301 Ibid. p. 25.

302 Ibid.

303 Peter Pham, 'A Viable Model for International Criminal Justice: The Special Court for Sierra Leone' (2006) 19 *New York International Law Review* 37, 88.

Importantly, extensive efforts were made from the beginning by SCSL Prosecutor David Crane of the United States and Registrar Robin Vincent of the United Kingdom, to enter into dialogue with civil society groups and the wider population on the work of the Tribunal. This increased local support of the Court and resulted in the initiation of local programmes designed to promote the rule of law within the wider society.[304] These efforts constituted the first effective outreach programme in an international court. Ultimately, the viability of the hybrid institutional form was confirmed as the SCSL arrested suspects and convicted 10 indictees from 2003 to 2013.[305] This included the trial of the sitting head of state, Charles Taylor, in 2012.[306]

Expressive and Communicative Dimensions of the SCSL

The SCSL procedural framework was modelled on that of the ad hoc Tribunals. Thus, victims were only able to participate in trial proceedings as witnesses called by the parties. McGonigle Leyh recorded accounts of 'prosecutorial insensitivity' to victims within a prosecution narrative providing a 'politically skewed reading of the conflict'.[307] The prosecution opposed the hearing of victim impact statements in sentencing proceedings on the basis that they constituted new evidence.[308] Furthermore, reparations were not dealt with by the SCSL, but were left to the national courts.

However, the instrumental nature of the role of victims at the Court was offset in some ways by the formation of the Sierra Leone Truth and Reconciliation Commission (SLTRC). The Commission was able to investigate events outside the Court's temporal jurisdiction and provided an avenue for victims to share their experiences in narrative form. The greater scope for victim inclusion during the proceedings permitted creation of a broader historical record.[309]

In all, the SCSL presented a new trial form combining international and national criminal justice *in situ*. While the Court focused on bringing convictions, its outreach efforts contributed to lessening the remoteness of trial outcomes from their social context. The community interactions through outreach brought a communicative dynamic to the hybrid court which complimented the dialogue between victims and perpetrators made possible by the work of the SLTRC.

---

304 Ibid. pp. 104–107.

305 See Residual Special Court for Sierra Leone website: http://www.rscsl.org (accessed 30 May 2016).

306 *Prosecutor v. Charles Ghankay Taylor (Judgment)* (Special Court for Sierra Leone, Trial Chamber II, Case No. SCSL-03-01-T, 18 May 2012).

307 McGonigle Leyh, above n. 41, p. 149.

308 Sluiter, above n. 22, p. 1329.

309 McGonigle Leyh, above n. 41, pp. 150–151.

Thus, transitional justice in Sierra Leone permitted engagement with the past beyond the expressivism of conviction and punishment.

3.6.2.2. *The Special Tribunal for Lebanon*

Political Action Creating the Court

Political tensions were running high in Lebanon as the May 2005 elections approached. Prime Minister Rafiq Hariri, who had close ties with Western powers (US, France) and Saudia Arabia, was expected to lead the opposition party to victory in the election.[310] However, on 14 February 2005, he and 22 other people were killed when his motorcade was bombed in central Beirut. Mass demonstrations followed with demands for the withdrawal of Syrian troops from Lebanon and investigation of the attack through an international tribunal.[311] The sustained protests and international pressure brought the withdrawal of Syrian forces in April 2005 after 35 years of occupation of Lebanese territory.[312]

In December 2005 the Lebanese government requested UN assistance to establish a tribunal of international character to try the alleged planners of the assassination of Hariri in February, and a number of purportedly related terrorist acts.[313] Pursuant to Security Council Resolution 1644, an Agreement between the UN and the government of Lebanon for creation of a tribunal modelled on that of the SCSL was signed by the parties on 23 January and 6 February 2007 respectively.[314] However certain political machinations transpired in Lebanon which prevented ratification of the enabling legislation by the parliament. In response to the national impasse, the Security Council passed Resolution 1757 under its Chapter VII power in view of the perceived threat to international peace and security posed by the assassination of Hariri.[315] This made way for formal establishment of the Special Tribunal of Lebanon as a hybrid court based

---

310 UNSC Resolution 1599 had already been adopted calling for 'the withdrawal of foreign forces from Lebanon and for strict respect for the sovereignty, territorial integrity, unity and political independence of Lebanon.' UNSC Res. 1559 UN Doc. S/2004/1559 (2 September 2004) paras. 1–2.

311 Williams, above n. 1, p. 73.

312 Ibid.

313 'Letter of the Prime Minister of Lebanon to the Secretary-General on the 13 December 2005' UN Doc. S/2005/783 (2005).

314 The Agreement is annexed to the resolution and is referred within it as the 'annexed document' Negotiation of an agreement to Establish a Special Tribunal for Lebanon was recommended by the UN Secretary-General in the Report of the Secretary-General pursuant to paragraph 6 of Resolution 1644 (2005) para. 5. UN Doc. S/2006/176 (21 March 2006).

315 UNSC Res. 1757 (2007) UN Doc. S/RES/1757 (30 May 2007) Preamble para. [13].

in The Hague by 11 June 2007 if the Agreement remained unratified before then, which it did.[316]

Despite five abstentions from the Security Council vote, international criminal justice as an instrument in the hands of the Council may have evolved to become a logic in its own right.[317] Instead of sovereignty defences being raised against Security Council action, the Resolution was carried based on threats to Lebanese sovereignty and democracy by alleged Syrian interference in national governance.[318] Previously, the criteria of international peace and security had justified the creation of international criminal courts, but in this case the expressive value of international criminal justice arguably informed interpretations of international peace and security.[319]

The subject-matter jurisdiction of the STL is limited to domestic crimes under the Lebanese Criminal Code relating to terrorism. These are 'acts of terrorism', 'offences against life and personal integrity', 'illicit associations and failure to report crimes and offences'.[320] However, in an interlocutory decision, the STL Appeals Chamber ruled that in construing the Lebanese law the Court was entitled to take account of the international treaties and customary law that bind Lebanon. Therefore, the Court would have regard to the relevant international rules on terrorism in view of the gravity and transnational dimension of the facts at issue, which the Security Council had considered grave enough to justify establishment of the Court.[321] Furthermore, Article 3 of the STL Statute makes provision for individual responsibility on the basis of joint criminal enterprise and command responsibility, both of which are forms of participation in systematic crime generally derived from international law.[322] Thus, excision of the institution from its national context brought internationalised judicial proceedings within the hybrid court.

There was some retention of the applicable national law, such as the possibility of holding trials *in absentia*, subject to safeguards protecting the rights of the accused.[323] In addition, the application of Lebanese law activated some

---

316 Williams, above n. 1, pp. 76–77.

317 Frédéric Mégret, 'A Special Tribunal for Lebanon: The Council and the Emancipation of International Criminal Justice' (2008) 21 *Leiden Journal of International Law* 485, 485.

318 Ibid. pp. 494–495.

319 Ibid. pp. 498–499.

320 United Nations Security Council Resolution 1757 (30 May 2007) Attachment: Statute of the Special Tribunal for Lebanon art. 2(a).

321 *Prosecutor v. Ayash et al.*, Interlocutory Decision on the Applicable Law: Terrorism, Conspiracy, Homicide, Perpetration, Cumulative Charging, AC, No. STL-11-01 (16 February 2011) 'Summary of President Cassese's Remarks', available: http://www.stl-tsl.org/en/media/press-releases/summary-of-president-cassese-s-speech, paras. 14, 18.

322 *Statute of the Special Tribunal for Lebanon* S/RES/1757 (2007) art. 3(1)(b). [SLT Statute]; See Williams, above n. 1, p. 234.

323 Cecile Aptel, 'Some Innovations in the Statute of the Special Tribunal for Lebanon' (2007) 5 *Journal of International Criminal Justice* 1107, 1121; See SLT Statute art. 22(2), (3).

aspects of criminal procedure in the Romano-Germanic civil law tradition; for instance there is a Pre-Trial Judge, who, while not an investigative judge, may issue investigative orders as part of pre-trial procedure.[324] Other procedural features characteristic of inquisitorial trials include: scope for judges to control proceedings, to question witnesses first, and to access certain documents ahead of the trial.[325]

Communicative Dimensions of the STL

The mixed composition of judicial officers, consisting of a majority of internationally appointed judges working with Lebanese judges, of the Trial Chambers and the Appeals Chamber signals representation of the national interest in the prosecutions. The communicative benefits of local knowledge combined with international expertise flow from hybridity at that level; even though the Prosecutor is an international appointee, and the pre-trial procedure is controlled by one international judge.[326]

In addition, the framers of the STL Rules of Evidence and Procedure considered carefully how the Court could do justice to and uphold the dignity of victims of the crimes before the Court. In this, they sought to strike an 'adequate balance between the legitimate judicial, reparative and symbolic interest of victims on the one hand and the fairness and efficiency of trial proceedings on the other.'[327] The judicial interest stemmed from victims' contributions to establishing the truth through raising relevant facts and evidence that might assist the prosecution process. Reparative effects could flow to victims through being heard in Court, with the opportunity to express their suffering at appropriate stages of proceedings recognised as contributing to victim rehabilitation and restoration.[328] Finally, involving victims in proceedings, rather than keeping them extraneous to the trial except for their instrumental value as witnesses had symbolic or expressive purpose.[329]

Under the STL RPE, a victim is a 'natural person who has suffered physical, material, or mental harm as a direct result of an attack within the Tribunal's jurisdiction'.[330] In the STL's first pre-trial decision on victim participation, the

---

324 McGonigle Leyh, above n. 41, p. 161.

325 Ibid.

326 Aptel, above n. 323, p. 1120.

327 Jérôme de Hemptinne, 'Challenges Raised by Victims' Participation in the Proceedings of the Special Tribunal for Lebanon' (2010) 8 *Journal of International Criminal Justice* 165, 179.

328 Ibid. p. 168 citing War Crimes Research Office (Washington College of Law) Victim Participation Before the International Criminal (WCL Legal Analysis and Education Project Report 1, November 2007) at pp. 8 and 9.

329 Ibid.

330 STL RPE Rule 2.

Pre-Trial Judge held that the requirement of a 'direct result' referred to causation and that the definition of victim extends to indirect victims, such as the victim's close relatives.[331] In order to participate in proceedings victim applicants must be screened by the Pre-Trial Judge. A 'victim participating in proceedings' (VPP) is a 'victim of an attack within the Tribunal's jurisdiction who has been granted leave by the Pre-Trial Judge to present his views and concerns at one or more stages of the proceedings after an indictment has been confirmed.'[332] The decision to grant victim participation rights turns on specific and discretionary considerations.[333] The Pre-Trial Judge must consider:

> whether the applicant has provided prima facie evidence that he is a victim ... whether the applicant's personal interests are affected ... whether the applicant's proposed participation is intended to express his views and concerns; and ... whether the applicant's proposed participation would be prejudicial to or inconsistent with the rights of the accused to a fair and impartial trial.[334]

Discretionary considerations include: 'whether the proposed participation by the applicant would jeopardise the appearance of ... objectivity of the proceedings'; 'cause unnecessary delay or inefficiency in the proceedings'; or 'impact negatively on the security of the proceedings or any person involved'. While the range of additional considerations that may be taken into account suggests considerable scope for denial of participation rights, in the *Ayash* decision, the discretionary factors were not applied to 'limit' victim participation; rather an inclusive approach to victims was evident.[335]

Victims are also unable to claim reparations through the STL process, but may subsequently make a claim in national proceedings.[336] Victim participants are excluded from the investigation process at the STL and cannot acquire civil party status, but the Pre-Trial Judge must ensure that the Trial Chamber has the necessary information on their major interests and concerns.[337] A report is prepared addressing the VPPs' arguments on both facts and applicable law, the probative matter introduced by them, and details of witnesses they seek to have called by the Trial Chamber.[338]

---

331 *Prosecutor v. Ayash et al.* (Case No STL-11-01/PT/PTJ, 8 May 2008) pp. 38–46.

332 STL RPE Rule 2.

333 Sluiter, above n. 22, p. 1306.

334 STL RPE Rule 86(B); See further *Prosecutor v. Ayash et al.* (n. 331 above) pp. 89–90, 96 and 100.

335 Sluiter, above n. 22, p. 1306.

336 McGonigle Leyh, above n 41,. p. 162.

337 STL RPE Rule 95.

338 Sluiter, above n. 22, p. 1324.

At trial, VPPs may present their views and concerns at stages of the proceedings determined to be appropriate by the Chamber and in a way that is not prejudicial to the rights of the accused.[339] Through their legal representatives, VPPs may make opening statements;[340] request that specific questions be put to the accused;[341] examine and cross-examine witnesses and file motions and briefs;[342] and make closing arguments.[343] In addition, other rights accrue to ensure their effective and meaningful participation, such as rights to receive documents filed by the parties.[344]

Thus, the VPPs are factored into the procedural apparatus with scope for representation of their views and hearing of their voices on evidentiary matters. The absence of a reparations mandate, although available under Lebanese law, is a further limit on the nature of communication possible in STL proceedings. However, in the STL's separate sentencing proceedings, subject to authorisation by the Trial Chamber, a VPP may be heard on the personal impact of the crimes or may file written submissions as to impact.[345] Clearly, the STL constrained the dialogue of its trials in order to protect the rights of the accused, as well as ensure impartiality and security of process. Nonetheless, the deliberate inclusion of the voice of the victim and their respectful treatment expanded the communicative capacity of STL trials.

3.6.2.3. *The Iraqi High Tribunal*

In 2003, in the circumstances of the occupation of Iraq by the United States, France, China and Russia considered the occupation to be unlawful. The three states indicated their intention to veto Security Council action to create an international tribunal to prosecute the crimes of the regime of Saddam Hussein.[346] The Iraqi High Tribunal (IHT) was subsequently created by decree of the Coalition Provisional Authority (CPA) as a national court with the assistance of the United States. The United States President attached expressive ideals to the Tribunal. President George W. Bush stated that the Tribunal

339 STL RPE Rule 17.

340 STL RPE Rule 143.

341 STL RPE Rule 144(B).

342 STL RPE Rule 146.

343 STL RPE Rule 147.

344 STL RPE Rule 87(A).

345 STL RPE Rule 171(B).

346 Williams, above n. 1, p. 114.

would permit Iraq to assume responsibility for trials of the former regime's operatives with CPA assistance, help Iraq build local legal capacity and the rule of law and, importantly, send the message that systematic abuse of the civilian population was intolerable.[347] However, reminiscent of the Tokyo IMT, the IHT was expressive of unilateral political action without discernible communicative dynamics.

3.7. CONCLUSION

The complexity of expressivism is evident in the development of the transitional trial. Expressivism is manifestly positive and negative through the political action of creating institutions to prosecute international crimes. The Allied Powers' actions in creating the post-WWII International Military Tribunals brought the first cracks in the otherwise impenetrable edifice of national jurisdiction over such crimes. When the ad hoc Tribunals began enforcing international humanitarian law, an expressive deterrence vehicle was created. As the courts operated, the contours of universal norms were refined by expressive judicial analysis. However, the political contingencies of creating transitional courts mean that the enforcement of international criminal law is selective and equivocal. Not all situations of international crime will be addressed, and institutional legitimacy may be compromised by the bias of victors' justice or unilateral state action on grounds of political expediency, as illustrated by the IMTFE and the IHT. As the abrupt end to the East Timor Special Panels demonstrated, the expressivism of transitional trials is also susceptible to domestic political manoeuvring to divert efforts to prosecute higher-level suspects.

While the governing instruments of transitional courts are expressive of the global norm of accountability, the procedural regimes of individual courts may undermine the legitimacy of the courts in the eyes of subject communities. At the ad hoc Tribunals, the exclusion of the victim's voice except as witness limited the communicative potential of trial proceedings which might otherwise have built trust in the authority of the courts among the affected populations. At the ICC, despite the implementation difficulties of incorporating victim participation rights, the *sui generis* scheme expanded the representativeness of trial proceedings and gradually enhanced the quality of international justice.

The emergence of the hybrid and internationalised court offered the potential for evaluation of the transitional trial on the basis of its communicative

[347] M. Cherif, Bassiouni, 'Post-Conflict Justice in Iraq: An Appraisal of the Iraq Special Tribunal' (2005) 38 *Cornell International Law Journal* 327, 344.

potential within the affected communities. The SCSL showed the viability of justice process shared between national and international authorities *in situ*. It also demonstrated that justice outcomes may be enhanced by communication initiatives between the Court and local communities, as well as linkages with complimentary restorative justice mechanisms. The hybrid STL sought protection of the rights of the accused as being of paramount importance while advancing the communicative capacity of its trials by recognising victim participants' rights to justice and voice. At the same time, the steady internationalisation of STL proceedings blocked the communicative dynamics that might have emerged had Lebanon's inquisitorial trial procedure been activated more fully.

In Chapters five to seven, the communicative dimensions of the ECCC's inquisitorial procedure are explored. As a prelude to this, in Chapter four, the historical and political factors affecting the creation the ECCC are discussed.

CHAPTER 4

THE CREATION OF THE EXTRAORDINARY CHAMBERS IN THE COURTS OF CAMBODIA

4.1. INTRODUCTION

The transitional courts and tribunals discussed in the last chapter exhibited an expressive surplus as a consequence of the dominance of the international in terms of their composition, applicable law and procedure. This chapter introduces the Extraordinary Chambers in the Courts of Cambodia (ECCC), an internationalised court established to try senior leaders and those most responsible for crimes of mass atrocity under the government of Democratic Kampuchea (Khmer Rouge regime), which ruled Cambodia from 17 April 1975 to 6 January 1979.

The chapter explores the background to the creation of the ECCC by traversing Cambodia's history and political culture. After Cambodia secured independence from France in 1953, a complex mix of national and geopolitical factors determined the course its national governments would take. The same factors compromised law and justice in Cambodia and preserved a place in Cambodian society for the Khmer Rouge long after the demise of the government of Democratic Kampuchea. The longevity of the Khmer Rouge also shaped the negotiations for the Agreement for the establishment of the ECCC. In the absence of any national justice and reconciliation mechanism to address the political crimes of the Khmer Rouge era, the creation of the locally situated ECCC finally offered Cambodians both the promise of some justice and scope for engagement with the past. Against this background, the chapter aims to highlight the socio-political imperatives underpinning the adjudication of crimes before the internationalised Court.

4.2. POLITICAL CULTURE AND *REALPOLITIK*

From their ancient origins as an animistic, subsistence society, the Khmer people of Cambodia endured many political transformations. The language of the Khmer peasant, which belongs to the family of languages known as Mon-Khmer of Southeast Asia, survived as the national tongue.[1] Cambodia's predominantly rural majority accommodated each political transformation due to an abiding cultural acceptance of subordination in exchange for protection from governing elites so that crops could be harvested and family ties maintained.[2] The continuity of kinship ties and connection to the land, even if subject to the exigencies of patron–client relationships, sustained a sense of Khmer identity despite the fall of the Angkorean Empire, loss of Cambodian territory to Thailand and Vietnam, and subjection to French colonial power (1864–1954).[3]

The presence of a righteous ruler at the apex of a moral hierarchy underpinned the Cambodian conception of social order, albeit subject to cyclical change under Buddhist philosophy.[4] However, Cambodia's culture and traditions masked fear of territorial encroachment – the possibility of imminent extinction, and the sense of racial superiority. A long line of despotic rulers capitalised on these factors for political gain.[5]

In the twentieth century, Cambodia's feudal hierarchies were challenged by militant nationalist movements to oust the French colonial power, and in the context of communism taking hold in Southeast Asia. In Cambodia, the nationalist Khmer Issarak movement against French rule gradually became allied to the insurgent Viet Minh communist resistance in Vietnam during the First Indochina War (1946–1954).[6] In 1951, the Khmer People's Revolutionary Party (KPRP) was formed under the sponsorship of the Vietnamese communist movement. The KPRP eventually gained ascendency over the more democratic Issarak nationalists.[7]

---

1 David Chandler, *History of Cambodia*, 4th ed. (Westview Press, 2008) pp. 13–14.

2 Ibid. pp. 3, 171–173.

3 Patron client groupings were characteristic of the hierarchical political cultures of the Hinduised kingdoms of Southeast Asia through which wealth was redistributed and 'patrons were expected to lead, teach, educate, and provide for their clients.' Karl D. Jackson, 'Introduction: The Khmer Rouge in Context' in Karl D. Jackson (ed.), *Cambodia 1975–1978: Rendezvous with Death* (Princeton University Press, 1986) pp. 3, 5; Ledgerwood noted that in Cambodian villages 'reciprocity between patrons and clients' established the social bonds that underpinned community. Judy Ledgerwood and John Vijghen, 'Decision-Making in Rural Villages' in Judy Ledgerwood (ed.), *Cambodia Emerges from the Past: Eight Essays* (Center for Southeast Asian Studies, Northern Illinois University, 2002) pp. 109, 115.

4 Judy Ledgerwood, 'Ritual in 1990 Cambodian Political Theatre' in Anne Hansen and Judy Ledgerwood (eds), *At the Edge of the Forest: Essays on Cambodia, History and Narrative in Honor of David Chandler* (Southeast Asia Program [SEAP], Cornell University, 2008) pp. 195, 197.

5 Elizabeth Becker, *When the War was Over: the Voices of Cambodia's Revolution and its People* (Simon & Schuster, 1986) p. 16.

6 Ben Kiernan, *How Pol Pot Came to Power: Colonialism, Nationalism, and Communism in Cambodia, 1930–1975*, 2nd ed. (Yale University Press, 2004) p. *xx*.

7 Chandler, above n. 1, p. 222.

Against the background of war between France and Vietnam and the anti-royalist sentiment of the communists, the Cambodian monarch, King Norodom Sihanouk, negotiated partial independence from France in October 1953.[8] In 1954 at the Geneva Conference, following the defeat of France by the Viet Minh forces, Cambodia secured full independence under the monarch.[9]

However, the end of French colonial rule in Indochina was followed by the Vietnam War (1960–1975), which enmeshed Cambodia in a geopolitical web of conflict. The war to remove the French colonial power and to end United States intervention in Vietnam had united traditional regional enemies. However, it also froze long-standing hostility over territorial claims between China and Vietnam, and Cambodia and Vietnam.[10] These complicated the intense national political rivalries within Cambodia after independence, and led to armed struggle against the Cambodian government, and eventual civil war.

4.2.1. ROYALIST RULE AND *REALPOLITIK*

In 1955, prior to the national election, Sihanouk abdicated as monarch and began his personal political crusade. His movement, known as the Sangkum Reastr Niyum (Popular Socialist Community), stood for royalist, Buddhist socialism without class conflict.[11] Francophile in orientation, Sihanouk placed himself in the middle of the pluralist political spectrum introduced by the French between the radical pro-communist Krom Pracheachon Party, whom he dubbed the red Khmer (Khmer Rouges) and the Democrats (blue Khmer). He saw himself as the white Khmer; his party was conservative and aligned with the ancient Khmer respect for royalty.[12]

Sihanouk modernised the Cambodian economy, building a commercial sector composed largely of Chinese businesses, and established a trade-based market economy from the capital, Phnom Penh. For the first time an urban Khmer population developed.[13] With foreign aid from France, the United States and the Sino-Soviet power block, he invested extensively in educational infrastructure, hospitals, public transportation and the arts. He was extremely popular among the Cambodian peasantry, who saw him not only as royalty but as the personification of Cambodia itself.[14] Sihanouk was criticised by his

8 Ibid. p. 227.

9 Kiernan, above n. 6, p. xxi.

10 Nayan Chanda, *Brother Enemy: The War after the War* (Harcourt Brace Jovanovich, 1986) p. 11.

11 Michael Vickery, *Cambodia 1975–1982* (South End Press, 1984) p. 22.

12 Chandler, above n. 1, p. 240; Ibid.

13 Vickery above n. 11, p. 18.

14 Evan Gottesman, *Cambodia after the Khmer Rouge: Inside the Politics of Nation Building* (Yale University Press, 2003) p. 18.

political opponents for condoning inequity and corruption throughout what became effective monopoly rule for 15 years after independence. His populist movement overcame opposition by intimidation, violence and propaganda. Gottesman argued that Sihanouk's style of government and campaigning became the model for the national political power struggles that followed the Cambodian revolution of 1975–1979.[15] However, Sihanouk could not control the external events that embroiled Cambodia in the Vietnam War as Cold War tensions played out in Southeast Asia.

While Sihanouk initially asserted Cambodian neutrality in the Vietnam War, he subsequently allowed North Vietnam to establish bases in Cambodia to feed supply lines to their troops in South Vietnam.[16] From 1965, after American troops landed in South Vietnam, Cambodia was destabilised by intense aerial bombardment in the region of the border with South Vietnam. As North Vietnamese National Liberation Front (NLF) troops sought refuge and supplies direct from Cambodian peasants, government tax revenues and exports were affected.[17] In 1967, the Cambodian government faced a serious peasant revolt, known as the Samlaut Uprising, against action to control the price of rice in Battambang. The riots were attributed to local communist dissidents, and spread to other villages. Sihanouk, already cracking down on suspected communist opposition in Phnom Penh, was then perceived as vulnerable to a communist threat by some government members.[18]

Further destabilisation occurred from 18 March 1969 as a result of the massive United States B52 bombing campaign (code named 'Menu') of bases established in Cambodia by North Vietnam.[19] The bombing of Cambodia continued until August 1973, inflicting great loss of life conservatively estimated at 600,000 and producing refugee contingents in multiples of that figure in urban centres, particularly Phnom Penh.[20]

Sihanouk's alignment with the North Vietnamese blocked the Sino-Cambodian commercial sector from the Southeast Asian economic boom.[21] Although Sihanouk renewed diplomatic relations with the United States in 1969, the Phnom Penh commercial elite resolved to move against him as the economy weakened, social unrest increased and corruption in government ranks grew.

---

15 Ibid.

16 David Chandler, *Brother Number One: A Political Biography of Pol Pot* (Westview Press, 1992) p. 71.

17 Ibid.

18 Ibid. p. 82.

19 William Shawcross, *Sideshow: Kissinger, Nixon and the Destruction of Cambodia* (Andre Deutsch, 1979) pp. 28–33.

20 Aaron Buckley, 'The Conflict in Cambodia and Post-Conflict Justice' in M. Cherif Bassiouni (ed), *Post-Conflict Justice* (Transnational Publishers, 2002) pp. 635, 637, citing Christopher Hitchens, *The Trial of Henry Kissinger* (Verso, 2001) p, 35.

21 Chandler, above n. 16, p. 87.

On 17 March 1970, Sihanouk was ousted in a 'bloodless coup' led by his Prime Minister Lon Nol, who then formed a new government, the Khmer Republic.[22] The United States supported the Lon Nol regime and they became allies in an offensive to remove Vietnamese forces and citizens from Cambodia.[23] Sihanouk in turn made an alliance with the growing communist Khmer Rouge insurgency in Cambodia and secured support from North Vietnam and China.[24]

4.2.2. THE RISE OF THE KHMER ROUGE

The 'Khmer Rouges' were urban Cambodian communists influenced by the ideas of an elite group of Khmer students who had studied in France during the 1950s, where they participated in a Marxist Study Circle, in Paris. The faction included Saloth Sar, who became known as Pol Pot, Ieng Sary, Khieu Thirith and Khieu Samphân. They were acquainted with the French Communist Party and adhered to a mix of radical political theory derived from the work of Fanon, Amin, Stalin, Marx and Mao.[25] On their return to Cambodia this elite group became teachers in formal positions, but also informally through public discussion groups and seminars reminiscent of their Paris experience.[26] Their intellectual approach attracted monks, students, schoolteachers and members of the new class of urban workers to an ideology which condemned Sihanouk's feudalist autocracy as in league with foreign capitalist elites.[27] In this way they offered an indigenous revolutionary path distinct from the militaristic Vietnamese approach that had hitherto dominated Cambodian communism.

By 1966, the new communist faction wrested the party from Vietnamese influence and changed its name to the Communist Party of Kampuchea (CPK). Following the Samlaut uprising the CPK leadership fled the capital as

22 Ibid. p. 81.

23 Buckley, above n. 20, p. 637.

24 Ibid.

25 Karl D Jackson, 'Intellectual Origins of the Khmer Rouge' in Karl D. Jackson (ed), *Cambodia 1975–1978: Rendezvous with Death* (Princeton University Press, 1989) pp. 241, 250.

26 *Saloth Sar* taught French, history, geography and civics at a private college, Chamraon Vichea ('Progressive Knowledge') in Phnom Penh after marrying Khieu Ponnary, sister of Khieu Thirith in 1956. Ieng Sary married Khieu Thirth in 1953. On his return to Cambodia in 1957 he became a teacher of history and geography at Kampuchea Bot High school until 1963. Thirith taught English literature at the Norodom Lycée. Khieu Ponnary taught Cambodian literature at the Lycée Sisowath. See Chandler, above n. 16, pp. 50–52. As professor of political economics, Khieu Samphân taught at a private college, the Kamputh Bot, and was editor of the *Observateur*, a review espousing progressive political views. See Francois Ponchaud, *Cambodia: Year Zero* (Reinhart and Winston, 1978) p. 159

27 Chandler, above n. 16, p. 83.

Sihanouk crushed their urban networks.[28] From that time Pol Pot, Ieng Sary, Khieu Samphân and other party members moved to the Northeastern provinces of Cambodia, adopting a policy of armed struggle against the Phnom Penh government.[29]

The provinces were populated by animistic tribal peoples and Buddhist peasants already opposed to the government's programmes of roads, rubber plantations and timber harvesting in their area, and so were initially receptive to the new revolutionaries.[30] However, moving from village to village, the Khmer Rouge terrorised inhabitants by killing up to 10 people per village, purging commune or village chiefs, and appointing revolutionary leaders to take their place. The murderous tactics used in the provinces became the hallmark of the Khmer Rouge during the decades that followed.[31]

Pol Pot and Ieng Sary drew up a plan for the zoning of the country into administrative and military sectors under the revolutionary government they envisioned. By 1970, their growing insurgent forces, from bases in the northeast and northwest, occupied or controlled nearly a fifth of Cambodian territory, albeit without military support from the North Vietnamese, who viewed the Khmer communist role solely as maintaining supply lines through Cambodia to their forces in South Vietnam.[32]

Ultimately, the CPK path to power was fostered by large swathes of village populations swelling their ranks as the Vietnam War spilled over into Cambodia. Kiernan has chronicled the flood of Khmer and Vietnamese refugees fleeing South Vietnam into Cambodia as the United States' intervention escalated the Vietnam War.[33] In May 1970, United States troops invaded Cambodia in pursuit of Vietnamese communist forces as the bombing of the countryside continued.[34] The devastation, dislocation and massive loss of Cambodian civilian lives made surviving villagers easy prey for the CPK, whose propaganda condemned the US imperialists and the government for what was happening. Many were recruited to CPK ranks and indoctrinated in its network of training camps. Radicalised youths became the CPK's agents of social change under a totalitarian ideology.[35] From 1974, refugees fleeing the Southeast of Cambodia into Vietnam and other

---

28 Ibid. p. 84.

29 Report of the Group of Experts for Cambodia established pursuant to General Assembly Resolution 52/135 18 February 1999 UN Doc. A/53/850; S1999/231 (15 March 1999) [Group of Experts Report] [14].

30 Craig Etcheson, *After the Killing Fields: Lessons from the Cambodian Genocide* (Praeger Publishers, 2005) p. 5.

31 Ibid.

32 Chandler, above n. 16, pp. 86–88.

33 Kiernan, above n. 6, pp. 350–371.

34 Shawcross, above n. 19, pp. 128–149; 280–299.

35 Etcheson, above n. 30, p. 321.

areas spoke of the climate of fear engendered by the growing rule by terror at the hands of fanatical youths. There were also numerous media reports of Khmer Rouge brutality in other parts of the country including reports of executions for infringement of 'reconstructing' processes in the camps.[36]

The CPK also profited militarily from corruption among Lon Nol's army officers, who used their positions to amass wealth by devising schemes to sell American armaments.[37] This included channnnelling ammunition to CPK forces which grew in strength as a result. Ammunition was vital because the North Vietnamese communists remained unwilling to arm their Cambodian comrades. By 1974, with increased military power the Khmer Rouge abandoned the fiction of a united national front with the exiled Sihanouk. They accused him of 'living too long in comfort in Peking and of supporting the hated Vietnamese.'[38]

In April 1975, the Khmer Rouge army of 60,000 easily defeated Lon Nol's forces, from whom American military assistance had by then been totally withdrawn. With the foreign forces evacuated, the Khmer Rouge filled the power vacuum in Cambodia. After taking Phnom Penh on 17 April 1975 they began to implement their revolutionary agenda for Cambodia.[39]

4.2.3. CAMBODIA UNDER DEMOCRATIC KAMPUCHEA

Suspicion of Vietnamese intentions towards Cambodia as the Vietnam War ended informed Khmer Rouge policies from the outset. The country was blockaded from all foreign influence, except that of Khmer Rouge allies, China and North Korea. The CPK declared a national policy of complete independence and self-reliance.[40] An offer of reparations from the United States and international aid in the wake of the massive carnage wrought by years of extensive bombing and civil war was refused.[41] Instead, the Khmer Rouge relied on the rhetoric of moral purity to distinguish themselves from their predecessors and justify radical political action to deconstruct Cambodian society. Proclamations through radio broadcasts announced the new government's plans to restore the true national spirit and identity of Cambodians by clearing the society of the corruption of the Lon Nol regime and the decadence of American imperialism.[42]

---

36 Shawcross, above n. 19, pp. 321–322.

37 Chandler, above n. 1, p. 252; Shawcross, above n. 19, p. 318.

38 Ibid. (Shawcross) p. 321.

39 Group of Experts Report, above n. 29, para. [14].

40 Karl D. Jackson, 'The Ideology of Total Revolution' in Karl D. Jackson (ed.), *Cambodia 1975–1978: Rendezvous with Death* (Princeton University Press, 1989) pp. 37, 41–45.

41 Ibid. p. 45.

42 Alexander Hinton, 'Songs at the Edge of Democratic Kampuchea' in Anne Hansen and Judy Ledgerwood (eds.), *At The Edge of the Forest: Essays on Cambodia, History and Narrative in Honor of David Chandler* (SEAP, Cornell University Press, Ithaca NY 2008) pp. 71, 78.

In the week following the seizure of Phnom Penh, the new government forced two to three million people from the cities and towns into the countryside to live and work in regional collectives. Many thousands died from lack of food, water and medical assistance during forced marches to CPK-controlled administrative or functional units.[43]

Forced labour and inhumane living conditions characterised life in the cooperatives. Under armed supervision, people were also forced to work on large-scale infrastructure construction projects in work teams for long hours and with meagre food rations. Communal life was highly regulated. Marriages required CPK approval and existing families were broken up. Children were separated from their parents and taught that their first allegiance was to the party apparatus known as 'Angkar.'[44] Proclamations of the CPK assigned mystical status to Angkar as the all-knowing and supreme Organisation which was transforming Cambodian society.[45]

Khmer Rouge cadres in the cooperatives re-educated new party members and were responsible for purifying party ranks of potential traitors. Quinn concluded from accounts of those with direct experience of the camp leaders, referred to as *chlorbs* (those who ensure security), that Pol Pot and CPK leaders relied on the youngest and least literate elements of Cambodian society to implement their revolutionary agenda. Incapable of discussion with their older and more educated charges, with little stake in the old society and shaped themselves by strict indoctrination in the pre-revolutionary years, the *chlorbs* used terror, violence and death to satisfy their superiors who had given them status and power in the new Kampuchea.[46] However, the local cadres were unable to meet Angkar's unrealistic demands of rapidly increasing rice production. Fearful of incurring the wrath of the Party, they deprived inmates of the collectives of sufficient rations. Upon investigation of the production levels and the conditions of the collectives, the CPK, unwilling to concede flawed policies and expectations, blamed apparent failings on sabotage by 'class enemies'. The leadership became increasingly convinced that subversives were plotting the overthrow of the regime and began purging party ranks.[47]

Apart from the deaths of hundreds of thousands caused by the privations of communal rural life, the regime targeted for elimination certain groups classed as enemies of the revolution: officials of the former regime, the Khmer Republic; ethnic minorities, including Cham Muslims, ethnic Chinese and Vietnamese;

---

43 Group of Exports Report, above n. 29, para. [17].

44 Hinton, above n. 42, p. 79.

45 Ibid.

46 Kenneth Quinn. 'Explaining the Terror' in Karl D. Jackson (ed), *Cambodia 1975–1978: Rendezvous with Death* (Princeton University Press, 1989) pp. 215, 238–239.

47 Hinton, above n. 42, p. 85.

teachers; students; and the educated. Also targeted were religious leaders, and organised religion was banned. Buddhism in particular was condemned for having mystified and exploited the poor.[48]

In addition, the existing legal system, modelled on the civil law system of France, was completely dismantled. Courthouses, the law school, and other legal institutions were either vandalised or converted to the new government's uses.[49] The Cambodian legal profession became a prime target for elimination as representatives of the old regime. Of the 400–600 legal professionals estimated to have been in Cambodia prior to the Khmer Rouge assuming power, as few as 12 were alive and still in Cambodia by January 1979.[50] In April 1976, a new constitution and organs of state were announced as the country was renamed Democratic Kampuchea.[51] However, there is no evidence that any judges held office or that a legal system existed in Cambodia from April 1975 to January 1979.[52] Under the administration of Party committees, CPK directives from Phnom Penh became the nation's laws.[53]

Extensive purging of Party ranks and committees began in March 1976 and continued at an accelerated rate throughout 1977 and 1978.[54] Suspects were accused of being agents of the CIA, KGB or of Vietnam, and were then transferred to interrogation facilities located throughout the country. The largest and most important of these, because of its close association with the Central Committee of the CPK, was the Tuol Sleng complex in Phnom Penh, designated S-21. Up to 14,000 people were incarcerated at S-21, a former school building. S-21 was portrayed by the CPK as purifying the society through incarceration, interrogation, and extraction of confessions from the dangerous 'microbes' that were undermining the revolution. Execution was implicit following arrest, the all-knowing Angkar having already determined the guilt of detainees.[55] Only seven people survived incarceration at S-21, due to skills they possessed which were deemed useful to the Party by the Director of the institution, Kaing Guek Eav (alias Duch).

---

48 Kenneth Quinn, 'The Pattern and Scope of Violence' in Karl D. Jackson (ed.), *Cambodia 1975–1978: Rendezvous with Death* (Princeton University Press, 1989) pp. 179, 194; Hinton, above n. 42, p. 81.

49 Ibid.

50 Kathryn E Neilson, 'They Killed All the Lawyers: Rebuilding the Judicial System in Cambodia' (Centre for Asia Pacific Studies, University of Victoria, British Columbia Occasional Paper No. 13, October 1996) 1.

51 Group of Experts Report, above n. 29, para. [16].

52 Timothy Carney, 'The Organisation of Power' in Karl D. Jackson (ed.), *Cambodia 1975–1978: Rendezvous with Death* (Princeton University Press, 1989) pp. 79, 90–91.

53 Ibid. p. 97.

54 Ibid. p. 96.

55 Hinton, above n. 42, p. 87.

Records of confessions systematically extracted from prisoners were structured to confirm plots and treachery within CPK ranks and to explain away economic failings as the famine affecting the population deepened. Chandler's analysis of the surviving records of S-21 confirmed the brutal nature of interrogation techniques and the fear, confusion and disorientation suffered by prisoners as they were forced through violence to inhabit a 'liminal space' where they were regarded as less than human.[56]

There was also wholesale purging of party ranks in particular sectors or military divisions.[57] One attempted purge from May to September of 1978 led to a prolonged insurrection against government forces in the eastern zone. Government forces were suspected of killing at least 100,000 people in the region, including village dwellers and their families.[58]

In 1999, the UN appointed a Group of Experts to examine the pattern of human rights abuses under the government of Democratic Kampuchea. From the available evidence, the Group concluded that Cambodia's indigenous communist revolution of 1975–1979 had resulted in the deaths of 20 per cent of the April 1975 population, or an estimated 1.7 million people, from execution, starvation, overwork or disease.[59] Records from the network of interrogation centres, and excavation of multiple 'killing fields' throughout the country, provided ample testimony to the relentless brutality of the regime in its uncompromising drive to secure 'ideological purity and internal security.'[60] While the rhetoric of the CPK was not out of step with other revolutionary cliques of the period, what distinguished the Khmer Rouge regime was the merciless literalism with which its revolution was implemented in the face of the enormous deprivation it imposed on the Cambodian population.[61]

4.2.4. DEFEAT OF DEMOCRATIC KAMPUCHEA

Throughout the regime Democratic Kampuchea received unconditional military and technical support from China.[62] The Chinese leadership viewed Cambodia as an important hedge against the risk of Vietnamese advance in the

56 Ibid. pp. 88–89 citing David Chandler, *Voices from S-21: Terror and History in Pol Pot's Secret Prison* (University of California Press, 1999).
57 Group of Experts Report, above n. 29, para. [29].
58 Ibid. para. [30].
59 Ibid. para. [35]; Other sources put the total figure at as many as two million people nearly one third of the Cambodian population of 7.3 to 7.9 million in April 1975. See Buckley, above n. 20, p. 641.
60 Jackson, above n. 3, p. 3.
61 Jackson, above n. 40, pp. 44–45.
62 John D. Ciorciari, 'China and the Pol Pot Regime' (2014) 14 *Cold War History* 215, 223.

region backed by the Soviet Union.[63] Although Maoist ideology informed CPK policy, the leadership refused advice from the Chinese to moderate domestic programmes. In foreign policy too, the CPK vehemently asserted independence from other communist powers.[64]

From its first days in power in 1975 the Khmer Rouge pressed their claims against Vietnam for control of Cambodian islands, and disputed the delineation of Cambodia's border with Vietnam under agreements made between Sihanouk and the Vietnamese in 1967.[65] Incursions into Vietnam met with retaliation by Vietnamese troops.[66] Attempts to negotiate a settlement failed. In September 1977, Democratic Kampuchea initiated fresh attacks on villages in which hundreds of Vietnamese were killed.[67] Vietnam responded by sending troops into Cambodia in December 1977 and progressively built up forces along the Cambodian border.[68] This prompted purges of the CPK eastern zone leaders, leading to an uprising in May 1978. Some of the Khmer Rouge leaders fled to Vietnam and formed the Kampuchean United Front for National Salvation, later referred to as the Salvation Front.[69]

In December 1978, Vietnam launched a full-scale war on Cambodia and advanced towards the capital. On 6 January 1979, Vietnamese troops supported by the Cambodian dissidents took Phnom Penh.[70] As Democratic Kampuchea collapsed, surviving Khmer Rouge leaders and cadres fled the capital with many relocating to the northwest border areas between Cambodia and Thailand.[71]

4.3. CAMBODIA AFTER THE KHMER ROUGE

Vietnam promptly installed a new government in Cambodia, the People's Republic of Kampuchea (PRK). The PRK was composed of Cambodian leaders of the Salvation Front which had formed on 2 December 1978 to overthrow the Khmer Rouge regime. It included Heng Samrin, who became Head of State, Chea Sim as Minister of the Interior and Hun Sen, as Foreign Minister. Also included were Cambodian communists who had stayed in Hanoi after the division of

63 Ibid. p. 220.

64 Ibid. pp. 221–222.

65 Jackson, above n. 40, pp. 40–41; Chanda, above n. 10, pp. 9–20.

66 Ibid. Jackson added that Vietnamese troops resisted attempts by both Lon Nol and Khmer Rouge troops to reassert sovereignty in eastern Cambodia prior to 1975. The CPK feared that Cambodia would be colonised by Vietnam after the United States withdrew from Indochina.

67 Group of Experts Report, above n. 29, para. 37.

68 Ibid.; Chanda, above n. 10, p. 6.

69 Tom Fawthrop and Helen Jarvis, *Getting Away with Genocide: Elusive Justice and the Khmer Rouge Tribunal* (University of New South Wales Press, 2005) pp. 12–13, fn. 12, p. 275.

70 Ibid. p. 12.

71 Group of Experts Report, above n. 29, para. 38.

Vietnam in 1954, other Khmer Rouge dissidents, members of Cambodian ethnic minorities and individual Cambodians without communist connections.[72] In the years directly following the overthrow of the Khmer Rouge, the intellectual and professional vacuum in Phnom Penh was filled by Vietnamese experts, as well as advisors from the Soviet Union, Eastern Europe and Cuba.[73]

4.3.1. GEOPOLITICS AND KHMER ROUGE LONGEVITY

Vietnamese influence in Cambodia stirred Cold War tensions. This ultimately ensured a role for the Khmer Rouge in Cambodia's future and isolated the Cambodian population from Western support for the next two decades. A few days before the Vietnamese invasion, Pol Pot, who was Chairman of the CPK Central Committee and Prime Minister of Democratic Kampuchea, sent Sihanouk to New York to make the case for recognition of Democratic Kampuchea before the United Nations.[74] In September 1979, eight months after the Heng Samrin government was installed, the Credentials Committee of the General Assembly voted in favour of Democratic Kampuchea over the PRK submission. The General Assembly vote on the issue produced a majority of 71 in favour of Democratic Kampuchea, with 35 against and 34 abstentions.[75] While India warned that recognition of a phantom regime would undermine UN credibility, there was no reference to genocidal evidence against the Khmer Rouge throughout the process.[76] The voting outcome reflected a new united front within the Assembly between China, the United States and ASEAN countries against Vietnamese ambition to create an Indochinese Federation and perceived Soviet hegemony in Southeast Asia.[77] Thus, although the remnant Khmer Rouge remained in exile, no longer exercised significant control over Cambodian territory or commanded political or administrative authority, and were still committed to the continuation of a criminal agenda, the General Assembly granted recognition to Democratic Kampuchea.[78]

---

[72] Chandler above n 1, p. 273; Chandler above n 16, 157; Gottesman above n 14, p.37 ff.

[73] Fawthrop, above n. 69, p. 184.

[74] After the Vietnamese invasion Sihanouk, once again in exile (this time in North Korea), lobbied member states to leave the Cambodian seat in the UN vacant on the basis of the Khmer Rouge's genocidal reign, but this fell largely on deaf ears. See 'Open Letter to Member States of the UN From Prince Norodom Sihanouk', from Pyongyang September 1979 reproduced in Fawthrop and Jarvis at p 28 (from Peter Schier and Manola Oum-Schier, *Prince Sihanouk on Cambodia: Interviews and Talks with Prince Norodom Sihanouk*, 2nd ed. (Institut fur Asienkunde, 1985) pp. 75–80.

[75] *First Report of the Credentials Committee of the General Assembly*, New York, UNGA 34th Session: UN Document A/34/500 (September 1979) para. [21].

[76] Fawthrop, above n. 69, pp. 28–33.

[77] Gottesman, above n. 14, 43.

[78] Fawthrop, above n. 69, p. 32.

The forces of *realpolitik* therefore secured diplomatic advantage for the Khmer Rouge, whose militancy continued from the refugee camps near the Thailand border among the very people they had terrorised under their regime.[79] In the camps the Khmer Rouge mixed with troops of Sihanouk's royalist National Army and Lon Nol's Khmer People's National Liberation Front (KPLNF). In 1982, the Khmer Rouge National Army of Democratic Kampuchea joined forces with its former enemies by forming the Coalition Government of Democratic Kampuchea (CGDK) to remove the Vietnamese from Cambodia. The CGDK served several purposes for its chief architects China, Thailand, Singapore and the United States. First, it linked former king Sihanouk once again to the Khmer Rouge and created a non-communist faction against the purportedly expansionist Vietnam. This shifted international focus away from past Khmer Rouge crimes.[80] Secondly, it permitted the external powers to channel humanitarian and non-lethal military aid to the Khmer Rouge's coalition partners from the refugee camps to service opposition forces against the new government in Phnom Penh. International assistance was given through the United Nations Border Relief Operations rather than the body normally equipped to distribute aid to refugees, the Office of the United Nations High Commissioner for Refugees. This placed the Khmer Rouge in a position to control distribution of aid as the lawful representative of the Kampuchean nation from 1979 to 1981 and the CGDK from 1982.[81] The non-recognition of the PRK by the international community meant Cambodia was deprived of Western economic aid and isolated once more from the non-communist world.[82]

From 1979 to 1989 China supported the Khmer Rouge guerrilla war against the PRK politically and militarily.[83] For their part, the United States also provided the Khmer Rouge and other resistance forces with substantial aid in order to destabilise the Vietnamese-dominated government, thus making it possible for the guerrilla movement to gain strength throughout the 1980s.[84] At the same time, ASEAN member countries in the General Assembly railed against Vietnamese occupation of Cambodia, while repeated appeals from the Phnom Penn government to bring the Khmer Rouge to trial went unheeded.[85]

---

79 Gottesman, above n. 14, p. 41.

80 Fawthrop, above n. 69, p. 69.

81 Ibid. p. 39.

82 Gottesman, above n. 14, p. xiv.

83 Buckley, above n. 20, p. 645.

84 US military support of Khmer Rouge and allied war efforts were financed at US$17–32 million per year. See Buckley, above n. 20, p. 646.

85 Fawthrop, above n. 69, pp. 82–83.

4.3.2. THE PEOPLE'S REVOLUTIONARY TRIBUNAL

The founding document of the Salvation Front declared that 'all reactionary ringleaders, who stubbornly oppose the people and owe a blood-debt to them, should be sternly punished,' but offered clemency towards those willing to repent and help reconstruct the society.[86] In 1979, amidst the social upheaval following the Khmer Rouge regime, the new government of Cambodia established the People's Revolutionary Tribunal. The level of organisation required to hold trials for Khmer Rouge leaders while the country was in ruins indicated the level of priority attached to them.[87]

A pre-trial investigation began in January 1979 from a legal unit comprising lawyers who survived the Khmer Rouge regime. A legal delegation was sent from Vietnam to advise on the projected trials. In July, the PRK passed Decree Law No. 1 to establish the People's Revolutionary Tribunal to try Pol Pot and Ieng Sary for genocide.[88] The trial procedure that emerged was a blend of the civil law system criminal procedure inherited by Cambodia from the French, overlaid with the element of the pre-determined verdict of the Soviet model applied by the Vietnamese.[89]

The degree of selectivity in prosecutions was expressive of political intent. Limiting the number of indictees to two senior leaders allowed the new regime to distinguish the top Khmer Rouge leadership from the thousands of lower-level cadres whom the government sought to co-opt into the new state apparatus.[90] Restricting the Tribunal's jurisdiction to the crime of genocide had particular expressive value. On the eve of the trial, the Presiding Judge, Cheo Chenda, spelled out the objective of the charges:

> Trying the Pol Pot–Ieng Sary clique for the crime of genocide will on the one hand expose all the criminal acts that they have committed and mobilise the Kampuchean people more actively to defend and build up the people's power, and on the other hand, show the peoples of the world the face of the criminals who are posing as the representatives of the people of Kampuchea.[91]

The apparent pre-determined outcome of the trial was aided by the weakness of the defence counsel, who instigated virtually no cross-examination of witnesses

---

86 *Declaration establishing the Kampuchean United Front for National Salvation* [Salvation Front] (2 December 1978) para. [8] cited in Fawthrop, above n. 69 at p. 40.

87 Fawthrop, above n. 69, p. 40.

88 *Decree Law No. 1: Establishment of the People's Revolutionary Tribunal at Phnom Penh to Try the Pol Pot-Ieng Sary Clique for the Crime of Genocide* reproduced in Howard J. De Nike, John Quigley and Kenneth J. Robinson (eds.), *Genocide in Cambodia: Documents of the Trial of Pol Pot and Ieng Sary* (University of Philadelphia Press, Philadelphia PA 2000).

89 Fawthrop, above n. 69, p. 47.

90 Gottesman, above n. 14, p. 61.

91 Fawthrop, above n. 69, p. 44.

and made no effort to refute the individual responsibility of those accused. Instead they supported the prosecution's case which laid the blame for Khmer Rouge atrocities on Chinese influence. The prosecution argued that through a 'thick network of advisers' China gave encouragement to the Khmer Rouge 'to carry out a savage genocidal policy against our people … [and a] war of aggression against Vietnam.'[92]

Pol Pot and Ieng Sary were convicted of genocide *in absentia* and sentenced to death. The western media paid little attention to the trials or their outcome. Because of their perceived political purposes they were dismissed internationally as mere show trials.[93] There was also criticism of the trial stemming from unfamiliarity with the civil law procedure by those acquainted with common law criminal procedure; for instance, the brevity of the trial which was held from 15–19 August 1979 seemed inappropriate, even though it followed an extensive pre-trial investigation over several months.[94]

However, the trials produced a substantial body of reliable evidence. In addition, the proceedings in inquisitorial mode had communicative elements. The trials were held in an auditorium which was filled to overflowing. Victims of the crimes were entitled to join the criminal proceedings as civil parties and to be represented by legal counsel. Witnesses provided graphic details of what they had seen and experienced during the regime. The audience was keen to both listen during the proceedings, and afterwards to talk openly together about what they had suffered at the hands of the Khmer Rouge. The proceedings were broadcast by loudspeakers attached to the building and throughout Cambodia via radio. The weekly newspaper, *Kampuchea*, provided reports and photographs of the emotionally-charged trial.

The proceedings were controlled by a presiding Cambodian judge and 10 lay people's 'assessors', the latter adding to the representative nature of the proceedings. Foreign observers and selected international organisations were invited to attend.[95] John Quigley, a United States lawyer, was engaged to provide international legal opinion on the extent to which genocide had been proven with reference to the 1948 Genocide Convention.

In the year 2000, Quigley and De Nike assembled the Tribunal documents and provided commentary on the proceedings which they viewed as a clear effort to

92 Ciorciari, above n. 62, p. 2, citing 'Judgment of the People's Revolutionary Tribunal, 19 August 1979' translated and reprinted in Howard J. De Nike, John Quigley, and Kenneth Robinson (eds.), *Genocide in Cambodia: Documents from the Trial of Pol Pot and Ieng Sary* (University of Philadelphia Press, 2000) pp. 523, 545–546.

93 Fawthrop, above n. 69, p. 47.

94 John Quigley, 'Editor's Note' and 'Introduction' in Howard J De Nike, John Quigley and Kenneth J. Robinson (eds.), *Genocide in Cambodia: Documents of the Trial of Pol Pot and Ieng Sary* (2000) pp. viii–ix, 1, 10–11.

95 Fawthrop, above n. 69, pp. 43–45.

mount the first prosecution of genocide, albeit in idiosyncratic style.[96] While the context of opposition from the CGDK resistance and international rejection of the Vietnamese government imported unapologetic political purpose to the proceedings, the Tribunal's founders expressed the hope that it constituted a tribunal of 'mankind's conscience.'[97] Today the trials are recognised, at least, as an accountability or truth-seeking mechanism which provided a substantial evidentiary base from which the ECCC could operate 30 years later.[98]

4.3.3. LAW, JUSTICE AND CIVIL WAR 1979–1989

The new government established courts in Cambodia from 1980, but they functioned largely to uphold the policies of state without means of appeal, and with the executive branch of government empowered to review verdicts and sentences.[99] In 1985, the People's Supreme Court was established, but the judiciary, subject to executive control, routinely consulted with the Ministry of Justice in the performance of its functions.[100]

As the PRK fought the civil war against the CGDK, the country was regulated largely by national security laws. This enhanced the power of the police and the military over civilians and other legal authorities, including the Ministry of Justice itself which became subservient to the Ministry of the Interior and the Military.[101] Citizens had no reason to expect that the justice system would uphold their individual rights or check the exercise of power of the security forces. They relied on traditional local dispute resolution mechanisms through village or district officials and submitted to the inequities inherent in patronage systems.[102]

Heder recorded that in 1981 as the civil war in Cambodia continued, the PRK called for accountability for a broader base of Khmer Rouge leaders for crimes of the Democratic Kampuchea era before an international Tribunal in the mode the Nuremburg IMT.[103] In 1988, Hun Sen wrote to the United Nations

---

96 Howard J. De Nike, John Quigley and Kenneth J. Robinson (eds.), *Genocide in Cambodia: Documents of the Trial of Pol Pot and Ieng Sary* (University of Pennsylvania Press, 2000).

97 Fawthrop, above n. 69, p. 51, citing President Heng Samrin at the close of the trials.

98 William Schabas, 'Cambodia: Was it Really Genocide?' (2001) 23 *Human Rights Quarterly* 470, 471.

99 Neilson, above n. 50, p. 2.

100 Ibid. p. 3.

101 Ibid. p. 4; Gottesman, above n. 14, pp. 244–245.

102 Ibid.

103 Steve Heder, 'Review of the Negotiations Leading to the Establishment of the Personal Jurisdiction of the Extraordinary Chambers in the Courts of Cambodia', *Cambodia Tribunal Monitor* (1 August 2011) pp. 1, 4.

Secretary-General identifying a list of Khmer Rouge leaders who should be brought to trial for genocide. The list included Pol Pot and Ieng Sary, whose 1979 convictions remained unenforced; top level CPK leaders Nuon Chea, Ta Mok, Son Sen, Khieu Samphân; and less senior CPK members, Sàm Bĭt and Meas Mut.[104] While the first request was likely to fall on deaf international ears, the second was made at a time when Hun Sen might have expected a more favourable response in the context of easing Cold War tensions. In addition, change to the power balance in Cambodia was on the horizon as the dissolution of the Soviet Union and the end of the Warsaw Pact brought an end to Soviet aid for their long-standing ally Vietnam, and consequently the PRK in Cambodia. As the Cambodian government had not subdued the militancy of the Khmer Rouge, whose leadership still controlled troops and Cambodian territory, the prospect of further political instability loomed.[105]

In April 1989, the Vietnamese government announced that it would withdraw its troops from Cambodia by the following September.[106] As the Vietnamese prepared to withdraw from Cambodia a new Constitution was enacted to facilitate greater Cambodian self-rule under the newly created State of Cambodia (SOC), with Hun Sen as Prime Minister.[107]

4.3.4. PEACE NEGOTIATIONS AND UNTAC

In July 1989, France and Indonesia convened the Paris Peace Conference to negotiate a settlement to the Cambodian civil war.[108] The Conference included the five permanent members of the UN Security Council, the six ASEAN states, foreign ministers of other interested states, including Australia, two members of the International Control Commission (India and Canada), the chair of the non-aligned movement (Zimbabwe) and representatives of all four Cambodian warring factions.[109] Hun Sen attended the Conference armed with his list of eight CPK leaders liable for prosecution, expecting trials of Khmer Rouge suspects to form part of the peace settlement. The negotiations stalled over a proposal for a quadripartite power-sharing arrangement. Hun Sen rejected any notion of power-sharing with the remnant Khmer Rouge faction.[110]

---

104 Ibid.

105 Trevor Findlay, *The Legacy and Lessons of UNTAC* (Oxford University Press, 1995) p. 4; Gottesman, above n. 14, p. 302.

106 Ibid. (Findlay) p. 5.

107 Gottesman, above n. 14, pp. 302–303.

108 The war was also known as the Third Indochina War. See Chanda, above n. 9, p. 7.

109 The six ASEAN states were Brunei, Indonesia, Malaysia, the Philippines, Singapore and Thailand. See Findlay, above n. 105, p. 5.

110 Ibid.

As the Conference adjourned, diplomatic efforts by Australia, Japan, Indonesia, France and other states of the permanent five members of the Security Council brought a peace proposal which included the creation of a transitional authority to temporarily administer Cambodia prior to holding a national election. Meanwhile, in Cambodia the Khmer Rouge forces remained militant. Their ambush of several trains, which resulted in the deaths of dozens of civilians and security guards, came to world attention. In July 1990 the United States announced it would no longer continue to support the CGDK as the legitimate representative of Cambodia in the General Assembly. Thereafter, the Assembly declared the Cambodian seat temporarily vacated.[111]

By August 1990, a framework for settlement document had been formulated by the five permanent members of the Security Council.[112] As negotiations resumed, the Khmer Rouge, represented at that time as the *Party of Democratic Kampuchea* (PDK), remained entitled to a place at the negotiating table and to share power within a new government. Throughout the peace process, Khmer Rouge responsibility for international crimes was repeatedly side-lined either in preference for the view that a new national government should deal with it, or the belief that the peace process itself would foster national reconciliation.[113] In light of the precedent of exclusion of former Nazi leaders from the peace process after the Second World War, it would not have been inappropriate to exclude the Khmer Rouge from the negotiations, but human rights was not a determinant in the composition of parties deemed fit to represent the future of Cambodia. Although the Paris Peace Agreements, signed on 23 October 1991 contained a framework for human rights in Cambodia, they only obliquely referred in the Preamble to the atrocities committed under the government of Democratic Kampuchea.[114] The Agreements recognised the need for measures to ensure the 'non-return to the policies and practices of the past' but contained no sanctions, penalties, exclusions or reference to genocide in the final text.[115] The Agreements are thus expressive by omission, and reflect the drafters' support for Chinese interests over and against compliance with the Genocide Convention.[116] They ensured ongoing Khmer Rouge impunity, and as Hun Sen protested during

---

111 Fawthrop, above n. 69, pp. 93–94.

112 UNSC Resolution 668 UN Doc. S/RES/668 (20 September 1990) and UNGA Res. 45/3 UN doc. A/RES/45/3 (15 October 1990).

113 Findlay, above n. 105, p. 6.

114 The Paris Peace Agreement consists of four documents: *Final Act of the Paris Conference*; *Agreement on a Comprehensive Political Settlement of the Cambodian Conflict*, with five annexes; *Agreement Concerning the Sovereignty, Territorial Integrity and Inviolability, Neutrality and National Unity of Cambodia* and the *Declaration on the Rehabilitation and Reconstruction of Cambodia* (1992) 31 ILM 174.

115 Fawthrop, above n. 69, p. 100.

116 Ibid. pp. 89–100.

the negotiations, effectively provided the Khmer Rouge with reward for their atrocities.[117]

The Cambodian factions accepted the draft Agreements under sustained international pressure.[118] Fawthrop concluded that Hun Sen and the State of Cambodia delegates had little option but to accept the peace terms imposed by the other states.[119] After two decades of war and a genocidal regime, and without military and economic support from former allies, the SOC went along with a deal that would at least usher in a new era of peace, aid and development once the UN-organised election had taken place.[120]

In 1992, the United Nations Transitional Authority in Cambodia (UNTAC) was established to administer a 'comprehensive, just and durable political settlement.'[121] This included holding elections to form a new government and drafting a Constitution. However, UNTAC's broad mandate was only partially realised. The PDK reneged on its commitments under the Agreements, claiming that Vietnamese forces had not been completely withdrawn from Cambodia, and resumed its policy of armed struggle. UN peacekeepers came under fire, territory under UN control was seized and civilians, particularly ethnic Vietnamese, were targeted for attack.[122] Despite violence between factions throughout the election campaign, and an estimated 100 deaths at the hands of the PDK, more than 4.2 million Cambodians (or 90 per cent of the electorate) voted in the May 1993 election.[123]

The royalist National United Front for an Independent, Neutral, Peaceful and Cooperative Cambodia (FUNCINPEC) led by Prince Norodom Ranariddh, secured a majority in the election.[124] However, post-election disputation between the political parties resulted in threats of secession, a constitutional coup by Sihanouk and a military coup by Hun Sen, leader of the Cambodian People's Party (CPP).[125] Ultimately, the volatility was subdued by formation of a coalition government, the Royal Government of Cambodia (RGC). The coalition comprised FUNCINPEC and the CPP, with the Prince and Hun Sen as first and second Prime Ministers, and with Sihanouk returned as Cambodia's constitutional monarch.

---

117 Ibid. p. 90; Stephen P. Marks, 'Forgetting "The Policies and Practices of the Past": Impunity in Cambodia' (1994) 18 *Fletcher Forum of World Affairs* 17, 28–29.

118 Findlay, above n. 105, pp. 7–8.

119 Fawthrop, above n, 69, p. 100.

120 Ibid.

121 UNSC Res. 745, UN Doc S/RES/745, (28 February 1992).

122 Joseph Zasloff, and MacAlister Brown, *Cambodia Confounds the Peacemakers 1979–1998* (Cornell University Press, Ithaca NY 1998) p. 297.

123 Buckley, above n. 20, p. 643.

124 *Front Uni National pour un Cambodge Indépendent, Neutre, Pacific et Coopératif.* See Heder, above n. 103, p. 5.

125 Zasloff, above n. 122, pp. 165–189.

The Constitution established a pluralist constitutional monarchy, the Kingdom of Cambodia, an independent judiciary and a framework for the protection of human rights in Cambodia.[126] With the new Constitution in place, UNTAC was dismantled and Cambodia's sovereignty restored.[127] Apart from a UN Military Liaison Team and personnel to handle residual non-military matters, by the end of 1993, UNTAC had withdrawn from Cambodia.[128]

The United Nations High Commissioner for Human Rights established a UN Field Office for Human Rights in Cambodia.[129] Subsequently, Justice Michael Kirby was appointed UN Special Representative of the Secretary-General on the situation of human rights in Cambodia. While the Special Representative established a formal human rights presence in Cambodia, Kirby's mandate was forward-looking only. He reported to the United Nations High Commissioner for Human Rights and the General Assembly on the state of human rights in Cambodia from 1994–1996.[130] While Kirby's reports provided extensive analysis of the contemporary human rights situation in Cambodia and advocated reform of the legal system, prisons and courts, they did not address the crimes of the Khmer Rouge era.[131]

The Paris Peace Agreements envisioned a system of liberal democracy for Cambodia with a Constitution enshrining human rights consistent with international instruments and the establishment of an independent judiciary empowered to enforce those rights.[132] However, successive Special Representatives on human rights in Cambodia and the UN Group of Experts sent to Cambodia in 1998 reported the absence of a trained, fair and impartial judiciary, inadequate legal infrastructure and the politicisation of legal process in the country.[133] Charlesworth argued that Cambodia adopted the practice of

---

126 Steven R. Ratner, 'The Cambodian Settlement Agreements' (1993) 87 *American Journal of International Law* 1, 27.

127 Findlay, above n. 105, p. 97.

128 Ibid. p. 98 per UN Security Council Resolution 880, UN Doc. S/RES/880 4 November 1993. The team stayed until 15 May 1994 and was replaced by a group of three military advisers from Belgium, France and Malaysia.

129 Zasloff, above n. 122, pp. 165–189.

130 *Report of the Special Representative of the Secretary-General on Human Rights in Cambodia, Mr Michael Kirby*, UN Doc. E/CN.4/1995/73 (21 February 1994) and Doc. E/CN.4/1995/73 Add.1 (24 February 1994); And see Kirby's later reports *Situation on Human Rights in Cambodia*: UN Doc. A/49/535 (3 November 1994), UN Doc. A/CN.4/1995/87 (24 January 1995), UN Doc. A/CN.4/1995/87 Add.1 (13 February1995); *Recommendations made by the Special Representative of the Secretary-General for Human Rights in Cambodia on Matters within his Mandate*, UN Doc. A/50/681 (26 October 1995); *Situation of Human Rights in Cambodia: Report of the Special Representative*, UN Doc. E/CN.4/1996/93 (26 February 1996).

131 Fawthrop, above n. 69, p. 108.

132 Neilson, above n. 50, p. 5.

133 Group of Experts Report, above n. 29 [126]–[130].

human rights ritualism. This involves states becoming parties to human rights treaties ostensibly to gain international approval, while resisting participation in the human rights system through unwillingness to implement treaty commitments domestically, or by not genuinely meeting international reporting requirements. Furthermore, in Cambodia, the international community may have 'tacitly endorsed this ritualism' by adopting a largely educative approach to human rights in the face of the government's reluctance to uphold human rights claims.[134]

However, impetus for creating a human rights culture in Cambodia came from a burgeoning civil society that emerged after the peace settlement as the country opened up and international NGOs were permitted to operate in the country. At the same time, a social movement begun by the Cambodian refugee diaspora and a coalition of NGOs which opposed the United States' support of the CGDK alliance throughout the 1980s began to effect a change in foreign policy towards the impunity of the Khmer Rouge.[135] The Campaign to Oppose the Return of the Khmer Rouge (CORKR) lobbied the Congress and the State Department from 1991 to introduce the Cambodian Genocide Justice Bill to support efforts to bring Khmer Rouge members to justice. The Bill was passed by the Congress on 1 April 1994 and signed in May by President Clinton. It directed the State Department to engage researchers to investigate and document the alleged crimes of the Khmer Rouge. Lawyers were commissioned to investigate the culpability of the Khmer Rouge for war crimes, genocide and crimes against humanity.[136] Yale University's Cambodian Genocide Program (CGP) secured the public tender contract for research, documentation and training, and the Documentation Center of Cambodia (DC-Cam) was established as the Program's office in Phnom Penh. By 1997, DC-Cam had amassed and organised tens of thousands of documents, photographs and maps pertaining to the Khmer Rouge period. These included S-21 records, the court documents of the 1979 national trial, reports of interviews with witnesses, and evidence of the location of over 500 killing sites in 20 Cambodian provinces. DC-Cam also disseminated information about the regime throughout the country and ran education programmes for victims of the Khmer Rouge as the prospect of trials became real.[137]

---

134 Hilary Charlesworth, 'Swimming to Cambodia: Justice and Ritual in Human Rights after Conflict' (2010) 29 *Australian Yearbook of International Law* 1, 11–13.

135 Fawthrop, above n. 69, p. 109.

136 Ibid. p. 110. Lawyers Jason Abrams and Stephen Ratner presented their findings and discussed legal options at a Conference organised by CGP and DC-Cam in 1995 in Phnom Penh, and at which the Co-Prime Ministers also spoke. See Steven R. Ratner, Jason Abrams and James L. Bischoff, *Accountability for Human Rights Atrocities in International Law*, 3rd ed. (Oxford University Press, 2009) pp. 305–361.

137 Fawthrop, above n. 69, pp. 111–112.

4.4. POLITICS AND THE CREATION OF THE ECCC

4.4.1. THE POLITICAL CURRENCY OF IMPUNITY

Change in the geopolitical tide towards an end to the impunity of the Khmer Rouge met with the strong cross currents of national politics. The new government still had the remnant Khmer Rouge leadership and their troops to deal with. In June 1994, in the context of continuing militancy by the PDK, Co-Prime Minister Hun Sen called for trials of those responsible for the 'genocidal crimes of the Khmer Rouge.'[138] In July 1994, the Cambodian National Assembly passed legislation outlawing the Khmer Rouge revolutionary organisation and military forces.[139] Article 3 of the Law made leaders and members of the organisation and military forces of the Democratic Kampuchea Group subject to the criminal law for secessionist activities, armed combat and destructive acts against the government or public authorities. The Law provided a six-month amnesty permitting surrender to the government before 7 January 1995. While Article 6 of the legislation provided that amnesty did not apply to Khmer Rouge leaders, Article 7 declared that the King, under the Constitution, could grant partial or full amnesty or pardon.[140] The amnesty deadline was extended in January 1995 for an indefinite period as the government declared that soldiers and ordinary citizens subject to Khmer Rouge control would escape prosecution if they came over to the government side. Defections in the thousands were added to those who had already defected in 1994. From April 1996 division commanders of Khmer Rouge strongholds along with their troops went over to the government.[141]

The success of the government's renewed defection strategy hastened the implosion of the Khmer Rouge leadership, which was already withering on the vine due to internal ructions. Throughout 1995 and early 1996, the government asserted that that the top leadership remained liable to be tried before an international tribunal. Early in 1996, Hun Sen repeatedly urged officials of Yale University's Cambodian Genocide Project to draft a law for the Cambodian parliament requesting the international community to form an international tribunal to try the Khmer Rouge. Hun Sen made clear that if the international community did not act on the request the Cambodian government would convene a domestic court for senior Khmer Rouge leaders.[142]

---

138 Heder, above n. 103, p. 8.

139 Law to Outlaw the Democratic Kampuchea Group Law No. 064, 15 July 1994.

140 Law to Outlaw the Democratic Kampuchea Group Law No. 064, 15 July 1994, arts. 3, 6–7.

141 By the end of 1996 … almost 18,000 of the Government's troops were Khmer Rouge defectors. This included mid-level Khmer Rouge, Sàm Bĭt, Meas Mut and Sou Mĕt. See Heder, above n. 103, pp. 9, 12.

142 Etcheson, above n. 30, pp. 134–135.

However, the draft law was shelved when the government negotiated an amnesty with Ieng Sary in August 1996. Ieng Sary, formerly Deputy Prime Minister and Foreign Minister of Democratic Kampuchea, remained the mouthpiece of Democratic Kampuchea abroad and a leader of the CGDK. He was the 'exclusive interlocutor with the Chinese regarding military and financial assistance to Democratic Kampuchea in exile.'[143] In the 1990s, he fell out with Son Sen, a senior Khmer Rouge military leader, over military tactics and with Pol Pot over who would replace Pol Pot as leader should he die. Khmer Rouge troops loyal to Sary defected in the thousands to the government. In September 1996, Sary was granted a royal pardon for his 1979 conviction before the People's Revolutionary Tribunal.[144]

4.4.2. DRAMA AND THE DEATH OF AN OLD ACTOR

By June 1997, amidst the government's efforts to secure further defections, Pol Pot suspected Son Sen of being in league with Hun Sen. When Son Sen failed to attend a meeting with himself, Nuon Chea and Ta Mok, Pol Pot reportedly ordered Son Sen's execution along with his wife and children.[145] Ta Mok and his troops then seized control of Pol Pot's base at Anlong Veng. Pol Pot fled north with Nuon Chea and Khieu Samphân toward the Thai border. However, Pol Pot capitulated to Ta Mok a few days later and by apparent agreement presented himself before a 'rally of the masses' at Anlong Veng where he was publicly denounced as a traitor. Ta Mok assumed the leadership of the remnant Khmer Rouge forces and kept Pol Pot in custody. Then, in March 1998 Ta Mok came under attack in Anlong Veng from forces associated with another defecting senior ex-CPK cadre, Ke Puak. Ta Mok fled to Thailand where he was placed under Thai military house arrest along with Nuon Chea and Khieu Samphân.[146]

---

143 *Nuon Chea, Ieng Sary, Khieu Samphân, Ienh Thirith* (Closing Order) (Extraordinary Chambers in the Courts of Cambodia, Office of the Co-Investigating Judges, (Case File No. 002/19-09-2007/ECCC-OCIJ, 15 September 2010) paras. 1592–1593.

144 Etcheson, above n. 30, p. 130.

145 Heder, above n. 103, p. 13; Nuon Chea was not part of the Paris Marxist Circle, but became involved in revolutionary activities on his return to Cambodia after living in Thailand where he joined the Thai Communist Party. He became a member of the Central Committee of Democratic Kampuchea and was active in promoting the government in exile at international conferences during 1981. Khieu Samphân went to France to study in 1953, and in 1957 completed a doctoral thesis entitled 'Cambodia's Economy and Industrial Development.' He was President of the Presidium of Democratic Kampuchea, and from 1979–1986 represented Democratic Kampuchea at diplomatic missions and UN and other international meetings. He was present as President of the PDK at the signing of the Paris Peace Agreement in 1991. See *Nuon Chea and Others* (Closing Order) 002/19-09-2007/ECCC-OCIJ (15 September 2010) paras. 1577–1604.

146 Heder, above n. 103, pp. 13–14.

While these events were occurring, the United States explored ways to apprehend Pol Pot in order to remove him to another country as a preliminary measure to trials before a UN-approved judicial institution.[147] However, in April 1998 Pol Pot died mysteriously at Anlong Veng.[148] While Pol Pot was 73 years old, known to be in poor health and needing the use of oxygen equipment, no autopsy was carried out by the Thai military authorities who controlled access across the border to his place of death. Fawthrop recorded that in 2002 General Surayud, the Thai commanding officer, admitted that Pol Pot had not died of natural causes.[149] Scheffer described this period as one where events had spiralled out of control and that the opportunity to ascertain what had been done with Pol Pot's body was lost.[150] Seeking to keep the prospect of international trials for Khmer Rouge leaders alive, the United States pressed Hun Sen to locate and capture Ta Mok and the remaining leadership.[151]

4.4.3. THE INTERNATIONAL PLAYERS

The national political machinations prompted by the amnesty for Ieng Sary brought the first formal UN engagement on the impunity of the Khmer Rouge with the Cambodian government.[152] On 21 June 1997, at the instigation of the UN Secretary-General's Special Representative for Human Rights in Cambodia, Thomas Hammarberg, a joint request for assistance from the UN to Cambodia to prosecute those responsible for genocide and crimes against humanity during the Khmer Rouge regime was signed by Cambodia's Co-Prime Ministers, Hun Sen and Prince Norodom Ranariddh.[153] In response to Cambodia's letter, the UN General Assembly requested the Secretary-General's examination of the request including the appointment of 'a group of experts to evaluate evidence and propose measures' to address the impunity of the Khmer Rouge.[154]

---

147 David Scheffer, *All the Missing Souls: A Personal History of the War Crimes Tribunals* (Princeton University Press, 2011) p. 346.

148 Fawthrop, above n. 69, pp. 122–123.

149 Ibid.

150 Scheffer, above n. 147, p. 361.

151 Ibid. pp. 370–371.

152 Heder, above n. 103, p. 12.

153 Prince Norodom Ranariddh and Hun Sen, 'Letter to Kofi Annan, United Nations Secretary-General', UN Doc. A/51/930-S/1997/488, 24 June 1997; And see Steven Ratner, 'Justice for the Khmer Rouge? Sir Ninian Stephen and the United Nations Group of Experts for Cambodia' in Timothy L.H. McCormack and Cheryl Saunders (eds.), *Sir Ninian Stephen: A Tribute* (Melbourne University Publishing, 2007) pp. 206, 207.

154 UNGA Res. 52/135 UN Doc. A/RES.52/135 (27 February 1998) para. [16].

The request from Cambodia was sent at a time when a common position against Khmer Rouge leaders may have preserved the existing delicate balance of power within the fragile coalition government.[155] However, the defections strategy had political currency within the political parties to the Coalition. In July 1997, after FUNCINPEC recruited Khmer Rouge defectors to its ranks, Hun Sen staged a violent coup to head off the threat posed by his political opponent's actions as the 1998 national elections approached.[156] After the July 1998 national elections, FUNCINPEC once again entered a governing coalition with the CPP, but as the junior partner with a reduced share of seats in the Cambodian National Assembly.[157]

Most of the remaining lower-level Khmer Rouge cadres surrendered to the government between May and December of 1998. On 25 December, Nuon Chea and Khieu Samphân were surrendered to the Phnom government by Thailand.[158] Neither Nuon Chea nor Khieu Samphân was arrested, and both were publicly welcomed back to Cambodian society by Prime Minister Hun Sen, who proclaimed that Cambodia should now 'dig a hole and bury the past' for the sake of peace and national reconciliation.[159] Hun Sen added later that while this did not rule out holding trials for Khmer Rouge leaders, their nature was not yet settled.[160]

4.5. NEGOTIATING A TRIBUNAL TO PROSECUTE THE KHMER ROUGE

The Group of Experts Report provided a basis from which the UN was prepared to negotiate with the Cambodian government on the creation of a justice mechanism to address the crimes of the Khmer Rouge. The UN negotiators were the Secretary-General, Kofi Annan and his legal counsel led by Hans Corell. On the Cambodian side was Prime Minister Hun Sen, Sok An, Chairman of Cambodia's Council of Ministers and Senior legal advisor to the Prime Minister, as well as Om Yentieng, advisor to Hun Sen. The United States remained in

155 Daphne Shraga, 'The Second Generation UN-Based Tribunals: A Diversity of Mixed Jurisdictions' in Cesare P.R. Romano (ed.), *Internationalized Criminal Courts and Tribunals: Sierra Leone, East Timor, Kosovo, and Cambodia* (Oxford University Press, 2004) pp. 15, 16.

156 Zasloff, above n. 122, pp. 262–263; Etcheson, above n. 30, pp. 145–146.

157 Etcheson, above n. 30, p. 152; Suzannah Linton, *Reconciliation in Cambodia* (Documentation Center of Cambodia, 2004) pp. 84–85.

158 Fawthrop, above n. 69, p. 134.

159 Heder, above n. 103, p. 17; Craig Etcheson, 'Fair and Public Trial: A Political History of the Extraordinary Chambers' (2006 Spring issue) *Justice Initiatives* 7, 8.

160 Scheffer, above n. 147, p. 372, citing Seth Mydans, 'Cambodian Denies He Opposed Trial for Khmer Rouge', *New York Times* (2 January 1999): http://www.nytimes.com/1999/01/02/world/cambodian_denies_he_opposed_trial_for_khmer_rouge.

communication with the Cambodian government as negotiations proceeded, and provided diplomatic consultants to work with the negotiating teams. David Scheffer, United States Ambassador for War Crimes within the Clinton administration, and Senator John Kerry played important roles in resolving impasses between the negotiators over the four years following the release of the Group of Experts Report.[161]

The Group of Exports Report took seven months to complete and was delivered to the Secretary-General on 22 February 1999. It recommended the creation of an international tribunal modelled on the ad hoc Tribunals to try Khmer Rouge officials for international crimes committed between 17 April 1975 and 6 January 1979.[162] The proposed court would be located near, but not in Cambodia.[163] The possibility of domestic trials was ruled out because of Cambodia's lack of adequate legal infrastructure, a qualified legal profession and a 'culture of respect for an independent criminal justice system.'[164] The Report also cited a lack of confidence among the population concerning local judicial process for Khmer Rouge leaders.[165]

4.5.1. EXPRESSIVE NEGOTIATING POSITIONS

The Cambodian government rejected the report's recommendation for an international tribunal and claimed China would veto a Security Council resolution proposing to create such an institution.[166] Hun Sen asserted that more comprehensive justice was due to the Cambodian people and called for the investigation of crimes over an expanded period, 1970–1998.[167] He also began discussing the possibility of creating a form of truth and reconciliation commission as an alternative to internationally assisted trials.[168] The government then arrested Ta Mok and switched its position again. Hun Sen declared that a domestic trial for Ta Mok alone would be held as representative of the entire Khmer Rouge movement.[169] Ta Mok was the expressive capital the

161 Senator Kerry was Chairman of the East Asian Subcommittee of the Senate Foreign Relations Committee. See SCHEFFER, above n. 147, pp. 370–400.

162 Group of Experts Report, above n. 29, para. [219].

163 Ibid. para. [171].

164 Ibid. paras. [127]–[129].

165 Ibid. para. [134].

166 ELIZABETH BECKER, 'Cambodia Spurns U.N. Plan for Khmer Rouge Tribunal', *New York Times* (14 March 1998) p. 4.

167 SCHEFFER, above n. 147, p. 382.

168 ETCHESON, above n. 159, p. 8.

169 Ibid. Note Ta Mok was a military commander described as the 'hammer' of the CPK Central Committee. He was also known as the 'butcher' for his role in overseeing mass killings of the regime. See SCHEFFER, above n. 145, p. 349.

government needed at that stage. He was the major remaining symbol of the Khmer Rouge era, who was also capable of mobilising troops and stirring up old regime sympathisers against the government. Scheffer observed that Hun Sen's preferences were first, for the 'fading away' of the Khmer Rouge leaders now that their troops were being 'neutralised' and second, a trial or justice mechanism he could control.[170]

Defending the Cambodian position for national trials, Hun Sen cited Cambodia's sovereign legal obligation under the Genocide Convention to try the international crime within its jurisdiction. He reminded the Secretary-General of the UN's long-term recognition of the Khmer Rouge and the inclusion of their representatives as equals at the Paris Peace meetings of 1989–1991.[171] The Cambodian position was also justified by reference to the national process of reconciliation made possible by surrender to the government of senior Khmer Rouge leaders and the integration of lower-level cadres into society.[172] The possibility of the prosecution of Khmer Rouge leaders could sow confusion and panic among other cadres, threatening peace and stability in Cambodia.[173]

In April 1999, when Senator Kerry was in Phnom Penh he introduced the idea of a 'mixed tribunal' composed of national and international judges to the negotiations. Details as to the inclusion of international judges and prosecutors could be decided by negotiation. The Cambodian government was amenable to the proposal.[174]

In early May 1999 Kaing Guek Eav, alias Duch, former Chairman of S-21, emerged from hiding to speak to foreign journalists. On 9 May, he was imprisoned with Ta Mok and subsequently charged under Article 3 of the 1994 Law outlawing the Democratic Kampuchea group.[175] With two former Khmer Rouge leaders under arrest in Cambodia the government's position strengthened.

4.5.2. TOUGHING IT OUT

Thomas Hammarberg shifted his support from the Group of Expert's recommendation to support for a mixed tribunal created under Cambodian law.[176] In August 1999, a UN draft proposal for a mixed tribunal comprising a

[170] Scheffer, above n. 147, p. 370.
[171] Etcheson, above n 159, p. 10.
[172] Ibid; Linton, above n. 157, pp. 82–87.
[173] Daniel Kemper Donovan, 'Joint U.N.-Cambodian Efforts to Establish a Khmer Rouge Tribunal' (2003) 44 *Harvard International Law Journal* 551, 558.
[174] Scheffer, above n. 147, p. 383.
[175] Ibid.
[176] Ibid. p. 387.

majority of international judges and an international prosecutor was rejected by Hun Sen. At a meeting between Hun Sen and Kofi Anann in September in New York, Cambodia's position was clear. The UN could provide a legal team to participate in Cambodian trials or withdraw from the negotiations.[177] Scheffer's mediation at this point produced a draft proposal for a tribunal created under Cambodian law, but of 'international character' by virtue of foreign participation with respect to judges and prosecutors, and due process standards characteristic of international trials. To resolve the disagreement over the Cambodian judicial majority, Scheffer advocated that judicial decisions be subject to the affirmative vote of at least one international judge of the bench, or a supermajority. The innovation was designed to provide a minimum degree of 'international oversight' in the decision-making of the judges while retaining the Cambodian majority.[178]

In December 1999, the UN General Assembly urged Cambodia to accept a tribunal governed by international standards of justice and due process of law.[179] When the negotiations resumed in the year 2000 there were other differences between the negotiators. These included the relevant definition of genocide and the legal status of Ieng Sary's amnesty. The UN also wanted assurances from the government that Khmer Rouge leaders would be arrested and surrendered to the proposed tribunal.[180]

The negotiations stalled again when in 2001 the Cambodian Law enabling creation of the tribunal within Cambodia was passed without the procedural guarantees sought by the UN.[181] In February 2002, Hans Corell broke off negotiations, citing continuing concerns over the independence, impartiality and objectivity of the tribunal envisaged by Cambodia.[182] However, the action was considered premature by some UN Member States.[183] The UN General Assembly requested the resumption of talks with the Cambodian government and establishment of a tribunal in accordance with international standards followed.[184]

Renewed negotiations in early 2003 produced an Agreement for an internationalised tribunal as a special court within the Cambodian court

177 Ibid. p. 386.

178 Ibid. p. 387.

179 UNGA. Resolution 54/171, UN Doc. A/RES/54/171 (17 December 1999) para. [11].

180 Scheffer, above n. 147, p. 394.

181 *Law on the Establishment of the Extraordinary Chambers in the Courts in Cambodia for the Prosecution of Crimes Committed during the Period of Democratic Kampuchea*, Reach Kram No. NS/RKM/0801/12 (2 January 2001).

182 Donovan, above n. 173, p. 564.

183 Scheffer, above n. 147, p. 402.

184 UNGA Resolution 57/228 *Khmer Rouge Trials* UN Doc. A/RES/57/228 (27 February 2003).

system.[185] The Agreement cemented the compromises struck between the parties. These were reflected in the applicable law, composition, judicial decision-making scheme and sharing of prosecutorial and investigative functions between national and international court actors. Provision in the Agreement was also made for dispute resolution between the national and international prosecutors and the investigating judges before a Pre-Trial Chamber.[186] The Agreement and subsequently, the Cambodian enabling law incorporated procedural standards consistent with Articles 14 and 15 of the 1966 International Covenant on Civil and Political Rights.[187] The Agreement provided that the scope of the pardon previously granted to Ieng Sary was a matter for the new Tribunal.[188]

At the instigation of the United States, creation of the ECCC by the Security Council was mooted, but was opposed by China, Russia and France on the ground that in the absence of a threat to international peace and security, the proposed tribunal was not a justifiable enforcement measure under Chapter VII of the UN Charter.[189] The ECCC does not, therefore, have the same legal basis as the Special Court for Sierra Leone or the Special Tribunal for Lebanon. The General Assembly initiated the negotiation process, approved the terms of the Agreement, and confirmed UN support of the Court.[190] However, while the General Assembly can create subsidiary organs pursuant to its functions, it lacks the enforcement power of the Security Council and cannot compel a state to establish a court.[191] It can recommend, but not compel a state to do so. Thus, with the consent of the Cambodian National Assembly, the enabling legislation became the constitutive instrument creating the ECCC.[192] The Agreement provides a legal basis for a regime of cooperation between the UN and Cambodia.[193]

---

185 *Agreement between the United Nations and the Royal Government of Cambodia Concerning the Prosecution under Cambodian Law of Crimes Committed During the Period of Democratic Kampuchea*, signed 6 June 2003, adopted by General Assembly Resolution 57/228B (13 May 2003) available at: http://www.eccc.gov.kh/english/Agreement_between_UN_and_RGC.pdf; The Agreement was adopted by General Assembly Resolution 57/228B (13 May 2003) [ECCC Agreement].

186 ECCC Agreement Art. 7.

187 *Law on the Establishment of the Extraordinary Chambers in the Courts in Cambodia for the Prosecution of Crimes Committed during the Period of Democratic Kampuchea Reach Kram with amendments promulgated on 27 October 2004* NS/RKM/1004/006 (27 October 2004) [ECCC Law]; See also 1966 *International Covenant on Civil and Political Rights*, opened for signature 16 December 1966, 999 UNTS 172 (entered into force 23 March 1976).

188 ECCC Agreement Art. 11(2).

189 Scheffer, above n. 147, p. 367.

190 The UN General Assembly passed Resolution 57/228B of 13 May 2003 approving the draft Agreement between the UN and the Cambodian government.

191 *1945 Charter of the United Nations* (adopted 26 June 1945) [1945] ATS 1, art. 22.

192 Sarah Williams, *Hybrid and Internationalised Criminal Tribunals: Selected Jurisdictional Issues* (Hart Publishing, 2012) p. 295.

193 ECCC Agreement art. 1.

4.5.3. PROTEST, CYNICISM AND OPTIMISM

The Agreement has been described as a less than perfect but reasonable outcome in the face of the 'insularity' of the government of Cambodia and the 'stubborn priorities' of the UN negotiators.[194] The UN Secretary-General highlighted ongoing serious concern with the 'precarious' state of the judiciary in Cambodia, recalling findings of the UN Special Representative to Cambodia and the General Assembly on problems related to rule of law observance and the independence of the judiciary in Cambodia.[195] Luftglass argued that the Agreement ought to be abandoned in the interests of international law enforcement and Cambodian stability.[196] Other scepticism centred on the Agreement's lack of guarantees as to prosecutorial, investigative and judicial independence, ill-defined applicable law and unclear investigative and decision-making procedures.[197] Linton outlined the systemic problems of Cambodia's legal system, and warned that affording a high profile to ECCC trials would not guarantee judicial independence and impartiality.[198] Human rights groups criticised the provision for two Co-Prosecutors as opposed to a single international prosecutor. They argued that it raised the same issue of potential executive interference, lack of professionalism and corruption that occurred routinely in the work of the Cambodian judiciary.[199]

Others supported the Agreement because of the perceived potential benefits to Cambodia of properly conducted trials; not as a backward-looking exercise but a future-oriented process which might transform the existing culture of impunity.[200] Lieberman, while acknowledging some substantive and procedural flaws in the Tribunal's design, viewed them as remediable through legal strategies and measures which the international community could take to

---

194 SCHEFFER, above n. 147, p. 343.

195 *Report of the Secretary-General on the Khmer Rouge Trials* [11] UN Doc. A/57/769 (2003).

196 SCOTT LUFTGLASS, 'Crossroads in Cambodia: The United Nation's Responsibility to Withdraw Involvement from the Establishment of a Cambodian Tribunal to Prosecute the Khmer Rouge' (2004) 90 *Virginia Law Review* 893, 896.

197 HUMAN RIGHTS WATCH. *Serious Flaws: Why the UN Should Require Changes to the Draft Khmer Rouge Tribunal Agreement*, April 2003; AMNESTY INTERNATIONAL, *Position and Concerns Regarding the Proposed Khmer Rouge Tribunal*, 25 April 2003; KATHERYN KLEIN, 'Bringing the Khmer Rouge to Justice: The Challenges and Risks Facing the Joint Tribunal in Cambodia' (2006) 4 *Northwestern Journal of International Human Rights* 549.

198 SUZANNAH LINTON, 'Safeguarding the Independence and Impartiality of the Cambodian Extraordinary Chambers' (2006) 4 *Journal of International Criminal Justice* 327, 327–328.

199 HUMAN RIGHTS WATCH REPORT, above n. 197, p. 4; AMNESTY INTERNATIONAL REPORT, above n. 197, p. 9.

200 RATNER, above n. 153, p. 218; SARAH WILLIAMS, 'The Cambodian Extraordinary Chambers: a Dangerous Precedent for International Justice?' (2004) 53 *International and Comparative Law Quarterly* 209, 227.

influence the proper carriage of trials.[201] Horsington also maintained that many of the concerns raised were manageable and argued that the hybrid operation of the ECCC might accommodate Cambodian sovereignty while increasing the legitimacy of the Court in the eyes of the Cambodian people. This might also force members of the government with links to the Khmer Rouge to confront the truth of the atrocities as they were revealed.[202] She also identified the ECCC's potential to deliver legal-capacity-building and other benefits which would not accrue in either a purely international or domestic tribunal.[203]

As for the national government, Ratner concluded that ultimately the benefits to Cambodia of cooperation in international justice for genocide were assessed in terms of increased foreign aid and credibility in regional fora and the UN General Assembly.[204] Hun Sen shrewdly judged the level of international interest in creating the ECCC, and achieved important foreign policy goals through the negotiation process including:

> reconciliation with China (which, due to its long support for the Khmer Rouge, clearly endorsed Hun Sen's delaying tactics), control of Cambodia's UN seat, and membership of ASEAN – without having to compromise significantly on the trial issue. [Furthermore,] to assuage a few states like Japan and the United States, [Hun Sen] participated in the talks with the UN and reached agreement with it.[205]

While such gains may have accrued to the Cambodian government, the ultimate form of the ECCC reflects Khmer Rouge longevity and the struggle for power between contending political elites.[206] However, this is not the whole story. In the Cambodian negotiating team were Sok An and Om Yentieng, who, along with citizens from almost all strata of Cambodian society were victims of the Khmer Rouge regime and sought an end to the impunity of its key leaders.[207] Both men hid their identities and professional backgrounds from the Khmer Rouge during the regime, witnessed the death of their children or other relatives by Khmer Rouge cadres, and watched as people were traumatised into submission during the revolution. As Scheffer worked with the men on the shape of the proposed tribunal in private during the negotiations period, he asked Om Yentieng how they had sustained hope during those years. Yentieng laughed and replied:

---

201 Michael Lieberman, 'Salvaging the Remains' (2005) 186 *Military Law Review* 164; Helen Horsington, 'The Cambodian Khmer Rouge Tribunal: the Promise of the Hybrid Tribunal' (2004) 5 *Melbourne Journal of International Law* 462.

202 Helen Horsington, 'The Cambodian Khmer Rouge Tribunal: the Promise of a Hybrid Tribunal' (2004) 5 *Melbourne Journal of International Law* 462, 473.

203 Ibid.

204 Ratner, above n. 153, p. 216.

205 Ibid. p. 216.

206 Linton, above n. 157, p. 84.

207 Scheffer, above n. 147, p. 390.

'There was no hope. Hope had died. The task was to live each day to survive to the next day.'[208]

4.5.4. AFTER THE STORM

In the first quarter of 2004 further work through a UN technical assessment team and Cambodian officials brought consensus around amendments to the Cambodian Law on establishment of the ECCC so that it conformed to the main Agreement.[209] The Cambodian National Assembly ratified the Agreement on 4 October 2004 and promulgated amendments to the 2001 Cambodian Law to ensure consistency between the two instruments.[210] The Secretary-General's progress report to the General Assembly reiterated the ECCC's anticipated contribution to national reconciliation and sought to mobilise the resources needed for, *inter alia*, the special training of judges, outreach and media activities.[211] Implementation of the Agreement was delayed while pledges for the funding of the tribunal were secured. On 29 April 2005 the Agreement entered into force. Following the swearing-in of the Cambodian and international judges, co-prosecutors and co-investigating judges in July 2006, the investigation phase of the first ECCC trial began.[212] By June 2007, the ECCC rules of evidence and procedure, known as the Internal Rules were adopted.[213]

Former Khmer Rouge leaders Ke Pauk and Ta Mok died before the ECCC became operational in 2007.[214] Comrade Duch remained in custody in the Cambodian Military Court from May 1999 until his indictment by the ECCC. His trial, referred to as Case 001, commenced in February 2009. The ECCC Trial Chamber found Duch guilty of war crimes and crimes against humanity, and imposed a sentence of 35 years' imprisonment.[215] On 3 February 2012, the

208 Ibid.

209 *Agreement between the United Nations and the Royal Government of Cambodia Concerning the Prosecution under Cambodian Law of Crimes Committed During the Period of Democratic Kampuchea*, signed 6 June 2003, ratified 19 October 2004) [ECCC Agreement]. Ratification in the National Assembly was delayed until 4 October 2004 because of a year-long deadlock over formation of the government following the 2003 elections. The amendments were promulgated on 27 October 2004.

210 Scheffer, above n. 147, p. 403.

211 *Report of the Secretary-General on Khmer Rouge Trials* A/59/432 (12 October 2004) paras. [22], [31].

212 Scheffer, above n. 147, p. 404.

213 *Internal Rules* (Extraordinary Chambers in the Courts of Cambodia) (adopted 12 June 2007) [ECCC Internal Rules].

214 Ke Pauk was Deputy Chief of General Staff, Revolutionary Army of Democratic Kampuchea and Commander in Chief of the Central Zone armed forces. Ta Mok died in custody in July 2006. Scheffer, above n. 147, p. 405.

215 *Kaing Guek Eav alias 'Duch'* (Judgment) 001/18-07-2007ECCC/TC (26 July 2010) paras. 214–216.

ECCC Supreme Court Chamber increased the sentence to life imprisonment, bringing the first trial to completion.[216]

Between September and November 2007, the Cambodian government arrested Khieu Samphân, Nuon Chea, Ieng Sary and Ieng Thirith and delivered them to the ECCC detention facility.[217] On 15 September 2010, all four were indicted under the Closing Order of the Co-Investigating judges for genocide (against the Muslim Cham and the Vietnamese), crimes against humanity and grave breaches of the 1949 Geneva Conventions during the Khmer Rouge regime. The Open Society Justice Initiative which monitored the ECCC proceedings reported that the initial hearing of 27–30 June 2011 generated enormous public interest locally and internationally. The 'huge symbolic and legal significance' of bringing the surviving leaders of the Khmer Rouge to trial 32 years after their regime could not be overstated, and the hearing provided the opportunity for the public to see the four accused persons who were all before the court.[218]

Their trial, known as Case 002, began in January 2011 as a joint trial. The Closing Order addressed a diverse range of charges and amassed evidence of multiple crime sites throughout the territory of Democratic Kampuchea.[219] However, the case was severed by order of the Trial Chamber into a series of separate trials, each targeting segments of the indictment. The intervention was in the interests of justice, including safeguarding the interests of victims in achieving meaningful and timely justice, and the right of all the accused to an expeditious trial.[220] The frailty of the elderly accused, who were all experiencing various ailments as the trial proceeded, and the "scale and complexity of Case 002" were other factors underlying the severance order.[221]

The severance order produced Case 002/01, the first severed mini-trial limited to addressing alleged crimes and criminal policy related to the forced movement of the population from Phnom Penh in April 1975 and from September 1975 to late 1976, together with the Khmer Republic soldier killings at the execution site, Tuol Po Chrey immediately after the Khmer Rouge took power in 1975.[222]

---

216 *Kaing Guek Eav alias 'Duch'* (Appeal Judgment) 001/18-07-2007/ECCC/SC (3 February 2012) para. 382.

217 Scheffer, above n. 147, p. 405.

218 Open Society Justice Initiative, *Recent Developments at the Extraordinary Chambers in the Courts of Cambodia* (February 2012) p. 15.

219 *Nuon Chea, Ieng Sary, Khieu Samphân, Ieng Thirith* (Closing Order) Office of the Co-Investigating Judges, (Case File No. 002/19-09-2007-ECCC-OCIJ, 15 September 2010).

220 Severance Order Pursuant to Internal Rule 89ter Trial Chamber, 002/19-09-2007-ECCC/TC (22 September 2011) para 8.

221 *Nuon Chea and Others* (Decision on Severance of Case 002 Following Supreme Court Chamber Decision of 8 February 2013) 002/19-09-2007-ECCC/TC (26 April 2013) para 38.

222 *Nuon Chea and Others* (Decision on Co-Prosecutor's Request to Include Additional Crime Sites within the Scope of Trial in Case 002/01 (E163) and deadline for submission of applicable law portion of Closing Briefs ECCC-TC) 002/19-09-2007-ECCC/TC (8 October 2012) para. 3.

In response to an appeal by the Co-Prosecution arguing that the order was not reasonably representative of the indictment, the Supreme Court Chamber (SCC) overturned the severance order. The SCC ruled that the Trial Chamber should reassess its approach to severance after hearing the submissions of all parties and balancing their respective interests. The Trial Chamber should also explain how it planned to adjudicate on the outstanding charges in the indictment.[223] Thereafter, and as Case 002/01 proceeded, the Trial Chamber considered the submissions of all the parties on severance. Ultimately, the Chamber concluded that the proposals made by the parties did not significantly advance the representativeness of Case 002/01 and on balance, may hinder the delivery of a timely verdict in relation to the accused.[224] Consequently, the scope of the case in its existing form was reaffirmed by the Chamber. In addition, the Trial Chamber provided a provisional outline for future Case 002 trials contingent upon the health of the Co-accused and ongoing donor support of the Court.[225] These were matters of particular urgency given case developments, including the accused Ieng Thirith being found unfit to stand trial due to the onset of advanced dementia in November 2011, and the death of Ieng Sary on 14 March 2013.[226]

Case 002/01 was concluded under the slightly revised severance order. On 7 August 2014 the Trial Chamber found Nuon Chea and Khieu Samphân guilty of the crimes against humanity of extermination (encompassing murder), persecution on political grounds, and other inhumane acts (comprising forced transfer, enforced disappearances and attacks against human dignity). They were both sentenced to life imprisonment.[227]

On 23 November 2016, the SCC quashed the convictions in part, but affirmed the sentence for each of the accused persons.[228] Nuon Chea and Khieu Samphân's convictions for the crime against humanity of extermination in the course of the population movement immediately following the fall of Phnom Penh in April 1975 (Phase 1), was reversed.[229] The convictions for crimes against humanity of murder, persecution on political grounds and other inhumane acts

223 *Nuon Chea and Others* (Decision on the Co-Prosecutor's Immediate Appeal of the Trial Chamber's Decision Concerning the Scope of trial in Case 002/01) 002/19-09-2007-ECCC/SC Document No. E/163/5/1/13 (8 February 2013) paras. 41, 48–52.

224 *Nuon Chea and Others* (Decision on Severance of Case 002 Following Supreme Court Chamber Decision of 8 February 2013) 002/19-09-2007-ECCC/TC (26 April 2013) 149, 159–161.

225 Ibid. Annex; See Cambodian Center for Human Rights, *Severence of Proceedings in Case 002 at the Extraordinary Chambers in the Courts of Cambodia* (CCHR, October 2013) pp. 6–7.

226 Ibid. paras. 11, 28.

227 *Nuon Chea and Khieu Samphân* (Judgment) 002/19-09-2007/ECCC/TC, (7 August 2014) p. 622.

228 *Nuon Chea and Khieu Samphân* (Appeal Judgment) 002/01-002/19–09-2007-ECCC/SC (23 November 2016) p. 519 [Case 002/01 Appeal Judgment].

229 Case 002/01 Appeal Judgment para 845.

were affirmed with respect to Phase 1.[230] However, the SCC found that separate convictions for 'forced transfers' and 'attacks against human dignity' ought not to have been entered as these acts formed part of the crime against humanity of 'other inhumane acts.'[231]

In relation to the second phase of population transfers, the SCC reversed the conviction for the crime against humanity of extermination, and upon re-characterisation of the facts entered a conviction for the crime against humanity of murder.[232] The SCC also reversed the conviction for the crime against humanity of persecution on the basis that the Trial Chamber had not established that the Phase 2 transfers were 'discriminatory or an emanation of persecutory intent.'[233] In addition, the SCC found that it had not been established beyond reasonable doubt that 'a [CPK] policy contemplating the execution of Khmer Republic soldiers and officials existed at the time of the events' surrounding the deaths of at least 250 Lon Nol soldiers at Tuol Po Chrey.[234] Therefore the convictions for crimes against humanity of extermination, murder and persecution on political grounds in relation to those events were reversed.[235] However, the SCC concluded that the identified errors of law should not result in the life sentences being overturned. This was based on the roles of the accused, gravity of the established crimes, including their extended duration, and the fact that there had been a 'complete lack of consideration of the fate of the Cambodian population, especially those from the most vulnerable groups.'[236] The Appeal Judgment is discussed further at Sections 5.3.1, 7.5.3.2, and 9.6.

The scope of Case 002/02 took account of submissions made by the Co-Prosecution as to the range of charges and crimes sites. The Lead Co-lawyers were in agreement with the Co-Prosecutors' request to expand the Trial Chambers' provisional workplan and sought as a matter of priority to expand the charges of forced marriage (including rape) to nationwide scope and to include alleged crimes at additional worksites, as well as a third phase of forced movement of the population.[237] Nuon Chea's Co-Defence counsel sought the inclusion of certain alleged crime sites in order to adduce exculpatory evidence.[238] The Khieu Samphân Co-Defence opposed severance of the outstanding charges, arguing that his right to be tried without undue delay was compromised by the delay involved in running a severed trial.[239] Ultimately, at the second mini-trial,

230 Ibid paras 846–862.
231 Ibid paras 589 et seq, 845.
232 Ibid paras 864–868.
233 Ibid paras 705–706.
234 Ibid paras 902, 914, 972.
235 Ibid para 972.
236 Ibid paras 1117–1120.
237 *Nuon Chea and Khieu Samphân* (Decision on Additional Severance of Case 002 and Scope of Case 002/02) Trial Chamber, 002/19-09-2007- ECCC-TC (4 April 2014) para 8.
238 Ibid para 9–10.
239 Ibid para 11.

Khieu Samphân and Nuon Chea face charges of genocide against the Cham and Vietnamese communities, forced marriage and rape (nationwide), internal purging, crimes in a number of Khmer Rouge security centres, worksites and cooperatives, and crimes against Buddhists at Tram Kok Cooperative.[240] Case 002/02 proceedings began efficiently with both Nuon Chea and Khieu Samphân actively engaged despite intermittent health issues affecting their attendance.

The severance issue was but one of the trial management considerations facing the Court. As discussed further in Chapter seven, changes to the ECCC's Internal Rules following the 'Duch' trial raised a number of fair trial concerns in the proceedings of Case 002/01 and Case 002/02. In addition, the progress of two new investigations brought to light a large store of new evidence relevant to Case 002/02. The procedural implications of the newly admitted material affecting the rights of the accused are discussed at Chapter 5, section 5.4.3.

Cases 003 and 004 remain at the investigation stage despite their initiation by the international Co-Prosecutor in 2009. Both investigations sought to widen the net of prosecutions beyond the five initial suspects surrendered by the government to a cluster of former Khmer Rouge cadres of middle rank. In 2009, the Cambodian government made known its opposition to the initiation of the new investigations. The government asserted that the new cases would stir up civil strife among sectors of the population still loyal to the Khmer Rouge.[241] In due course, the national Prosecutor and the national Co-Investigating Judge withdrew cooperation from their international counterparts, leading to a stalemate in the work of the respective Court offices.[242] In the context of perceived political interference, one Co-Investigating Judge after another resigned their post and the morale of international staff flagged as the UN failed to effect any clear change to the pattern of obstruction that emerged.[243] It seemed as though the UN negotiators' and the ECCC Agreement's critics' worst fears had been realised. However, the ECCC continued the investigations and through the work of successive international Co-Investigating Judges has gradually moved the cases to an advanced stage. Initially four suspects were charged *in absentia* due to the government's failure to execute arrest warrants. In 2015, following private discussions between the UN and government officials about apparent violation

240 Ibid. p. 21.

241 'ECCC ruling risks unrest: PM', *Phnom Penh Post* (8 September 2009): http://phnompenpost.com/index.php/2009090828258/National.

242 Open Society Justice Initiative, *Political Interference at the Extraordinary Chambers in the Courts of Cambodia* (July 2010) p. 16; Neth Pheaktra and George Wilkins, 'Judges Should Focus on Current KR Suspects: Gov't.', *Phnom Penh Post* (12 March 2008): http://www.phnompenhpost.com/national/jusdges_should_focus on_current_KR_suspects_govt.

243 Asian Human Rights Commission, *Cambodia: Civil Society Expresses Concern over Recent Developments in the Extraordinary Chambers in the Courts of Cambodia and Urges the International Community to Speak Out* (AHRC, 20 May 2011); Mark Ellis, *Safeguarding Judicial Independence* (International Bar Association, September 2011) pp. 1–30.

of the ECCC Agreement through lack of cooperation, two of the charged persons presented at the Court voluntarily.[244]

4.6. CONCLUSION

The deconstruction of the society under the invisible, all-knowing Angkar disconnected individuals, families and communities from their traditional social underpinnings. After the Khmer Rouge regime was ousted in 1979, a proxy war in Cambodia, instigated by foreign powers, from 1979–1989 inhibited any true reconciliation or open public discourse on the Khmer Rouge era. The Khmer Rouges were able to re-group during this time and for another decade influenced the Cambodian political agenda. The history of the Khmer Rouge regime was erased from school curricula and forgetting the past became the political mantra of reconciliation for a society deprived of voice, rights and memory. The long-term impunity of the Khmer Rouge entrenched a culture of impunity in Cambodia. If there was no justice for genocide, citizens could have no confidence in the national justice system's capacity to address ordinary crimes. However, hope for many returned as civil society groups and the UN began to represent the justice interests of Cambodians in the years following the UNTAC mission.

In 2003, the UN sought creation of a model court in Cambodia to bring Khmer Rouge leaders to justice, but the government would not permit international control of the ECCC. As David Scheffer noted, the international side could only negotiate a range of procedural safeguards to counter foreseeable threats to legitimate legal process in a largely Cambodian court.[245] The UN negotiators aimed to achieve a credible justice mechanism for those who had suffered under the Khmer Rouge. Fair and expeditious trials for a few high-level perpetrators would have important expressive effects, but it seems unlikely that the creators of the ECCC envisioned the dominance of the national in the Court's composition, law and procedure as producing a platform for the suppressed voice of the Cambodian community. In the next chapter, the legal framework of the controversial Court is examined in more detail. Aspects of the Court's procedure are discussed as they affect the communicative as opposed to expressive value of ECCC trials.

---

244 Open Society Justice Initiative, *Recent Developments at the Extraordinary Chambers in the Courts of Cambodia* (OSJI, December 2015) pp. 5–6.

245 David Scheffer, 'The Extraordinary Chambers in the Courts of Cambodia' p. 19: http://www.cambodiatribunalmonitor.org/history_history-analysis-scheffer-english.pdf (an abridgement of a book chapter in M. Cherif Bassiouni, *International Criminal Law*, 3rd ed. (Martinus Nijhoff Publishers, 2008).

CHAPTER 5

INQUISITORIAL CRIMINAL PROCEDURE AT THE ECCC

5.1. INTRODUCTION

Controversy, missteps and delays formed part of the implementation phases of all of the Courts described in Chapter three. The ECCC had the additional challenge of instituting credible criminal procedure within a national legal system and administrative structure known for questionable justice processes and outcomes. Under these conditions, the ECCC judiciary began the delicate task of drafting the Court's rules of evidence and procedure, the Internal Rules. This chapter discusses the fusion of Cambodian inquisitorial criminal procedure with elements of international criminal procedure to support the ECCC's internationally assisted trials.

The ECCC Internal Rules instituted inquisitorial criminal procedure based on Cambodian law, but incorporating international standards of due process. The rules also gave effect to the intricate compromises contained in the ECCC Agreement between Cambodia and the UN, discussed in Chapter four. In this chapter, the legal framework of the ECCC and the procedural scheme implemented by the Internal Rules are examined. This includes the role-sharing among senior court actors, incorporation of the civil party action within the criminal proceedings, and the supermajority formulae in judicial decision-making. The judiciary's recognition of the ECCC's reconciliatory purpose during the early stages of Cases 001 and 002 is also discussed. The analysis reveals the potential of these procedural features to produce representative and discursive trials. While the Court encountered difficulties in implementing victim participation rights, and the Cambodian government opposed the opening of investigations into Cases 003 and 004, the procedural regime proved sufficient to support the first internationalised trials of former Khmer Rouge leaders. The chapter highlights elements of the ECCC's structure and procedure that may have been instrumental in producing not only expressive but communicative trials.

5.2. LEGAL FRAMEWORK OF THE ECCC

The legal framework includes the Cambodian enabling law and the ECCC procedural rules, known as the ECCC Internal Rules. In Chapter three, I noted that the ECCC from its inception was described as a hybrid court, not unlike the Special Court for Sierra Leone (SCSL).[1] However, closer analysis of the ECCC's founding instruments suggested categorisation of the ECCC as an 'internationalised' court, being one derived from national law but with international elements underpinned by a bilateral agreement.[2]

The scope for, and nature of representation at the ECCC flows from the legal framework agreed between the UN and the Royal Government of Cambodia (RGC). The Cambodian government succeeded in securing a majority of national judges in all Chambers: the Pre-Trial and Trial Chambers; and the Supreme Court acting as the court of appeal. The roles of investigating judge, prosecutor and defence counsel are shared equally between Cambodian and international officers. Senior administrative roles are similarly shared, except that there is a Cambodian director of the Office of Administration appointed by the RGC and an international deputy director appointed by the UN Secretary-General.[3] The extent of role-sharing at senior levels at the ECCC exceeds that of all other UN-supported Courts.

5.2.1. THE AGREEMENT AND THE ECCC LAW

Unlike the circumstances surrounding creation of the SCSL by treaty, described in Chapter three (sections 3.6, 3.6.2.1), the Cambodian government insisted on national ownership of the ECCC and adopted a law to enable its creation within the national legal system.[4] This was an assertion of Cambodian sovereignty and

---

1 Laura A. Dickinson, 'The Promise of Hybrid Courts' (2003) 97 *American Journal of International Law* 295; Helen Horsington, 'The Cambodian Khmer Rouge Tribunal: the Promise of a Hybrid Tribunal' (2004) 5 *Melbourne Journal of International Law* 462; Frédéric Mégret, 'In Defence of Hybridity: Towards a Representational Theory of International Criminal Justice' (2005) 38 *Cornell International Law Journal* 725; David Cohen, 'Hybrid Justice in East Timor, Sierra Leone, and Cambodia: "Lessons Learned" and Prospects for the Future' (2007) 43 *Stanford Journal of International Law* 1.

2 Sarah Williams, *Hybrid and Internationalised Criminal Tribunals: Selected Jurisdictional Issues* (Hart Publishing, 2012) p. 299; Guido Acquaviva, 'New Paths in International Criminal Justice: The Internal Rules of the Cambodia Extraordinary Chambers' (2008) 6 *Journal of International Criminal Justice* 129, 129–130.

3 *Agreement between the United Nations and the Royal Government of Cambodia Concerning the Prosecution under Cambodian Law of Crimes Committed During the Period of Democratic Kampuchea* signed 6 June 2003, adopted by General Assembly Resolution 57/228B (13 May 2003) available at: http://www.eccc.gov.kh/english/Agreement_between _UN_and RGC.pdf [ECCC Agreement] art. 8.

4 Acquaviva, above n. 2, p. 130.

exercise of the national duty to investigate and prosecute serious violations of human rights and international humanitarian law within sovereign territory.[5] The national enabling law is the constitutive instrument creating the ECCC.[6] Concomitantly, the Agreement between the UN and the Cambodian government constitutes an international treaty pursuant to which the 2004 amendments to the initial Cambodian law (ECCC Law) were passed to reflect the international elements insisted upon by the UN during the negotiations.[7] A hierarchy of authority between the Agreement and the ECCC Law was suggested by the Secretary-General following the final negotiations, based on the Agreement's operation by law within Cambodia, and the government's obligation to ensure that the national law conformed to the Agreement.[8] The Agreement provides that where amendments to the ECCC Law are 'deemed necessary, such amendments shall always be preceded by consultations between the parties.'[9] Of primary concern to the UN is maintenance of the fine-tuning of the Agreement to ensure that the ECCC functions in accordance with international standards of due process, in the knowledge that the institution will be evaluated internationally on that basis.[10]

The two instruments may be read together as providing the governing framework of a joint venture, each having a specific purpose. The ECCC Law is the Court's working instrument establishing Cambodian ownership of the Court.[11] The Agreement has the specific purpose of regulating cooperation between the UN and the RGC in bringing suspects before the ECCC to be prosecuted for serious violations of Cambodian penal law, international humanitarian law and custom, and international conventions recognised by Cambodia, that were committed during the period 17 April 1975 to 6 January 1979.[12] Cohen took the view that the ECCC was created by the Agreement but noted from an interview with Michelle Lee, the international Deputy Director of Administration at the

5 Williams, above n. 2, p. 293.

6 Ibid. p. 295.

7 *Law on the Establishment of the Extraordinary Chambers in the Courts in Cambodia for the Prosecution of Crimes Committed during the Period of Democratic Kampuchea* Reach Kram No. NS/RKM/0801/12 including amendments promulgated 27 October 2004 available at: http://eccc.gove.kh/english [ECCC Law].

8 *Secretary-General's Report on the Khmer Rouge Trials 31 March 2003* UN Doc. A/57/769 [10]; see also Ernestine E. Meijer, 'The Extraordinary Chambers in the Courts of Cambodia for Prosecuting Crimes Committed by the Khmer Rouge: Jurisdiction, Organization, and Procedure of an Internationalized National Tribunal' in Cesare P.R. Romano, Andre Nollkaemper and Jann K. Kleffner (eds.), *Internationalized Criminal Courts and Tribunals: Sierra Leone, East Timor, Kosovo and Cambodia* (Oxford University Press, 2003) pp. 207, 209–210.

9 ECCC Agreement art. 2(3).

10 Acquaviva, above n. 2, p. 131.

11 Williams, above n. 2, p. 295.

12 ECCC Agreement art. 1.

ECCC, that there was wide acceptance of Cambodian ownership from the UN side of the Court administration 'which views its role as in essence, one of support for the process in accordance with international standards.'[13]

Reflecting the tense negotiations and doubts of the UN as to the Cambodian government's intentions, Article 28 of the Agreement provides for UN withdrawal of cooperation in the venture 'should the RGC change the structure or organisation of the ECCC or otherwise cause them to function in a manner that does not conform to the terms of the Agreement.' The provision appears to provide the UN with an exit strategy should the Cambodian government act in bad faith. In practice, the provision is largely expressive in light of the complex political and economic factors involved in withdrawing from or withholding support for a Court of such historic significance.[14]

5.2.2. JURISDICTION

5.2.2.1. *Temporal Jurisdiction*

Consistent with practice in other internationalised courts, the temporal jurisdiction of the ECCC covers a limited period: 17 April 1975 to 6 January 1979. While the Cambodian conflict began before, and continued after this period, the limitation is explicable, at least in part, by a pragmatic concern not to overburden the ECCC and the desire to permit the Court's prompt and cost-effective functioning.[15] It was foreseeable however, that a more expansive view of the conflict, encompassing larger regional conflict supporting geopolitical interests beyond the Khmer Rouge regime itself would engage the defence. A challenge to the legitimacy of the proceedings could come by means of the 'rupture defence.' Developed by Jacques Verges in the war crimes trial of Klaus Barbie in France, the controversial defence strategy was designed to attack the legitimacy of the prosecuting authorities by suggesting they do not bring the proceedings with entirely clean hands.[16] In Case 002/01, Nuon Chea's international Co-Defence counsel challenged the historical analysis undertaken by the Co-Prosecution, by asking 'which history' was included. And, 'why did the Co-Prosecution describe the CPK's alleged violence prior to 1975 with almost no mention of the atrocities committed by Lon Nol's forces against CPK cadres? Was the CPK fighting a phantom or an enemy?'[17] This supported his argument

---

13 Cohen, above n. 1, p. 27 from notes on Cohen's interview with Michelle Lee on 30 May 2006.
14 Williams, above n. 2, p. 297.
15 Meijer, above n. 8, p. 212.
16 *Federation Nationale des Deportes et Internes Resistants et Patriots v. Barbie* (1985) 78 ILR 125.
17 Closing Statement of Co-Defence Counsel, Koppe Trial Transcript Day 224, Case File NO. 002/19-09-2007-ECCC/TC (31 October 2013) p. 45.

that Nuon Chea could not be fairly judged in the context of a form of victors' justice. Added to the issue of fairness was the fact that the Court had not issued a summons for Heng Samrin, an important character witness for Nuon Chea.[18] In this, the Co-Defence alleged that the Co-Prosecutors were 'in the clutches of the [Cambodian] government.' Thus, 'this trial is fundamentally political.'[19]

While the use of the strategy arguably amplifies the risk taken by the UN in supporting the creation of the Court, challenges to jurisdiction are not uncommon in international criminal proceedings.[20] Moreover, raising relevant contextual matters forms part of the inquisitorial truth-finding process the Court is engaged in. The narrative tropes of the Co-Prosecution and Co-Defence are integral to Cambodian society's discursive engagement with its past through the process of prosecution.[21] The defence strategy might undermine the work of the Court to some degree by affecting public opinion but simultaneously, it sheds more light on the Khmer Rouge era with its ongoing effects.[22]

5.2.2.2. *Subject-Matter Jurisdiction*

The ECCC is empowered to try alleged perpetrators of both national and international crimes during the designated period. The ECCC Law lists the crimes of homicide, torture and religious persecution as the relevant domestic crimes under the 1956 Penal Code of Cambodia.[23] The Code is applicable national law, as it remained in force 'following the promulgation of both the Constitution of the Khmer Republic on May 1972 and the Constitution of Democratic Kampuchea on 5 January 1976.'[24]

As to international crimes, the relevant sources of law include 'customary and conventional international law and the general principles of law recognised by the community of nations.'[25] Accordingly, the core international crimes of genocide,

---

18 Heng Samrin is President of the National Assembly of Cambodia.

19 Closing Statement of Co-Defence Counsel, Koppe Trial Transcript Day 224, Case File NO. 002/19-09-2007-ECCC/TC (31 October 2013) p. 44.

20 For example, there were challenges to the jurisdiction of the ICTY and the SCSL.

21 Mark Osiel, *Mass Atrocity, Collective Memory and the Law* (Transaction Publishers, 1997) p. 73.

22 Robert Cryer, *Prosecuting International Crimes* (Cambridge University Press, 2005) p. 202; Other tactics may also be engaged such as the Case 002/02 defence team of Khieu Samphân's boycott of the trial proceedings until the Trial Chamber addresses their allegations of bias on the part of several of its judges. 'Khmer Defense Teams a no Show at Meeting to End Boycott', *Cambodia Daily*, 22 October 2014.

23 ECCC Law art. 3 *new*, the relevant provisions of the 1956 Penal Code are cited as Homicide (arts. 501, 503–508), Torture (art 500), Religious persecution (arts 209–210).

24 *Kaing Guek Eav alias 'Duch'*, (Judgment) 001/18-07-2007/ECCC/TC (26 July 2010) para. 29.

25 Ibid. para. 30; See Article15(2) of the 1966 *International Covenant on Civil and Political Rights* 999 UNTS 172 (signed by Cambodia on 17 October 1980 and acceded to on 26 May 1992) See also *Statute of the International Court of Justice* art. 38(1).

crimes against humanity and grave breaches of the Geneva Conventions of 12 August 1949 come within the jurisdiction of the ECCC.[26] In addition, the ECCC may prosecute suspects most responsible for the destruction of cultural property during an armed conflict under the 1954 Hague Convention for the Protection of Cultural Property in the Event of Armed Conflict and crimes against internationally protected persons under the 1961 Vienna Convention on Diplomatic Relations.[27]

By the enforcement of Cambodian and international law, the ECCC aims to end impunity for some domestic crimes and fulfil its primary obligation to enforce human rights and international humanitarian law through the internationally approved Court, and before the Cambodian people. This represents at least partial fulfilment of the Office of the High Commissioner for Human Rights in Cambodia's objective of furthering the rule of law in Cambodia, the slow progress towards which is recorded in Reports of the Office and those of the Secretary-General's Special Representatives.[28] In addition, application of domestic law by the ECCC not only activates accountability for criminal violations but also a remedy and for victims, as discussed further at 5.6.5 below.[29]

5.2.2.3. *Personal Jurisdiction*

More politically contentious than either temporal or subject-matter jurisdiction is the personal jurisdiction of the ECCC. The ECCC Law and the Agreement limit ECCC prosecutions to 'senior leaders' of Democratic Kampuchea and those 'most responsible' for violations of Cambodian penal law, international humanitarian law and custom, and international conventions recognised by Cambodia during the period of temporal jurisdiction.[30] Neither the Agreement nor the ECCC Law defines 'senior leaders' or 'those most responsible.' However,

---

26 ECCC Law arts. 1, 4–6.

27 ECCC Law arts. 7, 8; See *Hague Convention for the Protection of Cultural Property in the Event of Armed Conflict* opened for signature 14 May 1954–31 December 1954, 249 UNTS 240 (entered into force 7 August 1956); *Vienna Convention on Diplomatic Relations* opened for signature 18 April 1961 (1961) 500 UNTS 95 (entered into force 24 April 1964).

28 See *Advisory Services and Technical Cooperation in the Field of Human Rights: Report of the Special Representative of the Secretary-General for Human Rights in Cambodia, Yash Ghai* UN Doc. E/CN.4/2006/110 (24 January 2006); *Role and Achievements of the Office of the United Nations High Commissioner for Human Rights in Assisting the Government and People of Cambodia in the Promotion and Protection of Human Rights: Report of the Secretary General,* UN Doc. A/HRC/4/95 (18 January 2007); *Technical Assistance and Capacity-Building: Report of the Special Representative of the Secretary-General for Human Rights in Cambodia, Yash Ghai* UN Doc. A/HRC/7/42 29 (February 2008).

29 M. Cherif Bassiouni, *Introduction to International Criminal Law* (Transnational Publishers, 2003) p. 720.

30 ECCC Agreement, art. 1; ECCC Law arts. 1, 2.

as an international treaty, the Agreement is subject to the Vienna Convention on the Law of Treaties. As such, under Article 31(1) the ordinary meaning of these terms used in the Agreement, interpreted in 'good faith in accordance with the ordinary meaning to be given to the terms of the treaty in their context and in light of its object and purpose' guide the determination of ECCC jurisdiction over suspects.[31] Furthermore, as the ECCC Law is integrally linked to the Agreement, in accordance with Article 31(2) of the VCLT, it constitutes 'an instrument which was made by one or more parties in connection with the treaty.' As each instrument uses the same terminology, according to the rules of interpretation, the ordinary meaning of the terms used in context with reference to the object and purpose of the relevant instruments indicates that two categories of suspects fall within the jurisdiction of the Court: senior leaders of Democratic Kampuchea, and those most responsible for the commission of offences within the jurisdiction of the ECCC. Moreover, recourse to the drafting history of the instrument as a supplementary means of interpretation may be had under Article 32 in the case of ambiguity of terms.[32]

The 1998 UN Group of Experts Report first addressed the issue thus:

> The Group does not believe that the term 'leaders' should be equated with all persons at the senior levels of Government of DK or even of the CPK. The list of top governmental and party officials may not correspond with the list of persons most responsible for serious violations of human rights, in that certain top governmental leaders may have been removed from knowledge and decision-making; and others not in the chart of senior leaders may have played a significant role in the atrocities. This seems especially true with respect to certain leaders at the zonal level, as well as officials of torture and interrogation centres such as Tuol Sleng.[33]

The first batch of ECCC indictees reflected the dual categories envisaged by the Group of Experts. Four indictees can be categorised as senior leaders of Democratic Kampuchea, having held ministerial positions – Nuon Chea, Ieng Sary, Ieng Thirith, or a leading role within the CPK – Khieu Samphân. A fifth former Khmer Rouge member however, falls within the second category. While not a member of the Ministry or the CPK Central Committee, Kaing Guek Eav (alias Duch) was directly responsible to the Central Committee and controlled the administration of the Tuol Sleng interrogation centre, which implemented

31 *Vienna Convention on the Law of Treaties* opened for signature 23 May 1969, 1155 UNTS 331, (entered into force 27 January 1980) [VCLT] art. 31(1).

32 Steve Heder, 'A Review of the Negotiations Leading to the Establishment of the Personal Jurisdiction of the Extraordinary Chambers in the Courts of Cambodia', *Cambodia Tribunal Monitor* (1 August 2011) pp. 1, 1–2.

33 *Report of the Group of Experts for Cambodia established pursuant to General Assembly Resolution 52/135 dated 18 February 1999*, UN Doc. A/850-S1999/231 (15 March 1999) para. [109].

the CPK policy of 'smashing' (or destroying) enemies of the regime.[34] In the first trial, known as Case 001 or the Duch trial, the Trial Chamber confirmed the ECCC's personal jurisdiction as confined to those two categories, and prosecuted the accused as someone 'most responsible for the most serious violations of human rights during the rule of Democratic Kampuchea.'[35]

Scholarly analyses of the negotiating history of the ECCC's personal jurisdiction also confirmed the intention of drafters to identify two categories of suspects.[36] Separate analyses were published in the context of doubt cast on the reading of Article 1 as a result of the Appeal by Duch from his conviction in the first trial, and in the wake of delays in the investigation of Cases 003 and 004 due to perceived political interference by the Cambodian government.[37]

Reviewing the history of the ECCC's personal jurisdiction, Steve Heder recorded Prime Minister Hun Sen's public statements on those within Khmer Rouge ranks who were targeted for prosecution. Heder's study revealed that Hun Sen's preference was for prosecutions of former Khmer Rouge leaders to the mid-tier level, provided that those who overthrew the Regime were excluded from the net.[38]

David Scheffer stated that during the ECCC negotiations 'no concession was given that would permit interpretation of the language of ECCC personal jurisdiction to a pool of only five suspects.'[39] He concluded further that:

> There is no plausible way to interpret the personal jurisdiction language of the ECCC to narrow the field of suspects *only* to senior Khmer Rouge leaders who also were most responsible for the atrocity crimes of the Pol Pot regime. Duch's appeal challenging his designation within the personal jurisdiction is clearly refuted by the legislative history of the ECCC Law, by a common sense grammatical reading of the text, and by clear expressions of intent by the Cambodian Government and UN negotiators prior to enactment of that Law.[40]

The Cambodian government's opposition to continuing the investigation of Cases 003 and 004 highlights the political sensitivity around widening the net of prosecutions at the ECCC.[41] Cases 003 and 004 target an additional five suspects who held political and military authority within the CPK, or had zonal

---

34 *Kaing Guek Eav alias Duch* (Closing Order) 001/18-07-2007/ECCC-OCIJ (8 August 2008) paras. 31–33.

35 *Kaing Guek Eav (alias Duch)* (Judgment) 001/18-07-2007/ECCC/TC, 26 July 2010) para. 25.

36 David Scheffer, 'Negotiating History of the ECCC's Personal Jurisdiction' *Cambodia Tribunal Monitor* (22 May 2011) pp. 1, 11.

37 Heder, above n. 32, p. 1.

38 Ibid. p. 37.

39 Scheffer, above n. 36, p. 10.

40 Ibid. pp. 10–11.

41 Open Society Justice Initiative, *The Future of Cases 003/004 at the Extraordinary Chambers in the Courts of Cambodia* (OSJI, October 2012), p. 16.

responsibility at detention facilities.[42] Investigations may also involve government officials as witnesses and meet with government opposition. This happened in Case 002 when Cambodian officials refused to comply with summonses to appear as witnesses, in contravention of the duty of the government to cooperate with the ECCC.[43] This kind of problem is not unique to the ECCC. As discussed in Chapter three, section 3.4, the ICTY in its early years faced difficulties in securing the cooperation of Balkan states in the arrest of suspects.

The Open Society Justice Initiative criticised the UN for continuing to support the Court in these circumstances and asserted in expressive tones that it was weakening 'the UN brand' in the realm of internationalised accountability.[44] However, the UN did not exercise its right to withdraw cooperation from the tribunal as a whole, or in relation to Cases 003 and 004, under Article 28 of the Agreement. Instead, the UN deployed new personnel to the Office of the Co-Investigating Judges to 'continue pursuing the critical task of Khmer Rouge regime accountability' generally, while remaining invested in the completion of the less controversial Case 002.[45] The political storm surrounding the opening of Cases 003 and 004 deflected attention from the significant gains of the ECCC in establishing the Court and implementing an innovative scheme of criminal procedure under its Internal Rules, although this too was not without controversy.

5.2.2.4. The ECCC Internal Rules

If the ECCC had been a hybrid court with international majority composition like the SCSL the institution might have been mandated to adopt the procedure of one of the ad hoc Tribunals and adapt those rules to the local context as necessary. Such an approach would have activated predominantly adversarial procedure developed to address the requirements of prosecutions for international crimes. However, the ECCC Law and Article 12(1) of the Agreement instituted an essentially national with court procedure in accordance Cambodian law, albeit modified to permit the prosecution of mass crimes. The Internal Rules, pursuant to Articles 20, 23 and 33 *new* of the ECCC Law and Article 12(1) of the Agreement, have the stated purposes of consolidating multiple sources of Cambodian procedural law, resolving uncertainties or ambiguities as to their

---

42 Ibid. pp. 30–31.

43 Open Society Justice Initiative, *Political Interference at the Extraordinary Chambers in the Courts of Cambodia* (July 2010) [OSJI Report Political Interference] p. 15.

44 Open Society Justice Initiative, *Recent Developments at the Extraordinary Chambers in the Courts of Cambodia* (OSJI, November 2011) p. 21, citing Mark Ellis, 'Safeguarding Judicial Independence in Mixed Tribunals: Lessons from the ECCC and Best Practices for the Future' (International Bar Association, September 2011) p. 9.

45 'Deployment of International Co-investigating Judge' ECCC Press Release (30 July 2012).

application and where necessary, incorporating international standards to ensure the criminal procedure is not inconsistent with international fair trials.[46]

The process of giving effect to Cambodian law and international criminal procedural standards in the Internal Rules revived the tension inherent in the negotiations for the ECCC Agreement. As the national and international members of the Court negotiated the rules in plenary sessions, a major source of contention was the international view that international rules would need to apply in many cases, in contrast to the position of the national judges that Cambodian law must prevail.[47]

5.3. DRAFTING THE INTERNAL RULES

In July 2006 the Committee on the Rules of Procedure led by international Co-Investigating judge, Marcel Lemonde was formed to complete the negotiation and drafting of the ECCC Internal Rules.[48] Comprising five judges (three Cambodian and two international), the Committee circulated an initial draft to the larger ECCC judicial body, the Co-Prosecutors and other senior court officers as well as interested organisations and individuals.[49] The Court invited responses to the draft and various national and international non-governmental organisations made submissions on it. Over the following 11 months the draft was discussed further in closed plenary meetings. At the November 2006 meeting there was significant disagreement between the judges on how Cambodian law and international standards were to be integrated, as well as over the nature of victims' rights to be activated and the operation of the ECCC within the Cambodian court structure.[50] From January 2007, a newly constituted Rules Committee worked intensively to resolve the disagreements. By March 2007, the major impasses had been largely addressed and drafting of the Rules proceeded.[51]

However, disagreement remained between the Cambodian and international judges over the issue of access to international defence counsel for accused persons.[52] There were indications of government pressure on the Cambodian judges, through the Bar Association of the Kingdom of Cambodia (BAKC) to

46 *Internal Rules* Extraordinary Chambers in the Courts of Cambodia (adopted 12 June 2007) [ECCC Internal Rules] Preamble.

47 John D. Ciorciari and Anne Heindel, *Hybrid Justice: The Extraordinary Chambers in the Courts of Cambodia* (University of Michigan Press, 2014) p. 64.

48 Stan Starygin, 'Internal Rules of the Extraordinary Chambers in the Courts of Cambodia: Setting an Example of the Rule of Law by Breaking the Law' (2011) 3 *Journal of Law and Conflict Resolution* 20, footnotes xxxviii–xxxix; David Scheffer, *All the Missing Souls: A Personal History of the War Crimes Tribunals* (Princeton University Press, 2011) p. 404.

49 Ibid Starygin.

50 Ibid p.22.

51 Ibid footnote xxxviii.

52 Ibid.

limit international defence counsel activity to assisting Cambodian lawyers outside the Court.[53] The international judges on the other hand argued that international defence counsel must be able to represent accused persons in Court to meet international fair trial standards.[54] The compromise reached under what became Internal Rule 22 was that international lawyers could fully participate as defence counsel provided they acted alongside a Cambodian lawyer, and went through a registration process with the BAKC. Finalisation of the Internal Rules was further complicated by the late demand of the BAKC for registration fees for international counsel at 10 times the normal rate.[55] The final compromise of a flat registration fee of US$500 for all international counsel appearing before the ECCC cleared the way for implementation of the Internal Rules.[56]

5.3.1. THE LEGALITY OF THE INTERNAL RULES

Scholars reviewed the status and legality of the Internal Rules after their adoption on 12 June 2007. Acquaviva considered that the internationally appointed ECCC judges would view the Internal Rules as a sort of 'code' of its own, and that defence counsel would inevitably challenge perceived anomalies in the application of the relevant law and the 'policy considerations' of Court decisions.[57] Starygin argued that the Internal Rules deviated from existing Cambodian procedure in numerous respects, including civil party participation in proceedings, and doubted there was sufficient justification for such rules on the basis of consistency with international standards.[58] Others commentators advocated amendment to specific rules, notably those dealing with ECCC Appeals, to ensure their consistency with international human rights law.[59]

Revisions of the Internal Rules were released by the Court to address trial management issues as the cases proceeded. Nevertheless, in Case 002 the Co-Defence strategy included a challenge to the constitutionality of the Internal Rules. This included requests for the Court to determine whether specific procedural rules were applied in compliance with the Cambodian criminal procedure, as well as

53 Ciorciari, above n. 47, p. 65; See also Human Rights Watch, *Government Interferes in Khmer Rouge Tribunal - Donors Should Recognize How Government Tactics Threaten Entire Process* (5 December 2006).

54 OSJI Report Political Interference, above n. 43, p. 9, fn. 24.

55 *Internal Rules Governing Khmer Rouge Tribunal Reached*, 19 March 2007: http://www.voanews.com/english/news/a-13-2007-04-07-voa11-66547937.html; *Dispute Over Lawyers' Fees is Latest Threat to Long-Delayed Khmer Rouge Trial*, VOANews.com, 7 April 2007 26/10/2011: http://www.voanews.com/english/news/a-13-2007-03-19-voa19.html.

56 Ciorciari above n 47, p 66.

57 Acquaviva, above n. 2, p. 132–33.

58 Starygin above n 48, p 21-25.

59 Lily O'Neill and Goran Sluiter, 'The Right to Appeal a Judgment of the Extraordinary Chambers in the Courts of Cambodia' (2009) 10 *Melbourne Journal of International Law* 596, 627–630; ECCC Internal Rules (Rev 4) 11 September 2009) r. 104(3).

whether the body of rules adopted by the Plenary was consistent with both Article 90 of the Cambodian Constitution and Article 12(1) of the ECCC Agreement.[60]

In the Pre-Trial Chamber (PTC) Nuon Chea's defence counsel filed an appeal against an order of the Co-investigating Judges refusing the annulment of investigative actions. The Co-Defence sought clarification on the compliance with Cambodian law of the procedure for seeking annulment of investigative actions under the Internal Rules and the role of the Co-investigating judges thereto. In the course of deciding the appeal the PTC noted:

> [t]he Internal Rules ... form a self-contained regime of procedural law related to the unique circumstances of the ECCC, made and agreed upon by the plenary of the ECCC. They do not stand in opposition to the Code of Criminal Procedure the Kingdom of Cambodia(CPC) but the focus of the ECCC differs substantially enough from the normal operation of the Cambodian criminal courts to warrant a specialised system. Therefore, the Internal Rules constitute the primary instrument to which reference should be made in determining procedures before the ECCC where there is a difference between the procedures in the Internal Rules and the CPC.[61]

The Trial Chamber affirmed the PTC's formulation of the Internal Rules as it addressed Nuon Chea's further claim that Article 12(1) of the ECCC Agreement authorises the ECCC to refer to international standards on a case-by-basis, but not under a system of rules created by the plenary.[62] This issue was revisited by the Supreme Court Chamber (SCC) in the Appeal Judgment of Case 002/01. The SCC found that while the language of Article 12(1) anticipates deviation from Cambodian criminal procedure in articulated circumstances, this did not lead to the conclusion that the judges of the ECCC were prohibited from formulating a relevant body of procedural rules prospectively.[63] Moreover, the Internal Rules are an agreed interpretation of the applicable law adopted through a consultative process and as such hold persuasive value. The ECCC's specific structure and mandate at the interface with Cambodian law determines when resort to international standards is valid. Interpreting Article 12 too narrowly by 'adhering literally' to Cambodian procedure would run counter to the spirit of the ECCC agreement and render the Court inoperable.[64] Thus, the SCC rejected the claim that the Internal Rules 'usurp legislative powers' and are unconstitutional.[65]

---

60 Nuon Chea (Consolidated Preliminary Objections) 002/19-09-2007-ECCC-TC (25 February 2011) paras 66-68; Nuon Chea's Appeal Against the Judgment in Case 002/01 002/19-09-2007-ECCC-SCpara 15.

61 *Nuon Chea* (Decision on Nuon Chea's Appeal Against Order Refusing Request for Annulment) Pre-trial Chamber, 002/19-09-2007-ECCC/OCIJ (PTC06 26 August 2008) para 14.

62 *Nuon Chea* (Decision on Nuon Chea's Preliminary Objection Alleging the Unconstitutional Character of the ECCC Internal Rules Trial Chamber) 002/19-09-2007-ECCC/TC 8 August 2011) para 7.

63 *Nuon Chea and Khieu Samphân (Appeal Judgment)* Supreme Court Chamber, 002/19-09-2007-ECCC/SC, 23 November 2016) para 106 [Case 002/01 Appeal Judgment].

64 *Nuon Chea* Case 002/01 Appeal Judgment para 107.

65 *Nuon Chea* Case 002/01 Appeal Judgment para 106.

5.3.2. THE INTERNAL RULES AND OTHER SOURCES OF LAW

The Pre-Trial Chamber articulated a hierarchy of sources to be consulted on questions of procedure.[66] The Internal Rules are consulted first; then the Cambodian criminal procedural law. Where a gap or uncertainty remains regarding the applicable procedure, the ECCC looks to established international criminal procedure. On substantive issues, the Court first consults the ECCC Law, then the Agreement and lastly international criminal law precedent.[67]

A notable example of the ECCC's engagement with sources of law at domestic and international levels was the case challenging the continuing pre-trial detention of the Accused in Case 001, Kaing Guek Eav (alias Duch). While noting the ECCC's existence within the Cambodian court structure, the Trial Chamber distinguished the ECCC as a 'separately constituted, independent and internationalised court.'[68] As such the ECCC Law obliged the Court to apply Cambodian procedural rules but also to 'determine their conformity with international standards prescribed by human rights conventions and followed by international criminal courts.'[69] Moreover, the Court noted that the ECCC must take account of Article 31 of the Constitution of the Kingdom of Cambodia, which states:

> The Kingdom of Cambodia shall recognise and respect human rights as stipulated in the United Nations Charter, The Universal Declaration of Human Rights and covenants and conventions related to human rights.[70]

Articulation of this obligation of the Court in the Trial Chamber activated a legal requirement not hitherto routinely observed by the Cambodian judiciary. Furthermore, the Court pronounced upon the legality of the accused's prior detention over an eight-year period by the Cambodian Military Court, finding that Duch's prior detention had been in breach of Cambodian law and contravened 'his internationally recognised right to a trial within a reasonable time and detention in accordance with the law.'[71] As to the legality of continued

---

66 *Nuon Chea* (Decision on Nuon Chea's Appeal against Order Refusing Request for Annulment) 002/19-09-2007/ECCC/OCIJ (PTC06) (26 August 2008) paras. 12–14.

67 Richard L. Kilpatrick, '*Prosecutor v Kaing Guek Eav alias Duch*: In First Round of Proceedings, The Extraordinary Chambers in the Courts of Cambodia Convicts Former Chairman of Khmer Rouge Interrogation Center of Atrocity Crimes' (2011) 19 *Tulane Journal of International And Comparative Law* 660, 672.

68 *Kaing Guek Eav alias 'Duch'* (Decision on Request for Release) 001/18-07-2007-ECCC/TC-E39/5 (15 June 2009) para. 10.

69 Ibid. para. 15; Williams disputed the Chamber's categorisation of the ECCC arguing that 'the fact that the ECCC is a stand-alone institution does not change its legal basis which remains Cambodian law.' See Williams, above n. 2, p. 299.

70 Ibid. para. 15.

71 Ibid. para. 21.

detention by the ECCC in light of the circumstances of previous violations of his rights, the Court concluded the previous violations of Duch's rights were not so egregious as to preclude or restrain the exercise of ECCC jurisdiction.[72] Following the ICTR authority, *Prosecutor v. Barayagwiza*, the Court held that in the event of Duch's conviction, he would be entitled at the sentencing stage, not only to credit for time already spent in detention, but also to a reduction in sentence as a result of previous violations to his rights.[73]

While Cambodian criminal procedural law grants rights to prisoners in pre-trial detention, in practice such rights are frequently violated and subject to unprincipled practice by prosecutors and courts.[74] The reasoned decision of the ECCC reinforced the rights of accused persons against unwarranted and excessive detention and provided the Cambodian judiciary and national lawyers with a body of experience and precedent uncharacteristic of Cambodian domestic criminal justice practice.

5.4. IMPLEMENTING THE CRIMINAL PROCEDURE

One legacy of French colonial rule in Cambodia was a legal system based on the Western European civil law system. Cambodian criminal procedure is therefore inquisitorial in nature as opposed to the adversarial mode characteristic of the Anglo-American common law world.[75] With the exception of the Special Tribunal for Lebanon, international tribunals have applied predominantly adversarial trial procedure. The adversarial approach adopted by the creators of the International Military Tribunal at Nuremburg was similarly adopted under United States leadership following the Dayton Accords in the Balkans by the ICTY. This saw the new system of international criminal justice founded on that state's principles of adversarial procedure. However, judges from civil law countries, who have outnumbered those of common law jurisdictions at the ad hoc Tribunals, put the case for more inquisitorial elements in proceedings to offset the delay inherent in adversarial international trials and to provide more expeditious hearings.[76] Vogler described the emergence of a two-dimensional

---

72 *Lubanga* (Judgment on the Appeal of Mr Thomas Lubanga Dyilo against the Decision on the Defence Challenge to Jurisdiction of the Court pursuant to article 19(2)(a) of the Statute of 3 October 2006) ICC-01/04-01/06-OA4 (14 December 2006) paras. 29–35.

73 *Barayagwiza* (Appeal Judgment) Appeals Chamber, ICTR-97-19 (3 November 1999) para. 85; *Kaing Guek Eav alias 'Duch'* (Decision on Request for Release) 001/18-07-2007-ECCC/TC-E39/5 (15 June 2009) para. 35.

74 *Criminal Procedure Code of the Kingdom of Cambodia 2007* (adopted 6 August 2007) arts. 203–218; Yash Ghai, above n. 25, p. 7.

75 Christoph Safferling, *International Criminal Procedure* (Oxford University Press, 2012) pp. 52–57.

76 Richard Vogler, 'Making International Criminal Procedure Work: From Theory to Practice' in Ralph Henham and Mark Findlay, *Exploring the Boundaries of International Criminal Justice* (Ashgate, 2011) p. 106.

approach to international criminal procedure, which attempted to preserve the purest elements of both procedural systems.[77] The ECCC contributes to this debate by adding inquisitorial procedure with international elements in a way that is responsive to local law and conditions.

5.4.1. SHARED PROSECUTIONS: NATIONAL AND INTERNATIONAL

At the ECCC the prosecutorial role is subordinate to that of the Co-Investigating Judge.[78] This represents a departure from international trial practice, including the International Criminal Court (ICC), where the Prosecutor has full control of investigations.[79] Prospective prosecutions engage a two-stage investigative process. The first stage is the initiation of a prosecution by the Co-Prosecutors, one Cambodian and one international, at his or her initiative, or on the basis of a complaint received, to determine whether there is evidence that crimes within the jurisdiction of the ECCC have been committed, and to identify suspects and potential witnesses.[80] The sharing of the prosecutorial function combines the national Co-Prosecutor's knowledge of Cambodia, competence to assess local evidence and ability to communicate with witnesses, with the international Co-Prosecutor's knowledge and skills in applying international investigative standards.

Following preliminary investigations, if the Co-Prosecutors have reason to believe that crimes within the jurisdiction of the ECCC have been committed, they may forward an Introductory Submission to the Co-Investigating Judges, requesting a judicial investigation.[81] Should the case proceed to trial the Co-Prosecutors bear the burden of proving the guilt of the Accused 'beyond reasonable doubt'.[82] However, the importation of this standard is exceptional in inquisitorial procedure, pursuant to which the judges normally assess the evidence according to their 'innermost conviction (*intime conviction*)'.[83]

At trial, the teaming of the national with the international prosecutor engaged local knowledge of the Cambodian community in relation to Khmer

---

77 Ibid. p. 107.

78 ECCC Law Article 23 *new*.

79 Göran Sluiter, 'Due Process and Criminal Procedure in the Cambodian Extraordinary Chambers' (2006) *Journal of International Criminal Justice* 314, 323.

80 ECCC Internal Rules (*Rev 8*) (adopted 3 August 2011) r. 49(1), (2), 50(1).

81 ECCC Internal Rules (*Rev 8*) r. 53(1).

82 ECCC Internal Rules (*Rev 8)* r. 87(1).

83 Sergey Vasiliev, 'Trial Process at the ECCC: the Rise and Fall of the Inquisitorial Paradigm in International Criminal Law ?' in Simon M. Meisenberg and Ignaz Stegmiller (eds.), *The Extraordinary Chambers in the Courts of Cambodia: Assessing their Contribution to International Criminal Law* (Asser Press, 2016) p. 401, citing arts. 321 and 350 Cambodian Code of Criminal Procedure and art. 427 Code of Criminal Procedure of France.

Rouge impunity, with expertise in prosecuting international crimes. In Case 001, National Co-Prosecutor Chea Leang opened the prosecution case. Her remarks captured the historic nature and solemnity of the trial. Here was a Cambodian lawyer, in a Cambodian Court declaring that the time for justice had come, albeit over 31 years after the overthrow of Democratic Kampuchea.[84] She declared that for all of this time victims of the Khmer Rouge had demanded justice, accountability and answers to questions as to the fate of their lost family members and friends. Until now the government and the international community had failed them. The Court would, however, help end their suffering and establish how victimisation on a massive scale had occurred in Cambodia. 'History demands it' and the purpose of the tribunal was to establish the truth surrounding Duch's crimes so that such atrocities will never be repeated. Chea Leang sought to dispel myths concerning the Khmer Rouge and the version of history concerning them that many Cambodians had grown up with, noting that some still view the Khmer Rouge has having the 'best of intentions.'[85]

She spoke of peasants being inspired by Sihanouk to rise up against Lon Nol and to join the Khmer Rouge, thus swelling their ranks in a time of political flux in Cambodia. The Court was shown a film archive documenting the forced removal of hundreds of thousands of people from Phnom Penh, many of whom died of exposure or starvation during the journey.[86]

Chea Leang recounted that others were mercilessly purged as perceived enemies of the Khmer Rouge who claimed 'to keep you is no gain, to kill you is no loss.'[87] She explained the purpose of Khmer Rouge security centres throughout the countryside, and cited evidence from the DC-Cam archive of the existence of 380 mass graves linked to the centres. She then outlined the conditions under which detainees were held at S-21.[88]

Following Chea Leang's opening statement, the international Co-Prosecutor Robert Petit, argued the limits of Duch's confessions and acceptance of responsibility. While Petit acknowledged the benefits of Duch's cooperation with the Court in corroborating important evidence, he highlighted the gulf between Duch's present contrition and his past commitment to the Khmer Rouge revolutionary agenda. Petit described Duch's dedication and efficiency as Chairman of S-21 and argued that he exercised direct and independent control over the functioning of the institution, which was a major engine of the CPK's criminal machinery.[89] As Chairman, Duch had a close connection to the CPK

84 Transcript of Trial Proceedings *Kaing Guek Eav 'Duch'* 001/18-07-2007/TC, Day 2, (31 March 2009) p. 2.

85 Ibid. pp. 2–5.

86 Ibid. p. 4.

87 Ibid. p. 8.

88 Ibid. pp. 5, 9–11, 31–34.

89 Ibid. p. 55.

Standing Committee and knew of the importance of CPK's policy of smashing enemies of the regime through the S-21 apparatus he administered. Petit argued that this justified the mode of liability of joint criminal enterprise, in addition to the forms of responsibility specified in the Closing Order: commission, ordering, command responsibility, planning, instigation, aiding and abetting.[90] Bringing the skills of an international prosecutor to bear in the case, Petit argued that while guilt had been admitted, there was scope for further exploration of the facts in order to establish the truth.[91] Thus, the Co-Prosecution partnership broadened the representative nature of the proceedings of the ECCC through knowledge of the local context of the crimes and international prosecutorial experience.

The Internal Rules anticipate the possibility of disagreement between the Co-Prosecutors and make provision for review of the matter by the Pre-Trial Chamber (PTC).[92] There is no appeal from decisions of the PTC.[93] In December 2008, the international Co-Prosecutor filed a disagreement between himself and his Cambodian counterpart concerning the charging and judicial investigation of five new suspects whom he considered fell within the personal jurisdiction of the ECCC, and whose prosecution would lead to a more comprehensive accounting of Khmer Rouge crimes.[94]

However, the Cambodian Co-Prosecutor argued that new prosecutions should not be activated, on the basis of several factors: Cambodia's political instability and need for national reconciliation; the spirit of the ECCC Agreement and Law; and the temporary nature of the Tribunal and its limited budget. Prioritising the trials in progress of the five defendants already in detention was to be preferred, she contended, in light of the small number of trials envisioned in the founding documents.[95]

In reaching a decision on the disagreement, the PTC failed to achieve the necessary supermajority, (discussed at section 5.5.2), with the result that pursuant to Internal Rule 71(4) the action of the international Co-Prosecutor by default was executable. This meant that the international Co-Prosecutor could forward 'new Introductory Submissions to the Co-Investigating Judges with a request to open judicial investigations.'[96]

90 Ibid. p. 56.

91 Ibid. pp. 57–62.

92 ECCC Internal Rules (*Ver 8*) r. 71.

93 ECCC Agreement art. 7(4).

94 Pursuant to Rule 71 (2); See Robert Petit and Anees Ahmed, 'A Review of the Jurisprudence of the Khmer Rouge Tribunal' (2010) 8 *Northwestern Journal of International Human Rights* 165, 172.

95 'Statement of the Co-Prosecutors' (ECCC, Office of the Co-Prosecutors, 5 January 2009); And see Statement of the National Co-Prosecutor Regarding Case File 003, 10 May 2011, available at: https://www.eccc.gov.kh/en/articles/statement-national-co-prosecutor-regarding-case-file-003/, accessed 4 July 2016.

96 Consideration of the Pre-Trial Chamber Regarding the Disagreement between the Co-Prosecutors pursuant to Internal Rule 71 001/18-11-ECCC/PTC (18 August 2009) para. 45.

5.4.2. SHARED DEFENCE

Matching the Co-Prosecution, each accused may have Co-Defence counsel, one Cambodian and one international lawyer. The Co-Defence is supported by legal consultants and case managers. The Defence Support Section also supports the Co-Lawyers by undertaking legal research to assist in the preparation of cases, as well as providing office facilities and other practical assistance.

In Cases 001 and 002/01, the international defence lawyers all came with experience acquired at the ICTY, ICTR and SCSL where dual-party-led adversarial defence applied. Accustomed to vigorous testing of the prosecution evidence and actively seeking out exculpatory evidence, the international defence teams under the ECCC procedure could not conduct their own investigations or approach witnesses unless the Office of the Co-Investigating judges organised a confrontation.[97] While the national defence counsel brought their knowledge of the local procedural system to their task, the international defence lawyers seemed resistant to the inquisitorial investigation process. The international prosecutors from predominantly common law backgrounds also had difficulty adjusting to, and accepting the unfamiliar procedure, but international defence counsel dissatisfaction with their more restricted role at the ECCC generated ongoing tension between them and other organs of the Court, particularly as Case 002 proceeded.[98] While challenges in the interests of fair trial procedure are legitimate, the defence strategy in Case 002/01 stretched the boundaries of inquisitorial truth-finding to make it as adversarial as possible.[99] This is discussed further at Chapter seven, sections 7.5.3–7.6 and 7.6.3– and Chapter nine, section 9.6–9.7.

5.4.3. SHARED INVESTIGATIONS

The role of the Co-Investigating Judge is shared equally between a Cambodian and an international judge. Together they have a duty to conduct separate impartial and independent investigations, ensuring the protection of the rights of the accused.[100] Not bound by the Co-Prosecutors' submissions, the Co-Investigating Judges conclude an investigation by issuing a Closing Order, which either indicts a charged person and sends him/her to trial, or dismisses the case.[101]

---

97 Vasiliev, above n. 83, p. 403.

98 Ibid. pp. 401–403; Alex Bates, 'Transitional Justice in Cambodia: An Analytical Report' (Atlas Project, October 2010) p. 47.

99 Vasiliev, above n. 83, p. 406.

100 ECCC Internal Rules (*Rev 8*) r. 55(5).

101 ECCC Internal Rules *(Rev 8)* r. 67(1).

In inquisitorial proceedings the Investigating Judge may arrange site visits as investigative action to 'ascertain the truth' as to the allegations.[102] Confrontations may also be arranged between witnesses, civil parties and the charged person.[103] The pre-trial investigation of the trial of Kaing Guek Eav (alias Duch) included a visit to the former S-21 site, also known as the Tuol Sleng prison and now the Cambodian Genocide Museum, in Phnom Penh. They also arranged a re-enactment of alleged events at the Choeung Ek execution site on the outskirts of Phnom Penh. The Co-Investigating Judges took Kaing Guek Eav, his legal counsel and surviving detainees of the detention centre, two of whom were civil parties to the criminal action, to the S-21 prison site. Duch wept as he went with the Co-Investigating Judges through the former detention centre. He answered some questions put to him by the civil parties and publicly apologised to the S-21 victims.[104] The Choeung Ek visit was public and media coverage was permitted.[105] There, Duch cried openly and apologised to victims as he watched re-enactments of Khmer Rouge soldiers executing S-21 detainees, including babies by slamming them against a tree.[106] While this was a staged event, it marked the opening of dialogue around the crimes from the investigative stage.

At any time during an investigation, the Co-Prosecutors, a charged person or civil party (discussed at section 5.6 ff) may participate by requesting investigative actions which they consider useful for the conduct of the investigation.[107] The Co-Prosecutors and lawyers for the other parties also have a right to consult the original case file, subject to reasonable limitations, to ensure the continuity of the proceedings.[108] In Case 002, the multiple accused persons denied criminal responsibility and were less cooperative in the pre-trial investigation. They did not admit facts, refused interviews and exercised their right to remain silent throughout the investigation. In addition, a more combative defence strategy was engaged from the outset of the case.[109] There were multiple challenges to the case file and the decisions of the Co-Investigating Judges on requests for

---

102 ECCC Internal Rules (*Rev 8*) r. 55(5).

103 ECCC Internal Rules (*Rev 8*) r. 58(4), (5); Brianne McGonigle Leyh, *Procedural Justice? Victim Participation in International Criminal Proceedings* (Intersentia, 2011) p. 187.

104 Permissible under ECCC Internal Rules (*Rev 8*) r. 58(5).

105 ECCC Internal Rules (*Rev 8*) r. 56(2)(b); See 'Duch to Re-enact his Crimes', *Phnom Penh Post* (22 February 2008).

106 Ian MacKinnon, 'Khmer Leader Leads Judges to Killing Fields', *Guardian* (27 February 2008): http://www.theguardian.com/world/2008/feb/27cambodia.warcrimes; Rosalind Ryan, 'Torture Victims meet Top Khmer Rouge Inquisitor' (28 February 2008): http://www.theguardian.com/world/2008/feb27/cambodia.

107 ECCC Internal Rules (*Rev 8)* r. 55(10).

108 ECCC Internal Rules (*Rev 8)* r. 55(11).

109 Vasiliev, above n. 83, p. 404.

investigative actions, as well as allegations of partiality at the Office of the CIJ.[110] Some of the challenges were brought before the Trial Chamber. International defence counsel 'mistrust' of the confidential pre-trial investigation increased in the context of failure by the Cambodian authorities to summon senior officials as witnesses in Case 002 and to arrest suspects in Cases 003 and 004.[111] The ramifications in Case 002/01 are raised at Chapter nine, section 9.6.

As discussed at Chapter four, section 4.5.4, the judicial investigations of Cases 003 and 004 were stymied by the Cambodian government's opposition to the prosecution of additional Khmer Rouge members, and obfuscation in the Office of the Co-Investigating Judges.[112] In April 2011, Case 003 was closed by the Co-Investigating judges, You Bunleng and Siegfried Blunk.[113] The public outcry against the closure reflected the social significance the ECCC had acquired. Numerous civil society groups released a collective press release expressing concern at the closure, which they viewed as obstructing justice and hindering the people's right to know the facts of the Khmer Rouge regime.[114] Although the case was reopened by reserve international Co-Investigating Judge Kasper-Ansermet, the events exposed the fault-line in the ECCC cooperation scheme.[115] However, the public response and the UN's decision not to withdraw from the joint venture suggested a commitment to what the ECCC might achieve despite the government's desire to block some of its processes.

Following the appointment of international Co-Investigating Judge Mark Harman in October 2012, the investigations of Cases 003 and 004 were continued but without the cooperation of the Cambodian Co-Investigating Judge or the Cambodian Co-Prosecutor. By 2015, hundreds of witness interviews, and the investigation of multiple crime sites had been undertaken.[116] On 9 December

---

110 See *Nuon Chea and Others* (Decision on Ieng Sary's Appeal Against the Letter concerning Request for Information Concerning Legal Officer David Boyle) 002/19-09-2007/ECCC/PTC (28 August 2008); *Nuon Chea and Others* (Decision on Ieng Sary's Application to Disqualify Co-Investigating Judge Marcel Lemonde 002/19-09-2007/ECCC/PTC (9 December 2009); *Nuon Chea and Others* (Decision on Ieng Sary's Request for Appropriate Measures Concerning Certain Statements by Prime Minister Hun Sen Challenging the Independence of the Pre-Trial Chamber Judges Katinka Lahuis and Rowan Downing) 002/19-09-2007/ECCC/PTC (30 November 2009).

111 Vasiliev, above n. 83, p. 403.

112 OSJI Report Political Interference, above n. 43, p. 13.

113 'Statement of the Co-Investigating Judges' Extraordinary Chambers in the Courts of Cambodia, ECCC Press Release, (29 April 2011); Ciorciari above n. 47, pp. 175–184.

114 Cambodia: *Civil Society Expresses Concern over Recent developments in the Extraordinary Chambers in the Courts of Cambodia and Urges the International Community to Speak Out* Asian Human Rights Commission (20 May 2011): http:///humanrights.asia/new/forwarded-news/AHRC-FPR-025-2011.

115 Order on Resuming the Judicial Investigation 003/07-09-2009-ECCC-OCIJ (2 December 2009); 'Statement by the Co-Investigating Judges Regarding Case 003' (Extraordinary Chambers in the Courts of Cambodia, Office of the Co-Investigating Judges, 28 February 2013).

116 Open Society Justice Initiative, *Recent Developments at the Extraordinary Chambers in the courts of Cambodia* (OSJI, March 2015) p. 4.

2015, Yim Tith was charged with genocide, crimes against humanity and war crimes in Case 004.[117] He presented at the ECCC with defence counsel for the reading of the charges. On 27 March 2015 suspect Ao An was also arrested in Case 004.[118] Judge Harman also proceeded to charge suspects Im Chaem (Case 004) and Meas Muth (Case 003) *in absentia*, since the Cambodian authorities had failed to execute their arrest warrants.[119] There were renewed diplomatic discussions between Sok An, Cambodian Deputy Prime Minister, and Stephen Matthias, the UN's Assistant Secretary-General for Legal Affairs in November 2015 about the government's lack of cooperation in violation of the ECCC Agreement. On 14 December 2015, Meas Muth appeared voluntarily at the ECCC for the reading of charges against him.[120] With new international Co-Investigating Judge, Michael Bohlander in place from August 2015, the Court foresaw completion of the Case 003 and 004 investigations by the end of 2016.[121]

Expressive statements indicating a renewed spirit of cooperation between the parties raised hopes that the ECCC would complete its mandate despite the political obstacles strewn along its path. However, the standoff over the investigations has had consequences affecting the carriage of Case 002/02. These have been of both a positive and a negative nature. As reported by trial monitors, the new investigations have brought to light a large swath of evidence relevant to Case 002/02 which is still in progress. At a 'key documents' meeting held by the Trial Chamber in August 2015 the Co-Prosecutors were permitted to read out a number of Written Records of Interviews (WRIs) from the Case 003 and 004 investigations.[122] While many of those who made the statements will not be called as witnesses, the Co-Defence objected to the records being presented in view of the fact that those who made the statements had not been cross-examined. The Chamber admitted only the statements required for the purpose of corroboration and proof of facts other than those proving guilt, but soon after, Nuon Chea's international Co-Defence counsel walked out of the meeting.

117 Open Society Justice Initiative, *Recent Developments at the Extraordinary Chambers in the courts of Cambodia* (OSJI, December 2015) pp. 4–5.

118 ECCC, Statement of the International Co-Investigating Judge Regarding Case 004 (27 March 2015).

119 Open Society Justice Initiative, *Recent Developments at the Extraordinary Chambers in the courts of Cambodia* (OSJI, March 2015) p. 5; Open Society Justice Intitiative, Recent Developments at the Extraordinary Chambers in the courts of Cambodia (OSJI, October 2015) p. 6.

120 Open Society Justice Initiative, *Recent Developments at the Extraordinary Chambers in the courts of Cambodia* (OSJI, December 2015) p. 5.

121 Open Society Justice Initiative, *Recent Developments at the Extraordinary Chambers in the courts of Cambodia* (OSJI, October 2015) p. 6.

122 Open Society Justice Initiative, *Recent Developments at the Extraordinary Chambers in the courts of Cambodia* (OSJI, October 2015) p. 3.

Khieu Samphân's Co-Defence counsel also objected to the admission of the WRIs. They considered that the public reading was prejudicial and that there was no way to ensure the limited use of the material.[123]

In addition, the Co-Prosecution has submitted to the Co-Defence a large cache of documentary evidence from Cases 003 and 004 to be used against the accused in Case 002/02. Admitted to the proceedings as newly discovered evidence the documents may both build the Co-Prosecution case and can be used by the Co-Defence where they consider material is exculpatory. The volume of new material placed additional demands on the Co-Defence and overall the circumstances caused considerable angst between the Court and the parties as Case 002/02 proceeded. The Co-Defence argued it had an effect on the right of the accused to prepare an adequate defence. However, it also provided material for the Co-Defence in the preparation of its appeal in Case 002/01.[124]

5.5. THE COMPOSITION OF CHAMBERS AND JUDICIAL DECISION-MAKING

The ECCC Law established the Court within the existing Cambodian court structure of three Chambers.[125] The PTC consists of three Cambodian judges and two international judges responsible for the settlement of disagreements between the Co-Investigating Judges and Co-Prosecutors.[126] In the Trial Chamber there are a majority of three Cambodian judges and two international judges. The Supreme Court Chamber which serves as the Appeal Chamber has seven judges: four Cambodian and three international.[127] The ratio of national to international judges reflects the UN compromise over the Cambodian government's insistence on majority control of the trials.

5.5.1. THE JUDICIARY

All judges are appointed by the Cambodian Supreme Court of the Magistracy: the national judges according to existing Cambodian procedure; and the foreign judges from a list of nominations by the UN Secretary-General.[128] The

123 Ibid.

124 Ibid. pp. 3–4.

125 ECCC Law art 2 *new*, art 47 *bis* new. Simultaneously, Article 31 of the Agreement provides 'the present Agreement shall apply as law within the Kingdom of Cambodia following its ratification in accordance with the relevant provisions of the internal law of the Kingdom of Cambodia regarding competence to conclude treaties.'

126 ECCC Agreement art. 7.

127 ECCC Agreement art. 3.

128 ECCC Law art. 11 *new*.

selection of Cambodian judges from the existing domestic pool inevitably risked engagement of some judges with incomplete qualifications and/or histories of judicial bias. Indeed, the ECCC had some early judicial conduct challenges to face. These included allegations of judicial bias and executive interference, along with corruption among Court officials and government employees.[129] Exposure by court monitors of malpractice induced censure through the national and international media, and in January 2008, the introduction of ECCC's Code of Judicial Ethics.[130] While the adequacy of such measures is open to question, they nevertheless represent ECCC responsiveness to charges of impropriety, and recognition that Court officers are not above the law and international standards of fair trial process.

The ECCC measures also signal that the government is restrained from taking charge of politically sensitive cases, as it reportedly has in domestic cases, while publicly raising judicial independence as the imperative of fair prosecutions.[131] Where the measures adopted by the ECCC fall short of international expectations, it should be remembered that their target is national judicial competence, which has been undermined by governmental interference. The ECCC creates the opportunity for both training and correction in criminal process with international assistance, as an investment in Cambodia's future governance. As the Special Rapporteur noted, there is an expectation that the ECCC operating within the Cambodian legal system will function as a 'model Court', enabling the sharing of good practice within the wider judiciary in order to gradually lift standards which have hitherto been hampered by inadequate training in fundamental principles of natural justice, the rule of law and proper fair trial practice.[132]

5.5.2. DECISION-MAKING BY SUPERMAJORITY OR DEFAULT

The Cambodian majority in the Chambers is offset by the operation of a 'supermajority' in judicial decision-making to inhibit control of processes in compliance with executive dictates.[133] The ECCC Law and the ECCC Agreement provide that unanimous decisions are to be attempted in all Chambers, but

129 Ellis, above n. 44, p. 21.

130 *Code of Judicial Ethics of the Extraordinary Chambers in the Courts of Cambodia*: http: www.eccc.gov.kh/sites/default/files/legal-documents/Code_of_judicial_ENG.pdf (September 2008). An Independent Counsellor was also designated to address concerns surrounding the adequacy of anti-corruption measures in human resources administration.

131 Surya P. Subedi, *Report of the Special Rapporteur on the Situation of Human Rights in Cambodia*. UN Doc. A/HRC/15/46 (16 September 2010) paras. 40–45.

132 Ibid. para. 59.

133 Steven R. Ratner, 'Justice for the Khmer Rouge? Sir Ninian Stephen and the United Nations Group of Experts for Cambodia' in Timothy L.H. McCormack and Cheryl Saunders (eds.), *Sir Ninian Stephen: A Tribute* (Melbourne University Publishing, 2007) pp. 206, 213.

where this is not possible, a majority decision must include the affirmative vote of at least one international judge.[134] The requirement is the drafters' attempt to counteract the possibility of executive interference or decisions inconsistent with international standards. However, where a supermajority is not achieved, the decision simply reflects the views of the majority and the minority without legal force.[135] This creates the possibility of a prosecution failing by virtue of the Cambodian judges' refusal to convict a defendant because of judicial bias or political interference. It also risks the outcome of what could be perceived as an UN-sponsored mock trial.[136] However, such an outcome will also record judicial practice, which represents Cambodian legal culture (to its own detriment) before the Cambodian people generally and the victims of the Khmer Rouge in particular.

Focus on the potential of stalemate arising from a failed supermajority also distracts public attention from the positive element of the supermajority. The mechanism provides inherent scope for expanded communication between national and international judges. While there may be pressure on the international judges to persuade at least one national judge to adjudicate according to international legal precedent or principle, there is also scope for greater local wisdom and understanding to infuse judgments as the judges communicate with each other. This is explored further in Chapter nine.

Thus, while the composition of the judiciary and shared prosecutorial and investigative functions were the result of fraught negotiations between the UN and the Cambodian government, they bring to ECCC proceedings the benefits of local knowledge combined with international expertise. The communications integral to teamwork therefore underpin the investigation and prosecution of crimes. This may enhance the representation of national and international interests throughout the trials.

5.6. THE CIVIL PARTY ACTION

Almost every civil law jurisdiction makes provision for victims of crimes to join a civil claim to the criminal prosecution, or to initiate private prosecutions.[137] The civil party action recognises the accused person as answerable to both the individual harmed and the public law.[138] Lapie attributed the justification of the civil party action in France to the Frankish idea of monetary compensation as

---

134 ECCC Law art. 14; ECCC Agreement art. 4.
135 ECCC Agreement art. 4; ECCC Law art. 14.
136 Meijer, above n. 8, p. 220.
137 McGonigle Leyh, above n. 103, p. 79.
138 Ibid.

the first attempt at modifying the *lex talionis*, the law of retaliation.[139] Historically, the action merged the reformative and deterrent aims of punishment for crime with the idea of moral reparations designed to restore matters to conditions prior to the commission of the crime.[140] The notion of criminal justice as punitive and restorative is thus embedded through an action retaining civil character before the criminal tribunal within a common process. The Tribunal however, gives judgment on two separate actions: civil and criminal. In practice the civil petitioner may alert the prosecution to commission of a criminal offence; provide valuable evidence for the trial; and permit a degree of relief to victims by means of participation and reparation.[141]

The civil party action recognises certain victim participation rights in trial proceedings, including the pre-trial phase. These are generally available as an incident of the victim's claim for compensation. While the rights of civil parties vary between civil law jurisdictions, they may include the rights: to be heard in court without taking an oath; to examine the dossier or case file; to make requests for certain investigations (although limited to their civil claim); to be represented by counsel; to put questions to witnesses; to lead and challenge evidence; and to make closing arguments.[142] However, the civil claim is subordinate to the purpose of the criminal proceedings. In complex trials, or those where civil claims would delay or overburden the court, victims may be required to make their claim through a separate civil case.[143]

The civil party action of France should be distinguished from the status of victims in criminal proceedings as subsidiary or auxiliary prosecutors, or private prosecutors. Auxiliary prosecutors are used in Germany although on a limited basis. Where the state has decided not to prosecute, a victim may nevertheless force a prosecution, usually by securing the permission of the court and the public prosecutor, who is then required to take over the case alongside the auxiliary prosecutor and their legal counsel. The auxiliary prosecutor's participation rights are not limited to her compensation claim and she will not be obliged to pay the costs of the accused in the event of an acquittal.[144]

The auxiliary prosecutor may also be referred to as a private prosecutor. Private prosecutions are common to both civil law and common law jurisdictions. In Germany, private prosecutions are begun where a victim's counsel prompts investigations by the police or the judicial magistrate, and charges are brought as of right by victims who are also entitled to conduct a prosecution. The private prosecution was recognised under the English common law. Some State courts

139 P.O. Lapie, 'The Partie Civile in the Criminal Law of France' (1928) 10 *Journal of Comparative Legislation and International Law* 33, 45.

140 Ibid. p. 34.

141 Ibid. p. 36.

142 McGonigle Leyh, above n. 103, p. 80.

143 Ibid. pp. 80–81.

144 Ibid. p. 82.

of the United States also permit a private individual or their family to act as a prosecutor subject to the discretion of the trial judge.[145]

5.6.1. DESIGNING THE ECCC VICTIM PARTICIPATION SCHEME

Cambodian criminal procedure made provision for civil action in criminal proceedings.[146] In addition to acting as witnesses, direct victims of crimes may participate as civil parties in active criminal investigations, seek damages and contribute to the process of prosecution.[147] The ECCC's founding documents contained only a single reference to possible civil party rights by granting appeal rights to victims against decisions of the Trial Chamber under Article 36 *new* of the ECCC Law. Therefore, it fell to the drafters of the ECCC Internal Rules to determine the scheme of rights for victims before the ECCC. Against the background of recognition of victim participatory rights in ICC proceedings, it was logical that the internationalised ECCC would include some similar provisions. Thus, consistent with the spirit of Cambodian law and evolving international practice, the ECCC's Rules Committee, led by French civil lawyer and Co-Investigating Judge Marcel Lemonde, incorporated the civil party action within ECCC procedure. However, by virtue of the ECCC's special character within the Cambodian court structure, reparations were limited to collective and moral awards (see section 5.6.5 below).[148]

Under the ECCC victim participation scheme, a victim of a crime coming within the jurisdiction of the ECCC may apply to join a case under investigation by the Co-Investigating Judges or proceedings before the Trial Chamber as a civil party, provided he or she can demonstrate that they have suffered injury (physical, material or psychological) as a direct consequence of such crime.[149] The ECCC Internal Rules do not limit civil parties to residents or nationals of Cambodia, which allows for the participation of members of the Cambodian diaspora.[150]

As a civil party, a victim is permitted to participate in ECCC criminal proceedings by support of the prosecution and may seek collective and moral reparations.[151] Under the original version of the Internal Rules, the civil

---

145 Ibid. p. 83. McGonigle cites New York State and West Virginia as examples.

146 *Criminal Procedure Code of the Kingdom of Cambodia 2007* arts. 2, 5, 13.

147 David Boyle, 'The Rights of Victims: Participation, Representation, Protection and Reparation' (2006) 4 *Journal of International Criminal Justice* 307, 310.

148 Mahdev Mohan, 'The Paradox of Victim-Centrism: Victim Participation at the Khmer Rouge Tribunal' (2009) 9 *International Criminal Law Review* 733, 745.

149 ECCC Internal Rules (*Rev. 8*) 3 r. 23(1).

150 ECCC Internal Rules (*Rev. 8*) r. 23(2).

151 ECCC Internal Rules (*Rev. 8*) r. 23 *bis* (1).

petitioner's party status attracted procedural rights similar, though not identical to those of the charged person during the investigation, or the accused at trial.[152]

Victims may be called as witnesses, and also participate as complainants by lodging information or a written complaint with the Co-Prosecutors through the Victims Support Section, alleging crimes within the jurisdiction of the ECCC.[153] This may not only provide evidence for ongoing investigations, but lead to the initiation of new investigations.

5.6.2. ADMITTING CIVIL PARTIES TO ECCC TRIALS

The initial version of the ECCC Internal Rules adopted in June 2007 specified only that there must be sufficient information to allow the verification of the civil party applicant's claim as to injury, or that 'evidence tending to show the guilt of an alleged perpetrator was to be attached to applications.'[154] While the ECCC Internal Rules made provision for a Victims Unit to assist victims in lodging complaints and submitting civil party applications, due to funding problems the Unit did not come into existence until the middle of 2008, two years after the Court began its operations.[155] In the interim the ECCC authorised the Offices of the Co-Prosecutors and the Co-Investigating Judges to process victim applications.[156] In the absence of a fully resourced Victims Unit, Cambodian non-governmental organisations with very little guidance or assistance from the Court, worked with victims on a wide scale in almost every aspect of the civil party application and submission process; from educating potential applicants to helping them complete the necessary admission forms, to following up the progress of applications.[157] By the time the Unit opened its doors more than 500 victim complaints and civil party applications for Cases 001 and 002 had been received by the Court, largely as the result of the groundwork performed by Cambodian civil society organisations.[158]

---

152 ECCC Internal Rules (adopted 12 June 2007) r. 23(6).

153 ECCC Internal Rules (*Rev. 8*) Rule 12(1)(a).

154 ECCC Internal Rules (adopted 12 June 2007) r. 23(6).

155 ECCC Internal Rules (adopted 12 June 2007) art. 12(2)(c), (d).

156 'Practice Direction 001' Extraordinary Chambers in the Courts of Cambodia, (5 October 2007); See James P. Bair, 'From the Numbers who Died to Those who Survived: Victim Participation in the Extraordinary Chambers in the Courts of Cambodia' (2009) 31 *University of Hawaii Law Review* 507, 531, 538.

157 Eric Stover, 'Confronting Duch: Civil Party Participation in Case 001 at the Extraordinary Chambers in the Courts of Cambodia' (2011) 93 *International Review of the Red Cross* 503, 516.

158 *UN-Backed Tribunal Processing over 500 Complaints* UN News Centre (7 February 2008) http://www.un.org/apps/news/story.asp?NewsID=25544&Cr+cambodia&Cr1.

In vetting the applications the Co-Investigating Judges applied a *prima facie* standard of review by assessing applications as 'more likely to be true than not'.[159] The applications were assessed on the same basis when sent to the Trial Chamber.[160] However, at the initial hearing of Case 001 the Trial Chamber added the requirement of proof of identity of applicants, the sufficiency of which would be assessed by the Court on a case-by-case basis. As the trial commenced, 93 civil party applications were approved, activating all civil party rights to participation in the trial process. The civil parties were organised into four groups, each represented at trial by teams of national and international legal counsel. Towards the end of the trial, a defence challenge to the sufficiency of evidence of 24 civil party applications resulted in lengthy debates on the issue. The challenge was attributable at least in part to the ECCC's lack of preparedness to accommodate the large number of victims who sought inclusion in the trials, and inadequate vetting of civil party applications.[161] Concerned at the delay the issue was causing, the Court decided both matters should be resolved at the point of the trial judgment. This left the rights of the 24 civil parties intact for the remainder of the trial.

5.6.3. CIVIL PARTIES AND RECONCILIATION

While a number of population surveys revealed strong support for trials of the Khmer Rouge in the years before formation of the ECCC, they did not examine how victims would engage with the proposed court beyond witnessing retributive process.[162] The availability of the civil party action in ECCC proceedings brought victims forward as representatives of a previously hidden constituency. The victim constituency came from within and beyond Cambodia. It included members of the Cambodian diaspora who became refugees as a result of Khmer Rouge policies, Cambodian survivors still living within the country, and family

159 McGonigle Leyh, above n. 103, p. 182.

160 Ibid.

161 Youk Chhang, 'Sad Situation for Civil Parties', *Phnom Penh Post* (1 October 2009): http://www.phnompenhpost.com/national/sad-situation-civil-parties.

162 Suzannah Linton, *Reconciliation in Cambodia* (DC-Cam, 2004) pp. 60–61; Laura McGrew, 'Truth, Justice, Reconciliation and Peace in Cambodia: 20 Years after the Khmer Rouge' – Research Paper Presented to the Peace Research and Education Association 2000 Conference, Kingston, Ontario, 3 June 2000; *Voices of Cambodia: Calling the Khmer Rouge to Account – The Survey: Results and Recommendations*, at: http://advocacynet.org/resource/424#General_Recommendations; *Khmer Institute for Democracy. Survey of the Khmer Rouge Regime and Khmer Rouge Tribunal 2004*: http://www.bigpond.com.kh/users/kid/KRG-Tribunal.htm; William A. Burke-White, 'Preferences Matter: Conversations with Cambodian People on the Prosecution of the Khmer Rouge Leadership' in Jaya Ramji and Beth Van Schaak (eds.), *Bringing the Khmer Rouge to Justice: prosecuting Mass Violence before the Cambodian Courts* (Edwin Mellen Press, 2005) pp. 97–126.

members of Cambodians and foreigners who died at the hands of the Khmer Rouge.

In March 2008, the PTC linked civil party inclusion in trial proceedings with the ECCC's 'stated pursuit of national reconciliation.'[163] In a decision on the right of legally represented civil parties to participate in provisional detention appeals, the PTC ruled that civil parties could participate in all criminal proceedings, except those from which they were explicitly excluded. The Chamber also cited the relevant international standards on victim participation in criminal proceedings and examined the practices of other international criminal tribunals. The PTC found that the ECCC victim inclusion scheme was not modelled on the 'prescriptive procedure' adopted by the ICC. Rather, ECCC proceedings were to be 'fair and adversarial and preserve a balance between the rights of parties.'[164] Where the balance is in jeopardy the Chamber is empowered take action to restore it, and did so in the circumstances of the case by permitting the accused to make written submissions in response to oral submissions delivered without notice. Thus, the PTC enforced the international legal obligation to provide those who claim to be victims of human rights or international humanitarian law violations with equal access to justice.[165] The expressive action affirmed the civil party's right to be heard in proceedings and simultaneously expanded the discourse of the trial.

However, though the Internal Rules offered potentially broad participatory rights to victims from the pre-trial stage, it became clear that the ECCC would not permit civil parties to control or disrupt the proceedings.[166] The civil party right to address the court directly could only be exercised sparingly, and following amendments to the Internal Rules legally represented civil parties were required to make oral submissions to the Court through their lawyers.[167] More broadly, the Internal Rules required that ECCC proceedings be conducted 'within a reasonable time.'[168] Ultimately, this determined the nature and extent

---

163 *Nuon Chea and Others* (Decision on Civil Party Participation in Provisional Detention Appeals) 002/19-09-2007-ECCC/OCIJ (PTC01) (20 March 2008) paras. 37–40 citing United Nations General Assembly Resolution 57/228 and the ECCC *Internal Rules*, Preamble.

164 ECCC Internal Rules (*Rev. 1*) (adopted 1 February 2008) r. 21(1)(a).

165 *Nuon Chea and Others* (Decision on Civil Party Participation in Provisional Detention Appeals) 002/19-09-2007-ECCC/OCIJ (PTC01) 20 March 2008, paras. 30–31. See *Declaration of the Basic Principles for Victims of Crime and Abuse of Power*, Adopted by General Assembly Resolution 40/34, (29 November 1985), Principle 6(a); *Basic Principles and Guidelines on the Right to a Remedy and Reparation for Victims of Gross Violations of International Human Rights Law and Serious Violations of International Humanitarian Law*, adopted by the United Nations General Assembly by Resolution 60/147, 16 December 2005; (2006) 13 IHRR 907.

166 McGonigle Leyh, above n. 103, pp. 190–191 discussing civil party Theary Seng's statements and conduct in the Pre-Trial Chamber as she sought the right to address the Court directly and without legal counsel.

167 ECCC Internal Rules (*Rev. 8*) r. 23 *ter*.

168 ECCC Internal Rules (*Rev. 8*) r. 21(4).

of civil party participation at the ECCC. I discuss in Chapter seven how the Trial Chamber's approach to civil party participation nonetheless fostered dialogue in the proceedings between victims and other trial actors.

5.6.4. MODIFYING THE CIVIL PARTY SCHEME

With over 4000 civil party applications received as the second trial, Case 002, approached, the Court introduced measures to 'streamline' civil party participation in trial proceedings.[169] Pursuant to amendments to the Internal Rules, civil party participation during trials became collective, except at the pre-trial stage where individual civil party participation is still possible. At any time during an investigation, the civil party may 'request the Co-Investigating Judges to interview her, question witnesses, go to a site, order expertise or collect other evidence on her behalf.'[170] Civil party requests for investigative actions have had substantive effects. In Case 002, forced marriage charges were added to the indictment following a submission by civil party representatives.[171] Similarly, in Case 004, the international Co-Prosecutor's decision to investigate crimes against minority group the Kampuchea Krom, followed a civil party investigative request.[172]

The legal representation of civil parties was also modified by the appointment of two Lead Co-lawyers, one national and one international, who are authorised to manage the overall strategy, advocacy and interests of the body of civil parties as a single group.[173] The Lead Co-lawyers are expected to achieve consensus among the individual civil party lawyers and adopt a coordinated approach to victim representation.[174] In a study of civil party participation at the ECCC following Case 001, legal professional respondents associated with the Court considered that the stable presence in the courtroom and coordinating work of the Lead Co-lawyers 'facilitates communication between the court and the civil parties.'[175] Nevertheless, individual civil party representatives can no

---

169 '7th Plenary Session Concludes' Extraordinary Chambers in the Courts of Cambodia, Press Release (9 February 2010).

170 ECCC Internal Rules (*Rev. 8*) r. 59(5).

171 Co-Lawyers for the Civil Parties' Fourth Investigative Request Concerning Forced Marriages and Sexually Related Crimes, Case No. 002/19-9-2007-ECCC/OCJI (4 December 2009); See Order on Request for Investigative Action Concerning Forced Marriages and Sexually Related Crimes, Case No. 002/19-9-2007-ECCC/OCIJ (18 December 2009).

172 Ciorciari, above n. 47, p. 222 citing ECCC Press Release, Statement by the International Prosecutor Regarding Case File 004 (16 June 2011).

173 ECCC Internal Rules (*Rev 8*) r. 12 *ter* 23(3).

174 ECCC Internal Rules (*Rev 8*) r. 12 *ter* (3).

175 Elisa Hoven, 'Civil Party Participation in Trials of Mass Crimes: A Qualitative Study at the Extraordinary Chambers in the Courts of Cambodia' (2014) 14 *Journal of international Criminal Justice* 81, 100.

longer represent their clients' interests in court without the agreement of the Lead Co-lawyers. Where disagreement on the representation strategy occurs, the Internal Rules are silent on how such disputes may be resolved.[176] In Case 002/01, civil party lawyers for sexual violence victims felt aggrieved that they were not able to challenge the strategy of the Lead Co-lawyers in order to more directly represent the interests of those victims.[177]

However, even with the modifications to the victim participation scheme, the grant of procedural rights to victims of the Khmer Rouge exceeds the provisions of all other international courts, including the ICC. This is because the Court's reparations mandate kept approved civil parties integrated within trial proceedings as Case 002/01 commenced.

5.6.5. REPARATIONS

Reparations may only be awarded where the Chamber is satisfied that the harm suffered by civil parties was caused by the crimes committed by the accused.[178] In the Duch trial, civil parties described their harm and demonstrated the link with the crimes before the Court in the course of their narrative testimony, followed by examination by the judges and other parties. In Case 002, the Trial Chamber provided two avenues for the civil parties to communicate the nature of the harm they had suffered and causation. Civil parties called to provide testimony in the substantive proceedings were able to make general 'statements of suffering' at the end of their testimony. As discussed further at Chapter seven, section 7.5.3.1 such statements were not limited to issues within the scope of the case, 'to the extent that this [did] not infringe the accused's right to a fair trial.'[179] In addition, the court convened separate victim impact hearings for the purpose of reparations. The latter proceedings, while mediated by the judges, assumed a more rigorous adversarial character than the corresponding hearings of the Duch trial. The hearings are discussed in more detail at Chapter seven, sections 7.5.3.2 and 7.5.4.

The Court may award collective and moral reparations to acknowledge victim injury and provide benefits to address the harm.[180] Implicitly, by hearing civil

176 Ciorciari, above n. 47, p. 222.
177 Hoven, above n. 175, p. 101.
178 ECCC Internal Rules *(Rev 8)* r. 23 *quinquies*.
179 Memorandum from President Nil Nonn to All Parties (Case 002/02) on Information on (1) Key Document Presentation Hearings in Case 002/02 and (2) Hearings on Harm Suffered by the Civil Parties in Case 002/02, para. 8; Decision on Request to Recall Civil Party TCCP-187, for Review of Procedure Concerning Civil Parties' Statements of Suffering and Related Motions and Responses (E240, E240/1, E250/1, E267, E267/1 and E267/2) Trial Chamber, (Case File No. 002/19-09-2007-ECCC/TC, 2 May 2013) para. 14.
180 ECCC Internal Rules *(Rev 8)* r. 23 *quinquies* (1).

party statements of suffering through the communication vehicles described above, the Court made possible a further reparative benefit. The possibility of some civil parties being able to tell their stories as representatives of a victim collective in the presence of, and in some cases in conversation with the accused may constitute a non-material benefit.[181]

Reparations may not be monetary payments and there is no ECCC trust fund to finance awards made by the Court.[182] Initially, reparations could only be drawn against the assets of the accused. The limited scope for redress to victims probably resulted from a balancing of factors, including the large potential number of civil parties, the period that has elapsed since commission of the crimes, the diversity of needs among victims and the Court's capacity to provide workable forms of reparation.[183] However, the reparations provisions of the initial version of the Internal Rules were amended in 2010. The Court may now:

> recognise that a specific project sought by the [Civil Party] Lead Co-Lawyers' appropriately gives effect to [an] award and may be implemented. Such project shall have been designed or identified in cooperation with the Victims Support Section and have secured sufficient external funding.[184]

The revision of the scheme to collective participation rather than individual party status for civil parties was accompanied by changes to the Victims Support Section (VSS) powers. Changes to Internal Rules permitted the VSS to develop and implement 'non-judicial programs and measures addressing the broader interests of victims.'[185] Such measures where appropriate may be 'developed and implemented in collaboration with governmental and non-governmental organisations.'[186] The expansion of the VSS mandate was intended to offset the new restrictions on civil party rights and to extend the legacy of the ECCC.[187] The provision for non-judicial measures promised initiatives designed to serve a broader range of victims' interests, including those not directly connected with cases being heard at the ECCC.[188] The VSS, with funding from the UN Trust Fund to End Violence against Women, quickly began a collaborative project with local society organisations to promote gender equality and improve access

181 'The Purpose of Hearing Victims' Suffering': http://www.eccc.gov.kh/en/blog/2013/06/07/purpose-hearing-victims-suffering, citing reasons given by Lead Co-lawyers Pich Ang and Elisabeth Simmoneau Fort.

182 ECCC Internal Rules (*Rev 8)* r. 23 *quinquies* (1).

183 Acquaviva above n 2, 141.

184 ECCC Internal Rules (*Rev.* 8) r. 23 *quinquies* (3)(b).

185 ECCC Internal Rules (*Rev.* 5) rule 12 (*bis*) 3.

186 ECCC Internal Rules (*Rev.* 5) rule 12 (*bis*) 3.

187 Ciorciari, above n. 47, p. 227.

188 ECCC Internal Rules (*Rev.* 5) rule 12 (*bis*) 3; See Open Society Justice Initiative, *Recent Developments at the Extraordinary Chambers in the Courts of Cambodia* (OSJI, 26 March 2010) pp. 1, 26.

to justice for female victims of gender-based violence during the Khmer Rouge regime.[189]

The limited scope for reparations in Case 001 now stands in contrast to the Court's capacity to offer more tangible reparations that may result from communication and collaboration with victim of crimes and their supporters. In Case 002/01 the VSS worked with the Lead Co-lawyers of the civil parties in identifying reparations projects that the ECCC might endorse, and securing funding for projects from external donors in advance of the trial judgment.[190] The Trial Chamber's endorsement of all but one of the 13 proposed projects was for the stated purpose of demonstrating 'solidarity' with the civil parties of the case and other victims who may benefit from implementation of the approved projects.[191] Thus, while recognition of victims' rights at the ECCC was positive expressive action, the expanded representation made possible by the ECCC victims' participation and reparations scheme also had clear communicative value.

5.7. OTHER ECCC INQUISITORIAL ELEMENTS

In general, inquisitorial trial proceedings are more expeditious because the evidence has already been assembled in a case file prepared by judicial officers following an extensive judicial investigation of the alleged criminal matter. In addition, procedural motions known to delay adversarial trials are addressed at pre-trial hearings. At the ECCC with both the indictment and the case file before them, the trial judges have knowledge of the general form and direction of the case. While the accused and all other parties have access to the case file, the trial begins and proceeds under the tight control of the trial judges, who are vested with considerable discretion in the management of the proceedings.[192] This includes scope for consideration of issues before it in light of the ECCC's purpose of assisting reconciliation in Cambodia.[193]

The President of the Trial Chamber must inform the accused of his or her procedural rights and thereafter conduct the hearing.[194] The Trial Chamber hears the civil parties, witnesses and experts 'in the order it considers useful.'[195]

189 Rong Chhorng, 'Conflict's Female Victims Far From Forgotten', *Phnom Penh Post* (6 June 2012).

190 ECCC Internal Rules (*Rev 8*) r. 23 *quinquies* (3)(b).

191 *Nuon Chea and Khieu Samphân* (Judgment) 002/19-09-2007/ECCC/TC (7 August 2014) paras. 1152–1160.

192 Acquaviva, above n. 2, p. 144.

193 ECCC Agreement Preamble.

194 ECCC Internal Rules (*Rev. 8*) r. 90(1).

195 ECCC Internal Rules (*Rev. 8*) r. 91(1).

5.7.1. PARTICIPATORY PROCEDURE

At both the investigation stage and during the trial, the accused has the right of input into the processes whether or not his/her legal counsel is present.[196] At the investigation stage, this may include requesting the Co-Investigating Judges to take certain actions during the investigation.[197] The accused at trial may question witnesses through the President of the Chamber.[198] At the end of the trial the accused may also make a final statement. In these circumstances, counsel can be seen to assist rather than represent the client, who can thus influence the progress and tenor of the case.[199]

While the proceedings at trial are controlled by the judges, they are also dynamic by virtue of the participation of the complete range of trial actors. In Case 001, the judges led the examination of witnesses. This was followed by questioning of the witnesses by the Co-Prosecution, the Co-Defence and the Civil Party lawyers. In Case 002, the judges introduced and controlled the proceedings, but left the examination of witnesses to the parties to expedite the trials. All parties may make written submissions and put before the Court probative material which will be added to the case file.[200] The Chamber may in the course of the trial order new investigations to be carried out under conditions applicable at the pre-trial stage.[201] At the end of the hearings closing statements may be made not only by the prosecution and the defence, but by civil party lawyers and the accused.

The narrative testimony of witnesses and the scope for engagement between trial actors within proceedings raised the prospect of expanded dialogue within ECCC trial proceedings. The trials' discursive potential also flowed from the likelihood of ECCC judges applying, in Osiel's terms, a broader 'procedural brush', as they were empowered to take account of how the trials might contribute to reconciliation and justice.[202]

5.7.2. REPRESENTATIVE PROCESSES

Mégret's analysis of the hybrid international transitional trial highlighted the model's potential for greater representation of constituencies affected by the crimes prosecuted.[203] The representational function of the trial is observed by

196 Acquaviva, above n. 2, p. 139.
197 ECCC Internal Rules (*Rev. 8*) r. 58(6).
198 ECCC Internal Rules (*Rev. 8*) rr. 83(2), 91(2), 94.
199 Acquaviva, above n. 2, p. 139.
200 ECCC Internal Rules (*Rev 8*) r. 92.
201 ECCC Internal Rules (*Rev 8*) r. 93.
202 Osiel, above n. 21, p. 296.
203 Mégret, above n. 1, p. 742.

shifting the focus from the outcomes of trials to their procedure.[204] Focus on the proceedings of the ECCC from the investigative stage reveals an expanded range of voices in trial proceedings and scope for communication between international and national trial actors as they engage at all phases of the trial.

The ECCC's inquisitorial procedure and idiosyncratic features introduced communicative elements uncharacteristic of other transitional trials. The incorporation of the civil party action pursuant to Cambodian criminal law, and the ECCC's adherence to developments in human rights law, opened the ECCC trials to victim participation to an unprecedented extent. While the inclusion of victims as civil parties in the trial proceedings may lengthen the inherently complex trials and present certain procedural difficulties for the Court, their presence and legal representation marks the end of the silence imposed upon them since the end of the Khmer Rouge regime. The incorporation of international procedural rules and exchange of professional practice styles, flowing from the sharing of roles between national and international actors, suggests representation in more than expressive ways. Dialogue between national and international professionals may also enhance the communicative value of the trials by blending local knowledge with international standards.

Thus, when trial process is viewed in terms of its representativeness, due process in transitional trial procedure may be 'less a matter of imposing a ready-made model … than it is of re-interrogating the tradition of due process in light of the particular exigencies' of the transitional context.[205] For this reason the prospect of political interference which hovered over the progress of the Case 003 and 004 investigations ought not to deflect attention from the ECCC's 'peculiar adaptation' to produce trial procedure that is 'deeply in tune with its [local] environment.'[206]

5.8. CONCLUSION

The successful launch of the ECCC trials, engaging its novel procedure, demonstrated that internationalised criminal proceedings need not be based on the adversarial procedural model. Although national inquisitorial proceedings are arguably more expeditious than adversarial trials, it will not necessarily be so in cases involving the prosecution of international crimes. For this reason, as the ECCC quickly found, victim participation in trials must be limited. However, this does not mean that victim participation cannot be representative. As discussed further in Chapter seven, while there was rapid uptake of civil party rights in

---

204 Ibid.

205 Frédéric Mégret, 'Beyond Fairness': Understanding the Determinants of International Criminal Procedure' (2009) 14 *UCLA Journal of International Law and Foreign Affairs* 37, 76.

206 Ibid.

Case 002, not all civil parties sought direct participation in trial proceedings, but many of the concerns of the collective group were raised on a representative basis at various hearings organised by the Court.

Despite the substantial success of operationalising two internationalised transitional trials, the political furore surrounding the investigation of Cases 003 and 004 both undermined morale at the Court and distracted public attention from the ECCC's achievements. Even if viewed only in expressive terms, the political opposition to further investigations highlighted the importance of the process the Court had embarked upon. Fair trial considerations which surfaced as the Trial Chamber revised the civil party scheme also arose as the Court managed the ebb and flow of Case 003 and 004 developments. Balancing the legitimate interests of all the parties became the constant theme of trial proceedings.

As the ECCC wrestled with the complexities of civil party inclusion in trial proceedings, it was guided by the Court's reconciliatory purpose along with its retributive objectives. The opening of conversation on Khmer Rouge crimes during the investigations and the dialogic potential of inquisitorial proceedings introduced in this chapter heightened the sociological value of the trials. But how did the communicative dynamics of the ECCC's inquisitorial procedure work in practice? This question is considered in the next two chapters.

CHAPTER 6
TRIAL DIALOGUE IN CASE 001

6.1. INTRODUCTION

Exploring Osiel's conception of the transitional trial as a creative site wherein opposing accounts of the past are mediated by flexible application of procedural rules, this chapter examines the dialogue of the first trial in the Extraordinary Chambers in the Courts of Cambodia (ECCC), the trial of Kaing Guek Eav (alias Duch), known as Case 001. It begins with a discussion of the accused from the case file prepared by the Co-Investigating Judges. An outline of how the Court engaged with the accused as he gave his evidence is set out against the background of the Co-Prosecution and Co-Defence narratives. The chapter emphasises how the accused exercised his participatory rights and highlights the nature of the dialogue that emerged as the Court actors examined witness testimony. Sample exchanges between the judges and the accused, the accused and witnesses, and witnesses and counsel are used to illustrate the discussion that opened up within the trial proceedings. While the proceedings revolved around the Court's primary objective of establishing the individual guilt of the accused, the exercise of participatory rights expanded the frame of the trial and provided space for reflection on the context and causes of the crimes in a way not normally seen in the transitional trial. The argument is that the exercise of participatory rights and the nature of the Court's engagement with witness testimony moved the proceedings beyond the expressivism of due process to reveal the communicative value of the trial in its social context.

6.2. THE CASE FILE

As discussed in Chapter five, ECCC trials begin after an extensive pre-trial investigation led by the Co-Investigating Judges who produce the 'Closing Order' indicting the accused. For his role in the security apparatus of Democratic Kampuchea, Kaing Guek Eav (alias Duch) was indicted for planning, instigating, ordering, committing, aiding or abetting crimes against humanity and grave breaches of the Geneva Conventions of 1949. In the alternative his responsibility for the crimes operated by way of superior responsibility. Certain conduct found to constitute the domestic offences of homicide and torture under the 1956 Cambodian Penal Code were accorded the highest available legal classification and were subsumed under the aforementioned international crimes.[1]

Duch was transferred to the ECCC from the Military Prison in Phnom Penh on 30 March 2007. The Closing Order provided a profile of the life of the accused and outlined the ECCC's dealings with him prior to the commencement of his trial. The investigation included a summary of facts pertaining to the historical and political context of the crimes, the role of the accused in implementing policy of the Communist Party of Kampuchea (CPK), an outline of the legal characterisation of the alleged crimes and a psychological assessment of the accused. As noted in Chapter five, section 5.4.3, the investigation also involved visits to the scenes of the crimes, and re-enactments in the presence of the accused, his counsel and victims of the crimes.

The Closing Order also formed the case file from which the Trial Chamber examined the case against the accused. The investigation thus initiated dialogue around the crimes of the Khmer Rouge period and laid the foundation for further discussion at trial.

6.2.1. PROFILE OF THE ACCUSED

The Closing Order chronicled Duch's personal, political and professional evolution leading to his role as Chairman of S-21 during the Khmer Rouge regime. S-21 was the code name of the headquarters of *santebal*, the CPK's security police or special branch.[2] It was a secret interrogation centre and detention complex in Phnom Penh, operating within a former high school. The institution included a neighbouring facility known as S-24 at Prey Sâr, where prisoners were also detained and rice was farmed to supply S-21 needs. Large pits dug at Choeung Ek to the south of Phnom Penh supported S-21's system of executions.[3]

Duch was born on 17 November 1942 in the Cambodian village of Peovveuy in Kompong Thom province. He was the eldest child of poor peasants of Chinese origin. He was a small child and suffered from illnesses which he described as 'caused by poverty and living in the countryside.'[4] Aged nine years when he began

---

1 *Kaing Guek Eav alias Duch* (Closing Order) 001/18-07-2007-ECCC-OCIJ (8 August 2008) [Closing Order] para. 152.

2 Santebal is a compound word combining *santisuk* (security) and *norkobal* (police). David Chandler, *Voices from S-21: Terror and History in Pol Pot's Secret Prison* (University of California Press, 1999) p. 3.

3 Closing Order para. 20, p. 112.

4 Closing Order para. 163.

his schooling, he was a good pupil. After successfully finishing his junior and high school studies Duch completed the national Baccalauréate examinations in 1964 at the Lycée Sisowath in Phnom Penh. Duch was both fearful and enthralled by his teachers. He traced his later political activism to several of his teachers who condemned political corruption and social injustice.[5] Duch's sense of social injustice seemed to have been sharpened by the impoverished circumstances of his family and their suffering at the hands of a usurious relative.[6] When he joined the Khmer Rouge, Duch adopted his revolutionary name. He explained to the psychology experts who assessed his personality at the pre-trial stage, that Duch means 'student who stands straight when a teacher asks him to stand.'[7]

In 1964, Duch moved to Phnom Penh where he studied for a teaching certificate at the Institut de Pédagogie. The director of the Institut was Son Sen, a French-educated mathematician who soon fled the capital to join the CPK. Son Sen became a member of the CPK Central Committee and in 1975 was Duch's immediate superior at S-21. At the Institut, Duch also met Chhay Kim Hour, a professor and head of a communist cell in Phnom Penh. Chhay Kim Hour introduced Duch to the CPK and was a mentor to him.[8] While the two were close cadres during those years, when the CPK came to power Chhay Kim Hour was purged at S-21 which was then under Duch's administration.[9]

In 1965, Duch was appointed to the position of mathematics teacher at the junior high school at Skoun. His students described him as a sincere, devoted man, always seeking to help the impoverished.[10] While teaching he became increasingly engaged in the communist underground movement against the Sihanouk government. On 5 January 1968, Duch was arrested and sentenced to 20 years imprisonment for breach of state security. He was released from prison after the 18 March 1970 coup d'état by General Lon Nol against Sihanouk and thereafter resumed his activities as a member of the CPK.[11]

The Khmer Rouge policy of purging perceived enemies began long before the CPK came to power. In 1971, Duch was assigned to supervise a Khmer Rouge prison camp code-named M-13, where he implemented the CPK policy of executing detainees deemed enemies of the revolution. Duch told the Co-Investigating Judges, in his defence, that he had not joined the CPK to commit crimes but to liberate his people. He claimed that when he was 'forced to supervise M-13, [he] became both an actor in criminal acts and also a hostage

5 Closing Order paras. 163–164.

6 Closing Order para. 164.

7 Duch is also the name of the sculptor of the Great Buddha of the Pagoda of Povveuy in Siem Reap. Transcript of Trial Proceedings *Kaing Guek Eav 'Duch'* 001/18-07-2007/TC, Day 67, (31 August 2009), p. 19.

8 Nic Dunlop, *The Lost Executioner* (Bloomsbury, 2005) pp. 55–56.

9 Ibid. p. 56.

10 Closing Order paras. 163–164.

11 *Kaing Guek Eav alias Duch* (Judgment) 001/18-2007/ECCC/TC (26 July 2010) para. 112.

to the regime.'[12] Duch said it became clear to him that those who served the interests of their own people and not the CPK could be detained as opponents of the Party. This, he explained, made him increasingly fearful for his life. The fear continued after he was appointed by Son Sen first as Deputy, and then Chairman of S-21 in 1975. Son Sen became Minister for Defence of Democratic Kampuchea and was responsible for general state security.

In 1979, in the days following the Vietnamese defeat of the Khmer Rouge, two photo-journalists stumbled on the vacated S-21 facility. In addition to the bodies of recently killed prisoners and instruments of torture, they found thousands of documents, photographs and notebooks detailing how the institution had been administered.[13] Duch confirmed that the primary role of S-21 was the elimination of enemies of the regime and that this extended to their family members.[14] In addition to executing prisoners already condemned as traitors, S-21 had the overriding purpose of extracting confessions to justify arrests and to uncover further networks of enemies, perceived by the CPK leadership as 'boring from within.'[15] Duch was responsible for the content of detainee confessions, which were extracted by force, in the form of political biographies.[16] These formed a major part of the documentary evidence of Duch's crimes.

After the Vietnamese took Phnom Penh in January 1979, Duch fled the capital. By December he had joined Khmer Rouge cadres in Samlaut, where he resumed teaching. In October 1986, he was once again with Son Sen who sent him to China to teach Khmer to Chinese students. He remained there for two years and assumed the name Hang Pin. The Closing Order did not record when he returned to Cambodia. However, it noted that in 1992 Pol Pot assigned him to an economic post in a village in the far North West province of Banteay Manchey. Thereafter, he lost contact with the dispersing Khmer Rouge in the context of the progressive rupture within the leadership group and the ensuing defections to the Cambodian government. Duch became a school teacher again, as well as a trader in rice and breeder of pigs.[17]

In November 1995, Duch's wife was killed in a mysterious burglary at his home in which she was bayoneted, while he was only slightly injured. Duch suspected an assassination plot by Pol Pot. It was after her death that he began to attend meetings of the Evangelist Church of Battambang and his apparent conversion to Christianity ensued.[18] He also had his children baptised. He returned to live in Samlaut in 1996, but the population was evacuated across the Thai border in the

12 Closing Order para. 169.
13 Chandler, above n. 2, p. 3.
14 Closing Order paras. 34, 37.
15 Closing Order para. 43.
16 Ibid.
17 Closing Order para. 166.
18 Ibid. p. 166.

wake of Khmer Rouge hostilities against the Phnom Penh government. In July 1997, he began to work for the American Refugee Committee (ARC), an NGO operating in the Ban Ma Muang refugee camp. An ARC doctor recommended Duch, known by him as Hang Pin, for a vacancy for a community health worker. This was based on Duch's background as a teacher and his fluency in French, Khmer and Thai. Duch embraced his new humanitarian role and became well known in the camp, particularly when he acted to stem a typhoid outbreak which could have taken many lives.[19]

In late 1998, as Khmer Rouge combat subsided, Duch returned to Cambodia with other refugees. Dunlop recorded that Duch told his ARC supervisor, Tess Prombouth, that 'when I go back I really don't know what will happen with my life.'[20] In April 1999, journalists Nic Dunlop and Nate Thayer found Duch in Samlaut. Recognising Nate Thayer as the journalist who had interviewed Pol Pot, he declared 'now my future is in God hands,' and apparently resigned to his fate, began to talk about his life with the Khmer Rouge, saying 'I have done very bad things ... now it is time for *les représailles* (the consequences) of my actions.'[21] Soon after the interview, Dunlop heard that Duch had surrendered to the Cambodian authorities.[22]

The Closing Order recorded that throughout the investigation Duch recognised his responsibility for the crimes committed at S-21 under his command.[23] To the Co-Investigating Judges, Duch explained that he was bound to speak out about the Khmer Rouge years in 1999 'because it was impossible not to tell the truth about S-21 after he heard that Pol Pot denied its existence and claimed that it was an invention of the Vietnamese.'[24] The Closing Order also records that Duch repeatedly expressed remorse to the victims of S-21 and their families, as well as to the S-21 staff who were under his control. He stated that none of his staff were volunteers, or proud of what they had done, but rather were terrorised and constantly in fear for their lives.[25] Duch cooperated in the judicial investigation and attempted neither to implicate anyone who was under his command, nor to blame the senior leadership of the CPK alone in order to exonerate himself.[26] When presented with inconsistencies in his testimony before the Co-Investigating Judges, he indicated that they resulted from 'fear and embarrassment' at being reminded of an 'extremely painful history of crime.'[27]

---

19 Dunlop, above n. 8, p. 256.
20 Ibid.
21 Ibid. p. 272.
22 Ibid. p. 278.
23 Closing Order para. 167.
24 Ibid.
25 Closing Order para. 168.
26 Ibid.
27 Ibid.

The psychological examination of Duch commissioned by the Co-Investigating Judges was conducted by an international expert specialising in Geopolitical Clinical Psychology and by a Cambodian psychiatrist. The Closing Order cites their conclusion that Duch presented no psychopathology and that he was responsible for all his acts. While noting that Duch had developed powerful defence mechanisms and that there were remnants of the Khmer Rouge 'fabrication' processes in his language, thinking and behaviour, the experts perceived positive psychological progress despite a past pattern of 'disempathy'.[28] As to whether his expressions of regret regarding his crimes were sincere or circumstantial, they considered the explanation was not so clear cut. Their opinion was that 'Christianity, the West and the realm of international justice symbolised a new form of protection (also undeniably the most effective), because he suffered from insecurity.'[29]

The Closing Order thus introduced the case against Duch. It provided a sketch of the life of a Khmer Rouge perpetrator before, during and after the regime. It also made clear the role of S-21 within Democratic Kampuchea and presented a picture of Cambodia over at least four decades in continuous political turmoil.

With a factual record before them, the ECCC judges began the process of testing the evidence on the case file at trial. This included calling for additional evidence as they examined the accused and other witnesses. The next section discusses how the Court engaged with the accused and the evidence of expert witnesses.[30]

6.2.2. THE COURT'S EXAMINATION OF DUCH

Following an initial hearing, Duch's trial commenced on 30 March 2009. The trial ran for 22 weeks (77 sitting days). There were 38 witnesses of fact and eight expert witnesses. In addition, 22 civil parties made statements in support of claims for reparations.[31] Following the formal opening of the trial by President Nil Nonn, two Cambodian court officers read the Co-Investigating Judges' factual analysis of the case and the indictment. The proceedings were observed by a packed public gallery, seating 500, and broadcast to national and global television audiences. The transcript of the proceedings formally recorded the

---

28 Also referred to as 'alexithymia' to describe the inability to feel and express emotions. I discuss this further in section 6.4.4.

29 Closing Order para. 171.

30 The Court's analysis of Duch's responsibility for each of his crimes is discussed in Chapter eight.

31 Michelle Staggs Kelsall et al., *Lessons Learned from the 'Duch' Trial: A Comprehensive Review of the Frist Case before the Extraordinary Chambers in the Courts of Cambodia* (Asian International Justice Initiative, December 2009) p. 4.

reopening of a traumatic period in Cambodian history and represented the first official step towards social engagement with it.[32]

Although Duch assumed responsibility for the crimes with which he was charged, he faced a full trial. This was because unlike that of other international courts, the governing law of the ECCC made no provision for the acceptance of a guilty plea.[33] Duch chose to testify in his own trial even though, as the accused, he had a right not to be compelled to do so.[34] The benefit of his testimony towards findings of the truth relevant to crimes committed during the Khmer Rouge regime was acknowledged by the Trial Chamber in its Judgment as extending to assisting national reconciliation, one of the stated goals of the ECCC.[35]

As noted in Chapter five, section 5.7, all parties had access to the case file and rights to participate in the proceedings. The accused could participate either directly by way of reply following witness testimony, through legal counsel or by invitation from the Court.[36] The Court's task of establishing individual criminal responsibility for Duch's acts beyond reasonable doubt involved historical contextualisation of his conduct during the regime, as well as character analysis before and during the proceedings. Duch was an active player in his own defence as he exercised his inquisitorial procedural rights throughout the trial. In the next section, I describe how he engaged with the Court in both its narrow task of prosecution and broader purpose of assisting reconciliation. His willingness to cooperate in the investigation and trial proceedings, together with his readiness to exercise his participation rights, brought added dialogic dimensions to the proceedings.

6.2.3. DUCH AND CPK POLICY

The coercive nature of CPK policy before the establishment of S-21 was revealed by the Court's examination of Duch on his work as supervisor of the M-13 detention centre. Critically, Duch's testimony confirmed that the regime's policy of eliminating perceived enemies, known as 'smashing', was introduced at M-13 under his leadership. At M-13, Duch worked under the direction of Vorn Vet from July 1971 to mid-1973, and subsequently under Son Sen until January 1975. In August 1975, Son Sen initiated the establishment of S-21 and appointed Duch as deputy-in-charge of the interrogation unit. Duch testified that he

32 Transcript of Trial Proceedings – *Kaing Guek Eav 'Duch'* 001/18-07-2007/TC 1000H) Trial Day 1 (30 March 2009).

33 *Kaing Guek Eav alias Duch* (Trial Judgment) 001/18-07-2007 (26 July 2010) p. 48.

34 Guido Acquaviva, 'New Paths in International Criminal Justice' (2008) 6 *Journal of International Criminal Justice* 129, 147–148.

35 *Kaing Guek Eav (alias Duch)* (Judgment) 001/18-2007/ ECCC TC (26 July 2010) para. 609.

36 I discuss the exercise of the civil parties' participation rights in Chapter seven.

sought neither this position nor his subsequent promotion to Chairman. In fact, he wanted to work in the Ministry of Industry but his request was refused. Duch declared that he did not 'dare' to contest the new appointment on the grounds of duty to the Party.[37]

The Court sought clarification from Duch on the CPK policy of eliminating enemies. The policy of smashing was sanctioned by Article 10 (Chapter 7) of the 1976 Constitution of Democratic Kampuchea. Under the heading 'Justice', the Constitution stated that 'violations of the laws ... including dangerous activities in opposition to the people's State must be condemned to the highest degree.'[38] Duch described the policy as total, being applicable to 'S-21... the entire party, the military, the State authority in the bases, [and] the Police Offices throughout the country.'[39]

Duch testified that to 'smash' meant more than to kill:

> To smash ... means to arrest secretly ... [to interrogate] with torture employed, and then [to execute] secretly without the knowledge of the [detainee's] family members. [It also means that] the person was not to be released ... so if he is smashed ... this did not go through the judicial process because there was no law, no court, the Standing Committee [of the CPK] controlled all governmental powers.[40]

Moreover, smashing involved not merely physically smashing but breaking psychologically. Under Duch's supervision, S-21 was designed for the dehumanisation and psychological debasement of those detained there.[41]

As to his responsibility as a superior officer, Duch testified that as Chairman of S-21 from March 1976 to 6 January 1979 all his subordinates reported directly to him and that he in turn reported directly to the CPK Standing Committee (a Sub-Committee of the Party's Central Committee and the highest authority in Democratic Kampuchea).[42] During the trial Duch confirmed this reporting process by reference to documents tabled in Court that contained detainee confessions he had personally annotated. These he forwarded to Son Sen as his immediate superior, until Son Sen was replaced by Nuon Chea. Other annotated confessional documents revealed that Son Sen had sent those documents to Pol Pot or other Standing Committee Members. Duch also confessed that he met his superiors 'quite often' further to S-21 business.[43] He emphasised the vertical nature of the communication structure imposed by the CPK to maintain secrecy and control of information. Horizontal communications with officers

---

37 *Kaing Guek Eav (alias Duch)* (Judgment) 001/18-2007/ ECCC TC (26 July 2010) para. 122.
38 Ibid. para. 99.
39 Ibid. para. 100.
40 Ibid.
41 Ibid.
42 Closing Order para 32.
43 Ibid.

heading the Revolutionary Army of Kampuchea (RAK) units for instance, even if addressed directly to him, were delivered through Son Sen as the senior leader of both the military forces and S-21.[44]

S-21 was organised along hierarchical lines and Duch devised a reporting system at 'all levels to ensure that his orders were carried out immediately and precisely.'[45] Duch personally trained a team of interrogators to use physical and psychological violence to secure the confessions of detainees.[46] Because detainees were considered guilty by virtue of their arrests and presence at S-21, the contents of confessions generally followed a standard formula. The interrogators were instructed by Duch to establish links with the CPK's enemies and to force detainees to confess to association with the CIA, the KGB and/or Vietnamese agents.[47]

Duch and other witnesses explained the nature of torture techniques used at S-21 to secure confessions.[48] The Court also established the gruesome conditions under which prisoners were held and that inhumane practices, including the draining of blood from detainees, and the subjection of some to medical experimentation, occurred at S-21.[49] Duch and witnesses Him Huy and Prak Khorn all testified to the incidence of rape, though noted that the practice was not widespread.[50] Duch acknowledged the inhumane conditions in which detainees were held and recognised that excesses perpetrated by his staff went unchecked.[51]

The Court also clarified the demographics of S-21 detainees. Witnesses confirmed Duch's evidence of 48 prisoners from 11 countries other than Cambodia.[52] In addition, the detainee population consisted of former Lon Nol soldiers, members of the Khmer Rouge military forces and high- and low-ranking Khmer Rouge cadres, as well their family members, including children. At least 12,273 individuals appeared on the revised S-21 prisoner list, although the Court concluded that this was a minimum figure, and that the loss of records and the practice of not registering children meant that the actual number of detainees was likely to have been considerably greater.[53]

The vast majority of witnesses of fact as to what happened at S-21 under Duch's leadership were former employees of the institution. Many of Duch's former

44 Laura Macdonald, 'Duch and Expert Disagree on Khmer Rouge Communication Structure, But Disagree Regarding Responsibility', *Cambodia Tribunal Monitor* (7 May 2009) pp. 1, 2.
45 *Kaing Guek Eav (alias Duch)* (Judgment) 001/18-2007/ECCC/TC (26 July 2010) para. 144.
46 Ibid. para. 164.
47 Ibid. para. 155.
48 Ibid. paras, 241–255.
49 Ibid. paras. 273–275.
50 Ibid. para. 155.
51 Ibid. paras. 246–247.
52 Staggs Kelsall, above n. 31, p. 15.
53 *Kaing Guek Eav alias Duch* (Judgment) 001/18-2007/ ECCC TC (26 July 2010) paras. 141–142.

interrogators affirmed his testimony that he was neither present nor had taken part in interrogations.[54] However, they explained that they were fully aware he was the commander of the facility and that he trained the interrogators.[55]

Detainees of the re-education facility, S-24 also lived in inhumane conditions and faced the likelihood of execution. Duch testified that 'S-24 detainees were seldom released and that all were generally destined for execution regardless of their classification.'[56]

6.3. THE CO-PROSECUTION VOICE

The Co-Prosecutors dismissed Duch's expressions of remorse and his opinion of himself as a mere cog in the Khmer Rouge criminal machine.[57] National Co-Prosecutor, Chea Leang, highlighted the close connection of the S-21 complex with the CPK Central Committee and its distinctiveness from the other security centres for that reason. International Co-Prosecutor, William Smith, painted Duch as the efficient head of the famous torture centre whose diligence 'encouraged' the senior leadership of Democratic Kampuchea to arrest, detain and smash more than 12,000 detainees. Duch, he argued, along with his mentor and superior Son Sen, waged a misguided crusade sacrificing their hearts, souls and humanity in the process.[58] Smith grounded his argument for a 40-year sentence in the expressivism of criminal punishment. While acknowledging Duch's remorse and cooperation with the Court he argued that a long sentence would send the message that the ECCC was punishing the accused justly, and deterring the repetition of the grave crimes committed.[59]

6.3.1. THE CO-DEFENCE RESPONSE

In his closing statement, Duch's international Co-Defence counsel, François Roux, highlighted his client's assumption of responsibility for his crimes, expressions of remorse and repeated apologies to victims.[60] He reminded the Court that Duch was asked directly if he admitted implementing CPK policy at S-21, to which he replied

54 Staggs Kelsall et al., above n. 31, p. 14.

55 Ibid. p. 15; *Kaing Guek Eav alias Duch* (Judgment) 001/18-2007/ ECCC TC (26 July 2010) para. 132, fn. 224.

56 *Kaing Guek Eav alias Duch* (Judgment) 001/18-2007/ ECCC TC (26 July 2010) para. 198.

57 Staggs Kelsall et al., above n. 31, p. 16.

58 Ibid.

59 Transcript of Trial Proceedings – *Kaing Guek Eav 'Duch'* 001/18-07-2007/TC (Day 75, 25 November 2009) pp. 31–37.

60 Transcript of Trial Proceedings – *Kaing Guek Eav 'Duch'* 001/18-07-2007/TC (Day 76, 26 November 2009) pp. 9, 23–25.

'Yes, I admit it completely.'[61] Furthermore, his shame and remorse was ongoing. Roux recalled that Duch had acknowledged before the Court that he even betrayed his friends and that what he did at S-21 'transcends cowardice.'[62] Duch's crime was ultimately the 'crime of obedience', which he associated with a culture of submission to masters.[63] Roux maintained that Duch was himself a victim of a totalitarian regime leadership who fundamentally sought their own protection.[64] He asserted that Duch could not be portrayed as the conventional monster perpetrator of atrocity crimes, to be condemned in expressive terms, because international courts since the Nuremburg era recognised the contribution to reconciliation to be made by defendants who accept responsibility for their crimes and assist the truth-finding process through their cooperation with the relevant court. This had significance in communities for both victims and other former perpetrators.[65] In addition, the nature of Duch's participation in the proceedings had brought moments of truth more frequently associated with the work of truth commissions.[66]

Duch's national Co-Defence counsel, Kar Savuth, argued that an acquittal was in order because his client was not in fact one of the senior leaders of the Khmer Rouge and therefore not properly subject to the ECCC's personal jurisdiction. Duch was only one of the 196 prison chiefs within the *Santebal*. Savuth cautioned the Court against making Duch a 'scapegoat' for a great number of perpetrators some of whom had committed more egregious crimes than he had.[67] The reason for the apparent change of plea and the disagreement with Roux disclosed in Kar Savuth's closing statement is discussed at Section 5.

6.3.2. THE PARTICIPATION OF THE ACCUSED AT TRIAL

Duch took an active part in the proceedings. He was fully apprised of the documents in the case file and displayed an excellent memory of events. More

61 Transcript of Trial Proceedings – *Kaing Guek Eav 'Duch'* 001/18-07-2007/TC (Day 76, 26 November 2009) p. 32.

62 Transcript of Trial Proceedings – *Kaing Guek Eav 'Duch'* 001/18-07-2007/TC (Day 76, 26 November 2009) p. 32.

63 Transcript of Trial Proceedings – *Kaing Guek Eav 'Duch'* 001/18-07-2007/TC (Day 76, 26 November 2009) p. 17; David Scheffer, 'The Crime of Obedience' *Cambodia Tribunal Monitor* (26 November 200) pp. 1, 5.

64 Transcript of Trial Proceedings – *Kaing Guek Eav 'Duch'* 001/18-07-2007/TC (Day 76, 26 November 2009) p. 42.

65 Transcript of Trial Proceedings – *Kaing Guek Eav 'Duch'* 001/18-07-2007/TC (Day 76, 26 November 2009) pp. 11–15. Roux cited his experience as counsel in the *Prosecutor v. Obrenović* at the ICTY where Obrenović accepted responsibility as Commander of troops for persecution of the Muslim community at Srebrenica. See *Prosecutor v. Obrenović* (Sentencing Judgment) ICTY-IT-02-60/2-S (10 December 2003) paras. 144–157.

66 Transcript of Trial Proceedings – *Kaing Guek Eav 'Duch'* 001/18-07-2007/TC (Day 76, 26 November 2009) p. 9.

67 Transcript of Trial Proceedings – *Kaing Guek Eav 'Duch'* 001/18-07-2007/TC Day 75, 25 November 2009) pp. 76–109.

than once he resolved apparent inconsistencies in S-21 documents, explained their annotations and verified signatures. When testimony was confusing or erroneous he availed himself of opportunities to address the Court to resolve the issues. An example of this was his response to the testimony of a civil party who told the Court he had used an alias during the Khmer Rouge period and escaped from the Choeung Ek killing site. Referring to documents that showed that the named prisoner was detained at S-21 much earlier than the witness had stated, and that the prisoner was in fact killed, Duch declared that the witness could not be who he claimed to be.[68] Though participation of this kind clearly aided the truth-finding process, after several instances in which Duch appeared to slip into the role of teacher and controller of matters in dispute, the Court admonished him, reminding him that the role of analysing evidence lay with the judges.[69] Duch also made use of his right of reply to witness testimony. The following section illustrates how the exercise of this right mediated by the judges gave the proceedings a discursive tenor.

6.4. TRIAL DIALOGUE AND WITNESS TESTIMONY

In addition to the evidence of the accused, the Trial Chamber relied on the evidence of other eye- and expert-witnesses to establish proof of the elements of the crimes. The search for the truth in the inquisitorial proceedings traversed historical, psychological and social issues going to the context of the crimes and causation. Some of the matters raised tapped into live social debates, while others influenced the Court in its assessment of Duch's character and culpability. The Court's engagement with the evidence of some of the witnesses produced wide-ranging, nuanced and philosophical dialogue. A sample of trial dialogue resulting from witness testimony follows.

6.4.1. MAM NAI

In contrast to a tightly controlled adversarial process where the defendant generally speaks through defence counsel unless actually testifying, Duch's active engagement with the evidence provided dramatic and sometimes moving moments in the trial. An example was Duch's response to the testimony of Mam Nai, a witness called to give evidence on the functioning of S-21 and executions at Choeung Ek.

---

68 Open Society Justice Initiative, *Recent Developments at the Extraordinary Chambers in the Courts of Cambodia* (OSJI, August 2009) pp. 1, 16.

69 Ibid.

Mam Nai was 76 years old at the time he gave his evidence to the ECCC. Mam Nai was at M-13 with Duch and was one of his four senior interrogators at S-21. In February 2008, Mam Nai took part in the re-enactment at Choeung Ek, and the visit to S-21 organised by the Co-Investigating Judges. He stated then that he used whips and electric wire in his interrogation of detainees and made entries in a 300-page notebook, which included his dictations of lectures given by Duch to S-21 staff.[70] At trial however, Mam Nai testified that he had no knowledge of how the interrogation unit was operated, how many staff worked within it and what torture methods were used. He said he had interrogated 20 to 30 Vietnamese combatants and one or two civilian spies. Mam Nai conceded that he had been responsible for interrogating all the Vietnamese prisoners because of his language skills. However, he refused to confirm that he had interrogated prisoners on a list presented to him by to International Co-Prosecutor which documented the presence of 122 Vietnamese combatants and 144 Vietnamese spies at S-21.[71] Mam Nai's evasiveness slowed the proceedings and frustrated the Co-Prosecution.

In his examination of Mam Nai, François Roux asked the witness for his perspective on the government of Democratic Kampuchea. Mam Nai seemed to recall aspects of the regime fondly, stating that although conditions in Cambodia were difficult particularly because of food shortages, the Khmer Rouge ethic of independence and self-mastery were positive features. He also said he simply did not know how many people died under the Khmer Rouge. Roux then thanked the Prosecutors for providing such a witness.[72]

After listening all day to Mam Nai's testimony, Duch exercised his right of reply in emphatic fashion. He made a passionate plea to Mam Nai to fully testify to the events of the period in which they both participated as fellow revolutionaries. The plea consisted of a request to reform personally in view of the fact that over a million people died as a result of CPK policy and to 'tell the truth' for the sake of the particular victims involved and for the sake of humanity. Duch re-iterated that just as they had re-constructed themselves for the cause of communism, they must now change for humanitarian reasons.[73]

Duch reminded Mam Nai that the wife and daughter of Professor Phung Ton, the respected Law Professor and Dean of the University of Phnom Penh, who was interrogated at S-21, were present as civil parties and sought answers

---

70 Laura Macdonald, 'After Two Days of Questionable Witness Testimony, Duch Lectured His Former Subordinate: "Just Tell the Truth"', *Cambodia Tribunal Monitor* (15 July 2009) p. 1, 1.

71 Transcript of Trial Proceedings – *Kaing Guek Eav 'Duch'* 001/18-07-2007-ECCC/TC (Day 45, 15 July 2009) pp. 14–15.

72 Transcript of Trial Proceedings – *Kaing Guek Eav 'Duch'* 001/18-07-2007-ECCC/TC (Day 45, 15 July 2009) pp. 60–61.

73 Transcript of Trial Proceedings – *Kaing Guek Eav 'Duch'* 001/18-07-2007-ECCC/TC (Day 45, 15 July 2009) p. 64.

regarding the fate of their loved one. Duch told Mam Nai that he had accepted responsibility for the crimes at S-21 and said he wanted him to do the same, adding 'don't be afraid of death – just tell the truth.'[74]

Immediately following Duch's exchange with Mam Nai, civil party lawyer, Silke Studinsky, having previously failed to elicit information for her clients on the whereabouts of Phung Ton's remains, asked the Chamber to allow the witness an additional opportunity to address the issue.[75] The exchanges broke down Mam Nai's resistance. 'I wish to express my regrets to the family of Professor Ton' he declared.[76] As he sobbed, the witness said:

> I was enormously remorseful because my brothers and my parents suffered and died under the regime. My wife died. I think that it was a chaotic situation and that we can only be filled with regret. It's the only thing we can do. Now, I try to find solace by thinking about my karma; I turn to my religious faith. Of course I had many regrets and I believe that through this court, the family of Professor Ton is now aware of my feelings.[77]

Presiding Judge Nil Non then pressed Mam Nai for further details of the Professor's treatment at S-21, but the witness said he could recall nothing else.

Duch spoke firmly to his former colleague and with an authority that astounded those observing the proceedings.[78] The exchange between perpetrator and perpetrator introduced dialogue arguably more akin to restorative than retributive criminal process. In his closing arguments Francois Roux, reminded the Court that 'at times we had the impression [that] ... we were taking part in a truth and reconciliation commission in this courtroom.'[79] It was certainly a moment when the judges engaged their inquisitorial discretion to allow the drama to play out within the parameters of the legal proceedings. The rare form of trial dialogue allowed the perspectives of two Khmer Rouge perpetrators to be heard and reflected upon by the trial's public. Examples of Duch's exercise of his right of reply to victim testimony are discussed at Chapter seven, sections 7.5.1.2–7.5.2.6, 7.6.

---

74 Transcript of Trial Proceedings – *Kaing Guek Eav 'Duch'* 001/18-07-2007-ECCC/TC (Day 45, 15 July 2009) pp. 65–66; MacDonald, above n. 69, p. 3.

75 Transcript of Trial Proceedings – *Kaing Guek Eav 'Duch'* 001/18-07-2007-ECCC/TC (Day 45, 15 July 2009) p. 66.

76 MacDonald, above n. 70, p. 3.

77 Translation from Thierry Cruvellier, *The Master of Confessions: The Making of a Khmer Rouge Torturer* (Harper Collins, 2014) p. 239.

78 Stephanie Gee, 'What about the Duty to Say the Truth? Duch Lectures his former Subordinate', *CAAI News Media* (17 July 2009). http://khmernz.blogspot.com/2009/07/what-about-duty-to-say=truth-duc.html.

79 Transcript of Trial Proceedings – *Kaing Guek Eav 'Duch'* 001/18-07-2007/TC (Trial Day 76, 26 November 2009) p. 9.

6.4.2. FRANÇOIS BIZOT AT M-13

Although the charges against Duch did not extend to his management of the M-13, the Court called former staff of the centre as well as Professor François Bizot to testify on issues related to the functioning of the detention centre. In 1971, while researching Cambodian Buddhism with two Khmer assistants, Bizot was arrested as a CIA spy by Khmer Rouge cadres and detained for three months at M-13. Bizot's book, entitled *The Gate*, published in 2000, told the story of Bizot's detention at M-13 and its enduring effect on him.[80] At the ECCC, Bizot described the privations of life in the camp, the shackling of prisoners and the 'terrifying atmosphere of fear and death' that pervaded the camp.[81] As Duch interrogated Bizot on a weekly basis over at least two months, a strained form of friendship or 'familiarity' developed between the two men. Ultimately, Duch engineered Bizot's release when convinced of the prisoner's innocence, but not before securing approval from his superiors.[82] Bizot remarked that in the climate of constant terror, torture and death, Duch exhibited fear and suffering as he worked. Bizot explained that even as his transport out of M-13 was arranged, Duch feared an ambush by Ta Mok who had not agreed to let Bizot live, while Vorn Vet had supported Duch's recommendation for release.[83]

Before Bizot was set free Duch admitted to him that he beat prisoners to obtain confessions, not because he wanted to, but out of a sense duty to Angkar. Bizot was suddenly struck by the tragedy and terror of Duch's predicament and the humanity behind his work of writing up reports on people destined for execution.[84] Bizot's testimony lent support to the defence theory of Duch as a young Khmer Rouge cadre being been both a 'vector of state-institutionalised mass killing' and a dedicated revolutionary who had accepted the legitimacy of crime in the revolutionary cause.[85] The duality of Duch's existence and his inability to 'step back or out' of the regime he had committed himself to left a permanent imprint on Bizot's life, which he seemed compelled to communicate in court through his narrative testimony.[86] Under examination, Bizot explained

---

80 François Bizot, *The Gate* (Harvill Press, 2003).

81 Transcript of Trial Proceedings – *Kaing Guek Eav 'Duch'* 001/18-07-2007/TC (Day 7, 9 April 2009) p. 46.

82 Transcript of Trial Proceedings – *Kaing Guek Eav 'Duch'* 001/18-07-2007/TC (Day 7, 9 April 2009) pp. 48–49; Bizot, above n. 80, pp. 130–131.

83 Transcript of Trial Proceedings – *Kaing Guek Eav 'Duch'* 001/18-07-2007/TC (Day 7, 9 April 2009) p. 48.

84 Transcript of Trial Proceedings – *Kaing Guek Eav 'Duch'* 001/18-07-2007/TC (Day 6, 8 April 2009) pp. 70–71.

85 Staggs Kelsall above n. 31, p. 12; See Transcript of Trial Proceedings – *Kaing Guek Eav 'Duch'* 001/18-07-2007/TC (Day 6, 8 April 2009) p. 97.

86 Transcript of Trial Proceedings – *Kaing Guek Eav 'Duch'* 001/18-07-2007/TC (Day 6, 8 April 2009) p. 74.

that the view he had formed of Duch was part of a process of 'understanding the drama that took place in the forests of Cambodia' as well as in other national contexts, including those of more recent origin.[87] This point is discussed further at Chapter nine, section 3.2.

6.4.3. DAVID CHANDLER ON THE CPK IN HISTORY

David Chandler was a US diplomat in the 1960s and later became Professor of History at Monash University, Melbourne. The Court called him to elaborate on details in his book *Voices from S-21: Terror and History in Pol Pot's Secret Prison*, which was published 1999. The work provides his analysis of documents and publications retrieved from the S-21 complex, including over 1000 confessions of S-21 prisoners, together with records of interviews with several surviving detainees and security guards. In the course of his testimony, the Court asked Chandler to provide broad retrospective analysis of the CPK's policy and Duch's role as Chairman of S-21 as revealed in the institution's archive. Chandler was examined first by Judges Cartwright and Lavergne, followed by the Co-Prosecution, civil party lawyers and Co-Defence counsel. The Accused then exercised his right of reply. Some of the questions put to the witness and excerpts of his answers are reproduced in summary below to illustrate the breadth and nature of the dialogue that ensued.

6.4.3.1 S-21 – The Total Institution

In his book Chandler described S-21 as a 'total institution.' Judge Cartwright asked Chandler to elaborate on his use of the term. Chandler explained that he drew from the work of American sociologist, Erving Goffman who had applied the term to boarding schools, convents, monasteries and military units. Such places were described as 'sealed environments' in which rules were made from inside the institutions with little or no connection to the larger society. Chandler concluded that S-21 was such an institution. In the case of S-21, no information got out of the institution except to the senior leaders of Democratic Kampuchea.[88] What happened at S-21 was known only to those who worked or were imprisoned there and a few CPK members at the Party centre.[89] Chandler testified that this was consistent with the policy of secrecy which the leadership

---

87 Transcript of Trial Proceedings – *Kaing Guek Eav 'Duch'* 001/18-07-2007/TC (Day 7, 9 April 2009) p. 22.

88 Transcript of Trial Proceedings – *Kaing Guek Eav 'Duch'* 001/18-07-2007/TC (Day 55, 6 August 2009) p. 9.

89 Chandler above n. 2, p. 7.

viewed as essential to the survival of the regime.[90] To the leadership there could be no security without secrecy. This was reflected in the regime's choice of the words 'open' and 'secret' and in CPK documents rather than legal or illegal.[91]

Secrecy was also fundamental to the Khmer Rouge victory over the enemy.[92] Defending the Party's centre was all-important. In his book, Chandler concluded that for the CPK, the leadership had to be defended at all costs. Chandler cited Nuon Chea's statement that the movement could afford to lose 200–300 cadres but could not lose two or three leaders because the Party would not survive if there was damage at its centre.[93] In addition, a policy of continuous 'sweeping and cleaning' was necessary to ensure the safety of the Party leadership as well as preserve the purity of the revolution.[94] Judge Cartwright asked Chandler about the CPK's preoccupation with enemies of the regime and its increasing concern with purging enemies from within its own ranks. Chandler testified that the CPK Central Committee's approach to its enemies could be summarised as 'locate, question and destroy.'[95] To this end, S-21 was an interrogation and torture facility and not a prison operating according to law.[96] He described S-21 as the 'ante-room to death' that is, a waiting room for the fate of a forceful and violent death for all held there.[97] Confirming Duch's testimony, he concluded that the former S-21 Chairman had no role in arresting detainees; rather he was responsible for locating networks of other perceived 'traitors' through confessions extracted from detainees already determined as guilty by the leadership.[98] Duch's chief responsibility was to 'validate the verdict by extracting full confessions.'[99]

Judge Cartwright questioned Chandler on a CPK document that Duch had discussed as significant in confirming the nature of the phase of CPK purging of those perceived as enemies within its ranks.[100] Chandler said the document was discovered by chance in 1980 and was the closest thing we have to a 'smoking gun authorising the smashing of enemies' by the top echelon of the CPK hierarchy by way of a directive to all to security centres and CPK units throughout the

90 Transcript of Trial Proceedings – *Kaing Guek Eav 'Duch'* 001/18-07-2007/TC (Day 55, 6 August 2009) p. 10.

91 Chandler, above n. 2, p. 16.

92 Ibid.

93 Ibid.

94 Ibid, p. 41.

95 Transcript of Trial Proceedings – *Kaing Guek Eav 'Duch'* 001/18-07-2007/TC (Day 55, 6 August 2009) p. 12.

96 Chandler, above n. 2, p. 15.

97 Transcript of Trial Proceedings – *Kaing Guek Eav 'Duch'* 001/18-07-2007/TC (Day 55, 6 August 2009) p. 12.

98 Transcript of Trial Proceedings – *Kaing Guek Eav 'Duch'* 001/18-07-2007/TC (Day 55, 6 August 2009) p. 12.

99 Transcript of Trial Proceedings – *Kaing Guek Eav Duch'* 001/18-07-2007/TC (Day 55, 6 August 2009) p. 27.

100 The document was titled 'Decisions of the Central Committee Regarding a Number of Matters' and dated 30 March 1976. It was cited at page 51 of Chandler's book, above n. 2.

country. It was following the issue of the directive in the latter part of 1976, that the CPK began the purging of the 'internal enemy': party members and high-ranking Khmer Rouge.[101] This included some senior leaders such as Vorn Vet, Duch's superior at M-13.

Confessions to affiliation with external enemies including the CIA or the KGB were routinely extracted. Chandler testified that it was clear that the interrogators knew little of those organisations, but that the acronyms became catchphrases for the CPK's enemies. Vietnamese identity or connection was similarly condemnatory.[102] He noted further that the Vietnamese were automatically considered to be outside the human race and that female Vietnamese were particularly vulnerable to sexual violence by the Khmer Rouge as a result of this.[103]

6.4.3.2. Duch's Character and Conduct at S-21

Judge Cartwright questioned Chandler on Duch's character as revealed through the documentary evidence of his work at S-21 and his interviews with former S-21 staff. Chandler testified that Duch worked hard to control every aspect of the S-21 operation. He planned the interrogation methodology and was a proud and enthusiastic administrator who kept meticulous records, 'ferreting out problems and driving himself and his subordinates hard,' and frightening them in the process. As a mathematician he enjoyed drawing 'rationally pleasing models' and drew plans of this kind for S-21.[104] In answer to civil party lawyer Trusses Napprous, Chandler testified that Duch throughout his life was not concerned only with satisfying his superiors, but also sought to excel in everything he did so that he could be proud of himself.[105] While Duch was a dedicated revolutionary who would not deviate from the Party line, he became disillusioned as the internal purges eliminated some of his former mentors; the paranoia of the leadership knew no bounds and their decision-making became increasingly arbitrary.[106]

---

101 Transcript of Trial Proceedings – *Kaing Guek Eav 'Duch'* 001/18-07-2007/TC (Day 55, 6 August 2009) pp. 15, 26.

102 Transcript of Trial Proceedings – *Kaing Guek Eav 'Duch'* 001/18-07-2007/TC (Day 55, 6 August 2009) p. 28.

103 Transcript of Trial Proceedings – *Kaing Guek Eav 'Duch'* 001/18-07-2007/TC (Day 55, 6 August 2009) p. 85; and see CHANDLER, above n. 2, p. 38.

104 Transcript of Trial Proceedings – *Kaing Guek Eav 'Duch'* 001/18-07-2007/TC (Day 55, 6 August 2009) p. 11.

105 Transcript of Trial Proceedings – *Kaing Guek Eav 'Duch'* 001/18-07-2007/TC (Day 55, 6 August 2009) p. 70.

106 Transcript of Trial Proceedings – *Kaing Guek Eav 'Duch'* 001/18-07-2007/TC (Day 55, 6 August 2009) pp. 111–112.

When asked what the purpose of the large S-21 archive was, Chandler suggested several possible reasons. Chandler posited that Duch kept records in such precise detail to demonstrate that the CPK leadership's suspicions were justified – uncovering 'strings of traitors, Vietnamese agents and so forth.' Duch may have wanted to demonstrate to the leadership his professionalism and that S-21 was an efficient, responsible and productive unit in a country in otherwise total chaos. However, Chandler speculated that Duch may also have wished his records to be a significant historical source in the event that Democratic Kampuchea successfully held on to power over the longer term.[107]

6.4.3.3. *S-21 and Dehumanisation*

Judge Lavergne questioned Chandler on his description of the S-21 universe as being 'completely inhuman, dehumanised.' Chandler addressed the question as a philosophical one. He said the lives of S-21 employees were certainly restricted by virtue of the tightly controlled institution. However, the detainees were the subject of dehumanisation, being deprived of respect physically, mentally and psychologically from the moment they arrived at S-21. Judge Lavergne then asked Chandler to consider whether an atmosphere of cynicism or paranoia pervaded the S-21 administration particularly with respect to the authenticity of confessions. In response, Chandler said that while the accused knew that confessions were not authentic, he let the whole machinery of producing fabricated confessions 'run on', knowing that his life would be in danger if he resisted the leadership's policy.[108]

Chandler was pressed by civil party lawyer Trusses Napprous on the dehumanisation of defenceless detainees by their gaolers in history. Chandler replied that the behaviour of S-21 personnel was not unprecedented. He recounted other moments in history where the dehumanisation of perceived enemies occurred with the permission of authorities, citing the massacres in Indonesia in 1965, the Nazi concentration camps and the gaols of South America in the 1970s.[109] Chandler added:

> [De-humanising behaviour] is a global phenomenon … Euphemistic terms such as body count, collateral damage and smash are used routinely to disguise the brutality of warfare. The word 'kill' is not used … At S-21 when dehumanising practices became routine and the guards and interrogators were not punished, they did not exercise

107 Transcript of Trial Proceedings – *Kaing Guek Eav 'Duch'* 001/18-07-2007/TC (Day 55, 6 August 2009) pp. 24–25.

108 Transcript of Trial Proceedings – *Kaing Guek Eav 'Duch'* 001/18-07-2007/TC, Day 55, 6 August 2009) p. 73.

109 Transcript of Trial Proceedings – *Kaing Guek Eav 'Duch'* 001/18-07-2007/TC, Day 55, 6 August 2009) pp. 73–74.

> restraint and were able to operate with more and not less enthusiasm. It was the same among the Red Guard of the Cultural Revolution.[110]

François Roux raised with Chandler the analysis of S-21 in his book as a site giving rise to the 'crime of obedience.' Chandler explained that within S-21 and Democratic Kampuchea broadly, 'the people who gave orders were accustomed to giving them and the people who received the orders were accustomed to obeying.' Furthermore, in Cambodia there was little questioning of the commands of people in authority. The culture of obedience fed into the horror that was S-21, as it did in other contexts of mass atrocity.[111]

Roux also asked for Chandler's opinion on Duch's admission of guilt? Chandler replied that he 'was moved by his acceptance of responsibility for his crimes; it impressed me because Duch is the only senior member of the CPK to have willingly confessed. History will be served by it.'[112]

In his response to the wide-ranging testimony, Duch praised Chandler for his virtue as a researcher. Interviewed by the press afterwards, Chandler described this as fawning praise in view of Chandler's age, perceived seniority and the submissive culture he had described in Court.[113]

Chandler's testimony and the Court's engagement with his research shed light on the nature of the crimes committed at S-21 in a general historical sense as well as within the Cambodian context specifically. His reference to a culture of obedience in Cambodian society as it applied to Duch and others added a sociological dimension to the crimes. The issue resurfaced in the evidence of the psycho-political experts when they gave their testimony.

6.4.4. FRANÇOISE SIRONI-GUILBAUD AND KA SUNBAUNAT

The psychological examination of Duch commissioned by the Co-Investigating Judges addressed the political and cultural context of his life at the time of the facts at issue, and his current psychology. At trial the judges invited the experts to outline the findings of their initial report and provide an oral update having observed the accused during the trial proceedings.[114]

---

110 Transcript of Trial Proceedings – *Kaing Guek Eav 'Duch'* 001/18-07-2007/TC (Day 55, 6 August 2009) pp. 73–74.

111 Transcript of Trial Proceedings – *Kaing Guek Eav 'Duch'* 001/18-07-2007/TC (Day 55, 6 August 2009) p. 118.

112 Transcript of Trial Proceedings – *Kaing Guek Eav 'Duch'* 001/18-07-2007/TC (Day 55, 6 August 2009) pp. 105–106.

113 'Just a Series of Ghastly Screw-ups', *Phnom Penh Post* (10 August 2009) http://phnompenpost.com/national/just_a_series_of_ghastly_screw_ups.

114 Transcript of Trial Proceedings – *Kaing Guek Eav 'Duch'* 001/18-07-2007/TC (Day 67, 31 August 2009) p. 12.

The experts were Dr. Françoise Sironi-Guilbaud a specialist in Geopolitical Clinical Psychology and Ka Sunbaunat, Professor of Psychiatry and Dean of the University of Health Services, Phnom Penh. Sironi-Guilbaud had extensive clinical experience in Paris working with both victims and perpetrators of war crimes. Ka Sunbaunat lived through the Khmer Rouge regime and worked with Cambodian and international NGOs on mental health issues in Cambodia. He had treated other Khmer Rouge perpetrators and brought this experience to the proceedings as he fielded questions from the Court. Sironi-Guilbaud noted that Ka Sunbaunat's clinical experience as a psychiatrist and as a Khmer with knowledge of the political and cultural history of Cambodia was a necessary adjunct to the 'western way of understanding political crime' in their assessment of Duch.[115]

Sironi-Guilbaud explained the clinical geopolitical approach used to assess Duch's psychology. The analysis incorporated not merely an individual's personal history, but the articulation within the person of collective social history having regard to political, economic and historical factors weighing on the personality of the subject. She cited by way of example, the weight of personal events in Duch's life such as his family's poverty and his father's exploitation at the hands of a usurious uncle, as well as cultural and political factors which conditioned his life choices. The experts also highlighted the significance of teachers as mentors in Cambodian life. Ka Sunabunat explained that Cambodian children begin their education under the tutelage of monks who are afforded great respect. In Duch's case, respect for his teachers was transferred to Son Sen, the francophone intellectual and pedagogue. Duch came to view Son Sen as his master, and later, as his subordinate at S-21, sought recognition from him through his work at the institution.[116]

The experts' initial psychological report was submitted to the Co-Investigating Judges on 31 March 2008. The report was based on 13 interviews with the accused, each of approximately three hours in length. There were three further interviews to update the experts' assessment before they gave an oral report during the trial on 28 and 29 August 2009. Informing their report to the Court were video recordings of Duch's presentation of a letter of excuse to victims, the re-enactments at S-21 and Choeung Ek, and Duch's confrontations with witnesses, as well as other conduct by Duch during the proceedings that the experts had observed.[117] After the experts gave their report they answered questions from the bench, the Co-Prosecution and Co-Defence.

---

115 Transcript of Trial Proceedings – *Kaing Guek Eav 'Duch'* 001/18-07-2007/TC (Day 67, 31 August 2009) p. 15.

116 Transcript of Trial Proceedings – *Kaing Guek Eav 'Duch'* 001/18-07-2007/TC (Day 67, 31 August 2009) pp. 21–22.

117 Transcript of Trial Proceedings – *Kaing Guek Eav 'Duch'* 001/18-07-2007/TC (Day 67, 31 August 2009) p. 16.

Sironi-Guilbaud reported that while Duch was highly intelligent with an excellent memory, he was influenced by the ideologies of his mentors in pursuit of a necessary personal ideal. This included not questioning the decision of the CPK's leadership to execute a prisoner as an enemy of the regime who had been a former teacher and whom Duch admired for speaking out against corruption and social injustice. As a student, Duch discovered Stoicism, a doctrine that promoted indifference in the face of difficult personal emotions.[118] His practice of stoicism and the development of certain defence mechanisms helped Duch function as the dedicated administrator of S-21 despite the presence within him of doubt and fear.[119]

Judge Lavergne asked Sironi-Guilbaud to comment on the significance of the geopolitical psychological method of analysis to the justice process for international crimes. Sironi-Guilbaud began by noting that the Co-Investigating Judges wanted Duch's capacities such as his intelligence level and ability to exhibit empathy assessed in the interests of justice. She then explained that the methodology involved avoided the bias of other psychological assessment methods which are limited to a person's individual history without reference to the collective social history that affects a person.[120] Sironi-Guilbaud noted that Duch's personality and behaviour were shaped by the collectivist ideology of the Khmer Rouge.[121] This involved suppression of his personal identity for the sake of complete identification with the collective.[122] His personal psychological traits merged with his political conditioning. Always reasoning as a mathematician and dismissing what was not logical became a form of denial.[123] His obsessional tendencies derived from earlier life experiences of humiliation and disappointment made him meticulous and a perfectionist in carrying out his duties. Attention to detail and a rigid approach to his work provided a framework for his life in the context of chaos.[124] Significantly, Duch exhibited a disorder referred to as 'alexithymia,' the state where the emotions of compassion and concern for the suffering of others are not expressed. This stemmed from his family history, his culture and his encounter with Communism. Ka explained

118 Transcript of Trial Proceedings – *Kaing Guek Eav 'Duch'*. 001/18-07-2007/TC (Day 67, 31 August 2009) p. 44.

119 Transcript of Trial Proceedings – *Kaing Guek Eav 'Duch'* 001/18-07-2007/TC (Day 67, 31 August 2009) pp. 21–22.

120 Transcript of Trial Proceedings – *Kaing Guek Eav 'Duch'* 001/18-07-2007/TC (Day 67, 31 August 2009) pp. 37–38.

121 Transcript of Trial Proceedings – *Kaing Guek Eav 'Duch'* 001/18-07-2007/TC (Day 67, 31 August 2009) p. 12.

122 Transcript of Trial Proceedings – *Kaing Guek Eav 'Duch'* 001/18-07-2007/TC (Day 67, 31 August 2009) pp. 31–32.

123 Transcript of Trial Proceedings – *Kaing Guek Eav 'Duch'* 001/18-07-2007/TC (Day 67, 31 August 2009) pp. 31, 44.

124 Transcript of Trial Proceedings – *Kaing Guek Eav 'Duch'* 001/18-07-2007/TC (Day 67, 31 August 2009) p. 79.

that in Cambodian society children were educated to maintain silence rather express emotions openly so as not to reveal weaknesses. In addition, Duch had been very attracted to Stoicism.[125] Ultimately, the emotions he allowed himself to feel were those 'that corresponded to the communist ideal and what was expected of him by his society.'[126]

However, while he obeyed the CPK leadership, their order to execute his former mentor Vorn Vet in 1977 had a shattering effect on him. Vorn Vet had been a highly respected CPK leader and he had to have him smashed along with former friends and teachers. This undermined his attachment to the Party and he began to expect that he too would be killed in due course.[127] In 1978, he despaired and fell into depression as the frame of his life disintegrated.[128]

Francois Roux asked the experts to explain their use of the words 'paranoid drift of the regime' in their report. Sironi-Guilbaud explained that Duch, along with his countrymen, had to adapt to the traumatic change imposed on the society by the Khmer Rouge leadership's amplification of the presence of enemies as a manifestation of their own paranoia.[129] Ka concurred:

> During the regime, the whole population had to adapt psycho-politically. I remember when we were first sent to the so-called liberated zone it was clear that the Khmer Rouge inhabited a different mental world. They demanded that we be ever vigilant against pessimism and false notions of peace. They fostered a mindset of mistrust in everyone.[130]

Generalising the psychological adjustment that society had to make to survive in this way communicated the regime's impact on the society as a whole to the Court and the wider public viewing the proceedings. On the traumatic upheaval in the society as a result of the regime's policies, Sironi-Guilbaud noted that adaptation took different forms, depending on the position and personal psychology of the individual. Some, like Duch, adapted by being zealous, until denial no longer protected him.[131]

---

[125] Transcript of Trial Proceedings – *Kaing Guek Eav 'Duch'* 001/18-07-2007/TC (Day 67, 31 August 2009) p. 44–45.

[126] Transcript of Trial Proceedings – *Kaing Guek Eav 'Duch'* 001/18-07-2007/TC (Day 67, 31 August 2009) pp. 43–45.

[127] Transcript of Trial Proceedings – *Kaing Guek Eav 'Duch'* 001/18-07-2007/TC (Day 67, 31 August 2009) pp. 30, 69–71.

[128] Transcript of Trial Proceedings – *Kaing Guek Eav 'Duch'* 001/18-07-2007/TC (Day 67, 31 August 2009) pp. 79–80.

[129] Transcript of Trial Proceedings – *Kaing Guek Eav 'Duch'* 001/18-07-2007/TC (Day 68, 1 September 2009) pp. 18–19.

[130] Transcript of Trial Proceedings – *Kaing Guek Eav 'Duch'* 001/18-07-2007/TC (Day 68, 1 September 2009) pp. 20–21.

[131] Transcript of Trial Proceedings – *Kaing Guek Eav 'Duch'* 001/18-07-2007/TC (Day 67, 31 August 2009) pp. 19, 56.

The international Co-Prosecutor, Ahmed asked Sironi-Guilbaud to comment on the kind of remorse they could expect from the accused. She replied that while Duch's victims may expect that he would not appreciate what they had suffered, there was a perceptible 'evolution in his awareness' and that he was moving beyond the state of disempathy. Furthermore, the question of what he can do to repair the damage resulting from his crime is a very real one for him, which suggested development in his psychology.[132] The expert noted that while Duch continued to exhibit traces of the Khmer Rouge shaping process and faced difficulties stepping out of his mathematical mindset, she noticed a developing awareness of the 'other' including the 'victim'.[133]

Roux pressed the experts on the nature of the 'process' Duch had embarked upon and the role the trial had played in this. Sironi-Guilbaud replied that while the process includes inhibition as the subject faced difficulty dealing with new awareness:

> [Duch's] remorse at the Choeung Ek enactment, his response to the suffering of former S-21 detainee Bou Meng during the proceedings, and tears when speaking for his former teacher Phung Ton suggest internal change. Crying, for instance can reveal that [the defence mechanism] splitting is not watertight.[134]

Ka added that publicly crying over his respected teacher sprang from something overwhelming within him which could not be suppressed.[135] The experts also noted the effects of external factors affecting Duch's development since his departure from the Khmer Rouge. In this regard, Duch's new found Christian faith had proved therapeutic.[136]

Sironi-Guilbaud viewed Duch's shifts from Buddhism to Communism and subsequently to Christianity as in line with his quest to live according to an ideal, involving transcendent beliefs, through affiliation with groups. These were also logical choices for him. Communism appeared to resolve the social injustice he saw in Cambodia, but Christianity had defeated Communism in Poland.[137] While it was logical for him to align himself with the stronger belief system, she posited that the Christian emphasis on the value of the individual as opposed to

---

132 Transcript of Trial Proceedings – *Kaing Guek Eav 'Duch'* 001/18-07-2007/TC (Day 68, 31 August 2009) pp. 90–92.

133 Transcript of Trial Proceedings – *Kaing Guek Eav 'Duch'* 001/18-07-2007/TC (Day 68, 31 August 2009) p. 95.

134 Transcript of Trial Proceedings – *Kaing Guek Eav 'Duch'* 001/18-07-2007/TC (Day 68, 1 September 2009) pp. 16–17.

135 Transcript of Trial Proceedings – *Kaing Guek Eav 'Duch'* 001/18-07-2007/TC (Day 68, 1 September 2009) p. 17.

136 Transcript of Trial Proceedings – *Kaing Guek Eav 'Duch'* 001/18-07-2007/TC (Day 67, 1 August 2009) p. 96.

137 Transcript of Trial Proceedings – *Kaing Guek Eav 'Duch'* 001/18-07-2007/TC (Day 67, 31 August 2009) p. 27.

the collective was the essential reason for his choice. But there was also the issue of rebirth through faith in Christ and forgiveness for sins in Christianity that were important elements of his thought processes in the 1990s.[138]

Ka Sunbaunat, speaking in Buddhist terms, thought that Duch's conversion to Christianity stemmed from the belief that he would be released from the sins or bad 'karma' he had acquired and would receive instead the forgiveness of God.[139] However, as I noted earlier at section 6.2.1, Duch knew in 1999 that there would be consequences for his actions and said so to the journalists who found him in Samlaut at that time.

In her response to Roux's question as to Duch's sincerity in the process of psychological change, Sironi-Guilbaud noted that at no stage in the assessment phase did they have a sense of Duch manipulating the circumstances he found himself in before the Court.[140] Roux pressed her further on two points. First, what were Duch's prospects, as the author of collective violence, of rehabilitation or re-humanisation? Sironi-Guilbaud replied that while rehabilitation was not always possible, in Duch's case she believed it was.[141] Secondly, was the re-humanisation of an executioner an important element in the lives of his victims? Sironi-Guilbaud answered by communicating her experience of working with the victims of international crimes:

> There is a process to be gone through for victims which involves a lot of suffering. While I cannot speak for individual victims, from my twenty years of clinical practice treating migrants in Paris, I have observed that failure to bring perpetrators to trial and failure to recognise the plight of victims made their recovery more difficult. The collective process of acknowledgment of what happened in their country in the past is crucial.[142]

The question and the expert's response opened the dialogue to discussion of victims' interests and the significance of the justice process for them. In a way uncharacteristic of international criminal proceedings, the exchange highlighted the importance of collective recognition of the past and its social impacts.

Thus, the psychological report and the Court's engagement with the experts created space for reflection on Duch's actions and the social effects of the Khmer

---

138 Transcript of Trial Proceedings – *Kaing Guek Eav 'Duch'* 001/18-07-2007/TC (Day 67, 31 August 2009) p. 75.

139 Transcript of Trial Proceedings – *Kaing Guek Eav 'Duch'* 001/18-07-2007/TC (Day 67, 30 August 2009) p. 76.

140 Transcript of Trial Proceedings – *Kaing Guek Eav 'Duch'* 001/18-07-2007/TC (Day 68, 1 September 2009) p. 12.

141 Transcript of Trial Proceedings – *Kaing Guek Eav 'Duch'* 001/18-07-2007/TC (Day 68, 1 September 2009) p. 24.

142 Transcript of Trial Proceedings – *Kaing Guek Eav 'Duch'* 001/18-07-2007/TC (Day 68, 1 September 2009) p. 25.

Rouge regime. As the drama of analysis played out over two days, the court became a forum for in-depth discussion of a perpetrator in his social context rather than merely a venue for the expressive display of due process.

6.4.5. CHHIM SOTHEARA

More expert testimony on factors going to the interests of victims was given by Dr. Chhim Sotheara, when he was called to give evidence in support of claims for victim reparations. In 2002, Chhim, a psychiatrist, became the Cambodian Director of the Transcultural Psychosocial Organisation (TPO), an international organisation which has responded to the socio-psychological needs of Cambodians, particularly those traumatised by the Khmer Rouge regime. The TPO implemented specialised programmes and disseminated information to assist victims of the regime. The Organisation also provided counselling services to support the accused and victims participating in ECCC proceedings, whether as civil parties or witnesses.[143]

The ECCC reparations framework invited discourse on matters of current social significance to Cambodia and its future development. The Trial Chamber gave Chhim a platform to raise such matters beginning with the incidence of post-traumatic stress disorder in Cambodia. Chhim described to the Court the high levels of (PTSD) in Cambodia as stemming from the time of the Khmer Rouge and the lack of services in the country to assist people suffering from the condition. He attributed the high incidence in Cambodia of domestic violence and alcoholism to PTSD resulting from the regime.[144]

The Chamber President asked Chhim to outline the nature of the trauma suffered by victims of the Khmer Rouge regime. He replied that the regime's destruction of the entire infrastructure and social fabric of Cambodian life had undermined every aspect of victims' lives. Judge Lavergne asked Chhim whether participation in the trial proceedings might help victims overcome the trauma of the Khmer Rouge years. Chhim replied:

> Many victims of the Khmer Rouge face daily challenges as a result of what they suffered under the regime. The opportunity to express their trauma helps, but does not heal completely. Victims participate in the proceedings to seek justice for themselves or their dead, and the truth to resolve some of their trauma. Knowing the truth, seeing fair justice process and receiving an apology from the perpetrator are important factors in

---

143 Christoph Sperfeldt, 'From the Margins of Internationalised Criminal Justice: Lessons Learned at the Extraordinary Chambers in the Courts of Cambodia' (2013) 11 *Journal of International Criminal Justice* 1111, 1120.

144 Transcript of Trial Proceedings – *Kaing Guek Eav 'Duch'*. 001/18-07-2007/TC (Day 64, 25 August 2009) pp. 14–16.

> their healing. But honesty from former Khmer Rouge leaders and their acceptance of responsibility is critical. Denial places an additional burden on victims and makes them furious.[145]

Further questioning on the TPO's current work with victims within their communities confirmed the importance of the ECCC to the long-term process of reconciliation in Cambodia. Roux asked Chhim if he could tell the Court a little about the work his organisation was doing in what he described as small truth and reconciliation commissions throughout the country. Chhim said:

> The TPO's work to date has been with victims only. But in their communities victims go to the same pagoda and use the same community facilities as [former Khmer Rouge] perpetrators. It is difficult for them. But after these trials my organisation will try to initiate programs to reconcile victims and perpetrators in communities. The first step is justice at the national level.[146]

His testimony confirmed the significance of the national justice process, but also illustrated how the TPO and other civil society groups supporting the work of the ECCC may operate as the necessary 'critical yeast' of a network of relationships connecting the work of the ECCC with on-the-ground peace-building.[147] I discuss at Chapter 9, Section 9.6 how other civil society organisations collected evidence, conducted education programmes on the purpose of the ECCC, supported civil parties through the application process and helped fund their legal representation.[148]

Under examination, Chhim's testimony extended the trial dialogue to issues affecting social repair and reconciliation in Cambodia. The Khmer Rouge recruitment of children as enforcers of their policies has made the process of reconciliation in Cambodia more complex.[149] The matter was raised during the proceedings as a result of the Court's engagement with the issue of the lower level perpetrator as also being a victim of the coercive regime. Co-Prosecutor Vincent De Wilde D'Estmael revisited the issue when he asked Chhim if he

145 Transcript of Trial Proceedings – *Kaing Guek Eav 'Duch'* 001/18-07-2007/TC (Day 64, 25 August 2009) pp. 17–18, 38–39.

146 Transcript of Trial Proceedings – *Kaing Guek Eav 'Duch'* 001/18-07-2007/TC, (Day 64, 25 August 2009) pp. 53–54.

147 John P. Lederach, *The Moral Imagination: The Art and Soul of Building Peace* (Oxford University Press, 2005) p. 91; See also John Braithwaite and Ray Nickson, 'Timing, Truth, Reconciliation, and Justice after War' (2012) 27 *Ohio Journal of Dispute Resolution* 443, 456–457.

148 Brianne Mcgonigle Leyh, *Procedural Justice? Victim Participation in International Criminal Proceedings* (Intersentia, 2011) p. 220.

149 See discussion of the complexities of life as a result of the regime that continue for many Cambodians in Suzannah Linton, *Reconciliation in Cambodia* (Documentation Center of Cambodia, 2004) pp. 75–88.

could comment on the victim/perpetrator relationship raised in the proceedings. Chhim replied:

> Yes, I can answer this from my experience in treating former guards of S-21. The guards were generally aged around 12 or 13 years when they were made Khmer Rouge soldiers, but their removal from families, the surrender of their identities and indoctrination victimised them, as well as making them perpetrators of crimes.[150]

The Cambodian government's policy of integrating former Khmer Rouge cadres without reconciliatory processes – designed to improve social relations by allowing perpetrators space to confess and explain their crimes within the communities they joined – reinforced the political nature of the reconciliation policy imposed.[151] Chhim's evidence therefore confirmed the levels of victimhood permeating Cambodian society which had not been systematically addressed.

Chhim was also questioned on the notion of forgiveness in Cambodian culture. While the expert commented that forgiveness is both individual and communal, he, like Dr. Sironi-Guilbaud, highlighted the importance of the accountability process:

> It is still too early to resolve the issue of forgiveness for the crimes. This may happen for some after the trials, but it is part of a long-term process for each victim. The important thing is revelation of the truth as to the events of the regime which goes some way towards relieving the suffering of victims.[152]

Thus, the Court's engagement with the expert expanded the trial narrative and opened up dialogue publicly on the complexities of perpetration, victimhood and reconciliation in Cambodia.

6.5. DUCH'S BID FOR RELEASE

After cooperating with the Court throughout the proceedings, in the final hours of the trial Duch asked to be released. While he confirmed to the Court that he still accepted responsibility for his crimes, he now sought release. Duch left the reasoning for his decision to his national Co-Defence counsel. Kar Savuth departed from Roux's position and argued that Duch had been wrongly indicted because he could not be considered one of the most responsible, since he was

---

150 Transcript of Trial Proceedings – *Kaing Guek Eav 'Duch'* 001/18-07-2007/TC (Trial Day 64, 25 August 2009) p. 32.

151 Linton, above n. 149, pp. 75–78, 95.

152 Transcript of Trial Proceedings – *Kaing Guek Eav 'Duch'* 001/18-07-2007/TC (Day 64, 25 August 2009) pp. 56–57.

not part of the Khmer Rouge senior leadership. The request took the Court by surprise as it presented the legal impossibility of an accused who had pleaded guilty, but now sought acquittal. Duch's request did not flow logically from the case his counsel had run. It may simply have been a statement of what he wanted or saw as justified at the conclusion of the trial, having engaged with the evidence and participated in the dialogue of the trial. This might then be viewed as a rational request from one who genuinely viewed himself as someone also victimised by the Khmer Rouge. In his final words to the Court Duch said: 'I will leave it to the Court to decide. I would ask the Chamber to release me. I'm very grateful.'[153] Indeed, it was left for the Court to ponder the meaning of the events in their judgment. Whatever the motivation for his last minute plea, it presented the Court with an additional communication from the accused to factor into their assessment of his character and culpability affecting sentence (as discussed further in Chapter 8, section 8.4.1 and see Chapter 9, section 9.2.3).

6.6. CONCLUSION

As Mégret suggested, a focus on the direct outcomes of transitional trials in the form of verdicts and sentences is to overlook significant communications of the trial proceedings. In the inquisitorial forum, the Court delved deeply into the psyche of Duch as alleged perpetrator and victim of mass atrocity crimes. While this was arguably intrusive for the accused, it seemed to form part of his decision to cooperate with the Court. As he cooperated, the proceedings shed light on the nature of perpetration within a totalitarian regime, and its domino effects at different levels within the affected society. Simultaneously, the judges' broad-brush approach to establishing the veracity of the case against the accused revealed someone other than the archetypal 'monster' perpetrator of international crimes.

The importance of causal understanding of crime ought not to be underestimated in a society where discussion of social problems in the aftermath of atrocities and collective memory has been suppressed. Within the controlled courtroom environment, the trial dialogue allowed factors within Cambodian history, culture and suffering to surface as relevant to causation and the consequences of Khmer Rouge crimes. While the trial discussions may be have been at odds with some Cambodians' interpretation of what happened in their country, as Osiel suggested, trials provide space where dissension may be both made public and reflected upon with the possibility of the emergence of

153 Transcript of Trial Proceedings – *Kaing Guek Eav 'Duch'* 001/18-07-2007/TC (Day 77, 27 November 2009) p. 59; Beth Van Schaak, 'Closing Arguments Part II: Duch Addresses the Court', Intllawgrrls (21 January 2010): http://www.intllawgrrls.com/2010/01/closing-arguments-part-ii-duch.html.

a discursive solidarity. Analysis of Duch's mental condition during the regime and the nature of his acceptance of responsibility for his crimes were important elements of the trial that became the subject of discussion in the interests of justice and society.

The Court's flexible engagements with witness testimony permitted intermediaries to both represent the interests of victims of crimes, and discuss objectively the significance of the national justice process to communities still affected by the Khmer Rouge years. Examination of Chhim's testimony on the plight of Khmer child soldiers as the victim/perpetrators served this purpose. As the trial proceedings revealed, the ongoing denials of the former Khmer Rouge leadership infuriate victims of their crimes. By exercising his participation rights in trial proceedings and engaging with other Court actors, Duch added another dimension to the proceedings as he intercepted Mam Nai's denials. In the Durkheim-ian sense, Duch's plea to Mam Nai shifted the trial discourse to the interests of Cambodian society and humanity at large. Here was a moment of high drama within the theatre of ideas, for public reflection. Duch's clear communication from the heart of the trial to national and international audiences affected by the crimes brought to the Court's public something more than the expressivism of conviction and clinical due process. Thus, the proceedings revealed the social drama behind the crimes which may have exceeded the expressivism of establishing objective guilt. In the next chapter, the trial dialogue flowing from victim story-telling in Case 001, Case 002/01 and Case 002/02 is considered.

CHAPTER 7
THE VOICE OF THE VICTIM

7.1. INTRODUCTION

The trial dialogue around witness testimony within the inquisitorial procedural frame discussed in the last chapter was enlarged by the ECCC's civil party reparations scheme. This chapter examines the voice of the civil party in ECCC proceedings in the context of debate on the role of the victim and fair trial process. The chapter discusses the context in which the role of the victim in transitional trials has developed. Arguments advanced for minimising victim participation in adversarial international criminal proceedings, and the problems arising at the ECCC from victim participation in trial proceedings, are then raised.

The nature of civil party participation in the ECCC trial proceedings is then discussed. This includes the Trial Chamber's approach in the Duch trial to the hearing of civil party claims for reparation and the testimony of a number of victim-witnesses. The communicative dynamics of the ECCC's inquisitorial procedure are analysed as narrative testimony permitted a degree of victim story-telling within the proceedings, followed by the Court's examination.

The Court forum in Cases 002/01 and Case 002/02 under the revised civil party participation scheme is then discussed. These cases involve more complex indictments than the Duch case, and in each case the two remaining accused persons have not accepted legal responsibility for the crimes charged. Factors going to the fairness and expediency of trial proceedings are discussed to highlight the delicate balancing act in which the Court is engaged, in the context of ongoing civil party participation in the trials. The argument is that the scheme of victim inclusion adopted by the ECCC and the adaptations it has made go some way towards grounding a philosophy of the transitional trial on the basis of its communicative value in the interest of justice.

7.2. THE VICTIM AND TRANSITIONAL TRIALS

The role of the victim in the transitional trial may be conceived in expressive or communicative terms. Recalling the Argentinian transitional trial context, Osiel described the role of victims as witnesses, in communicative terms. Quoting

Vezzetti, who supported trials for the military juntas, Osiel argued that the criminal procedure of the Court permitted the victims of crimes as witnesses to not only testify before the Court, but implicitly communicate their experience to the larger community.[1] The Nuremburg trials, on the other hand, while admitting the testimony of a few Jewish victims and some graphic documentary films of the Nazi persecution of Jews in concentration camps and communities, on the whole treated the Jews as victims in the abstract. The priority of those criminal proceedings was the 'spectacle of legality' as the Court exhibited proof of extreme crimes followed by judgment and punishment for Nazi perpetrators under the 'neutral rule of law.'[2] Documentary evidence in very large part bolstered the expressive approach adopted by the Prosecution.

However, trials that are characterised by extensive victim testimonial evidence may be both expressive and communicative. The 1961 national trial of Adolf Eichmann in Israel for his role as an administrator of the Nazi 'Final Solution' is an example of this. The Prosecutor of the case aimed to educate both young Israelis, and the world at large on the enormity of the human and national catastrophe that was the Holocaust, through a 'living record' represented by the victim-witness.[3] The trial was also designed to justify Israel's right to conduct the prosecution.[4]

The Eichmann trial was challenged by contemporary commentators on legitimacy grounds. Critics at the time were dubious of the Court's authority to exercise universal jurisdiction in the circumstances of the defendant having been kidnapped in order to be present in court, and were concerned that prosecutions in peacetime for the international crimes of genocide and crimes against humanity involved application of law retroactively. There was also criticism regarding the fairness of the trial due to the limited availability of defence witnesses, and concerns as to the independence and impartiality of the Israeli judges.[5] However, in retrospect, and in view of modern international criminal law jurisprudence, the work of the Court has stood the test of time.[6] Schabas argued that critics of the trial were too negative in their assessment and 'possibly influenced by the famous, but harsh commentary of Hannah Arendt' in her articles in the *New Yorker* at the time.[7] Arendt, critical of the extent of the

---

1 Mark Osiel, *Mass Atrocity, Collective Memory and the Law* (Transaction Publishers, 1997) p. 30, translating Hugo Vezzetti, 'El Juicio: Un Ritual de la Memoria Colectiva' (1985) *Punto de Vista* 3, 5.

2 Lawrence Douglas, *The Memory of Judgment: Making Law and History in the Trials of the Holocaust* (Yale University Press, 2011) p. 41.

3 Ibid. p. 106.

4 Ibid.

5 William Schabas, 'The Contribution of the Eichmann Trial' (2013) 26 *Leiden Journal of International Law* 667, 668–686.

6 Ibid. p. 687.

7 Ibid. p. 668.

Court's use of victim testimony, insisted that the Court's primary purpose was to render justice to the accused as the protagonist in proceedings, and that even the noblest of other purposes could only detract from the 'law's main business' of weighing the charges, rendering judgment and meting out punishment.[8] Arendt's conception of the trial reflected her acceptance of the formal authority of law and the expressivism of criminal procedure in a narrow sense.[9]

In other post-war transitional trials, the inclusion of survivor testimony in proceedings did not jeopardise their legitimacy. Empirical research on the German war crimes trials of guards and officials of the Auschwitz concentration camp, in the 1960s, and the Majdanek camp trials from 1975 to 1981, indicates that far from being regarded as illegitimate, the inquisitorial trials were socially transformative. Karstedt noted the significance of the visibility of victims in those trials compared to their relative absence at the Nuremburg trials. The later domestic trials, through the agency of victim testimony, revealed truths that could no longer be denied by German society. This produced a shift in public consciousness from collective amnesia in relation to the crimes of the Nazi era, which reshaped the collective memory.[10] The moral burden of response to the social and political messages of the trials was taken up by young and educated elites who catalysed social change. Noting the timing of the trials two and three decades after the war as determinative of their impact, she suggested that trials in societies traumatised by civil conflict have communicative dynamics beyond the expressivism of clinical fact-finding and the judgment of individuals.[11]

7.3. FAIRNESS AND LEGITIMACY IN INTERNATIONAL TRIALS

Because the international trial is politically contingent, the fairness of the criminal proceedings and legitimacy of the relevant court has been considered paramount. As the institutions of the modern system of international criminal justice were developed, the expressivism of strict due process standards overrode any other purpose trials might serve, including the communicative value of victim-witness testimony. As discussed in Chapter three, international courts

---

8 Hannah Arendt, *Eichmann in Jerusalem: Report on the Banality of Evil* (Penguin Books, 1977) pp. 204–205, 233.

9 Judith Shklar, *Legalism: Law, Morals, and Political Trials* (Harvard University Press, 1964) p. 2.

10 Susanne Karstedt, 'The Nuremburg Trial and German Society: International Justice and Local Judgement in Post-Conflict Reconstruction' in David A. Blumenthal and Timothy L.H. McCormack (eds.), *The Legacy of Nuremburg: Civilising Influence or Institutionalised Vengeance?* (Martinus Nijhoff Publishers, 2008) pp. 13, 33–34.

11 Ibid. pp. 29–33.

have associated victim participation in proceedings with instrumental support of the prosecution and the expressivism of criminal justice. When victim participation in proceedings threatens the fairness of proceedings, the trials may be construed as negatively expressive. However, as practice at the ad hoc Tribunals has shown, the legitimacy of international courts may be undermined by their failure to include sufficient local voice in proceedings.

7.3.1. VICTIM-WITNESS TESTIMONY AT THE AD HOC TRIBUNALS

Dembour and Haslam's analysis of the victim-witness at the International Criminal Tribunal for the Former Yugoslavia (ICTY) revealed that Osiel's vision of the communicative potential of victim-witness testimony did not play out at the ad hoc Tribunal. The ICTY adhered unreservedly to the strictures of adversarial criminal proceedings for the purpose of exhibiting fair and legitimate trials. Analysis of the trial proceedings in *Prosecutor v. Krstic* showed that far from providing victims with a platform from which to communicate their knowledge and experience of the crimes, the testimony demanded of them involved telling only that which related to proof of facts going to establish the guilt of the defendant.[12] Instrumentalised for the purposes of the Prosecution, the victim voice at the ICTY was limited to that which was precise, quantifiable and structured within a dichotomy of truth or falsehood. Rendering facts and their context in narrative form or conveying deeper impressions or atmosphere fell outside the expressive framework which the Court adopted, and as such, was irrelevant.[13] Even as victims were invited by the Presiding judge, after giving their testimony, to make closing remarks, the judge's platitudinous responses appeared disconnected from the pleas the witnesses made to the Court.[14] In short, there was no broader engagement with the victims of international crimes than this. Stover's analysis of the victim-witness at the ICTY also highlighted the limited space afforded victims and concluded that their treatment as victims of crime by the Court should be more respectful.[15] As discussed in Chapter three, section 3.4.4, victim-witnesses at the International Criminal Tribunal for

12 Marie-Benedicte Dembour and Emily Haslam, 'Silencing Witnesses? Victim-Witnesses at War Crimes trials' (2004) 15 *European Journal of International Law* 151, 158–163; *Prosecutor v. Krstic* (International Criminal Tribunal for the Former Yugoslavia, Trial Chamber, Case No. ICTY-IT-98-33-T, 2 August 2001).

13 Ibid. pp. 162–163.

14 Ibid. pp. 172–173.

15 Eric Stover, 'Witnesses and the Promise of Justice in the Hague' in Eric Stover and Harvey M. Weinstein (eds.), *My Neighbour, My Enemy: Justice and Community in the Aftermath of Mass Atrocity* (Cambridge University Press, 2004) pp. 104, 118–119.

Rwanda (ICTR) complained of being poorly treated under a foreign procedural system.[16]

7.3.2. THE VICTIM AT THE ICC

As discussed in Chapter three (sections 3.5.3–3.6) the ICC's *sui generis* victim participation scheme expanded representation in trial proceedings through rights granted to victims at various stages of the Court proceedings. However, implementation of those rights was somewhat fraught because the theoretical embrace of victim participation under the Rome Statute was largely a product of the 'constructive ambiguity of diplomatic negotiations.'[17] Under the predominantly adversarial procedure of the Court, it fell to the ICC judges to construe the relationship between the rights of accused persons to a fair trial and the rights of victims to participation in the midst of continuous arbitration between the prosecution and defence narratives.

Victims as witnesses provide first-hand knowledge of the crimes and can be useful to the Prosecution in conveying how the crimes occurred, but at the ICC they cannot assume the role of auxiliary prosecutors because that would constitute a breach of the defendant's right to equality of arms in relation to the prosecuting authority.[18] Zappalà argued that for the judges it was not a matter of balancing rights between victims and the defendant, but ensuring that the rights of the defendant retained primacy. The possibility that victim participation rights could result in unreasonable delay also threatened the notion of fairness normally associated with the rights of defendants. This, in turn may affect the legitimacy of the judicial institution.[19] Therefore, in the procedural system of the ICC, the fair trial rights of defendants override any competing right.[20]

While the contribution of victims to ICC proceedings has been recognised, the pedagogical value of the ICC as the site of enforcement and interpretation of international norms has taken precedence.[21] The dominance the ICC's expressive goals and its remoteness from the communities affected by the crimes tend to minimise the communicative potential of its proceedings. However, Court consultations on reparations awards with victim representatives and

16 Alison Des Forges and Timothy Longman, 'Legal Responses to Genocide in Rwanda' in Eric Stover and Harvey M. Weinstein (eds.), *My Neighbour, Myself: Justice and Community in the Aftermath of Mass Atrocity* (Cambridge University Press, 2004) pp. 49, 56.

17 Salvatore Zappalà, 'The Rights of Victims v The Rights of the Accused' (2010) 8 *Journal of International Criminal Justice* 137, 141.

18 Ibid. pp. 149, 163.

19 Ibid. p. 164.

20 Ibid. pp. 143–151.

21 Ibid. pp. 162–163.

officers of the Victims Trust Fund engage communicative action external to the proceedings.

7.4. VICTIM PARTICIPATION AT THE ECCC

In Chapter five, I discussed the ECCC's procedural scheme of inclusion of the victim in trial proceedings through incorporation of the civil party action. Implementing the victim participation scheme involved the judiciary in the complex exercise of arbitrating between multiple priorities. In procedural terms, this included upholding the rights of the accused, civil parties and witnesses, while ensuring fair and expeditious procedure in accordance with international standards and securing 'local legitimacy.'[22] In this, establishing a record of the accused's crimes involved both adherence to the rules of procedure and attending to the vulnerability of individual victims whose testimony of harrowing events formed part of the Court's purpose of contributing to reconciliation.

As the trials began, the adaptation of procedure by the ECCC to its context involved a struggle to give concrete effect to the principles and fundamental goals it pursued. In particular, issues of fairness had to be adjudicated on as the civil parties through their legal counsel sought to express views and concerns during Case 001. Civil parties availed themselves of their rights to participation from the investigation stage onward. Having access to the case file, they exercised their right to submit requests for specific investigations, potentially reshaping the prosecution case by adding information to the Introductory Submission provided to the Co-Investigating Judges. Civil parties also made written and oral submissions in Pre-Trial Chamber (PTC) proceedings and appealed against the Court's decisions.[23] In addition, as described in Chapter five, some civil parties questioned Duch in interviews and participated in the re-enactment of conditions at S-21 and at the Choeung Ek killing field. Duch's engagement with the civil parties became emblematic of the trial. However, the liberality of civil party rights under the Internal Rules evolved in the face of challenges by the Co-Prosecutors and the Co-Defence as the trial proceeded.

7.4.1. CIVIL PARTY QUESTIONING OF WITNESSES

At Duch's trial 90 civil parties were ultimately represented by four teams of civil party lawyers who questioned witnesses in concert with up to five judges, the

---

22 Frédéric Mégret, 'Beyond Fairness': Understanding the Determinants of International Criminal Procedure' (2009) 14 *UCLA Journal of International Law and Foreign Affairs* 37, 76.

23 Brianne McGonigle Leyh, *Procedural Justice? Victim Participation in International Criminal Proceedings* (Intersentia, 2011) pp. 185–186.

Co-Prosecution and Co-Defence. While the civil party lawyers had a common goal, their questioning of witnesses was initially uncoordinated, repetitious and frequently strayed off topic.[24] The Trial Chamber President confirmed that civil parties were entitled to pose questions to witnesses 'in support of the prosecution' as long as they were not repetitious, 'long-winded,' or irrelevant.[25] The Court also imposed time-limits on witness questioning by the counsel teams, in the interests of fair and expeditious proceedings.[26]

However, the Co-Defence pressed the court to consider the limits of civil party questioning on the basis that those parties ought not to be considered second (auxiliary) prosecutors and as such able to draw out inculpatory evidence from the accused, because that was the sole province of the Co-Prosecutor.[27] The issue of the exclusivity of the role of the Co-Prosecutors was not specifically ruled on by the Trial Chamber at that stage, but it surfaced in rulings sought by the civil party representatives on the rights of civil parties to make submissions on sentencing, and to question the accused or certain witnesses as to the accused's character.

7.4.2. LIMITS ON CIVIL PARTY SUBMISSIONS ON SENTENCING

In response to the Co-Defence contention that civil parties had no part to play in the sentencing process, two of the civil party groups, through their lawyers requested a Trial Chamber ruling on the matter. The Trial Chamber by majority (4–1) ruled that the civil party right to participate in proceedings in support of the prosecution stemmed from the right to reparations upon a conviction of the accused. That right was not to be construed as conferring a general right of equal participation with the Co-Prosecutors, whose role is to represent the community, not individual or sectional interests:

> The Co-Prosecutors' responsibility is to ensure an appropriate sentence and the civil parties' is to seek reparations as provided in the Internal Rules. The Co-Prosecutors have no role in seeking reparation, and the civil parties have none in relation to sentencing.

24 Michelle Staggs Kelsall, et al., *Lessons Learned from the 'Duch' Trial: A Comprehensive Review of the First Case Before the Extraordinary Chambers in the Courts of Cambodia* (Asian International Justice Initiative, December 2009) p. 32.

25 Transcript of Proceedings – *Kaing Guek Eav Duch* 001/18-07-2007/ECCC/TC (Trial Day 31 22 June 2009) pp. 92–95.

26 Staggs Kelsall, above n. 24, p. 32.

27 Transcript of Proceedings – *Kaing Guek Eav Duch* 001/18-07-2007/ECCC/TC (Trial Day 31, 22 June 2009) pp. 92–93.

The latter is the preserve of the prosecution in the public interest and in the interests of justice.[28]

The majority ruling was a severe blow to the civil parties, who were shocked and disappointed with the majority's restrictive approach to their participation rights.[29]

7.4.3. CIVIL PARTIES AND CHARACTER EVIDENCE

In the same decision the Trial Chamber also ruled on the right of civil parties to give character evidence. The majority held that because such testimony was for the purpose of determining aggravating or mitigating circumstances in relation to any eventual sentence, and not related to reparation, this was the exclusive province of the Co-Prosecution.[30] In a strong dissent Judge Jean-Marc Lavergne disagreed with the distinction made by the majority between proceedings pertaining to guilt, and proceedings pertaining to sentence, which had the effect of denying standing to victims to participate. The distinction was particularly important at the ECCC, where trial and reparations proceedings are not separated.[31]

Judge Lavergne prefaced his findings by explaining the challenge facing the ECCC in maintaining a balance between, on the one hand, the requirement of fair and expeditious trial with respect for the rights of the accused, and on the other hand, the right of victims to participate in a trial which aims, *inter alia*, to contribute to the fight against impunity of the perpetrators of the most serious crimes.[32] While he noted the need for some change stemming from the difficulties in implementing a civil party system not designed for the trial of

---

28 Decision on Civil Party Co-lawyers' Joint Request for a Ruling on the Standing of Civil party Lawyers to make Submissions on Sentencing and Directions Concerning the Questioning of the Accused, Experts and Witnesses Testifying on Character 'Duch'. 001/18-07-2007-ECCC-TC (9 October 2009) para. 42.

29 Michael Saliba, 'Civil Party Participation at the ECCC: Overview', *Cambodia Tribunal Monitor* (6 November 2009) pp. 1, 4.

30 Decision on Civil Party Co-lawyers' Joint Request for a Ruling on the Standing of Civil party Lawyers to make Submissions on Sentencing and Directions Concerning the Questioning of the Accused, Experts and Witnesses Testifying on Character 'Duch'. 001/18-07-2007/ECCC/TC (9 October 2009) para. 47.

31 Decision on Civil Party Co-lawyers' Joint Request for a Ruling on the Standing of Civil party Lawyers to make Submissions on Sentencing and Directions Concerning the Questioning of the Accused, Experts and witnesses Testifying on Character 'Duch'. 001/18-07-2007/ECCC/TC (9 October 2009) Lavergne dissent, para. 32.

32 Ibid. (Lavergne dissent) para. 3.

mass atrocity crimes, and involving potentially large numbers of individual civil parties, he asked:

> How far can one go without breaching the spirit of the law, or fundamentally distorting the meaning of the involvement of civil parties before the ECCC and the purpose of the trial as a whole, characterised by the coexistence of two interrelated actions, namely criminal and civil actions?[33]

Excluding the civil parties from proceedings dealing with the character of the accused was not only at odds with Cambodian law and the ECCC Internal Rules but with the interest of justice. Lavergne argued that the interest of justice extends beyond establishing the objective culpability of the accused. All parties, including the civil parties, have an interest in understanding what motivated the relevant criminal conduct for the purpose of avoiding its repetition.[34] The Judge referred to the expert testimony of Chhim Sotheara, who described the plight of victims of the Khmer Rouge, and the high incidence of post-traumatic stress disorder in Cambodia as stemming from the time of the regime. Judge Lavergne argued that the inclusion of victim evidence in the interest of justice was particularly significant where justice had been delayed or crimes concealed.[35] He noted that it was not only important for victims to contribute to the trial process by putting questions and making comments, but that there should also be debate within the 'serenity of a court of justice' which included civil parties sharing their knowledge of the accused.[36]

Open informed debates also relieve the victims of some of their uncertainties and lack of knowledge of the accused. Earlier in the trial proceedings, the Court had recognised this by authorising civil parties to put questions to several expert witnesses called by the Co-Defence to testify on the practice of guilty pleas on the one hand, and the notion of forgiveness on the other. Continued participation in proceedings for the purpose of contribution to the Court's knowledge of the accused and the gaining of victim knowledge is arguably crucial in the context of ECCC proceedings because of the trauma suffered by victims of the Khmer Rouge at the hands of the abstract organisational entity, Angkar. Excluding victims from debates on the character of the accused was thus inconsistent with the Court's earlier practice of inclusion to further one of its fundamental goals of assisting reconciliation in Cambodia. Civil party participation in the Romano-Germanic tradition, encompassing the review of all evidence, including character

33 Ibid. (Lavergne dissent) para. 4.
34 Ibid. (Lavergne dissent) para. 32.
35 Ibid. (Lavergne dissent) para. 28.
36 Ibid. (Lavergne dissent) para. 30.

evidence, was not considered a violation of the equality of arms principle or at odds with the notion of fair trial.[37] Moreover,

> in a difficult context in which the credibility of the Chambers is scrutinised and in which the administration of justice by the ECCC is supposed to serve as an example for the Cambodian Courts, it is important to be able to maintain public trust; a goal which would be more easily attained if the Chambers ensure respect for the rights of victims who have applied to be joined as civil parties.[38]

Judge Lavergne's acceptance of the victim perspective in trial proceedings as integral to inquisitorial justice in the transitional context, adds to the debate in the wider realm of international criminal justice on the inclusion of victim views and concerns at trial. His argument that the ECCC should ensure respect for the rights of victims contrasts with Zappalà's assertion of the primacy of the rights of the accused at the ICC at all costs. Notwithstanding the different procedural underpinnings of the ICC and the ECCC, Lavergne's opinion invites reappraisal of the narrow rules-based conception of the administration of justice for expressive effect. His argument for wider discussion within substantive trial proceedings based on a broader view of criminal justice implicitly raised the value of communication through victim representation in trial proceedings as a crucial element in fair transitional trials. Added to this, where transitional courts operate *in situ* there seems to be no reason to overlook research findings indicating that local legitimacy and the notion of fairness in trials is enhanced by more representative proceedings.[39]

7.5. CIVIL PARTY STORY-TELLING: CASE 001 AND CASE 002

The Trial Chamber's majority ruling meant that civil party representatives did not participate substantively in the examination of the accused's character discussed in Chapter six. However, in the Duch trial the Court permitted extensive survivor story-telling as it examined the civil parties' claim for reparations. In addition, the judges fostered open engagement with victim-witnesses as they testified at other stages of the proceedings. In the following section I discuss the Court's

---

37 Ibid. (Lavergne dissent) para. 33.

38 Ibid.

39 Ray Nickson and John Braithwaite, 'Deeper, Broader, Longer Transitional Justice' (2013) 11 *European Journal of Criminology* 445, 454; Eric Stover, Mychelle Balthazard and K. Alexa Koenig, 'Confronting Duch: Civil Party Participation in Case 001 at the Extraordinary Chambers in the Courts of Cambodia' (2011) 93 *International Review of the Red Cross* 503, 531–532.

broad-brush approach to survivor testimony and consider the extent to which the resultant proceedings were either expressive or communicative.

While each witness was called for a substantive evidential purpose, the Court exercised latitude in relation to each person in recognition of the difficulty of recalling painful memories, and the individual reason/s each had for presenting in Court. Following their statements to the Court, the civil parties were invited to put their own questions to the accused. The accused was entitled to respond to the witness or civil party. Excerpts from victim stories are paraphrased below. They are not included to suggest the therapeutic value to victims of their participation in proceedings, but to illustrate what their presence and statements or testimony added to the proceedings. The Case 001 excerpts include the stories of victims testifying as either witnesses or civil parties. The civil party stories include direct and indirect victims. The discussion of Case 002 proceedings examines aspects of civil party participation following the Trial Chamber's severance orders and changes to civil party representation.

7.5.1. CASE 001: DIRECT VICTIMS OF S-21

Vann Nath, Chum Mey, and Bou Meng were the remaining survivors of the S-21 detention centre. As direct victims and eye-witnesses, they were each called to give evidence on the functioning of S-21. Vann Nath testified as a victim-witness. Chum Mey and Bou Meng had civil party status. The President invited each survivor to speak of their lives before 17 April 1975 and of how they came to be held at S-21. Each testimony therefore took the form of a narrative which was subjected to later examination by the Court. As examinations proceeded, each witness communicated their opinion on the past and their view of the Court's role in addressing it. As was the case with eye- and expert-witnesses, the Judges, and at times Counsel also sought to draw larger meaning from the survivors' experience beyond the purpose of objective proof of Duch's culpability.

7.5.1.1. Vann Nath

Vann Nath was called as a witness by the Trial Chamber. He did not seek civil party status because of its essential connection with an award of reparations. He viewed any such award as inadequate in the face of what he had lost and was opposed to the opportunism he perceived in some civil party applicants.[40] He

---

40 Mahdev Mohan, 'The Paradox of Victim-Centrism: Victim Participation at the Khmer Rouge Tribunal' (2009) 9 *International Criminal Law Review* 733, 763.

also suffered from ill health and was afraid he would not be able to attend regular hearings of the Court.[41]

On 17 April 1975 Nath was a painter in Battambang when the Khmer Rouge came to evacuate the city. He and his family relocated to O Mony Pir village where they worked in rice fields until he was arrested by Khmer Rouge cadres on 30 December 1977.[42] Accused of being a traitor to Angkar and the revolution, he was shackled, interrogated and tortured on the pretext of suspected involvement in treacherous networks.[43] On 7 January 1978, he was loaded with other prisoners into a truck which took them to S-21. There Nath was initially bound in leg-irons with other detainees, but one day he was taken to meet Duch, who ran the security complex. Duch gave Nath a photo of Pol Pot and asked him to produce portraits of the leader.[44] Nath was re-housed with Bou Meng, also an artist, in an area of S-21 that became their studio.

In his testimony Nath described the torture he directly observed at S-21 which he had also reproduced in paintings.[45] He conveyed the accounts of others who had been tortured, including a woman who said that she 'lost her female character'[46] and male prisoners who suffered water-boarding techniques.[47] The Court viewed a series of 14 of his sketches and paintings which captured his recollections of S-21. These included a painting of a thin, sick young man whose hands and feet were tied to a pole which was being carried by two guards, aged around 15 or 16 years, to be loaded onto a waiting truck.[48] Nath also captured the shackling of prisoners en masse at S-21 and the torture of Bou Meng by two guards who took turns in beating him.[49] The quietly spoken man's verbal descriptions and his art gave powerful expression to the inhumane nature of the institution that had imprisoned him.

Nath was examined by the Chamber President, three of the other judges, three civil party lawyers, the Co-Prosecution, and Co-Defence. Most of the

---

41 Ibid.

42 Transcript of Trial Proceedings – *Kaing Guek Eav 'Duch'* 001/18-07-2007/ ECCC/TC (Day 35, 29 June 2009) pp. 14–15.

43 Transcript of Trial Proceedings – *Kaing Guek Eav 'Duch'* 001/18-07-2007/ECCC/TC (Day 45, 15 July 2009) pp. 13–19.

44 Transcript of Trial Proceedings – *Kaing Guek Eav 'Duch'* 001/18-07-2007ECCC/TC (Day 45, 15 July 2009) pp. 19–21.

45 Transcript of Trial Proceedings – *Kaing Guek Eav 'Duch'* 001/18-07-2007/ECCC/TC (Day 45, 15 July 2009) p. 33.

46 Transcript of Trial Proceedings – *Kaing Guek Eav 'Duch'* 001/18-07-2007/ECCC/TC (Day 45, 15 July 2009) p. 45.

47 Transcript of Trial Proceedings – *Kaing Guek Eav 'Duch'* 001/18-07-2007/ECCC/TC (Day 45, 15 July 2009) pp. 43–44.

48 Transcript of Trial Proceedings – *Kaing Guek Eav 'Duch'* 001/18-07-2007/ECCC/TC (Day 45, 15 July 2009) p. 48.

49 Transcript of Trial Proceedings – *Kaing Guek Eav 'Duch'* 001/18-07-2007/ECCC/TC (Day 45, 15 July 2009) p. 46.

questioning concerned factual matters as to his arrest and detention. Some questioning was more expansive as the Court trawled beyond the facts. Judge Lavergne, for instance, asked the witness:

> How have you dealt with the trauma of your experience at S-21, and why did you choose to testify to events at S-21 through paintings, as well as the book you wrote, and by your involvement in a documentary film?[50]

The witness explained his determination from his days at S-21 that if he survived he would record the events so that the younger generation would know of the suffering and injustice which the innocent held at S-21 had endured. He sought to educate the young so that such history would never be repeated.[51] He explained further that as time passed he was challenged by children who had not been given any information by their parents about the acts of Khmer Rouge agents. He explained to them that their parents were perhaps so traumatised by those times that to recall the past would be painful for them.[52]

When asked what he was expecting from the trial, Vann Nath replied that he had never imagined a public trial would eventuate. It was a privilege to now be able to testify, and he hoped that the trial would achieve tangible justice.[53] At the end of his testimony he was asked what became of his family after he was taken from the Khmer Rouge collective that they had been sent to. He responded that though his wife survived, his two young children did not.[54]

7.5.1.2. Chum Mey

As a civil party, Chum Mey was not obliged to take an oath before testifying. While his testimony aided the Co-Prosecution case, questioning on the nature of his suffering also supported his claim for reparations. To establish their claim, the civil parties had to satisfy the Chamber of the existence of wrongdoing attributable to the accused which had a direct causal connection to the demonstrable injury they had suffered personally.[55]

---

50 Transcript of Trial Proceedings – *Kaing Guek Eav 'Duch'* 001/18-07-2007/ECCC/TC (Day 45, 15 July 2009) pp. 53–54.

51 Transcript of Trial Proceedings – *Kaing Guek Eav 'Duch'* 001/18-07-2007/ECCC/TC (Day 45, 15 July 2009) p. 54.

52 Transcript of Trial Proceedings – *Kaing Guek Eav 'Duch'* 001/18-07-2007/ECCC/TC (Day 45, 15 July 2009) p. 89.

53 Transcript of Trial Proceedings – *Kaing Guek Eav 'Duch'* 001/18-07-2007/ECCC/TC (Day 45, 15 July 2009) pp. 55–56.

54 Transcript of Trial Proceedings – *Kaing Guek Eav 'Duch'* 001/18-07-2007/ECCC/TC (Day 45, 15 July 2009) p. 53.

55 *Kaing Guek Eav (alias Duch)* (Judgment) 001/18-2007/ECCC/TC (26 July 2010) para. 637.

The Judges questioned Chum Mey on the events leading to his detention at S-21 and the torture he endured. Chum Mey was evacuated from Phnom Penh in April 1975 but later answered a call from Angkar for mechanics. In 1978, he and several of his fellow workers were arrested and taken to S-21 where he was accused of being a CIA or KGB agent. He described the physical pain he suffered, and his anguish at the dehumanising conditions in which detainees were kept. He was tortured over 12 consecutive days and nights before he confessed and implicated others as traitors.[56] At this the torture stopped. Like Vann Nath, Chum Mey escaped execution because of his occupational skills. He was sent to the S-21 workshop where he repaired typewriters and other machinery with several others who lived and worked there. As the Vietnamese approached Phnom Penh on 7 January 1979 they were all ordered out of S-21 by the guards. After the group scattered, Chum Mey managed to find his wife and baby at Prey Sar, but in a gun battle with a Khmer Rouge band his wife and baby born in prison were killed as they tried to flee.[57]

The judges asked Chum Mey to describe the long-term effects of his detention on his physical and mental health. While he was angry and depressed for a long time, the prospect of testifying before the Court and seeing justice done had relieved Chum Mey's anxiety. His participation in the trial had given meaning to his life. In an interview before his testimony he asked: What would the point of my life have been if I died before the trial? To Chum Mey the trial 'vindicated his survival.'[58] He attended all the proceedings.[59] In an interview with Eric Stover after he had given his statement in court, he expressed satisfaction and relief at having been able to 'tell the truth' about events at S-21.[60]

Chum Mey also communicated something common to most of the civil parties: a need to confront Duch.[61] During testimony on his treatment at S-21, he repeatedly lashed out at Duch who was sitting to the right of the witness stand with his Co-Defence counsel. The Chamber President asked him to cease being abusive towards the accused. At the end of Chum Mey's cross-examination he was given the opportunity he sought to put questions to the accused. His questions concerned the organisations which had been used to threaten him; the CIA, the KGB and Angkar. Who or what were they? Duch responded by describing the CIA and KGB as those perceived as opponents of the Central

---

56 Transcript of Trial Proceedings – *Kaing Guek Eav 'Duch'* 001/18-07-2007/ECCC/TC (Day 36, 30 June 2009) p. 29.

57 Transcript of Trial Proceedings – *Kaing Guek Eav 'Duch'* 001/18-07-2007/ECCC/TC (Day 36, 30 June 2009) p. 51.

58 Mohan, above n. 40, 763.

59 Transcript of Trial Proceedings – *Kaing Guek Eav 'Duch'* 001/18-07-2007/ ECCC/TC (Day 36, 30 June 2009) p. 35.

60 Stover, above n. 39, p. 521.

61 Ibid. p. 527.

Committee of the Communist Party of Kampuchea (CPK). Angkar was simply the Standing Committee of the CPK and among that group Pol Pot was referred to as Angkar.[62] The rare exchange between victim and perpetrator shifted the proceedings not only from the expressive to the communicative, but arguably in a tangible sense, towards restorative rather than retributive justice.

7.5.1.3. Bou Meng

Bou Meng was an artist and teacher who joined the CPK in 1971 when they were operating from jungle locations. There Bou Meng had drawn sketches of communist heroes: Karl Marx, Engels, Lenin and Mao Zedong.[63] However, by 1976, though he remained obedient to Angkar, he had lost faith in its purposes. He spoke of the hard physical labour he was assigned to perform and the frequent disappearances of people he worked with. After being relocated for re-education at the Ta Lei Cooperative, he and his wife were taken to S-21.[64] Although Bou Meng was severely tortured at S-21, he survived due to his skills as an artist. He, like Vann Nath was assigned to paint portraits of Pol Pot.

In contrast to Chum Mey, Bou Meng continued to live in despair and pain. He was overcome with emotion as he related his experience of S-21. As this happened the Cambodian Trial Chamber President, addressing him as 'Ta' (uncle), spoke at length to him about the importance of composing himself in order to tell the Chamber and the public of what befell him at the hands of former comrades and the suffering he had endured since then.[65] Both Bou Meng and his wife were orphans. They were separated when they arrived at S-21 and he never saw her again. When questioned about her, he said he heard that she had been sent to work in rice fields. One of the reasons he was testifying was to ask Duch what had happened to her. Duch was visibly moved by the anguish of Bou Meng and his weaker physical state attributed to the torture and hardship he had suffered.[66] He had no precise information as to the fate of Bou Meng's wife, but suggested that Comrade Huy may have had some details. He said he

---

62 Transcript of Trial Proceedings – *Kaing Guek Eav 'Duch'* 001/18-07-2007/ECCC/TC (Day 36, 30 June 2009) p. 76.

63 Transcript of Trial Proceedings – *Kaing Guek Eav 'Duch'* 001/18-07-2007/ECCC/TC (Day 37, 1 July 2009) p. 57.

64 Transcript of Trial Proceedings – *Kaing Guek Eav 'Duch'* 001/18-07-2007/ECCC/TC (Day 37, 1 July 2009) p. 59.

65 Transcript of Trial Proceedings – *Kaing Guek Eav 'Duch'* 001/18-07-2007/ ECCC/TC (Day 37, 1 July 2009) pp. 14–15.

66 Transcript of Trial Proceedings – *Kaing Guek Eav 'Duch'* 001/18-07-2007/ECCC/TC (Day 37, 1 July 2009) p. 67.

believed that she had been executed at Choeung Ek. He then asked Bou Meng to accept his deepest respect for her soul.[67]

Before the trial, Bou Meng had no time for Duch's due process rights, and the judgment of the Court seemed secondary in importance to compensation for what he had suffered.[68] After the trial however, he said that 'testifying had helped release some of his anger.'[69] The portrait of Bou Meng's life conveyed through the Court's engagement with him communicated something the proceedings did not otherwise focus on: the plight of a lower level Khmer Rouge cadre deeply damaged by his/her association with the regime. This added a further perspective on the crimes of the Khmer Rouge and their long-term effects on Cambodians still recovering from the regime.

7.5.2. CASE 001: INDIRECT VICTIMS

Civil parties who were indirectly harmed through the loss of family members or those closely associated with their families made statements to the Court. Through subsequent examination, the extent of the human cost of the Khmer Rouge era came into focus. Duch's engagement with those who sought to confront him was also revealing. He accepted the condemnation of those whose stories were verifiable and made some explicit apologies. Where their accounts raised doubts in his mind as to factual accuracy, he raised questions as to the authenticity of the claim. Though the Court had become familiar with this pattern in his behaviour, it was disconcerting to some of the civil parties.

7.5.2.1. Bou Thon

Bou Thon was called as a witness of fact on the functioning of S-24 where she had been detained. She was the wife of Phouk Hon who was detained at S-21. Though her story was fragmented, Bou Thon's tale of separation, loss and dehumanisation in Khmer Rouge camps conveyed the hardship and desperation of many Cambodians during and after those times. After the Khmer Rouge took power in Phnom Penh, Phouk Hon worked as a truck driver for the Ministry of Energy of Democratic Kampuchea. In 1976, Phouk Hon was taken to S-21 because the CPK leadership suspected him of being connected with Koy Thuon, whom they had determined to execute. At this time Bou Thon had given birth

---

67 Transcript of Trial Proceedings – *Kaing Guek Eav 'Duch'* 001/18-07-2007/ ECCC/TC (Day 37, 1 July 2009) p. 70.

68 Mohan, above n. 40, p.764.

69 Stover, bove n. 39, p. 530.

to her fourth child. The couple's other three children had already been sent to a Khmer Rouge child-minding centre, and she never saw them again. Bou Thon with her infant son worked in a Khmer Rouge collective before she was sent to S-24. Her youngest child died in her arms while she was on the run after the Vietnamese entered Phnom Penh in 1979.[70]

Cruvellier, observing her testimony, reported:

> Bou Thon talks and talks. But instead of making me drowsy, her story grips my attention. She uses fragments of dialogue and description to recreate the banality of camp life, and to evoke how the twin obsessions of hunger and interrogation hung over everything.[71]

The depth of Bou Thon's loss, and the hardship that she had endured under the regime resounded through the Court. Duch readily confirmed details of her story and commended her for her courage. He reflected that around million other people similarly lost their families under the Khmer Rouge. He concluded as Bou Thon herself had, that her husband and children had died at Choeung Ek.[72] In an emotional response Duch said:

> I want to be close to the Cambodian people, if they choose to condemn me, they can and I will accept it. I must accept it, no matter how heavy the sentence. I won't use a bucket to hide an elephant. At the time we thought that the Yuon [Vietnamese] were invading Cambodia. Now, finally, before all of you and before the Cambodian people, I would like to share this pain from the bottom of this heart. I will accept this court's judgment. I wish for the Cambodian people to condemn me as quickly as possible.[73]

The intensity of the illiterate woman's account filled the Court, affected the defences of the accused and resonated strongly in the transcript of the proceedings.

7.5.2.2. Antonya Tioulong

In the reparations proceedings, civil party Antonya Tioulong was asked by the President of the Chamber to describe the nature of the harm she suffered as an indirect victim of crimes before the Court. Antonya gave an eloquent and

---

70 Transcript of Trial Proceedings – *Kaing Guek Eav 'Duch'* 001/18-07-2007/ECCC/TC (Day 58, 12 August 2009) pp. 3–16.

71 Thierry Cruvellier, *The Master of Confessions: The Making of a Khmer Rouge Torturer* (Harper Collins, 2014) p. 204.

72 Transcript of Trial Proceedings – *Kaing Guek Eav 'Duch'* 001/18-07-2007-ECCC/TC (Day 58, 12 August 2009) pp. 46–47.

73 Cruvellier translation, above n. 71, pp. 205–206; *Transcript of Trial Proceedings – Kaing Guek Eav 'Duch'* 001/18-07-2007-ECCC/TC (Day 58, 12 August 2009) p. 47.

impassioned account of the loss of her sister and brother-in-law to the Khmer Rouge. Her sister Raingsy's admission that she was the daughter of Samdech Chakrey Nhoek Tioulong, a senior official of Sihanouk's government had sealed Raingsy's fate of detention at S-21 and death. As Phnom Penh was bombed in 1973, Raingsy and her husband sent their three children to France to join Antonya and her parents. Antonya described the suffering that the children and all the family experienced when the Khmer Rouge took Phnom Penh in 1975 and they had no word from Raingsy. She described her own attempts to impress upon the French government the need to take Cambodian refugees who were pouring into Thai camps.[74] News of Raingsy's detention at S-21 came through her cousins, who joined their family as refugees in France in 1979.[75] Antonya explained that although she tried desperately to trace what had happened to her sister, she and Raingsy's children had to endure almost two decades of silence due to the secretive nature of the regime, and the international community's failure to engage with Cambodia until the early 1990s. Only on her return to Cambodia in 1994 was Antonya able to discover more. On a visit to the Tuol Sleng Museum (formerly the site of S-21) Antonya found Raingsy's photo as a detainee.[76] The story of Antonya's relentless search communicated to the Court the void created at the micro-level by national oppression, and by inaction at the geopolitical level to press for Khmer Rouge accountability for their crimes.

Antonya, like other civil parties, clearly felt compelled to be her sister's advocate, to declare who she was and how much her family missed her. She asked the Court to show photos of Raingsy on the projector to Duch. She requested the Court to impose a sentence commensurate with the gravity of his crimes. When she completed her statement the Chamber had no questions for her. International Co-Prosecutor De Wilde declared that her statement recorded so much suffering and was delivered with such dignity and courage that he was speechless.[77]

Duch described her statement as a powerful testimony of a family's suffering and a document of living history of value to researchers seeking to understand crimes of the Khmer Rouge.[78] In answer to Antonya's specific questions to him about Raingsy's confession, Duch declared that the confession was obtained before he became Chairman of S-21. Therefore he had not overseen it or paid

---

74 Transcript of Trial Proceedings – *Kaing Guek Eav 'Duch'* 001/18-07-2007/ECCC/TC (Day 60, 18 August 2009) p. 13.

75 Transcript of Trial Proceedings – *Kaing Guek Eav 'Duch'* 001/18-07-2007/ECCC/TC (Day 60, 18 August 2009) p. 14.

76 Transcript of Trial Proceedings – *Kaing Guek Eav 'Duch'*. 001/18-07-2007/ ECCC/TC (Day 60, 18 August 2009) p. 21.

77 Transcript of Trial Proceedings – *Kaing Guek Eav 'Duch'* 001/18-07-2007/ECCC/TC (Day 60, 18 August 2009) p. 39.

78 Transcript of Trial Proceedings – *Kaing Guek Eav 'Duch'* 001/18-07-2007/ECCC/TC (Day 60, 18 August 2009) p. 40.

attention to it. He did however, know she had been detained. From other documents he had seen, he concluded she had died of illness.[79]

7.5.2.3. Hav Sophea

Hav Sophea became a civil party as the daughter of a Khmer Rouge soldier who was arrested in January 1976 and was taken to S-21. She testified that she was born 21 days after his arrest and lived a life of poverty with her mother from that time. Not knowing why he was arrested, her mother waited for her husband until 1991, when she learned he had been executed. In 2007, she visited the Tuol Sleng Museum (formerly S-21) with her mother and found a photo of her father. She and her mother were deeply distressed to know that this was where her father had been sent. When they came to the place where the clothes of detainees were stored her mother wanted to search through them to find her husband's clothes.[80]

Sophea's story captured the effects of the silence imposed on many Cambodian families under the regime and the lack of information available to them in its long aftermath. Hav Sophea asked Duch whether her father, Chen Sear was killed at S-21 or Choeung Ek. Duch confirmed that he had been executed but did not know at which site he had died. Duch reiterated his psychological and emotional responsibility for the barbaric acts committed at S-21 and accepted responsibility for the suffering of the civil parties. However, throughout the trial if documentary evidence did not support a civil party's story, Duch was inclined to challenge it. In his final response to the Court, Duch seemed to cast doubt on whether Hav Sophea was actually the daughter of Chen Sear, and suggested this was a matter for the Court to ascertain.[81]

7.5.2.4. Neth Phally

Civil party, Neth Phally was a 52-year-old farmer who spoke to the Court of his own and his family's suffering as a result of the death of his brother Bunthy at S-21. He asked Duch if he could explain what mistake his brother, who had been a Khmer Rouge soldier from the Eastern zone, had made that led to his arrest. Duch explained that the government of Democratic Kampuchea came to

79 Transcript of Trial Proceedings – *Kaing Guek Eav 'Duch'* 001/18-07-2007/ECCC/TC (Day 60, 18 August 2009) p. 37.

80 Transcript of Trial Proceedings – *Kaing Guek Eav 'Duch'* 001/18-07-2007/ECCC/TC (Day 60, 18 August 2009) pp. 46–51.

81 Transcript of Trial Proceedings – *Kaing Guek Eav 'Duch'* 001/18-07-2007/ECCC/TC (Day 60, 18 August 2009) p. 58.

mistrust their soldiers from the Eastern zone. As a result there was mass purging of those troops, with some being sent to S-21 for interrogation in order to trace other traitorous elements.[82]

Another rare moment of communication unrelated to evidentiary processes ensued after Neth Phally had given his statement and had been examined by the Court. With the permission of the Presiding Judge, Phally produced an 8 × 11 inch photo of his brother as a young man. Looking at the photo he said:

> It is like he is sitting next to me. I hope he is with me knowing that the accused is on trial ... I believe my brother will be at peace, knowing that justice is done through this Court ... I can never find your body ... this photo represents your body.[83]

Phally then quietly paid homage to his brother. From the evidence he had surmised that his brother was blindfolded when taken to S-21, as well as when executed. He wanted Duch to see the photo of his brother, and his brother's spirit to see the one responsible for his death. This small ritual was Phally's way of freeing his brother from the state of limbo imposed on him by the lack of a respectful burial, a feeling common to many whose relatives are among the 'disappeared.'[84] President Nil Nonn asked that the photo be projected so that all the parties and the public could see it.[85] The spontaneous gesture allowed the in-country Court to respectfully acknowledge the significance of the moment for Neth Phally without in any way undermining the legal process.

7.5.2.5. Robert Hamill

The testimony of indirect victims of the Khmer Rouge during the proceedings established the breadth and depth of the victim constituency. This was made clear by the statement of Robert Hamill on the circumstances and effects of the death of his brother Kerry at S-21. In 1978, Kerry Hamill, a New Zealand yachtsman, moored his vessel in the vicinity of Koh Tang Island in Cambodian waters. The yacht was fired upon by a Khmer Rouge gunboat and Kerry and John Dewhurst, an Englishman, were taken to S-21.[86] Both men made confessions and were executed according to the CPK policy of beating foreigners to death

82 Transcript of Trial Proceedings – *Kaing Guek Eav 'Duch'* 001/18-07-2007/ECCC/TC (Day 60, 18 August 2009) pp. 108–109.

83 Transcript of Trial Proceedings – *Kaing Guek Eav 'Duch'* 001/18-07-2007/ECCC/TC (Day 60, 18 August 2009) pp. 109–110.

84 Stover, above n. 39, pp. 506, 533.

85 Transcript of Trial Proceedings – *Kaing Guek Eav 'Duch'*. 001/18-07-2007/ECCC/TC (Day 60, 18 August 2009) p. 110.

86 Transcript of Trial Proceedings – *Kaing Guek Eav 'Duch'* 001/18-07-2007/ECCC/TC (Day 59, 17 August 2009) p. 84.

before burning their bodies to ashes.[87] Civil party Robert Hamill described the content of his brother Kerry's confessions as patently fictional and containing allusions to supposed CIA contacts such as Colonel Sanders of the fast-food Kentucky Fried Chicken fame. Other fictional references included one to a Captain Dodds, the surname being the name of one his friends from his hometown in New Zealand, and a Major Rouse. There was also mention of his public speaking instructor, Mr. S. Tarr. This Robert interpreted as a reference to their mother Esther. By this means, Robert concluded that Kerry sent a message of hope and love to his mother and had the last word over his captors.[88]

When Kerry's family had not heard from him for 14 months they feared he had drowned or met with a freak accident. Learning of his death by torture in the newspaper was devastating and paralysing for each of them. Eight months later one of his brothers committed suicide and the family seemed to progressively disintegrate. Suddenly the blanket of Khmer Rouge victimhood was spread to non-citizens of Cambodia. Robert laid bare the nature of their suffering. He said that when he contacted the sister of John Dewhurst she expressed feelings about the loss of her brother that captured his own toward Kerry. She said she could not say her brother's name out loud:

> When I first heard of my brother's death, and for a long time, I felt that if it was possible to die of emotional pain, then I would. I could not see how my heart could continue to pump and my lungs to breath. The physical pain was so intense and that pain continues. For me, it is all to do with how they were killed. Torture, I believe is dehumanising, both for the person who suffers and for the person perpetrating it.[89]

Communicating the nature of victim suffering stemming from the nature of the crimes of torture followed by execution was something Robert sought not only for himself but for the many Cambodian families unable to testify. However, Robert declared that it was now time to let go of his anger and suffering. Turning to Duch he said:

> Today in this courtroom I am placing on you the crushing weight of all that emotion – the anger, the grief and the sorrow ... It is you who should bear the burden. It is you who should suffer, not the families of the people you killed.[90]

---

87 Transcript of Trial Proceedings – *Kaing Guek Eav 'Duch'* 001/18-07-2007/ECCC/TC (Day 59, 17 August 2009) p. 110.

88 Transcript of Trial Proceedings – *Kaing Guek Eav 'Duch'* 001/18-07-2007/ECCC/TC (Day 59, 17 August 2009) pp. 85–86.

89 Transcript of Trial Proceedings – *Kaing Guek Eav 'Duch'* 001/18-07-2007/ECCC/TC (Day 59, 17 August 2009) pp. 102–103.

90 Transcript of Trial Proceedings – *Kaing Guek Eav 'Duch'* 001/18-07-2007/ECCC/TC (Day 59, 17 August 2009) p. 104.

In response, Duch acknowledged the suffering of the Hamill and Dewhurst families as well as the many Cambodian families who continued to suffer. He reiterated the responsibility he bears for commitment to a failed project which cost more than a million lives and continues to burden many. He declared that the remorse he feels was from his heart and that he accepted responsibility willingly.[91] These were highly-charged communicative moments with restorative elements within retributive proceedings, as one victim representing a large constituency confronted the accused.

7.5.2.6. Chum Sirath

Chum Sirath was a 68-year-old manager of an international technology company in Phnom Penh. He won a scholarship to study in France from 1960 to 1968 and returned to work there during the Khmer Rouge regime. Two of his eight siblings, his sister-in-law and probably her infant child were detained at S-21.[92] Like other civil parties, Chum Sirath sought more information about the fate of his family members than he had been able to trace from the available official records.

Sarith testified to the personal torment of having escaped the violence of the regime that had ravaged his family. His younger brother Narith had also been offered a scholarship to study in France, but had turned it down in order to support his family. Like Duch, Narith became a teacher and opposed the social injustice of the Sihanouk regime. Duch had known Narith and his younger brother Sinaret during those years. In 1973, Narith joined the communist guerrilla movement, known as the maquis, when Lon Nol's police force sought to suppress a revolt against perceived left-wing elements at the Institut de Pédagogie. From the research Sarith had conducted, he concluded that Narith opposed the CPK's collectivisation policy. Because of the family connection it appeared that Sinaret and Narith's wife and baby were arrested according to CPK policy.[93] In his statement, Sirath was scathing of Duch for his failure to assist his brothers when they and other contemporaries of his were detained at S-21.[94] Sirath also repeatedly impugned the sincerity of Duch's statements

---

91 Transcript of Trial Proceedings – *Kaing Guek Eav 'Duch'* 001/18-07-2007/ECCC/TC (Day 59, 17 August 2009) pp. 118–119.

92 Transcript of Trial Proceedings – *Kaing Guek Eav 'Duch'* 001/18-07-2007/ ECCC/TC (Day 62, 20 August 2009) p. 7.

93 Transcript of Trial Proceedings – *Kaing Guek Eav 'Duch'* 001/18-07-2007/ ECCC/TC (Day 62, 20 August 2009) pp. 17–19, 37–38, 46.

94 Transcript of Trial Proceedings – *Kaing Guek Eav 'Duch'* 001/18-07-2007/ ECCC/TC (Day 62, 20 August 2009) pp. 21–25.

of apology and expressions of remorse.[95] The President of the Chamber urged him not to try to provoke a response from the accused, and reminded him that it was for the Court to consider every aspect of the proceedings and evidence in its judgment.[96] Nevertheless, formulating a kind of curse drawn partly from the biblical story of Cain and Abel, Sarith asserted that Duch would find nowhere to hide from the eyes of the souls of the dead of S-21.[97]

In his response to Sirath's story and criticisms, Duch acknowledged that he betrayed many of his friends who were detained at S-21. He re-iterated that having been arrested, S-21 inmates were regarded as the enemy under CPK policy. Duch said he avoided contact with those he knew because he could not bear to face them.[98] He declared that his remorse was sincere and that he accepted the attacks of the civil parties.

Sirath's account of his brothers' imprisonment revealed the social breakdown that occurred in Cambodia that led to their execution at an institution overseen by a former friend, who himself could only survive by denial. The anomie of those times was exposed through profound exchanges between Sarith and Duch. Within a legal forum the Court did what justice it could through hearing an aggrieved citizen who sought some kind of explanation and even revenge of some kind.

A degree of forbearance is only reasonable in dealing with victims of mass crimes. Duch recognised that some civil parties would want to 'point the finger' at him and seemed to accept Chum Mey's anger, Chum Sirath's vengeful remarks and Robert Hamill's acting out. However, he would not yield his integrity to unverifiable statements. There is a line to be drawn by the Court when impulsive behaviour and unruly statements unfairly raise the emotional barometer of the courtroom and inject potential bias into the proceedings. Interventions of various kinds become necessary to retain an atmosphere of civility, respect and impartiality.[99] That this is a delicate balancing act was evident as the second trial proceeded. The Trial Chamber had to facilitate the legitimate contribution of victims to the proceedings, upholding their right to reparations, while also respecting the dignity and rights of the two remaining accused to a fair trial.

---

95 Transcript of Trial Proceedings – *Kaing Guek Eav 'Duch'* 001/18-07-2007/ ECCC/TC (Day 62, 20 August 2009) pp. 22–24; 29–30, 33–35.

96 Transcript of Trial Proceedings – *Kaing Guek Eav 'Duch'* 001/18-07-2007/ ECCC/TC (Day 62, 20 August 2009) pp. 26, 29.

97 Transcript of Trial Proceedings – *Kaing Guek Eav 'Duch'* 001/18-07-2007/ ECCC/TC (Day 62, 20 August 2009) pp. 21–25; The story of Cain and his brother Abel whom he murdered is from Genesis ch. 4: v. 8–16, *The Holy Bible* (New International Version, International Bible Society, 1973).

98 Transcript of Trial Proceedings – *Kaing Guek Eav 'Duch'* 001/18-07-2007/ECCC/TC (Day 62, 20 August 2009) pp. 42–43.

99 John D. Ciorciari and Anne Heindel, 'Victim Testimony in International and Hybrid Criminal Courts: Narrative Opportunities, Challenges and Fair trial Demands' (2015) 56 *Virginia Journal of International Law* 1, 22–23, 44–49 (forthcoming).

7.5.3. CIVIL PARTIES AND CASE 002/01

As discussed in Chapter five, a Trial Chamber severance order divided the Case 002 indictment to form a series of mini-trials.[100] Under the original order, the first of the mini-trials (Case 002/01), was to address the charges of crimes against humanity in relation to the forced population movements from Phnom Penh in April 1975 and from September 1975 to late 1976. The Lead Co-lawyers for the civil parties joined the Co-Prosecutors' appeal to expand the scope of the order on the grounds of reasonable representativeness of the indictment.[101] As a result, the Chamber expanded the severance order to include the killing of Khmer Republic soldiers at the Tuol Prey Chrey execution site immediately after the Khmer Rouge took power in 1975.[102] An effect of the severance order was a reduction of the number of civil parties eligible to claim reparations in the case.[103]

The breadth and complexity of the Case 002 indictment and the additional time needed for trial preparation appeared to precipitate modifications to witness examination in Case 002/01.[104] While the judges retained control of the proceedings, determined the topics that witnesses would be questioned on, and called the witnesses, they assigned the questioning to one of the parties.[105] There were times when the judges asked substantive questions, but generally, the trial in Case 002/01 was more party-driven than in Case 001.[106]

At the same time, the 2010 amendments to the civil party scheme were implemented. Nonetheless, the Trial Chamber maintained an inclusive approach to admitted civil parties by introducing additional means of giving them voice at trial. Civil parties were able to make statements of harm or suffering following their testimony in the substantive proceedings, and the Court convened separate

---

100 *Nuon Chea and Khieu Samphân* (Severence Order pursuant to Internal Rule 89*ter*) 002/19-09-2007/ ECCC/TC (26 April 2013).

101 *Nuon Chea and Khieu Samphân* (Urgent Request on the Scope of Trial One and the need for a reasoned Decision Following the Civil Parties Request for Reconsideration of the Severance Order) 002/19-09-2007/ECCC/TC (17 November 2011) para. 11.

102 *Nuon Chea and Khieu Samphân* (Decision on Co-Prosecutor's Request to Include Additional Crime Sites within the Scope of Trial in Case 002/01 (E163) and deadline for submission of applicable law portion of Closing Briefs) 002/19-09-2007/ECCC/TC (8 October 2012) para. 3.

103 Anne Heindel, 'Impact of Severence on Individual Civil Parties' Legal Status and Right to Reparations' *Cambodia Tribunal Monitor*, 22 February 2013 indicating 750 would be eligible under the original order.

104 Sergey Vasiliev, 'Trial Process at the ECCC: the Rise and Fall of the Inquisitorial Paradigm in International Criminal Law?' in Simon M. Meisenberg and Ignaz Stegmiller (eds.), *The Extraordinary Chambers in the Courts of Cambodia: Assessing their Contribution to International Criminal Law* (Asser Press, 2016) p. 422.

105 John D. Ciorciari and Anne Heindel, *Hybrid Justice: The Extraordinary Chambers in the Courts in Cambodia* (University of Michigan Press, Ann Arbour MI 2014) pp. 161–162.

106 Vasiliev, above n. 104, pp. 421–422.

victim impact hearings for the purpose of determining reparations. The suite of changes brought a certain tension to the proceedings as Counsel adapted to the new procedure.[107] The fact that Nuon Chea and Khieu Samphân had not accepted legal responsibility for the international crimes, and the multiple criminal policies contained in the indictment, sometimes added further complexity to trial communications.

7.5.3.1. Statements of Suffering

In Case 002/01, out of the 92 individuals who gave live evidence at trial 31 were civil parties.[108] After the civil parties had testified, President Nil Nonn gave each one the opportunity to speak of the suffering and harms they had sustained. These were general 'statements of suffering' not limited to the Case 002/01 charges, which the civil party could make 'freely' after testifying.[109] The right to make a general statement of suffering flowed from their civil party status.[110] In this, the Court accepted the submission of the Lead Co-lawyers that the harm and suffering of victims cannot be conveniently 'compartmentalised.'[111] Thus, the Chamber allowed the civil parties who wanted to make such statements to include their suffering and harm resulting from the Democratic Kampuchea era in a broad sense. However, where aspects of their 'statements' infringed upon the rights of the accused, the Chamber repeatedly recognised the Co-Defence right to object.[112] The Court declared that at all times it distinguished between testimonies given on the facts at issue in the case which are subject to adversarial examination, and the 'statements of suffering' a civil party may make after testifying.[113]

Furthermore, if the Co-Defence had not had sufficient opportunity to prepare a response to any new facts raised or alleged prejudicial matters in a 'statement of suffering,' the Court could grant an opportunity to recall the civil party to face examination on the allegation.[114] Such a situation arose when civil party Chau Ny introduced new and potentially inculpatory factual allegations against the

---

107 Ciorciari, above n. 105, pp. 161–162.

108 *ECCC, Guide to the First Trial in Case 002* (ECCC, April 2014) p. 1.

109 *Nuon Chea and Khieu Samphân* (Decision on Request to recall Civil Party TCCP-187 for Review of Procedure Concerning Civil Parties' Statements of Suffering and Related Motions and Responses (E240, E240/1,E250/1, E267, E267/1 and E267/2) 002/19-09-2007/ECCC/TC (2 May 2013) para. 14.

110 Ibid. para. 21.

111 Ibid. para. 5.

112 Ibid. para. 16, citing for example, the statements of Yim Sovann and Chum Sokha. See *Trial Transcript*, 22 November 2012, at pp. 2, 8–16 and 104 respectively.

113 Ibid. paras. 14–15.

114 Ibid. paras. 19–20.

accused, Khieu Samphân, in his 'statement of suffering'. Immediately prior to this Ny had given evidence as a witness on the forced evacuation of Phnom Penh, and his subsequent movements with family members to various cooperatives.

When it was time to make his statement of suffering stemming from the regime, Ny immediately sought to question Khieu Samphân about the fate of his beloved 'uncle', Chau Sau. Ny presumed the accused would know based on information he had received in 1979 through a third person, a Mr. Chhean, who had been his uncle's driver. Allegedly, Mr. Chhean had seen a letter written by Khieu Samphân on 17 April 1975 requesting Chau Sau's return to Phnom Penh. The letter was said to have been delivered by two Khmer Rouge soldiers. Mr. Chhean had also conveyed that after Chau Sau refused to go back to the city, the soldiers returned to ask him once more. He again refused and then told Mr. Chhean that he should now go to attend to his own family. Thereafter, Chau Sau disappeared and was never seen by Ny and his family again.[115]

Khieu Samphân elected to remain silent and left his response to his defence counsel. Ny expressed his disappointment at not being able to hear from the accused to garner information about the whereabouts of his uncle's remains so that he could arrange a ceremony in accordance with traditional Buddhist practice. After he was dismissed, the Co-Defence counsel objected strongly to the imputations in the statement. However, Judge Lavergne assessed the situation within the civil law framework. He concluded that Chau Ny in the context of expressing his suffering sought to air his concern for his uncle, who disappeared at the time of the evacuation of Phnom Penh, and in doing so was touching on material relevant to the subject-matter of the case. As a party to the proceedings, he was entitled to put questions to the accused, and the accused was entitled to remain silent. Counsel were also entitled to question the civil party at an appropriate time.[116]

Upon a Co-Defence request for the recall of Chau Ny, the Chamber convened a new hearing to allow for further examination of the civil party on the portions of his statement that the accused had not had an opportunity to properly respond to.[117] The actual hearing was more extensive because the Chamber also accepted the inclusion of additional facts submitted by the Lead Co-lawyers related to the allegations.[118] Ny recalled a radio broadcast he had heard on 17 April 1975 with his mother-in-law and other relatives, seeking the whereabouts of Chau Sau and

---

115 Transcript of Trial Proceedings – *Nuon Chea and Khieu Samphân* 002/19-09-2007/ECCC/TC (Day 133, 23 November 2012) p. 95.

116 Ibid p. 104–105.

117 *Nuon Chea and Khieu Samphân* (Decision on Request to recall Civil Party TCCP-187, for Review of Procedure Concerning Civil Parties' Statements of Suffering and Related Motions and Responses (E240, E240/1,E250/1, E267, E267/1 and E267/2) 002/19-09-2007/ECCC/TC, 2 May 2013) para. 19.

118 Transcript of Trial Proceedings – *Nuon Chea and Khieu Samphân* 002/19-09-2007/ECCC/TC (Day 183, 23 May 2013) p. 2.

two senior members of the Lon Nol regime: Cheng Heng and Sirik Matak.[119] In addition, Ny alleged the existence of a second letter to Chau Sau from Khieu Samphân, written a few days after the previously mentioned letter.[120] At the hearing, the international Co-Defence counsel examined Ny on the details and source of the letter he had described in his initial statement on 23 November 2012 and sought clarification on the second letter. Ny testified that Mr. Chhean was deceased, and confirmed that he had heard that two letters were sent to Chau Sau.

Khieu Samphân elected to respond to Chau Ny at the new hearing. He acknowledged that he knew Chau Sau in the 1960s before he had to flee Phnom Penh himself. He sympathised with Ny's suffering and desire to afford his uncle a traditional ceremony, but said that he had not sent the letters referred to and knew nothing of the man's fate.[121]

Aided by the questioning of his legal representative, Chau Ny explained his close connection with Chau Sau, who had brought him up from age five or six. Chau Sau had been a senior figure at the National Credit Bank in Phnom Penh in 1975. He was highly respected and well known for helping the Khmer Krom people in Phnom Penh. He had also formed a democratic political party.[122] Ny was also given another opportunity to make his statement of suffering. He explained that he had relatives connected at senior levels in the Lon Nol government but had lost them all during the period of Democratic Kampuchea. 'I lost everyone', he said. His elder siblings, his wife and nieces all died; all were Khmer Krom people, killed because of their origins, he added. Appealing to Khieu Samphân, he asked 'why' were the Khmer Krom killed?[123] At this, the Chamber President asked him to refrain from importing new facts and to only relate his direct suffering. Thereafter, although still dissatisfied at not securing information from the accused, Ny stepped down. As he did, President Nil Nonn thanked him for his additional testimony and assured him that his testimony would 'help ascertain the truth.'[124]

The Chau Ny case illustrates the truth-finding process at work at the ECCC. At the same time, it demonstrates the need for vigilance on the part of judges and counsel alike to respond to facts that may be raised by the civil parties, while respectfully constraining discourse which threatens the fairness of trial proceedings. In respect to defence counsel challenging the relevance or prejudicial nature of portions of statements, the Trial Chamber directed that such remarks be made only after the party had left the room so as not to embarrass the civil

119 Transcript of Trial Proceedings – *Nuon Chea and Khieu Samphân* 002/19-09-2007/ECCC/TC (Day 183, 23 May 2013) pp. 12–14.
120 Ibid.
121 Ibid. pp. 17–18.
122 Ibid. p. 28.
123 Ibid. p. 35.
124 Ibid. p. 36.

party.[125] This ruling followed an incidence of the Co-Defence interjecting and questioning the reason for a strong display of emotion by one civil party.[126]

In all, only 13 civil parties presented statements of suffering following testimony in Case 002/01.[127] The gratitude expressed by numerous civil parties for being able to make a public narrative statement of what they had seen and experienced under the regime suggests they derived reparative benefit beyond that flowing from witness testimony.[128] It was clear that their appreciation was heightened because of the absence of any other official mechanism providing recognition of this kind.[129] Their statements of usually 15 minutes each or less within a total of 222 trial days were not a significant time impost on the proceedings.[130] Rather, as discussed in the next section, the civil parties contributed to the truth-finding process by relating their experiences and the conditions under which they had to live and work when moved from one worksite or camp to another by Khmer Rouge officers.

7.5.3.2. Victim Impact Hearings

In addition to hearing the civil parties in the substantive proceedings as discussed above, the Trial Chamber also convened a series of 'victim impact hearings' from 27 May to 4 June 2013. This was in the course of the trial and separate from the sentencing hearings.

The purpose of the victim impact hearings was to provide opportunity for an additional group of civil parties to demonstrate by testimony and examination the effects of the crimes charged to substantiate reparations claims.[131] Thus, the hearings must be distinguished from the practice of some international courts of admitting written victim impact statements at the sentencing stage.[132]

The Lead Co-lawyers selected 15 civil parties as representatives of the victim collective of Case 002/01 to make statements demonstrating the 'diversity of

---

125 *Nuon Chea and Khieu Samphân* (Decision on Request to recall Civil party TCCP-187, for Review of Procedure Concerning Civil Parties' Statements of Suffering and Related Motions and Responses (E240, E240/1,E250/1, E267, E267/1 and E267/2) ECCC Case File No – 002/19-09-2007- ECCC/TC, 2 May 2013) para. 18.

126 See Yim Sovann's statement ECCC Case No 002/19-09-2007-ECCC/TC, Trial Day 121, Transcript 22 October 2012, pp. 22–23.

127 Case 002/01 Appeal Judgment para 317.

128 Ciorciari above n. 99, p. 64.

129 Ibid.

130 Ibid 66.

131 ECCC Internal Rules r. 23 *bis* (1)(b).

132 See ICTY, Rules of Evidence and Procedure IT-32/Rev.50 (8 July 2010) r. 92 *bis* (A)(1)(d); Göran Sluiter et al., *International Criminal Procedure: Principles and Rules* (Oxford University Press, 2013) pp. 1328–1329.

impacts' of the forced transfer of populations and executions at Tuol Po Chrey. The legal representatives explained that civil party statements provide evidence of the consequences of the crimes for the 'purpose of assisting the Chamber [to] assess the gravity of the crimes, in their proper context and determining the appropriateness of the reparations claimed to remedy these harms.'[133]

In addition, the hearings provided an opportunity for at least some of the civil parties to 'tell their stories in an official, judicial setting with the presence of (and sometimes exchange with) one or more of the Accused.'[134] In this way the hearings offered 'reparative benefit' to the victims representing the collective through the justice process itself; a benefit distinct from the value of any symbolic awards.[135]

As the first victim impact hearing began, the international Lead Co-lawyer, Elisabeth Simmoneau-Fort, requested the Court's patience and respect as the civil parties made their statements. In the circumstances, the Court should not expect the statements of what the civil parties had seen and experienced to be as 'clear-cut and specific' as factual testimonies.[136] Complete accuracy in the giving of dates and names for instance, was unlikely in the context of the task each civil party was undertaking in revisiting distressing history and painful personal experience. She added it should be understood that their giving voice to their pain, sorrow and at times, anger was not for themselves but for sake of the trial as a whole.[137]

In addition to presenting their statements, the civil parties were questioned first by the Lead Co-lawyers, before being examined by the Co-Prosecution and Co-Defence on the facts. The civil parties were permitted to put questions to the accused, although at the beginning of the hearings Judge Cartwright indicated that it should not be expected that all questions proposed would be answered.[138] The accused did not invoke their right to remain silent, and as the hearings proceeded they answered the civil parties' questions at their discretion. The judges mediated exchanges between counsel and the civil parties, but unlike their approach in the Duch trial, they did not interrogate the civil parties further.

Among the civil parties testifying were people who had been orphaned or permanently disabled during the regime.[139] The group represented those

---

133 'The Purpose of Hearing Victims' Suffering': http://www.eccc.gov.kh/en/blog/2013/06/07/purpose-hearing-victims-suffering, citing reasons given by Lead Co-lawyers Pich Ang and Elisabeth Simmoneau-Fort.

134 Ibid.

135 Ibid.

136 Transcript of Trial Proceedings – *Nuon Chea and Khieu Samphân* 002/19-09-2007/ECCC/TC (Trial Day 184, 27 May 2013) p. 8.

137 Ibid. pp. 8–9.

138 Ibid. p. 7.

139 See Aun Phally's statement of his mental suffering following the death of his parents, siblings and grandparents in Transcript of Trial Proceedings – *Nuon Chea and Khieu Samphân* 002/19-09-2007-ECCC/TC (Trial Day 184, 27 May 2013) pp. 36–38; And see Seng Sivuthu

categorised by the regime.as 'new people' or '17 April 1975 people.' It included those targeted for re-education due to their social status or association with the Lon Nol regime, and those considered closely linked with Vietnam, notably the Khmer Krom.[140] The impacts of the forced evacuation and attendant policies of the government of Democratic Kampuchea on a transgendered community in Phnom Penh were also represented.[141]

At each hearing, the civil parties were invited by the Chamber President to provide their statement of suffering and harms which were the direct result of the crimes charged and upon which their party status was based.[142] Common to all the statements were descriptions of the circumstances of their forced evacuation from Phnom Penh in April 1975 by armed Khmer Rouge soldiers. Their memories of home invasion and orders to leave temporarily while the city was made 'clean' of enemies and before the Americans dropped more bombs, remained vivid.[143] Similarly, the scene of families, the very young, the sick and disabled being driven without notice out of the city en masse with no transport, food or medical provisions was etched in their minds.

Civil party Nou Hoan described a huge crowd of shocked people being moved out of the city in the dry season heat. The situation was chaotic. The sick could not seek help from anyone. People were forced to keep moving and some had to leave their sick or elderly family members behind. There were swarming flies and no food supplies, medical services or toilet facilities.[144]

Civil party Thouch Phandarasa described how aggressive soldiers moved her family out of her parents' home, confiscated their belongings and forced them to join masses of people being moved along the roads out of Phnom Penh. She saw women giving birth on the road, sick people with intravenous drips in their beds 'under the burning sun' and others, unable to walk, left without aid. Children were forced to leave their parents behind. This was incomprehensible in a society where children are taught to venerate their parents. Seeing the children's distress was extremely difficult.[145]

---

who became blind from injuries she sustained, in Transcript of Trial Proceedings – *Nuon Chea and Khieu Samphân* 002/19-09-2007-ECCC/TC (Trial Day 187, 4 June 2013) pp. 93–116.

140 See statements of Thouch Phandarasa and Soeun Sovandy in Transcript of Trial Proceedings – *Nuon Chea and Khieu Samphân* 002/19-09-2007-ECCC/TC (Trial Days 185 and 187, 29 May 2013 and 4 June 2013) pp. 9, 18; 53–55 respectively.

141 See testimony of Sou Sotheavy in Transcript of Trial Proceedings – *Nuon Chea and Khieu Samphân* 002/19-09-2007-ECCC/TC (Trial Days 184, 27 May 2013) pp. 11–21, 26–27.

142 Transcript of Trial Proceedings *Nuon Chea and Khieu Samphân* 002/19-09-2007/ECCC/TC (Trial Day 184, 27 May 2013) p. 10.

143 See for example, Chan Socheat and Sophan Sovany's testimonies in Transcript of Trial Proceedings – *Nuon Chea and Others* 002/19-09-2007/ECCC/TC (Trial Days 185 and 186, 29 and 30 May 2013) pp. 42–43; 44 respectively.

144 Transcript of Trial Proceedings – *Nuon Chea and Khieu Samphân* 002/19-09-2007/ECCC/TC (Trial Day 186, 30 May 2013) pp. 6–7.

145 Transcript of Trial Proceedings – *Nuon Chea and Khieu Samphân* 002/19-09-2007/ECCC/TC (Trial Day 185, 29 May 2013) p. 6.

Illustrating the harm they suffered, the civil parties recounted the consequences of the evacuation policy on their lives. Additional forced movements by truck, train and boat or on foot to various camps or work sites were described. The respective accounts conveyed a pattern of repeated movement to new locations without explanation, continuous deprivation of liberty, violence or cruelty at the hands of Khmer Rouge cadres, and the loss of loved ones through starvation, disease or hard labour.[146] Civil parties who were children at the time of the evacuation spoke of lost childhoods, loss of educational opportunity, the pain of seeing parents waste away in the camps and the trauma of witnessing arbitrary killings.[147]

Civil party Yim Roumdoul was 10 years old in 1975. He recalled that on 17 April black-clad Khmer Rouge soldiers fired shots into the house opposite his family's home. In the evening, they began shooting at his home before firing a rocket launcher at the house. His family vacated the house and in the morning they saw dead bodies along the road as they left Phnom Penh.[148]

Rimdoul's father, Yim Sidarith, a professor and a senior public servant, disappeared when a Khmer Rouge village chief learned of his background. His mother was also killed in one of the Khmer Rouge communes they were sent to. He was tortured and beaten by Khmer Rouge cadres as he tried to survive alone. He testified that he had waited for 34 years to speak out about what he had witnessed. For all that time he had wanted the world to know what he, as a child, and the Khmer people had suffered during the regime. He also wanted to address the accused, and had prepared questions for them:

1. Were they aware of his father's arrest and disappearance?
2. Had they considered the consequences of the killings and disintegration of families that occurred under the Khmer Rouge?
3. As intellectuals did they dare to speak the truth about what had happened under the regime?
4. Would they express sorrow [about the regime] to the world, the nation and to himself?
5. To Khieu Samphân: As President of the State Presidium did you know the conditions the people were living under; of their hunger, of arbitrary arrest and torture, and killings?[149]

---

146 See for example, the testimony of Chan Socheap, who lost her entire family of 15, in Transcript of Trial Proceedings – *Nuon Chea and Khieu Samphân* 002/19-09-2007/ECCC/TC (Trial Day 186, 30 May 2013) pp. 43–52.

147 See the testimony of Yim Roumdoul in Transcript of Trial Proceedings – *Nuon Chea and Khieu Samphân* 002/19-09-2007/ECCC/TC (Trial Day 186, 30 May 2013) pp. 74–76.

148 Transcript of Trial Proceedings *Nuon Chea and Khieu Samphân* 002/19-09-2007/ECCC/TC (Trial Day 186, 30 May 2013) p. 72.

149 Transcript of Trial Proceedings – *Nuon Chea and Khieu Samphân* 002/19-09-2007/ECCC/TC (Trial Day 186, 30 May 2013) pp. 74–76.

Both accused replied to the questions. Khieu Samphân said he did not know Yim Sidareth and expressed his sorrow about his execution. He went on to say that while he had associated with the senior leaders of the regime, he did so initially to save his life. He was not a CPK ideologue; he sought only to develop and protect the country under the government of Democratic Kampuchea. Unfortunately, that had turned out to be a 'complete disaster.' He condemned the killings Roumdoul had witnessed and claimed he knew nothing of the atrocities he had recounted. He put his hands together and made an apology to Roumdoul for his loss as well as to the Cambodians across the country who had suffered under the regime. In answer to the final question, he said that while he had a title suggesting he held authority within the regime, in reality 'I had no power at all.'[150]

Nuon Chea also wished to answer Yim Roumdoul. He declared he wished to be 'frank' and respond from his heart and to bear some responsibility. He felt 'remorseful' about the crimes that were committed 'intentionally or unintentionally', and whether he knew about them or not, he wanted to take 'moral responsibility' for what had happened under Democratic Kampuchea. Furthermore, he wanted to express 'sincere condolences' for the loss of Roumdoul's family members. However, he wished to clarify that within the government of Democratic Kampuchea he was responsible for 'internal education and propaganda.' As for the executive branch, he had 'no power or authority.'[151]

These were not isolated responses. Both of the accused were generally cooperative throughout the hearings and showed sympathy to the civil parties as they expressed their suffering and questioned them. In the locally situated proceedings, the exchanges between victims and alleged perpetrators constituted a form of restorative justice within criminal proceedings. Any concessions made by the accused were in the absence of amnesties characteristic of truth commission processes, and both faced judgment by the Court. For the civil parties, apart from any reparative benefit they might have derived from making their statements and confronting the accused, the Court gave them opportunity to contribute directly to the retributive justice process on a representative basis.

Following the exchanges between the civil party and the accused, the Co-Defence counsel had no questions for Roumdoul. However, the Co-Prosecution sought clarification of certain matters. First, who had occupied the house opposite his family's home and what transpired there?

---

150 Transcript of Trial Proceedings – *Nuon Chea and Khieu Samphân* 002/19-09-2007/ECCC/TC (Trial Day 186, 30 May 2013) pp. 81–82.

151 Transcript of Trial Proceedings – *Nuon Chea and Khieu Samphân* 002/19-09-2007/ECCC/TC (Trial Day 186, 30 May 2013) p. 84.

Roumdoul knew that a military officer of the Lon Nol regime occupied the house and had exchanged fire with the Khmer Rouge attackers, but he did not know his fate because it occurred during the circumstance of mass evacuation of the city at gunpoint. In answer to a question on the evacuation scene, Roumdoul explained that it was one of human misery and that he had felt distressed at not being able to help the sick he saw along the road amidst the overall chaos.[152]

The Co-Defence tested the evidence in other civil party statements by more rigorous examination. In the case of Chan Socheap's statement, the Co-Defence examined her account of the killing of a person by a Khmer Rouge soldier on a boat on which she was travelling. She testified that as the boat with many families on board approached Phnom Penh, a man who was near her, stood and said 'Bravo, we got home to Phnom Penh now!' He was immediately called out by a Khmer Rouge soldier and following a short exchange there were gun shots and the man fell into the water.

Socheap was examined on the exact time between the man standing up and the time she heard the shots fired. While she could not be sure of the precise time span she knew that it was less than five minutes. Further questioning followed on her knowledge of the name and role of the soldier. She replied firmly that they were not told who he was, or what rank he had, but it was clear that he was in charge of the boat.[153]

In the Recall decision referred to above, the Court explained that while civil parties are exempt from taking the oath, where they testify their statements may be assessed by the Chamber as evidence if it is 'relevant and probative.'[154] In addition as noted at 7.5.3.1, Judge Lavergne explained the Court's truth-finding framework when questioned by Co-Defence counsel on civil party Chau Ny's statements concerning Khieu Samphân in the trial proceedings.[155] In Nuon Chea's appeal against the judgment in Case 002/01, he argued that 'each and every reference to victim impact testimony in the judgment for any purpose other than reparations and sentencing constituted an error of law.'[156] In examining the ECCC legal framework, the Supreme Court Chamber (SCC) found nothing

152 Transcript of Trial Proceedings – *Nuon Chea and Khieu Samphân* 002/19-09-2007/ECCC/TC (Trial Day 186, 30 May 2013) pp. 86–87.

153 Transcript of Trial Proceedings – *Nuon Chea and Khieu Samphân* 002/19-09-2007/ECCC/TC (Trial Day 185, 29 May 2013) pp. 62–63.

154 *Nuon Chea and Khieu Samphân* (Decision on Request to recall Civil party TCCP-187, for Review of Procedure Concerning Civil Parties' Statements of Suffering and Related Motions and Responses (E240, E240/1, E250/1, E267, E267/1 and E267/2) 002/19-09-2007- ECCC/TC (2 May 2013) para. 21.

155 Transcript of Trial Proceedings – *Nuon Chea and Khieu Samphân* (Trial Day 133, 23 November 2012) p. 104–105.

156 Nuon Chea's Appeal against the Judgment in Case 002/01 ECCC Case No. 002/19-09-2007-ECCC/TC) para. 193 [Nuon Chea Appeal Brief].

in the Internal Rules indicating that the questioning of civil parties during the investigative stage must be limited to matters relevant to reparations. In addition, civil parties along with other parties are included in proceedings as a means for establishing the truth and the Trial Chamber may rely on their testimony in making determinations of guilt.[157] Thus, the SCC found no error *per se* in the use of civil party testimony as material evidence.[158] The SCC also approved the Trial Chamber's approach in deciding the weight to be given civil party testimony on a case by case basis in view of both their special status and the fact that their testimony was unsworn.[159] As to Nuon Chea's claims of prejudice due to the extent of the Trial Chamber's reliance on civil party evidence, the SCC considered whether the relevant findings were reasonable in view of the adequacy of the totality of evidence relied upon.[160] This is also discussed in Chapter 9, section 9.6. The defence view that the Trial Chamber had over-relied on civil party evidence may explain their more robust examination of civil parties in Case 002/02.

7.5.4. CIVIL PARTIES AND CASE 002/02

In Case 002/02, the Court is hearing evidence of crimes occurring at multiple crime sites and involving more diverse systemic criminality. The charges include the crimes of genocide against the Cham minority in Cambodia and the Vietnamese (excluding crimes committed by the Revolutionary Army of Kampuchea on Vietnamese territory) as well as forced marriage and rape. While some scholars characterised the policies of the Khmer Rouge against the Vietnamese as genocidal, others considered that the attacks were motivated by politics rather than 'genocidal intent' under the 1948 Genocide Convention.[161] However, international Co-Prosecutor Andrew Cayley considered that with respect to Khmer Rouge and the ethnic Vietnamese 'it was difficult to conceive of a more pure expression of genocidal intent'.[162] He explained:

> [I]n the case of the Khmer Rouge genocide against the Vietnamese we have a rare instance in which the genocidal intent requirement need not be inferred. As early

---

157 *Nuon Chea and Khieu Samphân* (Appeal Judgment) 002/01-002/19-09-2007-ECCC/SC (23 November 2016) para 313.

158 Ibid. para 324.

159 Ibid. para 314.

160 Nuon Chea Appeal Brief paras 194–196.

161 Lyma Nguyen and Christoph Sperfeldt, 'Victim Participation in International Criminal Trials: Ethnic Viertnamese Civil Parties at the Extraordinary Chambers in the Courts of Cambodia' (2014) 14 *Macquarie Law Journal* 97, 112; William A. Schabas, Problems of International Codification: Were the Atrocities in Cambodia and Kosovo Genocide? (2001) 35 *New England Law Review* 287, 289–293.

162 Andrew T. Cayley, 'Prosecuting Mass Atrocities at the Extraordinary Chambers in the Courts of Cambodia' (2012) 11 *Washington University Global Studies Law Review* 445, 458.

as January 1978, the leadership began exhorting cadres and troops to prepare to exterminate the entire Vietnamese race.[163]

Ethnic Vietnamese civil parties of Case 002/02 have confirmed the escalating genocidal nature of the Khmer Rouge towards those of Vietnamese origin and knew of none who had remained in Cambodia under the regime.[164] Their statements of suffering will give voice to civil parties harmed by the forced expulsion of ethnic Vietnamese from Cambodian territory as well as many who suffered as a consequence of the policy of forced marriage.[165]

Civil party statements of suffering will be crucial to proving the charge of crimes against humanity including forced marriage, encompassing rape and sexual violence in forced marriage. The extent of sexual violence under the Khmer Rouge and its impact has been steadily documented.[166] Williams and Palmer argue that the reparations proceedings may shed more light on the 'ongoing impact of forced marriage on both men and women, including their freedom to marry and sexual autonomy.'[167] The criminal proceedings may have expressive effects through stigmatisation and reparative purpose for the victim collective. The victim impact hearings in particular will be concerned with establishing a causal link between the incidence of sexual violence under the regime and the harm and suffering of the civil parties. The ECCC's recognition of the crime and the harm through conviction and reparation may contribute to changing attitudes towards prevalent sexual violence in Cambodia.[168] Thus, the representative function of the civil parties as they make their statements during the proceedings may have significant long-term legal and social effects.

Against the background of the Co-Defence appeal in Case 002/01, and as the victim impact hearings in Case 002/02 approached, the role of civil parties in the proceedings was revisited as a trial management issue.[169] The Co-Defence pressed the Chamber for equal time to examine the civil parties on facts raised

---

163 Ibid. p. 457.

164 Nguyen, above n. 161, p. 113

165 Ibid.

166 See *A Study about Victim Participation at the Extraordinary Chambers in the Courts of Cambodia and Gender-Based Violence under the Khmer Rouge Regime* (Transcultural Psychosocial Organisation and United Nations Trust Fund to End Violence Against Women, September 2015) pp. 53–85; Theresa De Langis, Judith Strasser, Thida Kim and Sopheap Taing, *Like Ghost Changes Body: A Study on the Impact of Forced Marriage under the Khmer Rouge Regime* (Transcultural Psychosocial Organsiation, Phnom Penh 2014).

167 Sarah Williams and Emma Palmer, 'Transformative Reparations for Women and Girls at the Extraordinary Chambers in the Courts of Cambodia' (2016) 10 *International Journal of Transitional Justice* 311, 323.

168 Ibid. p. 327.

169 See Co-Defence questions to the Trial Chamber Judges in Transcript of Trial Proceedings – *Nuon Chea and Khieu Samphân* 002/19-09-2007-ECCC/TC (Trial Day 266, 31 March 2015) pp. 41–46, 65: And the Co-Prosecution debate in Transcript of Trial Proceedings – *Nuon Chea and Others* 002/19-09-2007/ECCC/TC (Day 267, 1 April 2015) pp. 10–19.

in their statements of harm.[170] The Chamber accommodated the request, while re-iterating that the practice of hearing general civil party statements of suffering and harm following civil party testimony on facts was continuing. As to victim-impact hearings, the Chamber determined that they would be held at the end of hearings for each trial topic, rather than in one round at the end of the entire substantive hearings.[171] Overall, this provides for representation by a select number of civil parties on each topic as it is addressed, rather than in one full sweep as was the case in the earlier trials.

As the hearings began, the proceedings were distinctly adversarial with each party examining the civil parties and the Co-Defence testing the veracity of facts by rigorous cross-examination. This included putting questions to an illiterate civil party on elements of her approved civil party application documents already on the case file and accessible to all parties.[172] As in the other trials, the civil parties' narratives were not completely cohesive, but they persevered nonetheless under the pressure of cross-examination. For instance, after civil party Loep Neang stated she had been forced to eat pork at a Khmer Rouge work camp, Co-Defence counsel raised the testimony of others who had told the Court they had only been given rice gruel and morning glory soup. Loep Neang replied that she and other Cham people were forced to eat thin rice gruel with pork and morning glory, which was deliberately given to them in the knowledge that pork was not eaten by them for religious reasons.[173]

As in the previous trials, some civil parties have spoken derogatively and prejudicially about the accused during their general statements of suffering following testimony in the substantive hearings. One civil party, for example, referred to the accused as 'criminals' in her statement, warranting defence interjection.[174] Although the Chamber directed the Lead Co-lawyers to instruct civil parties as to such matters, a burden remains on the Court, case-by-case, to mediate civil party story-telling during the proceedings in order to guard the rights of the accused.[175]

---

170 Transcript of Trial Proceedings – *Nuon Chea and Others* 002/19-09-2007/ECCC/TC (Trial Day 266, 31 March 2015) p. 65.

171 ECCC Memorandum from President Nil Nonn on Information on (1) Key Document Presentation Hearings in Case 002/02 and (2) Hearings on Harm Suffered by the Civil Parties in Case 002/02 (17 December 2014) para. 7.

172 Transcript of Trial Proceedings – *Nuon Chea and Khieu Samphân* 002/19-09-2007/ECCC/TC (Trial Day 268, 2 April 2015) pp. 11–17, 21.

173 Transcript of Trial Proceedings – *Nuon Chea and Khieu Samphân* 002/19-09-2007/ECCC/TC (Trial Day 269, 3 April 2015) p. 98.

174 Transcript of Trial Proceedings – *Nuon Chea and Khieu Samphân* 002/19-09-2007/ECCC/TC (Trial Day 233, 26 January 2015) pp. 41–42.

175 Rudina Jasini, *Victim Participation and Transitional Justice in Cambodia: The Case of the Extraordinary Chambers in the Courts of Cambodia* (Impunity Watch, Research Report, April 2016) pp. 57–58.

However, to be weighed against this risk is the benefit derived by the Court from victim testimony when freely given. As Judge Cartwright observed of the Duch trial:

> Any lawyer or judge will tell you that the dry words of an indictment charging an accused with serious crimes, come alive when the victim speaks in court ... More significantly for me, the victim testimony gave real vibrancy to the history of the regime and took us all back to the country as it was in the 1970s under Pol Pot's leadership ... Seeing and hearing the victims in person, also demonstrates clearly that the survivors of the regime continue to suffer the consequences of the Democratic Kampuchea regime.[176]

Stover recorded that for the majority of civil parties who participated in Case 001 the ECCC experience was generally positive, with most viewing the trial proceedings as fair and respectful.[177] A much larger study of victim-participation in Case 002 by the Cambodian Human Rights and Development Association found that, overall, the respondents strongly approved of the ECCC, with 92.5 per cent believing that the Court would help rebuild trust in Cambodia.[178] Participating in the trial had brought hope and solidarity among the respondents whose perception of the ECCC contrasted with their view of the Cambodian justice system.[179] Ryan's population survey of the ECCC's impact, encompassing Case 002, notes that 'civil parties often serve as information-sharing ambassadors' to families and communities who are remote from the operations of the Court.[180] Civil parties reported an increase in 'confidence, knowledge, rights, access to information, and networks as a result of their participation in the [Court] process.'[181] NGO representatives who had assisted the civil parties' participation observed a sense of empowerment, increasing rights awareness and understanding of Cambodian history among the civil parties.[182] One NGO respondent said:

> There are certain individuals who have grown through that experience as they understand the process, and there are may be room to use that more, to have a different

176 Silvia Cartwright, *International Criminal Trials: A Promise Fulfilled?* 2011 Annual Hawke Lecture, Adelaide 9 June 2011. Available at: http://www.unisa.edu.au/hawkecentre/ahl/2011AHL_Cartwright.pdf (accessed 25/5/2016).

177 Stover, above n. 39 at pp. 532–533.

178 Nadine Kirchenbauer et al., 'Victims Participation Before the Extraordinary Chambers in the Courts of Cambodia: Base-Line Study of the Cambodian Human Rights and Development Association's Civil Party Scheme for Case 002' (ADHOC, Phnom Penh January 2013) 32.

179 Ibid. p. 31, 33; Rachel Killean, 'Procedural Justice in International Criminal Courts: Assessing Civil Parties' Perceptions of Justice at the Extraordinary Chambers in the Courts of Cambodia' (2016) 16 *International Criminal Law Review* 1, 15–16.

180 Heather Ryan and Laura Mcgrew, *Performance and Perception: the Impact of the Extraordinary Chambers in the Courts of Cambodia* (Open Society Justice Initiative, 2016) p. 94.

181 Ibid.

182 Ibid.

voice vis-à-vis the commune chiefs, or even the courts. When people are called to appear, they now know something about fair trial rights.[183]

These responses point to the indirect outcomes of trial proceedings and the communicative benefits of the ECCC's procedure that are seldom considered amidst criticism of the Court's operational efficiency. While some commentators are not optimistic about the ECCC having an impact on rule of law development in Cambodia, the indirect effects of justice at grass-roots levels catalysed change in other transitional contexts when trials were held decades after violent, authoritarian rule.[184]

7.6. CONCLUSION

The role of the victim in transitional justice has evolved from ostensible exclusion at the International Military Tribunals at Nuremburg and Tokyo, thence instrumental support of the prosecution as victim-witness at the Ad hoc Tribunals, and limited participation at the International Criminal Court, to the grant of more substantive rights in the criminal proceedings at the ECCC. While it is clear that the exercise of victims' rights calls for careful mediation, what they were able to communicate during the ECCC proceedings was a major contribution to the justice process. Thus, Judge Lavergne's view of the transitional trial which values victim inclusion in proceedings on grounds of fairness and in the interest of establishing the truth, seems well founded. Without limiting the expressive value of the trial, Lavergne recognised the communicative value of the survivor's voice in its local context for the purpose of justice and reconciliation. In his view, substantive victim participation and fair trial process are not mutually exclusive.

The public nature of the ECCC proceedings and the space given to victims of crimes within the trials made possible wide transmission of what they communicated during the trial process. The narrative testimony of victims made clear the moral bankruptcy of the ideas of the architects of the regime that destroyed Cambodian society, and subjected their policies to public scrutiny. As the diverse groups of civil parties participated in the trial forum, they enlarged the moral canvass of Khmer Rouge crimes for deliberation within and beyond the walls of the Court in the sense envisioned by Osiel, but with arguably broader effect by virtue of trial dialogue accommodated under inquisitorial conditions.[185]

A safe, legitimate forum for discussion of the past seems critical in a society where transparency in legal proceedings and public deliberation over human

---

[183] Ibid.

[184] Karstedt above n 10, pp. 13, 33–34.

[185] Osiel, above n. 1, pp. 290–291.

rights violations has been virtually non-existent. As survivors of the Khmer Rouge testified in narrative form, the spatial and temporal frame of the courtroom drama expanded. Victim testimony controlled by the ECCC's mixed judiciary produced a forum for communication and debate on the human cost and broader social effects of the crimes. The trial dialogue under the inquisitorial procedure took on restorative justice elements as victims confronted perpetrators, and in some instances received sympathetic responses within the sanctity of the Court. Civil party accounts of what they witnessed and suffered under the regime were a major contribution to the retributive trial. In turn, the opportunity to make their statements within the trial proceedings offered a reparative benefit distinct from material reparations awards. Simultaneously, their story-telling became a legacy of the controversial Court.

While victim-witnesses and civil parties were not entirely protected from instrumentalisation by other court actors, Stover's research on civil parties who testified at the Duch trial confirmed that they assumed the risks of re-victimisation as they presented in court and faced examination following their testimony. In the controlled courtroom environment, victim statements and their responses to examination went beyond confirming or disproving facts. Their presence expanded the representative and dialogic nature of the proceedings, which, as discussed in the next chapter, also affected the process of judgment.

CHAPTER 8
THE VOICE OF THE COURT IN JUDGMENT: CASE 001

8.1. INTRODUCTION

Examining the process of judgment involves analysis of how the judiciary navigated the fault-lines of the trial, interpreted its narratives, and applied the relevant law. Drawing from Osiel's view of transitional courts as capable of accommodating divergent views of past violence, in this chapter, the ECCC's judgments are examined as sites where the social meaning of the trial was fleshed out within an internationalised legal framework. While the voice of the Court through its judgments is in a formal register, it is nonetheless a response to the dialogue of trial proceedings. The judgments also reflect the multiple levels on which transitional trials play out: legal and political, doctrinal and historical.[1]

The chapter highlights the communicative and expressive aspects of the process of judgment at the ECCC in both the Trial Chamber and the Supreme Court Chamber in Case 001. It examines the process of judgment by consideration of issues with social or political resonance in Cambodia, and to some extent in the international sphere. The chapter is structured around the grounds of appeal following the Trial Chamber finding of Duch's guilt for grave breaches of the Geneva Conventions and crimes against humanity, and its order of a fixed-term sentence. In addressing the grounds of appeal, the ECCC Supreme Court Chamber (SCC) interrogated the personal jurisdiction of the ECCC, interpreted the relevant international norms and reviewed the sentence imposed by the Trial Chamber. The SCC also ruled on appeals against the Trial Chamber's rejection of a number of civil party applications and the Trial Chamber's reparations award.

---

1 Mark Osiel, *Mass Atrocity, Collective Memory and the Law* (Transaction Publishers, 1997) p. 293.

8.2. PERSONAL JURISDICTION

In Chapters four and five, sections 4.5.4 and 5.4.3, I discussed the Cambodian government's opposition to the ECCC's opening of the investigations into Cases 003 and 004. The cases concerned former Khmer Rouge officials suspected as some of those most responsible for crimes within the jurisdiction of the ECCC, but who were not senior leaders of the regime. The government's resistance to expanding the net of prosecution highlighted the politically contentious nature of the ECCC's personal jurisdiction. The issue of jurisdiction was thrown into relief again as the Trial Chamber evaluated Duch's categorisation by the Co-Investigating Judges as one 'most responsible' for crimes within the ECCC's jurisdiction.

8.2.1. THE TRIAL CHAMBER'S DECISION

The Trial Chamber considered the ECCC's personal jurisdiction from the language of the ECCC Law which provides:

> The purpose of this law is to bring to trial senior leaders of Democratic Kampuchea and those most responsible for the crimes and serious violations of Cambodian penal law, international humanitarian law and custom, and international conventions recognised by Cambodia, that were committed during the period from 17 April 1975 to 6 January 1979.[2]

The Chamber concluded that the phrasing 'senior leaders of Democratic Kampuchea and those most responsible' referred to two separate categories of suspects based on the 1998 Group of Experts Report. The Report recommended that,

> any tribunal focus upon those persons most responsible for the most serious violations of human rights during the reign of Democratic Kampuchea. This would include senior leaders with responsibility over the abuses as well as those at lower levels who are directly implicated in the most serious atrocities.[3]

Referring to factors considered by the ICTY and the ICC Pre-Trial Chamber as grounding personal jurisdiction in similar circumstances, the Chamber found that Duch's effective control of S-21 as Deputy and subsequently Chairman, together with the gravity of the offences committed there established ECCC

---

[2] ECCC Law art. 1.

[3] *Report of the Group of Experts for Cambodia established pursuant to General Assembly Resolution 52/135 18 February 1999*, UN Doc. A/53/850-S/1999/231 (15 March 1999) [Group of Experts Report] para. 109.

jurisdiction over him as one of those most responsible for Khmer Rouge crimes during the period of temporal jurisdiction.[4] The fact that other individuals may have had equivalent seniority within Democratic Kampuchea did not preclude the accused from being indicted as one of those 'most responsible.'[5] This was sufficient to establish the jurisdiction of the ECCC without the necessity of examining whether the accused was also a senior leader of Democratic Kampuchea.[6] The Trial Chamber rejected the belated Co-Defence submission on Duch's request for acquittal.

8.2.2. THE SUPREME COURT'S APPRAISAL

Duch appealed the Trial Chamber decision in the Supreme Court Chamber. The accused claimed a jurisdictional error by the Trial Chamber on the grounds that he neither fitted the description of a 'senior leader' of Democratic Kampuchea, nor was one 'most responsible' for the crimes of that era.[7] His appeal went to the heart of ECCC personal jurisdiction. If he was neither a 'senior leader,' nor one 'most responsible,' then the Trial Chamber had no jurisdiction over him, his sentence would be invalid and he could be immediately released.

The Co-Prosecutors and one civil party group also exercised their appeal rights on the issue of personal jurisdiction. The Co-Prosecutors argued that the appeal was untimely and failed to meet minimum pleading standards.[8] The civil parties submitted that Duch's responsibility for M-13 had equipped him for his S-21 role of master interrogator, and requested the Supreme Court Chamber to treat the appeal as both out of time and unfounded.[9]

The Supreme Court addressed each allegation and interpreted the personal jurisdiction of the ECCC afresh. The judges saw their task as investigating whether the term 'senior leaders of Democratic Kampuchea and those most responsible' constituted a jurisdictional requirement to be evaluated by the ECCC, or a discretionary matter to guide the Co-Prosecutors and Co-Investigating Judges that was not subject to judicial review.[10] The Chamber undertook the task in two stages. First, the Chamber examined the scope of the terminology by reviewing the history of the negotiations relating to the intended targets

4 *Kaing Guek Eav alias Duch* (Judgment) 001/18-07-2007/ECCC/TC (26 July 2010) para. 25 [Duch Judgment].

5 Ibid. para. 24.

6 Ibid. para. 25.

7 Ibid. para. 23.

8 *Kaing Guek Eav alias Duch* (Appeal Judgment) 001/18-07-2007/ECCC/SC (3 February 2012) para. 24 [Duch Appeal Judgment].

9 Ibid. para. 25.

10 Ibid. para. 26.

for prosecution before the ECCC. Second, the Chamber conducted its own evaluation of the terms in the context of the purposes of the ECCC.

8.2.2.1. Scope of the Terminology 'Senior Leaders' and 'Most Responsible'

The SCC began its analysis by establishing the certain targets of ECCC prosecution. From the initiation of negotiations for creation of the ECCC, the historical record revealed the intention of the UN and the Cambodian government to focus finite resources on the criminal prosecution of certain surviving officials of the Khmer Rouge.[11] The SCC then considered whether the term 'senior leaders of Democratic Kampuchea and those who are most responsible' referred to two categories of Khmer Rouge officials. The Judges referred to documents reflecting the drafting histories of the ECCC Agreement and the amendments to the 2001 ECCC Law. They noted that the Group of Experts believed that the term 'leaders' should not be equated with all persons at senior levels of the government of Democratic Kampuchea or the CPK because that would remove from the reach of prosecution those who may also have played a significant role in Khmer Rouge atrocities. In addition, some top leaders may not have had knowledge of, or have been party to decision-making with respect to atrocities, particularly at the zonal level or the detention centres.[12]

The SCC also cited HE Deputy Prime Minister Sok An in the Cambodian National Assembly in 2004:

> Considering senior leaders, we refer to no more than 10 people, but we don't specify that they be members of the Standing Committee. This is the task of the Co-Prosecutors … However, there is still the second target. They are not the leaders, but they committed atrocious crimes. That's why we use the term those most responsible. There is no specific amount of people to be indicted from the second group. Those committing atrocious crimes will possibly be indicted.[13]

The Court examined recent scholarship on the terminology used to describe ECCC personal jurisdiction.[14] David Scheffer, who was involved in the ECCC

---

11 Ibid. para. 52.

12 Group of Experts Report, above n. 3, [109].

13 Cambodian National Assembly, (Proceedings) First Session, Third Term (4–5 October 2004) pp. 12, 23 cited in *Kaing Guek Eav alias Duch* (Appeal Judgment) 001/18-07-2007/ECCC/SCC, para. 53.

14 David Scheffer, 'Negotiating History of the ECCC's Personal Jurisdiction' *Cambodia Tribunal Monitor* (22 May 2011) pp. 1–11; Steve Heder, 'A Review of the Negotiations Leading to the Establishment of the Personal Jurisdiction of the Extraordinary Chambers in the Courts of Cambodia' *Cambodia Tribunal Monitor* (2 August 2011); See also Sean Morrison, 'Extraordinary Language in the Courts of Cambodia: Interpreting the Limiting Language and Personal Jurisdiction of the Cambodian Tribunal' (2008–2009) 37 *Capital University Law Review* 583.

negotiations as the US Ambassador at Large for War Crimes Issues from 1997–2001, recalled that in January 2000 Duch was already in custody and was a 'constant reference point for the negotiators as a likely defendant' before the proposed tribunal, being one recognised not as a senior leader within Democratic Kampuchea, but one who was allegedly most responsible for serious violations. Scheffer also confirmed an apparent consensus that de-linking leadership identity from responsibility identity by the use of the disjunctive 'or' in the personal jurisdiction terminology would have been unfair to senior leaders of Democratic Kampuchea who were not most responsible for atrocities.[15]

From the drafting history and analysis, the SCC concluded that the term 'senior leaders of Democratic Kampuchea and those who were most responsible' refers to two categories of Khmer Rouge officials that are not mutually exclusive.[16] A 'senior leader is not a suspect solely on the basis of his/her leadership,' but both a senior leader and a non-senior leader may be one most responsible for crimes within the ECCC's jurisdiction. Therefore, suspects targeted must be both Khmer Rouge officials and among the most responsible.[17]

The SCC then evaluated the terminology of ECCC jurisdiction. Using the guides to interpretation provided under both the Vienna Convention on the Law of Treaties and the ECCC Agreement, the SCC sought to establish whether the inclusion of the words 'personal jurisdiction' in Article 2(1) of the Agreement mandated that the term 'senior leaders of Democratic Kampuchea and those who were most responsible' operated exclusively as a legal requirement of the Trial Chamber's jurisdiction over an accused.[18]

8.2.2.2. *Interpreting the Terminology*

Article 2(1) of the ECCC Agreement provides in part:

> The present Agreement further recognises that the Extraordinary Chambers have personal jurisdiction over senior leaders of Democratic Kampuchea and those who were most responsible for the crimes referred to in Article 1 of the Agreement.[19]

Neither the ECCC Agreement nor the ECCC Law defines either the terms 'senior leaders' or 'those most responsible.' While the ordinary meaning given

15 Ibid. (SCHEFFER) pp. 4–5.
16 Duch Appeal Judgment para. 57.
17 Ibid. para. 58.
18 Ibid. para. 60.
19 Agreement between the United Nations and the Royal Government of Cambodia Concerning the Prosecution under Cambodian Law of Crimes Committed during the Period of Democratic Kampuchea' (signed 6 June 2003, ratified 19 October 2004) [ECCC Agreement] art. 2(1).

to the terms used suggested the exclusive prerogative of the Trial Chamber as to ECCC personal jurisdiction, the SCC considered whether the language used was consistent with the object and purpose of the ECCC Agreement and whether such interpretation would lead to a 'manifestly absurd or unreasonable result.'[20] In this the Chamber drew upon the content of and circumstances surrounding creation of preliminary documents constituting the *travaux préparatoires* to the Agreement, as well as international jurisprudence in other jurisdictions as legitimate sources of interpretive guidance.[21]

The ECCC background and drafting history revealed that the shared characteristic of those who might be prosecuted by the ECCC is that a suspect must be a Khmer Rouge official. The SCC concluded that the Trial Chamber is well suited to deciding a suspect's status as a Khmer Rouge official as a factual matter. However, deciding whether suspects are 'senior leaders' or those 'most responsible' is the subject of investigative and prosecutorial discretion.[22]

As to the term 'senior leaders,' the SCC reasoned that including former members of the CPK Central Committee and/or Standing Committee as senior leaders within the terminology of personal jurisdiction would have created a jurisdictional requirement which could be determined as a matter of fact by the Trial Chamber.[23] That the term is more flexible is indicated by the debates in the Cambodian National Assembly over the ECCC Agreement and the 2004 amendments to the ECCC Law.[24]

As to the term 'those most responsible', the SCC first gave reasons why treating the term as a jurisdictional requirement of the ECCC would be inconsistent with the object and purpose of the ECCC Agreement and would lead to an unreasonable result. Apart from the inability of the Trial Chamber to rank the criminal responsibility of all Khmer Rouge officials by objective method, the accused's effective submission that the Chamber should have embarked upon a relative assessment of his rank within Democratic Kampuchea amounts indirectly to a defence of 'superior orders' in contravention of Article 29 of the ECCC Law. Article 29 expressly confirms the international principle that 'superior orders' do not constitute a defence to crimes prosecuted by the ECCC. Additionally, the SCC pointed to the inherent discretion contained within the terminology of ECCC personal jurisdiction in contrast to the clearly defined parameters of the Court's temporal and subject-matter jurisdictions.[25]

---

20 *Vienna Convention on the Law of Treaties*, opened for signature 23 May 1969, 1155 UNTS 331 (entered into force 27 January 1980) art. 31(1). [VCLT]

21 Per VCLT Article 32(b); ECCC Agreement article 12(1).

22 Duch Appeal Judgment paras. 63–74.

23 Ibid. para. 76.

24 The First Session of the Third Term of the Cambodian National Assembly, 4–5 October 2004, p. 23.

25 Duch Appeal Judgment para. 62.

The SCC then found that the term 'most responsible' must be read with Articles 5(3) and 6(3) of the ECCC Agreement as a guide to the Co-Investigating Judges and the Co-Prosecutors respectively in exercising their independent discretion in investigating and prosecuting the most serious perpetrators of Khmer Rouge crimes. Revisiting the Group of Expert's Report, the Court found that the scope of investigations should be no more than a guide for prosecutors and not form an essential element of personal jurisdiction. Further support for treating the term 'most responsible' as investigatory and prosecutorial policy was drawn from the Rules of Evidence and Procedure of the ad hoc Tribunals. Those Rules provide limited scope for judicial scrutiny of the indictments by the Prosecutor so as to concentrate scarce resources on trying the most serious cases falling within the relevant jurisdictions.[26]

Thus, while the SCC noted that the Trial Chamber must consider all legitimate challenges to jurisdiction, it concluded that it was not reasonable to interpret 'most responsible' in the terminology of Article 2(1) of the ECCC Agreement as a justiciable issue before the ECCC Trial Chamber.[27] Rather, the terms

> operate exclusively as an investigative and prosecutorial policy to guide the independent discretion of the Co-Investigating Judges and Co-Prosecutors as to how to best target finite resources in order to achieve the purpose behind the establishment of the ECCC.[28]

Reviewing the jurisprudence of the Special Court for Sierra Leone (SCSL) in *Prosecutor v. Brima*, the SCC noted that SCSL had found that the only practical interpretation of the term 'greatest responsibility' within that Court's governing statute is that it 'guides the Prosecutor in the exercise of his prosecutorial discretion.' Furthermore, the SCSL Appeals Chamber stated:

> In the opinion of the Appeals Chamber it is inconceivable that after a long and expensive trial the Trial Chamber could conclude that although the commission of serious crimes has been established beyond reasonable doubt against the accused, the indictment ought to be struck out on the ground that it has not been proved that the accused was one of those who bore greatest responsibility[29]

While the SCC emphasised the wide margin of discretion in the investigative and prosecutorial functions, it concurred with international jurisprudence in holding that the discretion is subject to judicial review by the Trial Chamber when exercised in bad faith or according to unsound professional judgement.[30]

26 Ibid. para. 69.
27 Ibid. para. 74.
28 Ibid. para. 79.
29 Ibid. para. 73, citing *Prosecutor v. Brima* (Appeal Judgment) Appeals Chamber, SCSL-2004-16-A (22 February 2008) para. 283.
30 Duch Appeal Judgment para. 80.

With no suggestion of this in Case 001, the ground of the appeal of the accused on personal jurisdiction was found to be untenable and consequently dismissed in entirety.[31]

Duch's final-hour request for release brought the personal jurisdiction of the ECCC to centre-stage once more as it became the subject of further legal and historical scrutiny in the Supreme Court Chamber. From court documents and current academic discourse, the process of judgment by the SCC connected with the live debate surrounding the operation of the ECCC and conveyed to the Cambodian government the Court's interpretation of the Agreement it had entered into to end the impunity of indictable Khmer Rouge officials. The Chamber's engagement with the history of who the ECCC may prosecute was arguably communicative in its engagement with an issue of legal, social and political significance. It was also expressive in that the Supreme Court's legal analysis provided an authoritative statement on the independence of those authorised to perform ECCC investigations and prosecutions. Executive interference in those functions is therefore contrary to principle and the apparent original intent of the Cambodian side of the Court.

8.3. NORMATIVE ANALYSES OF DUCH'S CRIMES

8.3.1. IN THE TRIAL CHAMBER

As the first step in grounding the charges against Duch, the Trial Chamber examined the historical and political context of the crimes pursuant to the legality principle under international law.[32] The legality principle stated within Article 15(1) of the International Covenant on Civil and Political Rights (ICCPR) provides:

> No one shall be held guilty of any criminal offence on account of any act or omission which did not constitute a criminal offence, under national or international law, at the time it was committed.

The principle requires the offence with which an accused is charged to be 'sufficiently foreseeable' and the law providing for such liability to be 'sufficiently accessible to the accused at the relevant time.'[33] Preliminary issues for the Court therefore, were: whether crimes against humanity formed part of customary

31 Ibid. para. 81.

32 The principle of legality is a fundamental principle of criminal justice that prohibits persons from being convicted for acts which were not crimes under the relevant law at the time they were committed.

33 Duch Judgment para. 28.

international law by 1975; and whether grave breaches of the Geneva Conventions were crimes under national or international law during the period 17 April 1975 to 6 January 1979.[34]

Forms of individual responsibility must also conform to the legality principle.[35] The Chamber therefore considered the forms of responsibility provided under the ECCC Law that might establish Duch's individual criminal responsibility for crimes against humanity (Article 5) and grave breaches of the Geneva Conventions (Article 6):

> Any suspect who planned, instigated aided and abetted, or committed the crimes referred to in Articles 5 [and] 6 are to be found individually responsible.[36]

The Chamber then proceeded to establish that all the elements of the relevant offences were proved.

8.3.1.1. *Proving Grave Breaches of the Geneva Conventions*

As Cambodia and Vietnam ratified the four Geneva Conventions of 1949 on 12 August 1949 and 8 December 1957 respectively, the Chamber confirmed that Cambodia was bound by the conventions during the Khmer Rouge regime. This established ECCC jurisdiction to hear the case against Duch as to breaches of Article 6 crimes: grave breaches of the Geneva Conventions.[37]

Proving that grave breaches of the Conventions had been committed required: a finding of the existence of an international armed conflict; that there was a nexus between the acts of the accused and the armed conflict; that the accused had sufficient knowledge of the armed conflict and that the victims of the crimes had 'protected person' status under the Geneva Conventions. Furthermore, the ECCC Law required that the acts be committed during the period of 17 April to 6 January 1979.[38]

The Chamber traced Cambodia's enmity with Vietnam to Vietnamese encroachment on Cambodian territory from the fifteenth century. There were subsequent disputes over demarcation of the Cambodian border under the French, particularly the maritime boundary known as the Brevié line, which was drawn in 1939.[39] CPK resentment towards the Vietnamese was rooted in the non-recognition of Cambodian communist interests at the 1954 Geneva Conference,

---

34 Ibid. para. 402.
35 Ibid. para. 26.
36 ECCC Law art. 29.
37 Duch Judgment para. 404.
38 Article 6 of the ECCC Law requires that the acts be committed during the period of 17 April to 6 January 1979.
39 Duch Judgment para. 20.

and was exacerbated by differences between the brother communists in their combined resistance to the US-backed Lon Nol regime in the early 1970s. The CPK refusal to enter peace talks with the United States and Vietnam from 1972–1973 precipitated the United States' bombing campaign in Cambodia. Viewing the 1973 peace treaty between the Vietnam and the United States as Vietnamese betrayal, the CPK then attacked Vietnamese bases and a hospital within Cambodia, executing Vietnamese cadres. Further distrust and hostility stemmed from CPK fear that Vietnam intended to absorb and control Cambodia within a Vietnamese-dominated Indochinese Federation. The Vietnamese on the other hand, feared domination through the Khmer Rouge ally, China. The toxic climate of mistrust fostered border clashes and progressively hostile attacks on each state's interests from 30 April 1975.[40]

The Chamber concluded that Duch's acts were sufficiently related to the international conflict because they were the implementation of the policy of one of the parties to the war. Furthermore, Vietnamese prisoners of war and civilians as well as Cambodians perceived to be Vietnamese who were detained at S-21 were 'protected persons' within the meaning of the Geneva Conventions.[41]

Finally, the particular grave breaches with which Duch was charged were examined. The Chamber found that Duch's conduct towards protected persons amounted to the war crimes of wilful killing, torture or inhumane treatment, wilfully causing great suffering or serious injury to body or health, wilfully depriving a prisoner of war or civilian of the rights of fair trial and regular trial, and unlawful confinement of a civilian.[42] The Court's analysis was based on examination of Duch's leadership of S-21 within the context of the Khmer Rouge seizure of Phnom Penh in 1975, and the implementation of their communist state policy. Simultaneously, the CPK, as the emanation of the new government of Cambodia, engaged in armed hostilities with Vietnamese military forces until 6 January 1979.[43]

There was no appeal from the Chamber's finding on the Article 6 charge. The Chamber's historical contextualisation of the crimes established proof of culpability. It also created a new record of a turbulent period in Cambodian history from local and international sources, which was tested through legal process. Thus, the judicial process consisted of expressive norm interpretation, and the creation of a judicial record synthesising the factual evidence and expert opinion presented at trial. The ECCC expanded the judgment's communicative value by producing public copies for wide distribution throughout Cambodia.

---

40 Duch Judgment paras. 21–26.

41 Duch Judgment paras. 425–426.

42 Duch Judgment paras. 431–469.

43 Duch Judgment para. 423.

8.3.1.2. *Proving Crimes against Humanity Charges*

To ensure that the legality requirement of the crimes against humanity charges had been met, the Chamber had to establish the status of the crime during the period of the Court's temporal jurisdiction. The first prosecution of crimes against humanity in 1945 under Article 6(c) the IMT Charter required proof of a link with an armed conflict.[44] While the Chamber noted that the ECCC Law does not require a link between crimes against humanity and armed conflict, it considered the legality of the link in 1975. Referring to the jurisprudence of international tribunals that have considered when such link may have been dropped under international customary law, the Chamber cited the ICTY Appeals Chamber finding that the link was not required even in 1945, being a jurisdictional issue only.[45] In addition, the European Court of Human Rights found that a nexus may no longer have been relevant in 1956.[46] The Trial Chamber also noted the finding in the Group of Experts Report that the bond between crimes against humanity and armed conflict appeared to have been severed by 1975.[47] The Chamber concluded that the absence of any nexus with armed conflict within Article 5 of the ECCC Law 'comports with the customary definition of crimes against humanity during the period 1975–79.'[48]

Offences listed under Article 5 of the ECCC Law only constitute crimes against humanity if the *chapeau* or general elements are established. This involved establishing the existence of a widespread or systematic attack directed against any civilian population on national, political, ethnic, racial or religious grounds. There must also have been a nexus between the acts of the accused and the attack, and the accused must have had knowledge of the attack.[49]

The Chamber concluded that the seizure of power by the CPK, the forcible transfer of residents of cities to the countryside, the imposition of forced labour in collectives under harsh conditions and the dismantling of social structures constituted an 'attack.' It was under the circumstances of such attack that S-21 was created.[50] The Judges accepted the Co-Investigating Judges' conclusion that the magnitude and number of the crimes committed at S-21, together with the organised and prolonged character of the crimes, met the requirement of 'scale

---

44 Charter of the International Military Tribunal at Nuremburg – Annex to the Agreement for the Prosecution of the Major War Criminals of the European Axis ('London Agreement') (8 August 1945) 82 UNTS 279 art. 6(c).

45 *Prosecutor v. Tadic* (Appeal Judgment) ICTY-IT-94-1-A, (15 July 1999) para. 249.

46 *Korbley v. Hungary* (Judgment), (European Court of Human Rights, Grand Chamber, Application No. 9174/02, 19 September 2008) para.[82].

47 Duch Judgment para. 292.

48 Ibid.

49 Duch Judgment para. 297.

50 Duch Judgment para. 320.

and systematicity' of the *chapeau* element.[51] The systematic attack was mirrored in the purging process at S-21 which made no distinction between civilians and military personnel. All who were perceived as enemies of the regime were targeted and as result, the attack was found to have been directed against a civilian population.[52] Since there was no 'common linking factor among those detained' other than categorisation as 'enemies', the Chamber concluded that the attack was carried out at a minimum on political grounds.[53]

The Chamber was satisfied that the evidence established that S-21 was considered as 'vital to the achievement of the CPK's political objectives' including the 'smashing' of enemies.[54] Duch's awareness that S-21 was a site for the implementation of 'smashing' indicated to the Court that the nexus between his acts and the attack was established. The Court also found that Duch knew his acts contributed to the CPK attack.[55]

By majority the Trial Chamber found the accused criminally responsible for multiple underlying acts constituting crimes against humanity: murder, extermination, enslavement, imprisonment, torture (including an instance of rape), persecution on political grounds and other inhumane acts.[56] Judge Cartwright dissented from the majority finding on the offence of persecution. She argued that although Duch had implemented CPK policy unquestioningly, the evidence had not shown that he personally possessed the required discriminatory intent to support a conviction for persecution on political grounds.[57]

Citing ICTY jurisprudence, the Chamber noted the risk of prejudice to an accused arising from multiple convictions.[58] Therefore, the Chamber convicted Duch of persecution on political grounds as a crime against humanity (subsuming the other counts of the crime under the one head).[59] As to forms of responsibility the Chamber found that although Duch participated in at least some interrogations which included beatings or forms of torture, it was not satisfied that he committed these acts through physical perpetration or criminal omission.[60] However, he was found guilty of participating, instigating, ordering

---

51 Duch Judgment para. 321.
52 Duch Judgment para. 325.
53 Duch Judgment para. 327.
54 Duch Judgment para. 328.
55 Duch Judgment para. 329.
56 Duch Judgment para. 567.
57 Duch Judgment para 399; Richard L Kilpatrick, '*Prosecutor v Kaing Guek Eav alias Duch*: In First Round of Proceedings, The Extraordinary Chambers in the Courts of Cambodia Convicts Former Chairman of Khmer Rouge Interrogation Center of Atrocity Crimes' (2011) 19 *Tulane Journal of International and Comparative Law* 660.
58 Duch Judgment para. 560 *Prosecutor v. Delalić, Mucić, Delić & Landžo* (*'Celebici'*) (Appeal Judgment) IT-96-21A, 20 (February 2001) paras. 412–413.
59 Duch Judgment para. 568.
60 Duch Judgment paras. 483–486.

and aiding and abetting the offences. In addition, the Chamber concluded he had participated in a systemic joint criminal enterprise because he was 'deeply enmeshed' in the S-21 criminal system, aware of its criminal nature and acted with intent to further its 'criminal purpose.'[61]

8.3.2. IN THE SUPREME COURT

The Co-Prosecutors appealed the Trial Chamber findings on the specific findings of enslavement, rape, torture and persecution as crimes against humanity. For the purpose of this chapter, I limit the following discussion to the SCC's review of the Trial Chamber's findings on the crime of persecution and the decision to subsume the other offences as crimes against humanity under that crime.

On the question of subsumption, the SCC found that the Trial Chamber had rightly resorted to the *Celebici* test applied at the ICTY.[62] The test is applied in cases where the same factual conduct satisfies the definitions of multiple statutory offences. A Trial Chamber may enter multiple convictions with respect to those offences, but only where the crimes are considered sufficiently distinct or possess 'a materially distinct element' not found in the other offences. On the other hand, where multiple crimes do not each have materially distinct elements, the crime with the materially distinct element as the more specific crime subsumes the other and only one conviction is entered.[63]

The SCC found that the trial Chamber had erred in its application of the test. The Trial Chamber had placed emphasis on the factual circumstances surrounding the underlying conduct rather than each crime's distinct elements. The SCC held that with respect to the crimes which were subsumed under persecution, each had at least one materially distinct element from persecution. Furthermore, none of the offences carry a requirement of specific discriminatory intent, an element of the crime of persecution.[64] Subsuming the other crimes against humanity for which the accused was found responsible under the crime of persecution was therefore wrong in law. Consequently, the SCC ordered that separate convictions be entered for each of the other offences.[65]

In addition, after reviewing the legal definition of the crime of persecution, the SCC overturned the Trial Chamber ruling that all detainees at S-21 had been targeted on political grounds and were therefore victims of persecution. The SCC concluded that while Duch strove to implement the CPK policy of purging those considered to be traitors and political enemies at S-21, as the revolution

61 Duch Judgment paras. 515–516.

62 *Prosecutor v Delalić, Mucić, Delić & Landžo ('Celebici')* (Appeal Judgment) IT-96-21A, (20 February 2001) paras. 412–413.

63 Duch Appeal Judgment para. 288.

64 Duch Appeal Judgment para. 335.

65 Duch Appeal Judgment para. 336.

continued, individuals were arrested and executed indiscriminately without any rational or coherent justification on political grounds. Such action was not persecutory, but constituted a reign of terror where no discernible criteria applied to the targeting of victims. This resulted in the accused being responsible for the detention and execution of many individuals who were not in fact political enemies. The criminal activity of the accused towards such persons did not proceed from discriminatory intent on political grounds, but merely from attempts to demonstrate loyalty and efficiency to the Party. Therefore, the SCC found that the Trial Chamber had committed an error of law in categorising such conduct as persecution on political grounds.[66]

On the issue of subsumption, the SCC's normative analysis of the relevant law and the Trial Chamber's reasoning reflected expressive due process through judicial review. Review of the incidence of persecution at S-21 also constituted expressive norm interpretation. However, it was also communicative in its recognition of the climate of terror and dysfunction that characterised the institution in the Cambodian context of mass atrocity.

8.4. SENTENCE

8.4.1. THE TRIAL CHAMBER FINDINGS ON SENTENCE

The Co-Prosecutors had submitted that the gravity of Duch's crimes and various aggravating factors justified a life sentence. However, they added that conversion of the sentence to 40 years would be an adequate remedy in view of the mitigating factors and the accused's unlawful detention by the Cambodian military authorities. While the ECCC Agreement and the ECCC Law made provision for the maximum sentence of life imprisonment, they were silent as to the factors to be taken into account in sentencing. The Chamber ruled out reliance on Cambodian sentencing principles in light of uncertainties or complexity arising from their historical development since 1956. While noting the development of sentencing guidelines among international tribunals, the Chamber found there was no 'uniform approach to sentencing before these tribunals.'[67]

Ultimately the sentencing regime adopted by the Trial Judgment presented a holistic and responsive approach to what was communicated at the trial, subject to relevant sentencing principles and factors. In expressive tones the Judges explained:

> While an obvious function of a sentence is to punish, its goal is not revenge. The sentence must be proportionate and individualised such that it reflects the culpability

66 Duch Appeal Judgment para. 283.
67 Duch Judgment paras. 576–578.

> of the accused based on an objective, reasoned and measured analysis both of his or her conduct and its consequential harm.[68]

The Chamber then noted that international jurisprudence had established that the gravity of the crimes was the litmus test for the appropriate sentence, with consideration of both the particular circumstances of the case and the 'form and degree of the accused's participation in the alleged crime.'[69] Duch's crimes were of a particularly shocking and heinous character. He had managed and refined the S-21 system through which more than 12,000 people died. He worked 'tirelessly to ensure that S-21 ran as efficiently as possible and did so out of unquestioning loyalty to his superiors and CPK ideology, and without regard to the humanity of the detainees he oversaw.'[70] The testimony of survivors of S-21 and the family members of victims at trial had confirmed the long-term physical and psychological harm flowing from the accused's crimes.[71]

At the time, as an intelligent and educated man, Duch fully understood the nature of his acts. Aggravating factors were the sheer number of victims and the cruelty with which the crimes were committed. In addition, his exercise of power had a corrupting influence over the generally young S-21 staff as they were indoctrinated and trained to treat detainees inhumanely.[72]

As to mitigating factors, the Judges rejected the Co-Defence submission that Duch followed his superior's orders under duress. The extended period of time over which this occurred, the large number of victims and the diligence of the accused in his management of S-21 militated against such a finding. Nonetheless, the Judges attached weight, albeit 'limited', to the 'coercive climate of Democratic Kampuchea and [Duch's] subordinate position within the CPK.'[73]

Duch's cooperation with the ECCC as a mitigating factor was never disputed. It had both facilitated the trial proceedings and assisted the Court's contribution to national reconciliation.[74] However, his apologies to victims and expressions of remorse throughout the proceedings, while recognised as mitigating factors, were 'undermined by his failure to offer a full and unequivocal admission of responsibility', and his request for acquittal at the end of the trial diminished 'the extent to which his remorse would otherwise mitigate his sentence.'[75]

The Judges factored into their sentence Duch's propensity for rehabilitation. In this they relied on the psychological report of experts Françoise Sironi-Guilbaud

68 Duch Judgment para. 580.
69 Duch Judgment para. 582.
70 Duch Judgment para. 597.
71 The Chamber cited the testimony of Robert Hamill, Hav Sophea, Neth Phally, Antonya Tioulong, Martine Lefeuvre and Ou Savith.
72 Duch Judgment para. 602.
73 Duch Judgment para. 608.
74 Duch Judgment para. 609.
75 Duch Judgment para. 610.

and Ka Sunbaunat, supplemented by their own observations of Duch throughout the trial proceedings. The numerous quotations from the report of the experts in the judgment suggested the Judges' intention to widely communicate the analysis of the experts. The Chamber reiterated that the experts had drawn from their 'clinical and scientific research, as well as on cultural, religious and social factors relevant to the accused, considered by them to be vital for a comprehensive assessment of him.'[76] The Judges noted the experts' description of Duch as a 'dutiful person, readily influenced by [and] responding well to strong leadership,' with a 'need for affiliation, and for recognition and acknowledgment by his superiors.'[77] The Judges noted that during the proceedings Duch 'appeared anxious to please the Chamber, as well as to appease the victims of his acts.'[78] The judgment also cited the experts' observation that Duch's experience of 'successive and major assimilation of different cultural systems' included his radical affiliation with communism, which he described as a 'complete social order.'[79]

Marxist ideology satisfied his need for certainty and was subsequently replaced with an equally strong commitment to Christianity, described as a pragmatic and safe choice. In identifying with Marxism, the accused showed zeal and extreme allegiance, surpassing superiors' expectations in order to suppress his increasing doubts regarding Angkar's plans for smashing enemies, and his own fears of imminent death.[80]

The judgment also noted the experts' observation of Duch's lack of empathy, which they attributed in part to the 'fabrication' or conditioning process developed by the Khmer Rouge 'to eliminate emotions and to enhance self-control.'[81] They noted further:

> The accused was able to construct powerful defence mechanisms insulating him from emotional reactions and inner conflicts created by his external reality: mechanisms which they described as ultimately enabling him to nurture his own family whilst overseeing the deaths of children at S-21.[82]

Along with the experts the Chamber perceived and assessed positively Duch's greater capacity for self-reflection regarding his life and actions as the investigation and trial progressed.[83] The Judges accepted the experts' evaluation of Duch's rehabilitation and reintegration into society. Character evidence from

76 Duch Judgment para. 612.
77 Duch Judgment para. 613.
78 Duch Judgment para. 616.
79 Duch Judgment para. 613.
80 Ibid.
81 Duch Judgment para. 614.
82 Ibid. para. 614.
83 Duch Judgment para. 615.

two of Duch's former students and Pastor Christopher Lapel persuaded the Chambers of his commitment to his studies, professional vocation, and political and religious beliefs. However, there were no factors in his private or professional life that excused his criminal conduct.

By a majority, the Chamber decided upon a sentence of 35 years (Judge Lavergne dissenting).[84] The term however, was subject to a reduction of five years due to the violation of Duch's rights during his detention by the Cambodian Military Court between 10 May 1999 and 30 July 2007, as discussed in Chapter five, section 5.3.2. Furthermore, Duch was found to be entitled to credit for time spent in detention at both the Military Court and under the authority of the ECCC.[85] Together the reduction in sentence and credit for time spent in detention reduced his overall sentence to 19 years.

8.4.2. THE SUPREME COURT REVIEW

The Supreme Court as the ECCC court of appeal reviewed the Trial Chamber's sentencing decision. In their appeal against the Trial Chamber sentence the Co-Prosecutors argued that the mitigating factors had been afforded excessive weight.[86] In examining each of the mitigating factors, the SCC concluded that the effect the mitigating factors had had on the Trial Chamber's determination of sentence constituted an error of law.[87] Specifically, mitigation on account of the 'coercive climate in DK'[88] was of minimal degree because Duch failed to provide evidence that he had no choice in committing the crimes for which he was accused, or that he was personally threatened, or that he attempted to 'dissociate himself from his criminal conduct.'[89] Similarly, Duch's subordinate position in the hierarchy of Democratic Kampuchea was dismissed as a mitigating factor by the SCC on the basis of his knowledge that the orders he was given were unlawful and were not accompanied by actual threats causing duress.[90]

The Trial Chamber's treatment of Duch's cooperation as a mitigating factor because it had 'undoubtedly facilitated the proceedings … [and] assisted in the pursuit of national reconciliation' was challenged by the Co-Prosecutors.[91] They argued instead that the accused's cooperation was 'limited, scarcely facilitated

---

84 Judge Lavergne argued for a 30-year sentence consistent with Cambodian sentencing law. *Separate and Dissenting Opinion of Judge Jean-Marc Lavergne on Sentence* 001/18-07-2007/ECCC/TC (26 July 2010).

85 Duch Judgment para. 631.

86 Co-Prosecutor's Appeal at para. 216 cited in Duch Appeal Judgment para. 358.

87 Duch Appeal Judgment para. 363.

88 Duch Judgment para. 608.

89 Duch Appeal Judgment para. 364.

90 Ibid. para. 365.

91 Duch Judgment para. 609.

the economy of proceedings, and ultimately proved incomplete, selective and opportunistic.'[92] Upon their own review of Duch's conduct during the proceedings, the SCC ultimately agreed with the Co-Prosecutors and declared that the Court was not satisfied that his 'cooperation provided substantial information in terms of quantity and quality.'[93] Therefore, limited weight only could be attached to this factor.

The accused's expression of remorse and public apologies were also considered to be of limited weight. This was not because of Duch's late request for acquittal, which he had made without denying the facts or his culpability. The SCC held instead that because Duch's final statement placed emphasis on why he was outside ECCC personal jurisdiction, and not on his remorse for his actions, he had effectively given up his last opportunity to demonstrate the sincerity of his remorse.[94] The final mitigating factor, rehabilitation, was then examined. Considering ICTY jurisprudence with respect to this factor, the SCC held that only limited weight should be attributed to it in determination of sentence.[95]

The SCC declared that the mitigating impact of these factors, which was limited at best, was in fact neutralised when weighed against the outstanding aggravating elements and exceptional magnitude of the crimes for which the accused was found responsible.[96] The Trial Chamber had erred by attaching undue weight to mitigating circumstances and insufficient weight to the gravity of the crimes. Such an error was sufficient to invalidate the sentence pursuant to Internal Rule 104(1)(a) and an abuse of the Trial Chamber's discretion.[97]

In substituting the sentence of life imprisonment based on the gravity of the crimes and the aggravating circumstances, the SCC reasoned that the high number of deaths for which the accused was found responsible and the extended period of time over which the crimes were committed undoubtedly placed his case among the gravest before international tribunals.[98] While noting the Trial Chamber's capacity for close examination of the accused during trial proceedings as integral to the exercise of its discretion in sentencing, the SCC invoked two of the general purposes of criminal punishment: retribution and deterrence, as particularly relevant in this case in light of the gravity of the crimes in question.[99] As the Chairman of S-21, Duch had overseen a 'factory of death', where the lives of more than 12,272 people, including women and children, were mercilessly terminated.[100]

---

92 Duch Appeal Judgment para. 367.
93 Duch Appeal Judgment para. 368.
94 Duch Appeal Judgment para. 369.
95 Duch Appeal Judgment para. 370.
96 Duch Appeal Judgment para. 371.
97 Duch Appeal Judgment para. 373.
98 Duch Appeal Judgment para. 376.
99 Duch Appeal Judgment paras. 379–380.
100 Duch Appeal Judgment para. 380.

The crimes of the accused were described as deserving of the highest criminal penalty as a 'fair and adequate response to the outrage these crimes caused in victims, their families and relatives, the Cambodian people and all human beings.'[101] Furthermore, the passing of more than 30 years since the commission of the crimes does not lessen the necessity of the highest punishment, given that the Cambodian people still struggle to overcome the tragedies resulting from crimes which remain an 'affront to all humanity.'[102]

The imposition of a life sentence in this case also amounted to a statement that the passage of time neither eliminates impunity nor warrants undue leniency, and all the more so as numerous contemporary governments continue to violate the human rights of their constituent peoples.[103] Thus, the SCC by a majority authoritatively disavowed Duch's conduct and refused to acquiesce in any way in his crimes by entertaining less than the maximum sentence.[104] The language of the judgment on appeal seemed designed as the ritual performance of the process of punishment carrying 'manifest moral significance.'[105] The Chamber's reference to ongoing human rights violations in other countries invoked the socio-pedagogic value of sentencing as strengthening of the norm of accountability through consistent denunciation of inhumane conduct, reinforced by the expressive import of a maximum sentence.[106]

As the SCC delivered its judgment, DeFalco reported that the announcement of the life sentence was what the large audience assembled at the Court was waiting to hear.[107] This contrasted with the disappointment expressed by some civil parties at the prospect of Duch serving only 19 years of his sentence. However, as Osiel argued, assessing the significance of trials of mass atrocity calls for interpretation beyond the 'curative or even symbolic' meaning attached to punishment.[108] This is explored in Chapter nine through further discussion of the communicative dynamics of ECCC trials and their social impacts.

---

101 Ibid.

102 Duch Appeal Judgment para. 381.

103 Duch Appeal Judgment para. 382.

104 Robert D. Sloan, 'The Expressive Capacity of International Punishment: The Limits of the National Law Analogy and the Potential of International Criminal Law' (2007) 43 *Stanford Journal of International Law* 39, 71.

105 Ibid. pp. 89–90.

106 See Mirjan Damaska, 'What is the Point of International of International Criminal Justice?' (2008) 83 *Chicago-Kent Law Review* 329, 346.

107 Randle DeFalco, 'Case 001 Appeal Judgement: Duch Sentenced to Life', *Cambodia Tribunal Monitor* (4 or 5 February 2012) pp. 1, 5.

108 Mark Osiel, *Mass Atrocity, Collective Memory and the Law* (Transnational Publishers, 1997) pp. 50–51.

8.5. SCC REVIEW OF THE REMEDY FOR UNLAWFUL DETENTION

Though not a ground of appeal, the SCC made an *ex proprio motu* decision on the Trial Chamber's grant of a remedy to the accused for violation of his human rights while held in detention by the Cambodian Military Court between 10 May 1999 and 30 July 2009. Upon examination of relevant ICTR jurisprudence the SCC, by a supermajority of judges, declared:

> [V]iolations of human rights must constitute either an abuse of process or be attributed to the Tribunal in order to grant the Accused a remedy, and that also such remedies have always been granted in connection with failures by the Prosecution or other organ of the Tribunal.[109]

The majority determined that, while the Trial Chamber had enunciated the test, it had awarded the remedy based on a sole legal authority in which abuse of process had been established, whereas in the case of Kaing Guek Eav, neither abuse of process nor error attributable to the Tribunal was established.[110] The majority concluded that this constituted an error of law which made void the five-year reduction to sentence awarded by the Trial Chamber.[111] However, two out the seven SCC judges dissented and held that the remedy had been properly granted.

While concurring with the majority that a life sentence was warranted, international judges Klonowiecka-Milart and Jayasinghe could not support the majority decision, which denied a remedy for the severe violation of the accused's fundamental rights occasioned by his pre-trial detention.[112] The judges in the minority disagreed with the majority's 'mechanistic application' of the ad hoc Tribunal's jurisprudence to the circumstances of Duch's detention because of differences between the ECCC and the ad hoc Tribunals, and the national systems which had caused the violation of rights. The minority judges argued that the ICTY and the ICTR were established under the authority of the UN Security Council pursuant to Chapter VII of the UN Charter. There was no national legislation enacting the operation of the Tribunals and domestic rules of criminal law and procedure are inapplicable to those international courts. The ECCC, on the other hand, is an internationalised court which, although applying international law for some purposes, is a domestic court in key respects. Indeed the Cambodian had Government insisted upon having a national court

109 Duch Appeal Judgment para. 398.

110 *Barayagwiza v. Prosecutor* (Appeal Judgment) Appeals Chamber ICTR-97-19-AR72 (3 November 1999) para. 101.

111 Duch Appeal Judgment para. 399.

112 Duch Appeal Judgment Part 1X Partially Dissenting Joint Opinion para. 1.

with international assistance almost to the point of 'rupture.'[113] In view of the historical background to Duch's detention by the Military Court from 1999, it was clear that the case brought against Duch by the ECCC was 'functionally an extension of the charges originally brought by the domestic court.'[114] The clear nexus between the accused's pre-trial detention for eight years without any substantive proceedings contrasted with the relatively brief periods of detention ruled on by the ad hoc Tribunals, which involved jurisdictionally distinct authorities.[115]

The minority highlighted the decisions of the UN Human Rights Committee and the European Court of Human Rights where the gravity of the deprivation of liberty without sufficient grounds has been found to be a violation of a fundamental right in cases involving far shorter periods of unlawful detention.[116] The judges noted that the complexity of the case may dictate a lengthier period of detention, but that the authorities in Duch's case exceeded statutory limits and failed to proceed expeditiously over the extremely long period of eight years.[117] The minority agreed with the Trial Chamber that the ECCC is uniquely placed to grant a remedy to the accused that will not frustrate the mandate of the Court. Such remedy should be of a restorative nature to provide redress for excessive unlawful detention.[118] Redress in the form of sentence reduction has been found to be an appropriate remedy in such cases.[119] Consistent with the 2009 Cambodian Criminal Code and internationally recognised standards of fairness, the minority judges found that Duch's life sentence should be commuted to a fixed term of 30 years.[120]

The split decision demonstrated the accommodation of disagreement between the judges through expressive due process. The debate itself communicated different visions of transitional justice proceedings. The majority adopted a

---

113 Duch Appeal Judgment Part 1X Partially Dissenting Joint Opinion para. 9; And see DAVID SCHEFFER, 'The Extraordinary Chamber in the Courts of Cambodia' in M. CHERIF BASSIOUNI (ed.), *Introduction to International Criminal Law*, 3rd ed. (Martinus Nijhoff Publishers, 2008) pp. 219–255 at 224–239.

114 Duch Appeal Judgment, Part 1X, Partially Dissenting Joint Opinion para. 12.

115 Duch Appeal Judgment, Part 1X, Partially Dissenting Joint Opinion para. 13.

116 *Siewpersaud et al. v. Trinidad and Tobago*, United Nations Human Rights Committee, Views, UN Doc. CCPR/C/81/D/938/2000 (19 August 2004); *Dzelili v. Germany* (Chamber Judgment) European Court of Human Rights (Application No. 65745/01, 10 November 2005).

117 Duch Appeal Judgment Part 1X Partially Dissenting Joint Opinion) para. 14.

118 Ibid.

119 *Chraidi v. Germany* (Judgment) European Court of Human Rights (Application No. 65655/01, 26 October 2006) [24]–[25]; And see *Report on the Effectiveness of National Remedies in Respect of Excessive Length of Proceedings*, Study No. 316/2004, adopted by the European Commission for Democracy Through Law, 69th Plenary Session (3 April 2007) para. 228 ('taking into account the delays in the assessment of punishment must be considered an appropriate form of redress in criminal proceedings').

120 Duch Appeal Judgment, Part 1X, Partially Dissenting Joint Opinion paras. 29–32.

narrow, rule-based position, divorced from the local circumstances of Duch's detention and the ECCC as a model court within Cambodia. The minority, on the other hand, addressed the particular circumstances of the ECCC's creation and drew from a body of international precedent to assess the Trial Chamber's substantive decision to enforce Duch's human rights within the Cambodian justice system.

8.6. CIVIL PARTY APPLICATIONS

In Chapter five, section 5.6.2, I discussed issues surrounding the ECCC's management of the civil party application process and the Co-Defence challenge to the admissibility of 24 applications. The Trial Chamber deferred determination of the admissibility of the applications to the time of judgment. Subsequently, two civil party applicants withdrew their applications and one applicant abandoned his civil action, making the total number of admitted civil parties 90. The Trial Chamber's final determination of the applications in its judgment is outlined below.

8.6.1. TRIAL CHAMBER DETERMINATION

To substantiate claims for reparations the Chamber required each civil party to establish a causal connection between the criminal conduct of the accused and the injury they had suffered as a victim of his crimes.[121] Direct victims, or survivors of S-21 and S-24 were required to provide evidence of their internment or placement at the security centre.

The Chamber described its two-tiered approach to determining eligibility for civil party status: first, the Chamber assessed the credibility of information supplied by applicants at first instance on a *prima facie* basis. This initial process was distinct from the Chamber's subsequent determination of the merits of all civil party applications, taking account of all other evidence submitted in the course of the proceedings. In addition, indirect victims were required to substantiate their claims to injury based on kinship or 'special bonds of affection', or dependence on a direct victim of S-21 or S-24. In this, the Chamber was persuaded by the evidence of expert witness Chhim Sotheara regarding the often attenuated nature of familial relationships within Cambodian culture.[122]

At the judgment stage the Trial Chamber found that 24 civil party applicants had failed to substantiate a link with Duch's conduct at S-21 or S-24 and the harm

121 Duch Judgment paras. 640–641.

122 Duch Judgment para. 643.

they had suffered. Thereafter, 22 civil party applicants exercised their right of appeal to the Supreme Court against the rejection of their claims for reparations.

8.6.2. SUPREME COURT DETERMINATION OF CIVIL PARTY APPEALS

The appellants alleged errors of law by the Trial Chamber in determining the admissibility of their applications for civil party status. These were categorised by the SCC as error in the formulation of who is a victim before the ECCC, error in creating a two-tiered admissibility review of civil party applications, and error in determining the standard of proof applicable to civil party applications.[123]

8.6.2.1. The Definition of Victim at the ECCC

The appellants submitted that the test for admission as civil parties was too strict and outside the requirements of the Internal Rules. In addition, it was alleged that the Trial Chamber had jeopardised the fairness of the proceedings because the requirement of the 'special bonds of affection' criterion was not foreseeable at the point of application, and that notice of the test was not provided by the Trial Chamber before judgment.[124]

The SCC examined the requirement of injury in civil party claims under Article 13 the Cambodian Code of Criminal Procedure. The Chamber concluded that the meaning of injury with respect to indirect victims is 'congruent with many plausible scenarios involving a wide range of persons,' but 'the actuality of injury must be established in each case.'[125] The SCC found that the Trial Chamber's discretionary presumption that 'special bonds of affection or dependence' with the direct victim, as a criterion for admissibility for civil parties as indirect victims, was consistent with the notion of injury under Article 13. While the presumption took account of the attenuated nature of Cambodian familial relationships as described by expert Chhim Sotheara, only in exceptional circumstances will non-immediate family members be considered to have had special bonds of affection with or dependence on, direct victims. As to the narrowing of the scope of the presumption, the SCC found that this arose from the Trial Chamber's discretion and not the parties' right to benefit from it.[126] Furthermore, the appellants' rights were not affected by lack of notice as to the limitation because they had a continuing burden of proving their injury through

123 Duch Appeal Judgment paras. 406–502.
124 Duch Appeal Judgment para. 406.
125 Duch Appeal Judgment para. 417.
126 Duch Appeal Judgment para. 449.

the giving of evidence.[127] Questioning of civil parties by judges throughout the proceedings on the nature of their suffering was evidence of this.

8.6.2.2. Civil Party Application Process

The SCC reviewed the process of civil party application, including the letters of 'interim recognition' sent by the Greffier of the Co-Investigating Judges' Office to applicants, statements of Judge Lavergne to applicants at the Initial Hearing on 17 February 2009, and the Trial Chamber's summary of the two-tiered approach to determining applications. The Chamber also reviewed the applicable Cambodian law and found that it provided sufficient basis for the legality of the process adhered to by the ECCC. Specifically, ECCC Internal Rule 100(1) reflects Article 355 of the 2007 Code of Criminal Procedure, which provides:

> [I]n the criminal judgement, the court [of first instance] shall also decide upon civil remedies. The court shall determine the admissibility of the civil party application and also decide on the claims on the civil party against the accused and civil defendants.[128]

The SCC found that all civil party representatives, Cambodian and international, ought to have been familiar with Cambodian criminal procedure, which clearly empowered the trial court to finally determine the admissibility of civil party applications in the judgment. Thus, advance notice of the procedure and opportunity was available to the civil party appellants.[129]

Finding that the Trial Chamber was not in error as to procedure, the SCC also found that, whatever ambiguity may have arisen as to civil party standing before the ECCC, this had not prevented the civil party appellants from asserting their rights in trial proceedings.[130] Nevertheless, the SCC recognised that there had been a 'fundamental misunderstanding between the Trial Chamber and the civil party appellants as to the merits and legal effect of the initial review of their applications.'[131]

The SCC also conceded that the framework and the novel character of the ECCC victim participation scheme which made possible multiple civil parties to trials of mass crimes, conceivably lacked clarity as to the particulars of procedure. This may have been the source of confusion as to what was required of civil parties when submitting evidence in support of their application.[132] Noting the

127 Duch Appeal Judgment para. 450.
128 *Criminal Code of Procedure of the Kingdom of Cambodia 2007* art. 355.
129 Duch Appeal Judgment para. 496.
130 Duch Appeal Judgment para. 500.
131 Duch Appeal Judgment para. 501.
132 Ibid.

'anguish' caused by the unclear admission requirements, the SCC allowed the civil party appellants to submit further evidence of their eligibility during the appeal process. In light of the new evidence the Court received, the SCC found that 10 civil party applications which had been rejected by the Trial Chamber, were substantiated on appeal. They were therefore accepted by the SCC as civil parties and thus eligible for reparations.[133] The Chamber also accepted a submission of one civil party that clerical error had led to the omission of her child's name from the Trial Judgment.[134]

8.6.2.3. Trial Chamber Error in Determining the Standard of Proof?

The SCC confirmed the Trial Chamber's requirement that civil parties satisfy the Court of the injury they had suffered personally as a direct consequence of the accused's criminal conduct.[135] As to the correct standard of proof at the reparation stage, the SCC held that the Trial Chamber's application of the 'more likely than not to be true' or the 'preponderance of evidence test' was in accordance with international practice and the standard common to civil claims across the world.[136] Furthermore, the Trial Chamber had shown 'flexibility and broadly accepted any documentary evidence' that directly or indirectly supported a claim in light of the difficulties involved in obtaining official information in Cambodia.[137]

However, the SCC agreed with the civil party appellants that the Trial Chamber had failed to clearly inform the appellants of the standard of proof applicable at the reparations stage.[138] The lack of clarity as to which standard was to apply had 'caused confusion and frustration to civil party appellants' when the judgment was handed down. Nevertheless, it was found that any prejudice suffered by the affected appellants was cured by the SCC's acceptance of additional evidence in support of rejected claims.[139]

The SCC's review of the civil party admission process revealed the shortcomings in the ECCC's communications with victims and their representatives. The confusion sown by the fledgling Court could only be partially rectified by the SCC at the appeal stage. In the interim, some applicants had suffered a form of re-victimisation at the prospect of having their status as civil parties taken from them. However, the take up rate of applications from the earliest stages of

133 Duch Appeal Judgment paras. 535–628.
134 Duch Appeal Judgment para. 629.
135 Duch Appeal Judgment para. 522.
136 Duch Appeal Judgment para. 531.
137 Duch Appeal Judgment para. 534.
138 Duch Appeal Judgment para. 527.
139 Duch Appeal Judgment para. 534.

the Court's life, with strong support from local and international civil society groups, indicated that much more was required of the in-country justice process than it was designed to cater for. The strong demand for inclusion of victims of mass atrocity in the legal process speaks of the need for planning on the part of future transitional courts to incorporate infrastructure and personnel to serve the legitimate expectations of victims of crimes.

8.7. REPARATIONS

8.7.1. TRIAL CHAMBER RULING

Internal Rule 23(11) and (12) govern the award of reparations to civil parties. Such awards are against the accused and are moral and collective only in nature.[140] Civil party claims for reparations against Duch included: compilation and publication of his statements of apology; individual monetary awards or the establishment of a fund for victims' needs; requests for certain measures by the Cambodian government; requests for the construction of pagodas and other memorials; requests to preserve the S-21 archives, Vann Naths's paintings, and the S-21 and S-24 sites; as well as requests for the provision of free medical care and educational measures for victims.[141]

Most of the claims were beyond the mandate of the Court because the ECCC Rules do not allow for any monetary reparations, and requests involving the Cambodian government are not within the jurisdiction of the Chamber. The fact that the accused was indigent meant that the reparations order was limited to the publication of statements of apology or expressions of remorse as some satisfaction to victims, and as 'the only tangible means by which Kaing Guek Eav could acknowledge his responsibility and the collective suffering of victims.'[142] The only other forms of reparation secured were inclusion of the names of civil parties and recognition of the right to a remedy in the final judgment, and wide distribution of the judgment by the Court.[143]

8.7.2. SUPREME COURT REVIEW

The civil party appellants made extensive submissions to the SCC on the right to reparations under international law and requested orders for the enforcement of

140 ECCC Internal Rules, r. 23(11), (12).
141 Duch Judgment paras. 667–674.
142 Duch Judgment para. 668.
143 Duch Judgment paras. 667–675.

the reparations they had claimed. However, the SCC made no new reparations awards. Though recognising the right of victims of gross human rights violations to reparation, the Chamber re-iterated the constraints flowing from the ECCC reparations framework.[144] The SCC expressed the view that although collective and moral reparations may not fully compensate the victims of human rights abuses physically or economically, other general purposes of reparations are fulfilled under the ECCC scheme. This includes the Court's efforts to verify and disclose the truth surrounding the commission of the crimes in all of the Court's units, and disseminate information on the trial proceedings to support the social quest for 'historical truth.'[145] In addition, the wide circulation of the court's judgments may both promote 'public and genuine discussion on the past,' and help to reduce denial and distortions of the truth.[146]

Thus, the SCC limited itself to a didactic statement of the Court's contribution to victims of the Khmer Rouge and Cambodia generally. However, in Case 002/01, more tangible reparations were endorsed by the Court following the amendments to the Internal Rules which altered the victim participation scheme, and changed the powers of the Victims Support Section. These reparations awards are discussed at Chapter 9 Section 9.4.2.

8.8. CONCLUSION

The judgments of the Court give expression to the formal outcome of the trial in language respecting law and legal conventions. However, the authors have also been the judicial audience of the proceedings and exercise their voice in response to the trial's communications. The question is: who are the judges addressing in the judgment? The expressivist may say the judges' voices are addressed to all the world, as they enforce international criminal law and interpret international norms. From a communication perspective, the judicial voice may be one of engagement with local concerns that have surfaced in trial proceedings. Of course, given the monumental nature of their task in trials of mass atrocity, judges may also see themselves as addressing a society's future and speaking to history.

With the advantage of directly observing Duch throughout the proceedings, the Trial Chamber Judges in the process of judgment engaged with both the law and the dialogue of the trial. Their judgment is a composite of these inputs. While the Trial Chamber's determination of Duch's guilt demonstrated the expressivism of norm interpretation and due process, the judgment's coverage

144 Duch Appeal Judgment para. 717.
145 Duch Appeal Judgment para. 661.
146 Duch Appeal Judgment paras. 708–709.

of the history of armed conflict in Cambodia during the rule of Democratic Kampuchea was communicative in its detail. Justice proceedings held decades or more after the crimes may in fact demand a detailed historical record.

The determination of sentence by the Trial Chamber attempted to synthesise elements inhering in Duch from his personal and social conditioning in Cambodia, as well as his psychological shaping by the coercive Khmer Rouge regime under paranoid leadership. The Judges' attention to social and political factors affecting the accused, their direct observation of Duch and their analysis of the evidence perhaps reflected the inquisitorial trial's emphasis on the search for a form of ontological truth, as opposed to reasoning from the dualistic truth revealed in party-based proceedings. The court's reliance on the evidence of the psychological experts' report and the extensive references to its conclusions not only justified the fixed-term sentence, but suggested the importance of conveying aspects of the analysis to the Court's public. This, I suggest was indicative of a communicative approach to judgment.

The process of judgment in the Supreme Court largely reflected expressive due process, but had arguably communicative effects. Duch's final-hour request for acquittal brought the personal jurisdiction of the ECCC to centre-stage of the Court process, and became the subject of legal and historical scrutiny by the Supreme Court Chamber. The Chamber's engagement with the history of who the ECCC may prosecute put the Cambodian Government's protestations on the limits to possible Khmer Rouge convictions under a legal and historical microscope. The SCC provided a detailed response not only to Duch's appeal, but the challenge to ECCC jurisdiction posed by the Government to the investigations in Cases 003 and 004.

The SCC's retributive approach to sentencing based on the gravity of the crimes aligned with the expressivism of international criminal justice, particularly the international interest in ending impunity for mass atrocity crimes through deterrence of contemporary perpetrators. However, the split decision on the Trial Chamber's grant of a remedy for the violation of Duch's human rights when detained by the Cambodian Military Court reflected a plurality of views on the interpretation of standards of justice and fairness in the transitional context. The dissent arguably gave voice to one expression of what McEvoy described as a 'thicker understanding' of 'transitional justice process' at the judicial level.[147] The minority judges considered automatic reliance on the precedents of the ICTR as inappropriate in the case of the ECCC given its predominantly national character. They called instead for a less mechanistic approach to sentencing which admitted the possibility of restorative remedies when the defendant has in fact suffered violation of his or her human rights. While the dissent was part

147 Kieran McEvoy, 'Beyond Legalism: Towards a Thicker Understanding of Transitional Justice' (2007) 34 *Journal of Law and Society* 411, 440.

of expressive due process, the minority opinion seemed in tune with the more communicative spirit of the ECCC as discussed in previous chapters.

The processes of judgment outlined in this chapter marked the conclusion of the ECCC's first trial. The expressive and communicative value of the Case 002/01 Judgments are discussed in Chapter nine, section 9.6 and 9.7.

CHAPTER 9
CONCLUSION

9.1. INTRODUCTION

International criminal trials have been lauded for their expressive value. The expressivism of trials was tied to their legitimacy as impartial arbiters of fact as courts enforced international norms and modelled due process in societies transitioning to democratic governance. There is some conflation of expressivism with communication in the literature. Expressivists, for instance, argue that trials have a pedagogical or educative function.[1] While there is a degree of overlap in the nomenclature, expressive actions and statements do not equate with, and in fact may silence, dialogue which may be essential to societal reconstruction in the aftermath of atrocities. Shifting the focus to communication within transitional trials speaks to the rupture caused by past violence that still affects the society. Communicative processes are not merely didactic or concerned with message-sending. Communication carries an intention to engage another with the possibility of response in some form. The distinction made in this book is that communicative trials are concerned with the exchanges between trial actors that move from the didactic to something revelatory, affirming or restorative for those taking part in the discussion, and potentially for the society observing the process.

The significance of dialogue on the past within transitioning societies has been identified in studies of the Balkans communities which were consistently critical of the non-inclusive and non-communicative approach of the ICTY towards them as primary stakeholders in the justice process.[2] Dialogical transitional justice is more commonly associated with truth and reconciliation commissions or local justice processes. For uneasily transitioning societies like Cambodia, justice and dialogue go hand in hand, as trials open up conversation

1 Mirjan Damaska, 'What is the Point of International of International Criminal Justice?' (2008) 83 *Chicago-Kent Law Review* 329, 346; Mark Drumbl, *Atrocity, Punishment and International Law* (Cambridge, 2005) p. 175.

2 Stephan Parmentier, 'Dealing with International Crimes in Post-war Bosnia: A Look through the Lens of the Affected Population' (2012) 9 *European Journal of Criminology* 553, 555–557.

on the suppressed history of crimes. The isolation of the Cambodian people in the aftermath of the Khmer Rouge revolution, and government policies of reconciliation by forgetting, made the communication platform within ECCC trials a means of finally confronting the societal rupture caused by the Khmer Rouge in Cambodia.

The procedural regimes engaged by courts will have considerable impact on the communicative potential of trial proceedings. This chapter revisits aspects of the ECCC's proceedings that illustrate manifestations of the elements of communication: representation and trial dialogue. To demonstrate the discursive nature of the trials, debates emerging in proceedings on the topics of trauma and the victim/perpetrator relationship in Cambodia are discussed. Exchanges between trial participants are examined to show how the retributive proceedings at times assumed the character of restorative justice. Other factors enhancing the communicative value of the ECCC's trials are also discussed. These include aspects of civil party participation, role-sharing between international and national court officers and the engagement of civil society groups with work of the ECCC.

9.2. ELEMENTS OF COMMUNICATION: REPRESENTATION AND DIALOGUE

As discussed in Chapter two, in domestic criminal law philosophy we find some discussion of the notion of communication through trials.[3] International criminal justice has for the most part contained an expressivist emphasis on the prosecution and punishment of individuals responsible for core international crimes.[4] An expressivist account of the victim redress regime of the ICC suggested broader scope for the administration of transitional justice than the international model had hitherto supported, which implied some communicative effects within subject communities.[5] In addition, transitional justice theorists have argued for flexibility in transitional trial procedure to foster communicative trials.

As discussed at Chapter two, sections 2.5–2.5.3, a theoretical basis for a communication theory of the transitional trial may be derived from the work of Jürgen Habermas, Mark Osiel and Frédéric Mégret. Habermas emphasised

---

[3] Antony Duff, 'Punishment, Communication and Community' in Matt Matravers (ed.) *Punishment and Political Theory* (Hart publishing, 1999) 49; Simon Bronitt and Bernadette McSherry, *The Principles of International Criminal Law*, 3rd ed. (Lawbook Co., 2008) p. 21.

[4] Damaska, above n. 1, p. 331.

[5] Conor McCarthy, 'Victim Redress and International Criminal Justice: Competing Paradigms or Compatible Forms of Justice' (2012) 10 *Journal of International Criminal Justice* 351, 357–366.

the value of communicative action in social reconstruction. Both Habermas and Osiel recognised trials as communicative spaces that assist the building of social solidarity. Osiel argued that the transitional trial's platform for courtroom storytelling mediated by flexibly applied rules of legal procedure fostered communal engagement with the social breakdown arising from crimes of mass atrocity.[6] Through civil disagreement within trial proceedings, a discursive solidarity emerging from trial dialogue (not raised by Durkheim), provided the basis of new collective memory and a foundation for deliberative social recovery.[7] Osiel emphasised the value of the liberal trial to this end. While he drew no real distinction between national and international transitional trials in terms of preferable procedural models, he highlighted the social significance of trials following large-scale 'administrative massacre' over both the short and longer term.[8]

Osiel's conception of the transitional trial as a theatre of ideas surrounding the commission of mass atrocity is complemented by the work of Mégret. Making the case for more representation in trials by engaging national and international interests in transitional justice, Mégret proposed a normative basis for the hybrid or internationalised court based on a theory of the dual nature of international crimes. Simultaneously, he advocated a shift in focus from the outcomes of transitional trials in the form of expressive verdicts and sentences, to the communicative potential of hybrid court proceedings. Drawing from Durkheim, he suggested that transitional trials function to reconstitute the social through the theatre of court process.[9] While Mégret did not assign a specific role for the victim of international crimes within the hybrid court, the recognition of victims' right to participation in international trial proceedings sits well with the representational focus he advocated.

Drawing from Osiel and Mégret, the communicative trial has two distinctive elements: representation and trial dialogue. The following discussion examines manifestations of those elements in ECCC trial proceedings.

9.2.1. REPRESENTATION: CIVIL PARTIES

9.2.1.1. Fairness Concerns

In Case 001, the Trial Chamber judges' progressive restriction of civil party participation rights during the proceedings was a result of delays caused by

6 Mark Osiel, *Mass Atrocity, Collective Memory and the Law* (Transaction Publishers, 1997) 33–55.

7 Ibid.

8 Ibid. p. 299.

9 Frédéric Mégret, 'In Defence of Hybridity: Towards a Representational Theory of International Criminal Justice' (2005) 38 *Cornell International Law Journal* 725, 742.

poorly coordinated and repetitious questioning of witnesses by the four teams of civil party lawyers. Of concern to Duch's Co-Defence was the prospect of multiple represented civil parties acting as auxiliary prosecutors in breach of the equality of arms principle. The Chamber's response was to limit civil party participation rights so as to ensure that the accused faced only one prosecuting authority. This included their exclusion from making submissions on sentencing and the character of the accused. Better planning in advance of the trials would have permitted civil party inclusion on a representative basis with more constructive participation.

As to the problem of delayed proceedings, civil party lawyer Alain Werner believed that the ECCC, as the first internationalised court to apply predominantly civil law, was in a position to show that the inquisitorial procedure could work in theory, with a degree of adaption depending on the number of accused and civil parties.[10] Journalist and international tribunal monitor, Thierry Cruvellier, compared the poorly coordinated practice of civil party representation at the ECCC to the predicament of the victim at the ICTY:

> At the end of the day, even though it was messy and the representation was often poor, it seems that it did bring to the [Duch] trial a dimension considered missing at the other tribunals ... Anyone who says that this is not an interesting experiment here at the ECCC forgets how frustrated victims were in the ICTY.[11]

On civil party exclusion from sentencing and character proceedings, Judge Lavergne, dissented from the majority ruling and argued for the inclusion of civil parties out of concern for justice in the context of the transitional trial. Lavergne raised a duty in the court to civil parties particularly in the circumstances of delayed justice and in terms of what victims could add to the truth-finding process. Significantly, he highlighted the importance of debate within the 'serenity of the court room' to which civil parties could contribute substantively.[12] His argument was grounded in the principles underlying the civil party action, a conception of justice beyond strictly retributive or expressive outcomes, and the ECCC's stated purpose of assisting reconciliation in Cambodia. He acknowledged that the circumstances of trials for mass atrocity call for a wise approach to the principles at stake. However, he noted in particular that civil party participation

---

10 John D. Ciorciari and Anne Heindel, *Hybrid Justice: The Extraordinary Chambers in the Courts of Cambodia* (University of Michigan Press, 2014) p. 110.

11 Alex Bates, 'Transitional Justice in Cambodia: An Analytical Report' (Atlas Project, October 2010) p. 68, citing his interview record with Thierry Cruvellier, journalist and commentator on international trials, including the Duch trial.

12 Decision on Civil Party Co-lawyers' Joint Request for a Ruling on the Standing of Civil party Lawyers to make Submissions on Sentencing and Directions Concerning the Questioning of the Accused, Experts and Witnesses Testifying on Character 001/18-07-2007/ECCC-TC, 9 October 2009, Lavergne dissent, para. [30].

in proceedings on the character of the accused was generally not considered a violation of the equality of arms principle or the notion of the fair trial within civil law systems.[13]

The degree of convergence between adversarial and inquisitorial procedural modes in international courts indicates that the traditions can be revised to accommodate the exigencies of the transitional context.. In any case, reinvention at the domestic level proved possible, suggesting that the traditions are not as 'monolithic' as scholars and practitioners have presented them.[14] In common law jurisdictions, the elevation of the rights of the accused to an unassailable principle with the role of victims in criminal proceedings limited to that of victim-witness is not as legally pure as is sometimes suggested. As Stover pointed out, in nineteenth-century England 'the entire system of criminal law depended on prosecution by the individual and not the state.'[15] In most of the American colonies victims had central roles in the prosecution process and, if they succeeded in their claim against the wrongdoer, stood to benefit financially or in a psychological sense. The antecedents in common law systems suggest an exaggerated emphasis on the primacy of the rights of the accused when substantive victim participation is excluded in international criminal proceedings, except as witness.[16] This seems all the more so when the social value of inclusion is considered. Judge Lavergne's defence of civil party participation in proceedings (Chapter seven, Section 7.4.3) adds to the debate around restricting the role of the victim in criminal proceedings and retaining predominantly adversarial procedural form in international trials. Resistance to what may be seen as longstanding European authoritarianism through the inquisitorial trial should be viewed against modern fair trial standards under civil law systems, and informed by the extraordinary nature of transitional contexts elucidated in part by Lavergne's analysis.[17]

The Lavergne dissent, while not divorced from the expressivism of criminal justice, connects with the social purpose of trials in contexts where the foundations of trust and community have been destroyed. The nuanced notion of justice he articulated, which included debate in the courtroom with a significant role for survivors of crimes, recognised the role of dialogic truth in engaging communally with past atrocities. As noted in Chapter one, the

---

13 Decision on Civil Party Co-lawyers' Joint Request for a Ruling on the Standing of Civil Party Lawyers to make Submissions on Sentencing and Directions Concerning the Questioning of the Accused, Experts and Witnesses Testifying on Character. 001/18-07-2007/ECCC-TC, 9 October 2009, Lavergne dissent, para. [31].

14 Frédéric Mégret, 'Beyond Fairness: Understanding the Determinants of International Criminal Procedure' (2009) 14 *UCLA Journal of International Law and Foreign Affairs* 37, 75.

15 Eric Stover, *The Witnesses: War Crimes and the Promise of Justice in The Hague* (University of Pennsylvania Press, 2005) pp. 23–24.

16 Ibid. p. 24.

17 Richard Vogler, *A World View of Criminal Justice* (Ashgate, 2006) p. 159.

dynamic of dialogue or communication in social recovery has been recognised in transitional justice literature and peace studies. Borrowing imagery from Lederach in his work in the area of peace-building, the communicative theory posited herein invites us to another country 'whose geographies and realities' show us what 'destructive relationships produce and the legacies they leave.'[18] Nowhere was this more evident than in the statements made by the civil parties and victim-witnesses at trial.

9.2.1.2. *Narrative Statements*

As eye-witnesses to events occurring in Cambodia during the Khmer Rouge regime, victims as witnesses of fact and civil parties were able to provide evidence that indicated certain crimes formed part a larger criminal system. In Case 002, some civil parties made statements of suffering following testimony. In the victim impact hearings, selected civil parties presented their statements of suffering and thereafter faced examination by the Court. The transcripts of victim impact hearings in Case 002/01 reveal common conditions and patterns of crime in different camps and work sites that the civil parties were sent to after their evacuation of Phnom Penh in 1975. Some facts raised were relevant to substantive issues in the case and called for examination and further investigation. Thus, the various modalities of victim testimony contributed to the truth-finding process, but this is to underestimate their contribution to the proceedings.

The space created for victim story-telling in the proceedings produced a forum traversing personal and social histories, which gave concrete expression to the wide-ranging effects of the Khmer Rouge regime and the years of silence that followed its overthrow. In Case 001, the format adopted by the judges permitted the civil parties to put questions to the accused. In turn, the accused was able to exercise a general right of reply, as well as answer specific questions directed to him. Communication flowed from victim to the Court, victim to perpetrator, victim to lost family members, perpetrator to victim and from victims to the wider audience of the ECCC, including the vast victim constituency in and beyond Cambodia. The proceedings took on a restorative tenor as the proceedings, mediated by the judges, connected the civil parties to the accused. Something of the ritual value of the trial in Durkheim-ian terms emerged, not through the process of punishment, but rather through confrontation and dialogue. In Case 002, under the revised civil party representation scheme, the defendants frequently chose to engage with the civil parties. Nuon Chea, for

---

18 John Paul Lederach, *The Moral Imagination: The Art And Soul of Building Peace* (Oxford University Press, 2005) p. 5.

instance, indicated in a response to civil party Yim Roumdoul, that he held 'moral responsibility' for the events occurring during the regime and expressed his condolences to the victims suffering their effects.[19]

Though the civil parties made up only a fraction of the Khmer Rouge victim constituency, they spoke as special representatives of those they knew who died at the hands of the regime, and vicariously for those not chosen to speak. Theirs was not a token presence or one harnessed solely for the purpose of the prosecution. In various ways, they added something approaching the sacred to the justice process as they represented family members destroyed by the regime. Neth Phally's private ceremony to release his brother's spirit at the end of his testimony in which the court acquiesced was perhaps the best example of this. The exchanges between the civil parties, the judges and other court actors expanded the discussion of the victim perspective on the crimes within the sanctity of a respectful court. Intervention by the Chamber President was needed with a small number of civil parties to ensure the fairness of the proceedings, but generally, there was no seizing of the trial platform by any party to propagate views at odds with international criminal justice as predicted by Damaska.[20]

9.2.2. REPRESENTATION: OUTSIDER PERSPECTIVES

Mégret's thesis that some international crimes so 'threaten our sense of humanity' that international ownership of trials that address such crimes is justified had resonance in the Case 001 trial proceedings as two non-Khmer witnesses gave evidence.[21] The first was Frenchman François Bizot, who was conducting research on Cambodian Buddhism in 1971 when he was suspected by the Khmer Rouge of being a CIA spy. Khmer Rouge cadres imprisoned Bizot at the M-13 detention camp which was overseen by Duch. The second witness was American historian David Chandler who studied the S-21 archives.

As a detainee of M-13, Bizot was shackled along with two of his Khmer companions, kept in inhumane conditions and interrogated by Duch over a period of two months. Aware that other prisoners were beaten and disappeared, Bizot feared he would not escape death. However, when Duch was convinced that he was not a spy, he engineered Bizot's release through negotiations with his superiors Ta Mok and Vorn Vet. In a meeting with Duch just before Bizot was released, Duch admitted to him that he sometimes beat prisoners when there were inconsistencies in their testimonies. He added that while it was not at all

19 *Co-Prosecutors v Nuon Chea (Transcript of Trial Proceedings)* (Case No 002/19-09-2007-ECCC/TC, Day 186, 30 May 2013.) p. 84; And see *ECCC Court Report* (June 2013) p. 7.

20 Damaska, above n. 1, pp. 346–347.

21 Mégret, above n. 9, p. 737.

what he wished to do, it was his responsibility under Angkar. A kind of terror took hold of Bizot as he reflected on the truth he had to absorb. Bizot's book, *The Gate*, recorded his personal trauma of having known someone who was both a torturer and one who had protected him. Bizot communicated in narrative form the depth of a continuing sense of disquiet from his experience at M-13:

> Your Honour, I should say that until then, I had felt reassured. I believed that we were – that I was – on the right side of humanity; that some men were monsters and thank heaven, I could never be one of them. I believed that this was the state of nature, that some of us are born evil while the rest of us could never be. But that evening, Duch's response, combined with my perception of him throughout the course of various interrogation episodes opened my eyes … I had expected to encounter someone inhumane, as we are accustomed to think of such monsters. But I realised that this was far more tragic and infinitely more terrifying, because in front of me stood a man who looked like friends of mine: a Marxist who was prepared to die for his country and for the Revolution. The ultimate goal, for him, was the welfare of the inhabitants of Cambodia; he was fighting against injustice and inequity … And even if there was something insidious in the naiveté of the typical Khmer peasant, there was also a fundamental sincerity in his beliefs, as is the case with many revolutionaries. I myself had many friends in Paris at the time who were committed to this communist revolution and they were looking at events in Cambodia with an outlook that, to me was horrifying. But in their eyes, the ends justified the means – in this case Cambodia's independence, Cambodia's right to self-determination, the end to its citizens' misery, and so on. The Cambodians are not the only people that have killed in the name of fulfilling a dream. So here I was, looking behind the mask of the monster in front of me. His job was to write up reports on the people sent to be executed, and I saw that this monster was, in fact, human, which was just as disturbing and terrifying. I was no longer sheltered from this knowledge – we are no longer sheltered from this knowledge – and the worst mistake we could make would be to separate such monsters into a different category of being.[22]

Cruvellier, observing Bizot's demeanour and testimony, reported that it was in the 'solemn intensity' of the courtroom that Bizot had found the way to articulate the universal scope of his suffering and ongoing personal ambivalence. In perhaps an unexpected way Bizot represented our collective 'tormented conscience' in the internationalised proceedings.[23] Something additional to the Durkheim-ian conception of crime as offensive to the collective conscience and which will be avenged by punishment was imported to the proceedings as Bizot gave voice to the complex nature of the perpetration of international crimes and the depth of their effects.

Under examination, David Chandler also added nuance to the search for truth during the proceedings. He communicated that there existed inescapable

---

22 Translation from Thierry Cruvellier, *The Master of Confessions: The Making of a Khmer Rouge Torturer* (Harper Collins, 2014) pp. 163–164.

23 Ibid. p. 166.

universal truth with respect to the perpetration of mass atrocities. This testimony did not spring from a personal encounter with Duch, but from Chandler's analysis of the S-21 archive, accounts of mass atrocities in numerous historical contexts and modern psychological research on human conditioning. He opined 'in order to find the root of evil that was implemented at S-21, we should look no further than ourselves.'[24] Given the existence of extraordinary conditions, ordinary individuals will support systems that include the commission of atrocities. Such conditions existed at S-21 and reasonable people could be led to commit acts of the kind that took place there.[25]

Both witnesses of fact, from their personal and professional encounters with Duch's crimes, drilled beneath the facts to communicate their perspectives on them. In this, while the witnesses pointed to uncomfortable truths for all affected constituencies, their reflections added to our understanding of some of the structural dynamics of crimes against humanity. The trial's procedural form permitting narrative testimony and engagement with the evidence, gave broad representation to the nature of crimes of mass atrocity. This was evident from study of the communications of the proceedings rather than the trial outcomes.

9.2.3. REPRESENTATION: NATIONAL AND INTERNATIONAL ECCC STAFF

Role-sharing at the ECCC between international and national court staff reflected ownership of its trials by Cambodia and the international community as represented by the United Nations. This section considers the communicative dynamics of role-sharing between international and national judges and the similarly constituted teams of prosecution, defence and civil party lawyers.

Ciorciari reported from an interview with the former head of the ECCC Defence Support Section that national and international lawyers had exercised their respective skills and knowledge in a complementary fashion. The international practitioners had led the way in writing submissions, not normally a significant feature of Cambodian legal practice. This had the effect of developing the Cambodian professionals' competence in legal drafting and argument. On the other hand the Cambodian lawyers were adept at interviewing witnesses and reviewing documents in the Khmer language. They also ably explained the social and historical context of matters before the Court to their international counterparts. Thus, communication between the national and international staff fuelled the collaboration.

---

24 Transcript of Trial Proceedings – *Kaing Guek Eav 'Duch'* 001/18-07-2007/TC, (Day 55, 6 August 2009) p. 120.

25 Ibid. pp. 73–74, 115–121.

At the judicial level, Trial Chamber President Nil Nonn has said that he 'appreciated learning from the reasoning culture of his international counterparts on the bench and would seek to raise the capacity of the Cambodian judges he trains in the future.' If this occurs it will be significant information transfer to a system with negligible legal skills capacity. It is reasonable to conclude that this flowed from the communication and exchange of views between ECCC judges as they went about their judicial task.

Associated with this is the Court's production of reasoned decisions, which are made available on its website and which will help build a body of Cambodian legal precedent. Judicial practice in Cambodia has been reliant on oral tradition and judges' prior experience. The judgments from the internationalised court demonstrate to local practitioners and the community how human rights and fair trial principles may be interpreted pursuant to the Cambodian Constitution under which they apply. An example was provided in the Trial Chamber's and Supreme Court's analyses of Duch's civil rights during his period of detention. This engaged the judiciary in exchanges of views which were synthesised in the judgments.

Judicial management of proceedings involved articulation of fair trial concepts, including the presumption of innocence and the equality of arms, to local practitioners and the community at large in public proceedings. There was also the need to maintain civility and respect in the courtroom. Of course, there is overlap here between the expressivism of due process demonstration and communicative process dynamics, but perhaps there was a particular communicative element in authoritative pronouncements delivered by national President Nil Nonn as a role model for the Cambodian judiciary. The Cambodian judicial majority and the operation of the ECCC within the national court system arguably imported a strong local communicative dynamic because whatever positive lessons are learned by the Cambodian side may be acted upon independently after the internationals depart. Reportedly, Co-Investigating Judge, You Bunleng, has already overseen changes at the Cambodian Court of Appeals that both modernise trial processes and 'protect the rights of victims and accused.'[26]

Some communicative dimensions of role-sharing at the ECCC are less easily interpreted. The Co-Defence counsel partnership was communicative by reason of the professional differences between them and their opposing opinions on Duch's culpability. Francois Roux, a civil legal system lawyer, framed Duch's defence around his acceptance of responsibility for his crimes and penitence. This approach fell within the criteria for judicial assessment of crimes at the international level. Kar Savuth, who had been representing Duch since his detention in 1999, understood his client's position from a perspective incorporating the political and cultural forces making him a mere

26 Ciorciari, above n. 10, pp. 254–255.

cog in an unstoppable political machine. While at the end of the trial Duch left his fate in the hands of the Court, in his closing statement he revisited Khmer Rouge history and policy. This was perhaps an attempt to press his case to the end himself. His request for release at that point was, for him presumably a logical conclusion notwithstanding his confessions. After the trial Duch dismissed Roux and engaged a Chinese lawyer for his appeal. The apparent split in Co-Defence opinion may well have been the result of a lack of careful deliberation between the two lawyers as they pursued the task of defending their client. However, the divide may also be explicable in terms of the complexity and social character of the perpetration of crimes of mass atrocity. As noted in Chapter two, study of the genocide in Rwanda revealed that it was not amenable to analysis through the framework of Western trial models. This issue is revisited in the next section in the discussion of other communicative legacies of the trial.

The failure of national authorities to secure the attendance of certain Cambodian witnesses in Case 002, and Cambodian government opposition to the progress of the Case 003 and 004 investigations, were reminders of the authoritarian political culture affecting the administration of justice in Cambodia. The government's expressive action to prevent further ECCC prosecutions of lower level Khmer Rouge cadres brought to light the counterproductive effects of executive interference in Cambodia's legal system. The otherwise generally constructive collaboration between national and international staff in nationally important work was hampered by such action. This would have been amply clear to the Cambodian lawyers who were gaining significant professional experience and contributing to the development of their country's judicial system.

9.3. TRIAL DIALOGUE

The broader brush or discursive approach adopted by the ECCC judges in Case 001 admitted wider trial dialogue in the course of the inquisitorial search for the truth surrounding the crimes, and in the interest of the reconciliatory purpose of the ECCC. Exchanges between the judiciary and witnesses, and between witnesses and other actors in the trial process, including the accused, sometimes went beyond establishing legal proof. Dialogue at times encompassed historical, psychological or social issues of relevance to the context and consequences of the crimes. Dialogically based transitional justice processes have been found to more directly address issues of social concern in the aftermath of violent regimes.[27] Generally, trials have not been associated with dialogic mechanisms.

[27] Parmentier, above n. 2, pp. 554–557.

However, the Duch trial proceedings frequently touched matters of continuing social significance within Cambodia which have not been widely addressed in dialogic fora. One such issue is the victim/perpetrator relationship in Cambodia.

9.3.1. VICTIM–PERPETRATOR EQUATION

While the ECCC targeted senior leaders of the Democratic Kampuchea or those most responsible for crimes of the regime, the issue of the lower level perpetrator as victim of a coercive regime pervaded the proceedings. This was in part due to Duch's defence that he was a victim as well as a perpetrator under the regime. The issue had deep significance in Cambodia because the Khmer Rouge relied on Cambodian youths on a large scale to implement their policies in the system of agrarian collectives throughout the country and within their detention centres. After the regime, many Cambodians returned to their villages only to find themselves having to live in close proximity to Khmer Rouge cadres without any preliminary reconciliation process. In the course of the trial, the issue was visited from a number of angles through the dialogic format engaged by the judges.

During his examination, Chhim Sotheara was asked to comment on the victim–perpetrator equation which had surfaced in the proceedings. Chhim answered from his experience of clinically treating former guards of S-21 who were generally aged around 12 or 13 years when they became Khmer Rouge cadres. He explained their victimisation as a result of Democratic Kampuchea's policy of dissolution of family units, the assumption of a collective identity and other indoctrination which turned them into perpetrators of crimes.[28] The discursive proceedings illuminated the individual and social breakdown forced on a generation of Cambodians and gave some representation to the plight of less senior perpetrators during and after the regime.[29]

Bou Meng was a former Khmer Rouge cadre whose testimony revealed the nature of his suffering as a detainee at S-21 along with thousands of others as the CPK purged its own ranks. Duch's response to Mam Nai's evasive testimony displayed attitudes towards the past by older perpetrators 30 years after the Khmer Rouge regime. 'You can't cover an elephant with a rice basket', said Duch to Mam Nai as he implored him to now tell the truth about the regime they had been committed to, for the sake of humanity.[30]

---

[28] Transcript of Trial Proceedings – *Kaing Guek Eav 'Duch' Trial* 001/18-07-2007/TC (Day 64, 25 August 2009) pp. 56–57.

[29] See Suzannah Linton, *Reconciliation in Cambodia* (Documentation Center of Cambodia, 2004) pp. 57–66.

[30] Transcript of Trial Proceedings – *Kaing Guek Eav 'Duch'* 001/18-07-2007-ECCC/TC (Day 45, 15 July 2009) pp. 65–66.

The Court's wide-ranging examination of the expert evidence of Sironi-Guilbaud and Ka Sunbaunat became a forum for discussion of the mind-set assumed by the Khmer Rouge perpetrator, as well as the psychological adjustment faced by the population at large as a result of the regime. The discussion within nationally broadcast proceedings delved deeply into the psyche of a regime which had been virtually eliminated from Cambodian school curricula, but whose legacy continues to pervade the society. As discussed in Chapter 6, section 6.4.4, the experts testified that Duch, through the process of the trial and their engagement with him, was progressively coming to terms with his Khmer Rouge conditioning.

The trial proceedings were well attended, broadcasted and widely commented on in the media. The trial judgment, conveying the extent of the Court's engagement with the experts' report was distributed throughout the country. The scope for reflection within the society on the matters raised in the proceedings seems clear. The in-court debates and the Court's analysis also contribute to the building of a renewed collective memory through what Osiel described as 'discursive engagement with a society's past' which may be 'cultivated by trial process.'[31] Osiel added that recognition of the reality and the possible co-existence of conflicting interpretations of history, through collective engagement with the past may foster discursive solidarity as the communications of trial proceedings resonate beyond the walls of the courtroom.[32]

9.3.2. TRAUMA IN POST-KHMER ROUGE CAMBODIA

Trauma and victim recovery from the Khmer Rouge regime was examined from various perspectives during the proceedings. During the examination of Vann Nath's evidence, Judge Lavergne asked the survivor of S-21 to explain how he had dealt with the trauma flowing from his incarceration. Vann Nath spoke of the importance of confronting and recording the suffering and injustice of the regime in his creative works. He did this to educate the young on an important period in Cambodian history and to fill a void left by the silence of their parents for whom confrontation and dialogue had been too painful.

The civil parties, by virtue of their inclusion as parties to the proceedings, provided specific accounts of how the regime had affected them. Chhim Sotheara, a psychiatrist with the Transcultural Psychosocial Organisation (TPO) in Cambodia, was called to give evidence in relation to civil party reparations. Chhim represented the larger victim constituency as an intermediary between the group collectively and the court. Chhim faced broad examination by the Judges and other court actors. Chhim communicated his findings on trauma

31 Osiel, above n. 6, p. 39.
32 Ibid.

and post-traumatic stress syndrome based on decades of experience working with Cambodian survivors of the Khmer Rouge. He explained the particular manifestations of the conditions in Cambodian society and connected their incidence with specific social problems, such as alcoholism and domestic violence. In this he gave voice to the plight of a broad spectrum of victims who had little or no representation.

Chhim was also given opportunity to communicate the needs and expectations of victims in relation to the justice process which they had waited for, and were now participating in. In Chapter six I described how he articulated this for them. The opportunity to express their trauma helps them, but does not heal completely. Victims participate in the proceedings to seek justice for themselves or their lost relatives and to hear the truth. Honesty from former Khmer Rouge leaders helps them, while persistent denial angers them.[33]

Questioning on the TPO's work with victims within their communities connected the proceedings of the ECCC to the process of reconciliation in Cambodia. Chhim explained that thus far the TPO's work had been with victims only. He explained that because of the long-term impunity of the Khmer Rouge and conditions in villages, reconciliation in such communities had been inhibited by the lack of a credible justice process at the national level. However, programmes aimed at reconciling victims and perpetrators in communities were foreseeable now that the ECCC trials were under way.[34] The Court's engagement with the expert witness beyond strictly factual matters expanded the trial conversation on the effects of the crimes and revealed community perceptions of the role of the ECCC in the sequencing of transitional justice measures towards reconciliation in Cambodia.

9.4. COMMUNICATION AND JUDGMENT

9.4.1. CIVIL PARTIES

Judicial rulings will be expressive by virtue of the authority of the Court. If rulings are directed at an individual or a particular group, they may be met with a response and in that sense may be communicative. Perhaps this is more likely in representative proceedings, which may empower participants. The Trial Chamber's majority ruling which prevented civil party submissions in proceedings on Duch's character serves as an example. The ruling evoked a

---

33 Transcript of Trial Proceedings – *Kaing Guek Eav 'Duch'* 001/18-07-2007/TC (Day 64, 25 August 2009) pp. 14–38.

34 Transcript of Trial Proceedings – *Kaing Guek Eav 'Duch'* 001/18-07-2007/TC (Day 64, 25 August 2009) pp. 53–54.

strong reaction among the civil party group. With the solidarity gained from their collective participation in the trial proceedings they sent a joint letter to the President of the Trial Chamber expressing their discontent with the ruling preventing their participation.[35] A group of 28 civil parties announced they would not attend the proceedings dealing with character evidence as observers.[36] As those proceedings began, the group travelled to the Tuol Sleng Genocide Museum, where they conducted a public memorial service to the dead victims of S-21.[37] As discussed earlier in this chapter, their right to participate was supported by Judge Lavergne in his dissenting judgment. Thus, disagreement on the issue was aired through various channels of communication.

After the Trial Chamber delivered its judgment in Case 001 there was a strong response by the civil parties against Duch's sentence of 35 years imprisonment, which was reduced to approximately 19 years due to his long pre-trial detention, and the remedy granted by the Chamber for breach of his civil rights while detained by the Cambodian Military Court.[38] Generally, Cambodians viewed the sentence as too short.[39] The civil parties exercised their appeal rights, along with the Co-Prosecution, against the sentence. When the Supreme Court Chamber overturned the trial sentence and ordered a term of life imprisonment for Duch, the civil parties were jubilant.[40] Civil party, Bou Meng said 'I am fully relieved and fully satisfied with the Court's ruling … This court is a good model for the world.'[41]

Others viewed aspects of the Court's decision negatively. For instance, the appeal decision on sentence was read by one international non-governmental organisation as public opinion overriding human rights.[42] For Cambodians viewing the ECCC as a model court setting precedent in upholding fair trial rights, the SCC's reversal of the Trial Chamber ruling granting Duch a remedy for

---

35 See 'Letter of Civil Parties in Case 001 to the President of the Trial Chamber': http://www.eccc.gov.kh/sites/default/files/documents/courtdoc/E166.1_FR.pdf.

36 Eric Stover, Mychelle Balthazard and K. Alexa Koenig, 'Confronting Duch: Civil Party Participation in Case 001 at the Extraordinary Chambers in the Courts of Cambodia' (2011) 93 *International Review of the Red Cross* 513, 532.

37 Michael Saliba, 'Civil Parties Boycott Start of Character Witness Testimony while Experts Offer Psychological Assessment of Duch', *Cambodia Tribunal Monitor* (31 August 2009) pp. 1, 1–2.

38 Stover, above n. 36, p. 541.

39 Ciorciari, above n. 10, p. 121.

40 Randle DeFalco, 'Case 001 Appeal Judgement: Duch Sentenced to Life', *Cambodia Tribunal Monitor* (4 or 5 February 2012) pp. 1, 5.

41 'Former Khmer Rouge Jailer Gets Life Imprisonment', *Kyodo News Service* (3 February 2012).

42 Amnesty International, Press Release, 'Cambodia: Khmer Rouge Judgment Welcome, but Raises Human Rights Concerns' (8 February 2012).

breach of his rights while in pre-trial detention sent a contradictory message.[43] On the other hand, the SCC judgment included a strong dissenting opinion by two of the international judges against the majority ruling on the matter. Their more finely grained analysis synthesised human rights precedents applicable to the Cambodian case and framed the remedy as restorative. This contrasted with the relatively limited analysis of the majority which was confined to a narrow reading of a single ICTY precedent. As discussed earlier, the divergent judicial approaches will form part of the ECCC's legacy of legal reasoning in various shades which will be available to the Cambodian judiciary to reflect on in the future.

Reactions to the life sentences handed down by the Trial Chamber to Nuon Chea and Khieu Samphân in Case 002/01 were more subdued.[44] Ryan and McGrew's ECCC population perception survey in 2015 noted that 'only a handful of ordinary Cambodians ... interviewed disparaged the ECCC as mostly negative or potentially negative.'[45] Long trials and delays to proceedings may affect local attitudes to the trial verdicts, but the completion of Case 002/01 imparted a broad sense of accountability for Khmer Rouge crimes.[46] Other commentators concluded that 'the use of Cambodian law legitimised the verdict for many [Cambodians], making it more significant than a purely international verdict,' while others welcomed the verdict in accordance with international standards.[47]

Some commentators considered that greater public acknowledgement of the nature of harm occasioned by the crimes should have been included in the trial judgment.[48] They argued that for Case 002/02, proper recognition and detailing of the harm arising from forced marriage and sexual violence should be given because of its significance to victims and the society at large. The ECCC's stigmatisation of sexual violence as crime confined to the private sphere, and detailing of the effects of forced marriage in Cambodia has the potential to alter prevalent social attitudes towards the crimes.[49]

---

43 Cambodian Center for Human Rights, *Third Bi-Annual Report: Fair Trial Rights-One Year Progress Report* (January 2012) p. 44.

44 Sok-kheang et al.,'Villagers React to Verdict in Case 002/01' DC-Cam (7 August 2014) http://d.dccam.org/Prjects/Living_Doc/pdf/Villagers_React_to_Verdict_in Case_002-01.pdf; 'Reaction at Viewings Mixed', *Phnom Penh Post* (8 August 2014).

45 Heather Ryan and Laura McGrew, *Performance and Perception: the Impact of the Extraordinary Chambers in the Courts of Cambodia* (Open Society Justice Initiative, 2016) p. 96.

46 Ibid. p. 34.

47 Julie Kornfield, 'ECCC Case 002/01: The Effect off the Hybrid Court in Cambodia' MJIL Online: http://mjilonline.org/eccc-case-002-01-the-effect-of-the-hybrid-court-in-cambodia/ (26 September 2014).

48 Sarah Williams and Emma Palmer, 'Transformative Reparations for Women and Girls at the Extraordnary Chambers in the Courts of Cambodia' (2016) 10 *International Journal of Transitional Justice* 311, 326–327.

49 Ibid. p. 327.

9.4.2. REPARATIONS

Following the limited reparations award in Case 001 under the original version of the Internal Rules, several civil parties of Cases 001 and 002 expressed their determination to build a memorial at S-21, 'no matter what reparations may be awarded by the Court.'[50] Civil parties were also instrumental in forming victims' associations: the Association of Victims of Democratic Kampuchea and the Ksaem Ksan Association.[51] Their actions reflected a degree of survivor empowerment and also communicated how serious to them the issue of reparation was.

Due to the fact that Duch was indigent, the Trial Chamber declared that it lacked jurisdiction to order the Cambodian government to make reparations to civil parties and could, at best, only 'encourage' the government and other organisations to fund forms of reparation.[52] In the absence of any established alternative financing mechanism, the civil parties' reparations were restricted to the publication of the names of victims in the judgment as well as compilation and publication of Duch's apologies and statements of remorse throughout the trial process.[53] The Supreme Court did not overturn the lower court's order.

However, the issue of reparations in the Duch trial has to be viewed as part of the evolving civil party participation scheme. The revision of the civil party and reparations provisions of the Internal Rules also altered the powers of the Victims Support Section (VSS). The VSS may now develop and implement 'non-judicial measures' as reparations to address a greater range of victims' interests.[54] The amendments also provided that the VSS would work with the Lead Co-lawyers of the civil parties in identifying reparations projects that the ECCC might endorse, provided funding for those projects was secured from external donors in advance of the trial judgment. Shortly after the amendments were passed, the VSS, with funding from the UN Trust Fund to End Violence against Women began working with locally-based civil society organisations to implement a three-year project to promote gender equality and improve access to justice for female victims of gender-based violence during the Khmer Rouge regime.[55]

---

50 Phuong N. Pham, Patrick Vinck, Mychelle Balthazard, Judith Strasser and Chariya Om, 'Victim Participation and the Trial of Duch at the Extraordinary Chambers in the Courts of Cambodia' (2011) 3 *Journal of Human Rights Practice* 264, 284.

51 Christoph Sperfeldt, 'Cambodian Civil Society and the Khmer Rouge Tribunal' (2012) 6 *International Journal of Transitional Justice* 150, 157.

52 *Co-Prosecutors v. Kaing Guek Eav (alias Duch)* (Judgment) 001/18-2007/ECCC/TC, 26 July 2010) paras. 663–664 [Duch Trial Judgment].

53 Duch Trial Judgment, para. 668.

54 ECCC Internal Rules (Rev. 5) rule 12 (*bis*) 3.

55 Rong Chhorng, 'Conflict's Female Victims Far From Forgotten', *Phnom Penh Post* (6 June 2012).

In Case 002/01 the VSS and the Lead Co-lawyers submitted 13 projects as appropriate reparations schemes. Despite the low expectations of some commentators, the VSS ultimately secured over US$770,000 from individuals, governments and non-governmental organisations (NGOs) to fund the projects.[56] The Trial Chamber endorsed 11 of the 13 requested projects; with two projects going unsupported because the Court was not satisfied that sufficient external funding had been secured.[57] Under the new reparations provisions, the Court recognised the projects as 'contributing to the rehabilitation, reintegration and restoration of the dignity of civil parties,' and the support of donors as assistance demonstrating 'solidarity with victims of the Khmer Rouge era.'[58] The approved projects include public memorials, the construction and maintenance of a regional community peace learning centre, mental health programmes (one offering testimonial therapy), permanent exhibitions on aspects of Case 002/01, new educational material for teachers on the Khmer Rouge regime, and wide distribution of the trial judgment with accompanying informational material.

The approved projects of Case 002/01 were tangible responses to the civil parties' claim, their representations at trial and consultations with their counsel and the VSS. The projects are expressive outcomes, but were the product of representation and dialogue. While they are modest projects, they hold potential benefits for Khmer Rouge victims who did not participate in the trials, and their implementation harnesses the ongoing dynamic of communication. Mégret argued that collective reparations are future oriented and contemplate rebuilding social solidarity in transitional societies.[59] The ICC reparations principles applicable in the *Lubanga* case recognised the symbolic and transformative potential of reparations flowing from consultations with, and the participation of, victim groups.[60] Carefully designed reparations projects may also have a corrective and preventive function and create conditions in which 'communal and gender relations' may eventually be transformed.[61] The application of those principles in Case 002/02, in some measure in response to submissions made by victims of sexual and gender-based crimes, is now foreseeable.

---

56 'Wide Ranging Support Secured for the Reparations for Victims of the Khmer Rouge Regime' Extraordinary Chambers in the Courts of Cambodia, Victim Support Section, Press Release 21 April 2014) Attachment 1–3.

57 *Co-Prosecutors v. Nuon Chea and Khieu Samphân* (Judgment) 002/19-09-2007/ECCC/TC, 7 August 2014) paras. 1152–1160 [Case 002/01 Trial Judgment].

58 Case 002/01 Trial Judgment, para. 1116.

59 Frédéric Mégret, 'The Case for Collective Reparations before the ICC', Paper presented at McGill University Faculty of Law, 15 November 2012, p. 9 (SSRN2176911).

60 *Prosecutor v. Thomas Dyilo Lubanga* (*Decision establishing the principles and procedures to be applied to reparations*) (International Criminal Court, Trial Chamber 1, Case no. ICC-01/04-01/06, 7 August 2012) paras. [40] [209] [239]–[240].

61 (Mégret) above n 59 p. 9, citing the submission of the Women's Initiative for Gender Justice Submission in the *Lubanga* case.

In the 2010 Plenary Session, in which changes to the civil party scheme and the VSS mandate were discussed, Judge Silvia Cartwright in her opening speech said she believed that non-judicial measures 'will be a major legacy of the ECCC.'[62] Commentators on the changes to the VSS powers did not anticipate the ECCC's capacity to negotiate the reparations results achieved in Case 002/01.[63] At a deeper level the reparations represent the hopes of those who collectively fought for their realisation. Braithwaite's research on hope and governance describes institutions of hope as 'part of the family of enabling institutions that offset, loosen, or challenge the constraints imposed by regulatory institutions.'[64] The ECCC, as a temporary internationalised court, found a way to respond to the collective hope reposed in it by Khmer Rouge victim constituencies by dynamically accommodating at least some of the requests made of it through its institutional structures.[65] This together with the Court's policy of inclusion and dialogue in trial proceedings may account for the increasing local approval of the ECCC discussed in the next section.

9.5. CIVIL SOCIETY ENGAGEMENT WITH THE ECCC

A significant feature of the Cambodian transitional context was that civil society was comparatively well developed. As discussed in Chapter four, following the 1990 peace accords international NGOs aided the country's development and actively supported trials for Khmer Rouge leaders. They collected evidence of the crimes of the regime, disseminated information and conducted education programmes throughout the country. Local NGOs emerged to spread the word within regions where illiteracy levels were high, and justice and human rights conversation in communities was catalysed through their work. The readiness of Cambodian NGOs to make victims aware of their rights before the ECCC and to assist them brought civil party applicants and victim complainants to the Court before it was equipped to handle the applications. In the absence of sufficient funding for victims services and outreach at the ECCC, at least 15 civil society groups supported the Court in those areas.[66] In fact, in view of the ECCC's budgetary constraints in its early years, there was a conscious decision by ECCC staff to leave outreach work to NGOs to capitalise on their established networks and experience in local communities. The ECCC concentrated its

62 Silvia Cartwright, 'Opening Speech to the Extraordinary Chambers in the Courts of Cambodia, 7th Plenary Session' (2 February 2010).

63 Ciorciari, above n. 10, pp. 228–229.

64 Valerie Braithwaite, 'Collective Hope' in Valerie Braithwaite (ed.), *Hope, Power and Governance* (2004) 592 *Annals of the American Academy of Political and Social Science* 6, 7.

65 Ibid. p. 15.

66 Ciorciari above n. 10, p. 237.

efforts instead, at least until 2009, on public relations through its Public Affairs Section (PAS).[67]

Although the informal outsourcing of victim support and information dissemination on the work of the ECCC was uncoordinated, the NGOs remained invested in assisting the trial process as being pivotal to social development in Cambodia. Cambodian NGOs were particularly supportive of ECCC victim participation processes because they saw themselves as helping to reduce the gap between the internationalised court and Cambodian society, thus assisting reconciliation.[68] The NGOs assumed multi-faceted roles. The Transcultural Psychosocial Organisation (TPO) for example, provided expert testimony on victim trauma and, under a memorandum of understanding with the ECCC, provided psychological support to civil parties and witnesses during the trials.[69] This support, combined with the TPO's work within Cambodian communities and that of other local NGOS, arguably demonstrates their role as the 'critical yeast' of a network of relationships connecting the work of the ECCC with on-the-ground reconciliation processes.[70] Outside of the Court the TPO held events and participated in radio programmes to raise awareness about post-traumatic stress affecting many Cambodians as a result of the Khmer Rouge regime, and the lack of mental health services in Cambodia.[71]

NGOs initiated 'village forums' to both educate and foster dialogue within communities on issues surrounding the work of the ECCC. One local NGO, the Center for Social Development, for instance, held public forums on 'justice and history' and 'reconciliation and healing' which Court officials attended, and fielded questions from attendees. DC-Cam also ran village meetings and produced multi-media products to educate communities about the ECCC and promote dialogue on the Khmer Rouge era. The Khmer Institute for Democracy and the Cambodian Human Rights Action Committee (ADHOC) were also long-term purveyors of information about the work of the ECCC.[72] Youth for Peace tailored some educational programmes to particular communities, integrating Buddhist practices and ceremonies.[73] In addition, NGOs not only assisted civil party applicants through all phases of the trial, but also helped to fund their legal representation.[74]

---

67 Ibid. pp. 237–238.

68 Sperfeldt, above n. 51, p. 155.

69 Christoph Sperfeldt, 'From the Margins of Internationalised Criminal Justice: Lessons Learned at the Extraordinary Chambers in the Courts of Cambodia' (2013) 11 *Journal of International Criminal Justice* 1111, 1120.

70 Lederach above n. 18, p. 91; See also John Braithwaite and Ray Nickson, 'Timing, Truth, Reconciliation, and Justice after War' (2012) 27 *Ohio Journal of Dispute Resolution* 443, 456–457.

71 Ciorciari, above n. 10, p. 259.

72 Ibid. pp. 239–240.

73 Sperfeldt, above n. 51, p. 159.

74 Brianne Mcgonigle Leyh, *Procedural Justice? Victim Participation in International Criminal Proceedings* (Intersentia, 2011) p. 220.

In their study of a series of conflict contexts within the 'arc of instability' surrounding Australia, Braithwaite and Nickson noted that 'the most traumatised victims take longest to be ready to participate in transitional justice' and that 'it may take many years of traditional reconciliation work before perpetrators of the worst atrocities … can confess their crimes without fear of revenge.'[75] They concluded that the timing and sequencing of follow-up mechanisms ranging from national top-down initiatives to spontaneous local communal or spiritual rituals may constitute creative ways towards greater readiness for confession and/or forgiveness. They noted, however, that whatever justice mechanism is engaged first, whether it be through truth-telling, punitive justice or restorative process, what matters is that 'the flickering flame of reconciliation conversation' is kept alive in order to weather the societal 'long durée' of recovery following mass atrocity.[76] Despite fraught relations with the Cambodian government, civil society organisations have fanned the flame over the last three decades.[77]

Other transitional courts have been in significantly weaker positions with respect to grass roots connection to affected societies. As noted in Chapter three, neither the ICTY nor the ICTR initiated outreach programmes until several years after their creation, and by then the institutions had tarnished reputations within the respective local communities. The in-country Special Court for Sierra Leone (SCSL) promptly recognised the importance of establishing links with local communities, but did not have the level of established civil society support that the ECCC enjoyed and was hampered by the absence of mass media resources.[78] Although the ECCC was buffeted by the threat of political interference and suffered from inadequate funding, it has been bolstered by a vibrant and creative civil society which has built upon the communicative work of the trials.

As the ECCC trials proceeded, the presence of the internationalised court and the work it was engaged in gave impetus to civil society initiatives towards social healing and reconciliation in communities. Ryans' study of perceptions of the ECCC included the views of Cambodian NGO workers. The report reveals that the Court's criminal justice process and historical analysis of the Khmer Rouge era had helped to open the minds of people they were working with in communities, deepening their understanding of the past and producing a willingness to explore restorative justice solutions.[79] The view of a commune

---

75 John Braithwaite and Ray Nickson, 'Timing, Truth, Reconciliation, and Justice after War' (2012) 27 *Ohio Journal of Dispute Resolution* 443, 443–444; 456–457.

76 Ibid. p. 475; Susanne Karstedt, 'The Nuremburg Trial and German Society: International Justice and Local Judgement in Post-Conflict Reconstruction' in David A. Blumenthal and Timothy L.H. McCormack (eds.), *The Legacy of Nuremburg: Civilising Influence or Institutionalised Vengeance?* (Martinus Nijhoff Publishers, 2008) pp. 13, 28.

77 Ryan, above n. 45, p. 75.

78 Ciorciari, above n. 10, p. 234.

79 Ryan, above n. 45, p. 75.

chief involved in an NGO reconciliation programme who was interviewed for the study seems to confirm this:

> If we compare before and after, the victims and the perpetrators when they saw each other's faces felt angry, but now they have a better understanding of each other. They have shared their experiences, and see that there were rules and that the perpetrators had to follow orders – [the NGO] gave a space for them to talk … I know things have improved because now when they see each they embrace each other.[80]

NGO initiatives have also had an effect on education in Cambodian schools. In 2009, DC-Cam published a history textbook on the Democratic Kampuchea era and worked with the Ministry of Education to include the work in the history curriculum. With a teachers' guide attached, the work fills a major gap in the education of Cambodian youth about the Khmer Rouge regime.[81]

Even where the ECCC has failed, its presence has fostered communication initiatives and debates on important social issues. The ECCC was criticised for its prosecution strategy and judgments in the area of sexual violence, but the Court's shortcomings in this area galvanised a number of external initiatives which directly assisted victims of sexual violence during the Khmer Rouge.[82] In 2011, the Cambodian Defenders Project and the TPO initiated a series of Womens' Hearings designed to provide a forum for 'women and men' to talk about their experiences of sexual violence under the Khmer Rouge.[83] Between 2012 and 2014, the UN Trust Fund to End Violence Against Women funded the psychological support of civil parties participating in ECCC proceedings and various education programmes designed to improve the ECCC's responsiveness to victims of sexual violence.[84] The initiatives also precipitated engagement with VSS staff, which helped to reshape ECCC policy towards such victims, particularly with respect to reparations guidelines which may be applied in Case 002/02 where sexual violence charges have been laid.[85]

The ECCC failed in its early years to engage directly with communities affected by the crimes. However, it succeeded in making the proceedings of its trials accessible to the Cambodian public and to the national and international media. This flowed from a policy promoting transparency in trial proceedings, contained within the ECCC Law and the Internal Rules. The ECCC Law provided that trials should be open and public except where publicity may prejudice the interests of

---

80 Ibid. pp. 75–76.

81 Ibid. p. 89.

82 Ibid. p. 50; Sin Soworn and Silke Studinsky, 'Tribunal has Failed Victims of Sex Crimes', *Phnom Penh Post* (11 June 2012): http;//www.phnompenhpost.com/national/tribunal-has failed-victims-sex-crimes (accessed 15/4/2016).

83 Ibid. (Ryan) p. 76.

84 Williams, above n. 48, p. 329.

85 Ibid.

justice.[86] The Internal Rules provide that the ECCC's Office of Administration must ensure that the proceedings are publicly broadcast, except where a public hearing would threaten public order or violate protective measures sanctioned by the Court.[87]

As the Duch trial approached, the PAS arranged for public visits to the Court and free public transport to the site. The ECCC has the largest viewing area of all the international transitional courts, including the ICC. The SCSL viewing gallery seated around 20 people. During each day of the Duch trial, the viewing gallery and auditorium attached to the Trial Chamber, which seats up to 500 people, had a near to capacity audience.[88] In 2008, before the Duch trial commenced, the University of California at Berkeley Human Rights Center conducted an independent population-based survey which reported that 39 per cent of respondents in Cambodia had no knowledge of the ECCC. The Survey report indicated that 46 per cent of respondents had limited knowledge of the ECCC.[89] The data seemed to provide impetus to both ECCC and civil society outreach efforts.

The Court's outreach through the visitation programme was expanded to include an ECCC Study Tour. The one-day programme brought students, teachers and villagers to the ECCC from all regions of Cambodia. The guided Tour included visiting the Trial Chamber, the Tuol Sleng Genocide Museum, and the Choeung Ek killing-fields memorial site outside Phnom Penh. The programme was designed to deepen the understanding of the broader population about the Khmer Rouge trials, as well as to ensure that rural dwellers without the same level of access to media coverage of the trials were informed.[90] From the start of Case 001 to the end of 2011, over 100,000 people visited the ECCC either to view the proceedings or as part of the Study Tour.[91] On the day the Duch trial verdict was delivered an estimated 4000 people came to the ECCC. The rate of attendance of Case 002 from November 2011 to July 2013 was even greater.[92] At the very least this suggested that the predominantly Cambodian attendees did not wish to remain remote from the proceedings and increasingly availed themselves of the opportunity to participate as observers of the proceedings.

86 ECCC Law art. 34 *new*.

87 ECCC Internal Rules (Rev. 8) rules 77(6); 79(6)(b).

88 Ciorciari, above n. 10, pp. 240–241.

89 Phuong Pham, Patrick Vinck, Mychelle Balthazard, Hean Sokhom and Eric Stover, *So We Will Never Forget: A Population-Based Survey on Attitudes about Social Reconstruction and the Extraordinary Chambers in the Courts of Cambodia* (University of California, Berkeley, 2008) pp. 36–37.

90 Extraordinary Chambers in the Courts of Cambodia 'ECCC Study Tour': http://www.eccc.gov.kh/en/tags/topic/577.

91 Extraordinary Chambers in the Courts of Cambodia, 'ECCC Surpasses 100,000 Visitors Milestone': http://eccc.gov.kh/en/artcles/eccc-surpasses-100000-visitors-milestone.

92 Ciorciari, above n. 10, p. 241.

In 2010, after the Duch trial, the Berkeley team conducted another population-based survey focused on perceptions of the ECCC. The survey found that overall awareness of the ECCC among respondents had increased. This time, only 25 per cent of respondents indicated they had no knowledge of the ECCC, compared to the 39 per cent of the 2008 survey. There was a similar increase in the number of people who could adequately describe the nature of the Court and correctly name those detained at the ECCC.[93] The increase was attributable at least in part to the ECCC's efforts to make the proceedings accessible to both the media and the public at large through the visitation programme and live video feeds of the proceedings.[94]

However, the accessibility of the proceedings was also enhanced by the use of television to broadcast developments at the Court and make the content of trial proceedings digestible for the wider Cambodian audience. The initiative here was taken by the Asian International Justice Initiative (AIJI), in partnership with a local film production enterprise, Khmer Mekong Films and UC Berkeley's War Studies Center. The joint venture also secured the support of the Cambodian Television Network (CTN) to broadcast the programme as a public service. The programme, entitled 'Duch on Trial,' ran as a weekly series in a talk-show format. The programme included examination of complex trial issues with commentary provided by independent trial monitors. In the 2010 Berkeley survey, nearly 25 per cent of respondents had watched the programme.[95] A new series on Case 002, entitled 'Facing Justice' was produced but due to funding shortages was scaled back.[96]

The picture emerging as the Duch trial proceeded was one of civil society anticipating and creatively supporting the work of the ECCC. NGOs both responded to the Court's shortcomings and built upon its efforts to make the proceedings more accessible to Cambodians. This reflected an implied assumption by the NGOs that the ECCC trial proceedings had significant communicative value within the Cambodian community which perhaps exceeded their expressive value. In the second independent population survey conducted by UC Berkeley after the Duch trial, 75 per cent of respondents believed that the ECCC was 'neutral,' and 77 per cent believed that the trial had been conducted fairly.[97] In addition, 81 per cent saw the ECCC as helping to promote reconciliation and 76 per cent believed the Court would have positive effects for victims and their families.[98] The perceptions contrast with

---

93 Phuong Pham, Patrick Vinck, Mychelle Balthazard, Hean Sokhom, *After the First Trial: A Population-Based Survey on Knowledge and Perception of Justice and the Extraordinary Chambers in the Courts of Cambodia* (University of California, Berkeley, 2011) p. 21 [After the First Trial Survey].

94 Ciorciari, above n. 10, p. 242.

95 After the First Trial Survey, above n. 93, p. 22.

96 Christoph Sperfeldt, 'Broadcasting Justice: Media Outreach at the Khmer Rouge Trials', (June 2014) 15 *Asia Pacific Issues* 6–7.

97 After the First Trial Survey, above n. 93, pp. 26–27.

98 Ibid. p. 29.

the generally poor public opinion of Cambodian national courts. Nonetheless, the Cambodians interviewed for the Ryan study were 'hopeful that the ECCC will have positive effects on the judiciary and legal system in Cambodia.'[99] This suggests that the ECCC is becoming an enabler of individual and collective hope, and perhaps paradoxically, is more in tune with the social purpose of transitional justice than other international courts.

9.6. ASSESSMENT AFTER TWO TRIALS

Apart from the references to the reconciliatory aims of the ECCC in UN resolutions supporting the Court's formation, the ECCC negotiating parties sought expressive retributive justice for the surviving Khmer Rouge leadership and major perpetrators through less costly, expeditious and non-politically contentious proceedings. While the ECCC has moved steadily towards the realisation of its retributive objectives it has had to contend with numerous operational problems. As discussed in Chapter Three, each of the transitional courts described experienced practical problems in their early years and as their work continued. The ICTY, for example, could not secure the arrests of high-level perpetrators for want of cooperation from national and regional authorities. Mistakes in the choice of the applicable law for the Kosovo hybrid panels caused friction with the local population until the necessary adjustments were made by the institution's international representatives. When the ECCC was established, the merging of fragmented Cambodian criminal law and procedure with the necessary principles of international criminal trials produced an innovative body of rules and procedure which raised expectations of unparalleled participatory proceedings. However, the drafters of the ECCC Internal Rules did not make provision for contingencies such as the extensive take up of the civil party action by the Cambodian victim constituency. Nor did the designers of the ECCC make adequate provision for financing the Court or staffing the Victims Unit to provide services to civil party applicants as well as vet applications. This left the Court in the position of resolving such matters as the trials proceeded or, in the case of the disputed civil party applications, by ruling on them collectively at the stage of judgment.

The monumental single indictment of the ECCC's centrepiece case, Case 002, brought a further wave of procedural complexity and delay.[100] Structuring the original indictment into distinct trials or reducing the selection of criminal

---

99 Ryan, above n. 45, p. 83.

100 Sergey Vasiliev, 'Trial Process at the ECCC: the Rise and Fall of the Inquisitorial Paradigm in International Criminal Law?' in Simon M. Meisenberg and Ignaz Stegmiller (eds.) *The Extraordinary Chambers in the Courts of Cambodia: Assessing their Contribution to International Criminal Law* (Asser Press, 2016) pp. 426–27.

policies may have forestalled the need for severance, but instead the Trial Chamber had to decide the best way to split the indictment to expedite the trials for the multiple ageing accused. The severance orders inevitably blurred the topic distinctions between the first mini-trial and the next and embroiled the Chamber and counsel in seemingly endless wrangling and litigation.[101] As discussed further below, this also affected the levels of cordiality between the Judges and the Co-Defence during proceedings. Clearly, like other transitional courts, ideal functionality has eluded the ECCC. Nevertheless, the Court has proved adaptable and capable of innovation in the face of evolving demands. The ECCC's amended civil party participation and reparations scheme is just one illustration of this.

Of major concern to the ECCC's functioning has been the shadow of political interference which has hung over the Court. Case 001 was relatively uncontroversial, but before the end of the trial, media attention switched to coverage of the government's opposition to the investigation of Cases 003 and 004. Nevertheless, the verdict and the SCC's delivery of a life sentence were well covered. In Case 002, there were particular concerns when six senior government officials refused to participate in the case investigation.[102] Despite the assertion of Nuon Chea's Co-Defence counsel that at least one of the officials was crucial to his defence, the Trial Chamber did not call the witness to testify. Case 002/01 ended with Nuon Chea maintaining the Court had violated his fair trial rights, and Khieu Samphân declaring that he had felt pressured to admit guilt, but would leave his fate in the hands of the Chamber.[103] As discussed in Chapters Three and Five, there was resistance by the Cambodian government to widening the prosecutorial net to lower level suspects in Cases 003 and 004. Nuon Chea's Co-Defence counsel argued that the influence of the government over national staff at the ECCC had compromised the impartiality of the ECCC in all three investigations and this had affected Case 002 substantively.[104] A section of the Trial Chamber judgment in Case 002/01 is devoted to addressing various questions raised by the accused as to possible violations of fair trial rights.[105] The Chamber concluded that the alleged procedural defects and 'political interference' had not had tangible effects on the trial proceedings.[106]

---

[101] Ibid. p. 427.

[102] See Case 002/01 Appeal Judgment citing Pre-Trial Chamber Decision on Appeal Against Order on Requests to Summons Witnesses (D314/2/7, 314/1/8) para. 68.

[103] *Co-Prosecutors v Nuon Chea and Khieu Samphân* (Transcript of Trial Proceedings) ECCC No 002/19-09-2007-ECCC/TC, Trial Day 224 (31 October 2013) pp. 31–32; 72–73.

[104] Nuon Chea's Appeal against the Judgment in Case 002/01, 002/19-09-2007-ECCC-SC (29 December 2014) paras. 27–29.

[105] Case 002/01 Trial Judgment 002/19-09-2007/ECCC-TC-E313) Trial Chamber (7 August 2014) paras. 40–78.

[106] *Co-Prosecutors v Nuon Chea and Khieu Samphân* (Judgment) 002/19-09-2007/ECCC/TC (7 August 2014) para. 42 [Case 002/01 Trial Judgment].

In the months following the verdict a form of the rupture defence (discussed in Chapter Five, section 5.2.2.1) continued to play out as the Co-Defence teams appealed their clients' convictions, and Case 002/02 proceedings commenced.[107] The appeals briefs unleashed an arsenal of grievances against the Trial Chamber's management of Case 002/01 proceedings and alleged prejudice to the accused as a result of key defence witnesses not being summonsed.[108] Some trial monitors also considered that fair trial standards were threatened by perceived political machinations to protect witnesses in senior government positions from 'embarrassing testimony' and that there was insufficient response from the Trial Chamber.[109]

It fell to the Supreme Court Chamber (SCC) to determine whether the admission of additional evidence was in the 'interests of justice' in the sense of being 'conducive to ascertainment of the truth' in circumstances where there was a real possibility that the evidence, had it been put before the Trial Chamber, would have led the Chamber to enter a different verdict.[110] The SCC granted certain requests of the Co-Defence to admit additional evidence and scheduled three days of appeal hearings in November 2015. However, those hearings were adjourned without the presentation of legal arguments due to the absence of the international Co-Defence counsel from the hearings.[111] Disruptive tactics by defendants and attacks by defence counsel against the integrity of the court are not new to international criminal proceedings.[112] In due course, the SCC addressed the very serious allegations levelled against the Trial Chamber in the Appeal Judgment which was handed down on 23 November 2016.[113]

In the course of review of all the relevant evidence, the SCC found that the Trial Chamber had made procedural errors in deciding not to call certain witnesses.[114]

---

107 Nuon Chea's Appeal against the Judgment in Case 002/01, 002/19-09-2007-ECCC-SC (29 December 2014); Khieu Samphân's Defence Appeal Brief Against the Judgment in Case 002/01, 002/09-09-2007-ECCC/SC (29 December 2014).

108 Nuon Chea's Appeal Brief paras. 29, 41–53.

109 Ryan above n 45, p. 38; For an earlier report on the Case 003 investigation see Mark Ellis, 'The ECCC-A Failure of Credibility' (International Bar Association, February 2012).

110 ECCC Internal Rules r 104 (1); Case 002/01 Appeal Judgment para. 32.

111 Open Society Justice Initiative, *Recent Developments at the Extraordinary Chambers in the Courts of Cambodia December 2015* (OSJI, December 2015) p. 4.

112 Michael Newton, 'East-West Center's "Well-Reasoned Opinion?" Professor Michael A. Newton Offers Expert Analysis' *Cambodia Tribunal Monitor* (18 February 2016) 2 citing *Prosecutor v Milosevic* ICTY No. IT-02-54; *Prosecutor v Šeselj* ICTY No. IT-03-67; *Prosecutor v Krašjnik* ICTY. No. IT-00-39; *Prosecutor v Karadzic* ICTY No. IT-95-5/18/1; *Prosecutor Barayagwiza* ICTR No. 97-19-T; *Prosecutor v Taylor* SCSL No. SCSL-03-01; And see Marie Guiraud, 'A Well-Reasoned Critique? – Marie Guiraud Responds to East-West Center Report' *Cambodia Tribunal Monitor* (6 January 2016) challenging the Report's assertions on civil party evidence in the Case 002/01 judgment.

113 Nuon Chea and Khieu Samphân (Appeal Judgment) 002/01, 002/19-09-2007-ECCC/SC (23 November 2016) paras. 149, 158, 163.

114 Ibid. paras. 146–149, 156–158, 163.

This included Heng Samrin, formerly the Deputy Division Commander of the CPK Eastern zone and one of the 'few remaining high-ranking individuals with knowledge of the evacuation of Phnom Penh' and CPK policies pertinent to Case 002/01.[115] Where a procedural error was identified, the SCC then determined whether the defence was actually prejudiced by the error taking account of the proceedings as a whole, including action during the appeals phase to initiate investigations, secure specific evidence and hear defence submissions on the evidence as to its decisiveness with respect to the verdict.[116] While the SCC was critical of the judicial majority of the Trial Chamber for their failure to issue a summons to have Heng Samrin testify before the ECCC, on examination of all of the evidence secured, the appeal court concluded that it had not been established that the error resulted in a 'grossly unfair outcome' in the judicial proceedings.[117]

As to the various allegations of violation of fair trial rights, judicial scrutiny by the SCC generally brought their dismissal for lack of substantiation, being unreasonable in the circumstances, or failure to show actual prejudice.[118] Specific allegations of bias on the part of ECCC judicial officers were rejected and the argument that the ECCC's judicial independence was subject to the influence of the national government through the Cambodian judges' membership of the Supreme Council of the Magistracy was found to be 'hypothetical and weak.'[119]

On the other hand, some of the defence challenges to the sufficiency and adequacy of evidence brought the reversal of some Trial Chamber findings. For instance, the SCC found that the evidence relied on with respect to the existence of a CPK policy targeting Khmer Republic soldiers and officials was 'weak', of 'low probative value' or had been called into question by other evidence.[120] Thus, a 'common criminal purpose' in relation to the events at Tuol Po Chrey had not been established. Accordingly, Nuon Chea's and Khieu Samphân's convictions for the crime against humanity of extermination, murder and persecution on political grounds at Tuol Po Chrey under the responsibility doctrine of joint criminal enterprise (JCE) could not stand.[121]

The SCC's interrogation of the Trial Chamber's analytical framework and arguments of the defence also situated the crimes of the Khmer Rouge era within a broader historico-legal landscape. The Trial Chamber judgment encompasses the background to formation of the CPK and the evolution of its policies towards the common purpose of implementing 'rapid socialist revolution' through a 'great leap forward' which included defending 'the Party against internal and

115 Ibid. para. 145.
116 Ibid. para. 164.
117 Ibid. para. 155.
118 Ibid. paras. 110–209.
119 Ibid. paras. 113–119, 126.
120 Ibid. paras. 966–970.
121 Ibid. para. 972.

external enemies, by whatever means necessary.'[122] The Chamber ruled that in furtherance of the common plan, the CPK leadership saw the forced transfers of people from towns to rural areas as a top priority to sustain the revolution through the elimination of capitalist and feudalist classes.[123] The urban evacuations policy built upon the CPK's pre-1975 practice in regional areas. It was based on military, economic and ideological reasons so that the Party leadership could 'better control the people and prevent enemies from destabilising CPK forces.'[124] The forced movements could not be justified by claims of pre-existing food shortages or imminent threat of 'American bombings' as the humanitarian calamity that ensued was a result of the CPK's own actions.[125] The evacuations after April 1975 followed a consistent pattern of people being forcibly removed from towns without concern for their health or well-being. They were also subject to acts of terror and violence when removed to worksites or cooperatives for re-education by hard labour and indoctrination.[126]

In addressing some grounds of appeal, the SCC revisited the CPK policy of forced movement of the Cambodian population within two phases. The Trial Chamber convicted the accused of the crime against humanity of 'other inhumane acts' in the form of the specific criminal practices of forced transfer and attacks against human dignity as well as enforced disappearances (in Phase two only). Nuon Chea challenged his conviction in respect of the crimes of forced transfer and enforced disappearances on the basis that the offences did not exist under customary international law at the relevant time.[127] He submitted further that the Chamber had failed to correctly assess the gravity of the relevant acts as of similar seriousness to the other enumerated crimes against humanity.[128] The SCC's review of the status of the specific crimes in 1975 confirmed that 'enforced disappearances and forced transfer had not yet crystallised into separate categories of crimes against humanity.'[129] However, the Chamber found that the category of crimes against humanity of 'other inhumane acts' was well established and understood in 1975.[130]

In didactic mode, the SCC Judgment examines the crime against humanity of 'other inhumane acts' as a category of crimes with the residual function of preventing opportunities for the avoidance of the laws of humanity.[131] The SCC concluded that the Trial Chamber had erred in evaluating the relevant conduct

122 Case 002/01 Trial Judgment para. 722.
123 Ibid. paras. 777, 788.
124 Ibid. paras. 534, 794.
125 Ibid. para. 634.
126 Ibid. para. 794.
127 Nuon Chea Appeal Brief paras. 409–419.
128 Ibid. paras. 407–408.
129 Case 002/01 Appeal Judgment para. 589.
130 Ibid. para. 578.
131 Ibid.

in relation to the particular elements of the specific offences rather than the elements of the overarching offence of 'other inhumane acts.'[132] Concomitantly, the Chamber considered that restricting the scope of this residual category of crimes would foster consistency with the 'tenets of accessibility and foreseeability deriving from the principle of legality.'[133] Moreover, this was achievable by the interpretation of 'other inhumane acts' through a 'formal international unlawfulness' requirement with the identification of rights and prohibitions in human rights instruments applicable at the relevant time.[134] Adopting this approach, the appeal court proceeded to conduct its own holistic analysis of the Trial Chamber's reasonable findings for each phase of the population movement to determine whether the acts in question were of a nature and gravity similar to other enumerated crimes against humanity.[135] The SCC concluded that the evacuation of more than two million people from Phnom Penh in 1975 was

> legally unjustifiable, violated the right to liberty, the right to security of person, the right to freedom of movement and residence. In its physical circumstances, it infringed the right to freedom from cruel, inhuman or degrading treatment. As such, it caused serious mental and physical suffering and injury and constituted a serious attack against human dignity.[136]

The large number of individuals affected by the evacuation and that some were killed or died as a result of the circumstances is evidence that the criminality of Population Movement Phase 1 was of a nature and gravity similar to other enumerated crimes against humanity.[137] Similarly, during Population Movement Phase 2, involving the transfer of at least 300,000 to 400,000 people, there were killings, and displaced people endured poor conditions due to a lack of food, shelter, medical facilities or suffered serious mental or physical harm. Thus, the SCC held that the evidence established beyond reasonable doubt that the crime against humanity of other inhumane acts was perpetrated under the CPK's population movement policies which were inextricably linked to the common purpose of implementing a socialist revolution.[138] At the same time, the SCC articulated and gave practical effect to international human rights norms within a Cambodian court.

---

[132] Case 002/01 Trial Judgment paras. 547–552 for forced transfer; 640–643 for enforced disappearance.
[133] Case 002/01 Appeal Judgment para. 578.
[134] Ibid. para. 584.
[135] Ibid. para. 590.
[136] Ibid. para. 656.
[137] Ibid.
[138] Ibid. paras. 658–660, 816.

The appeals also invited further doctrinal analysis of the elements of JCE liability. International tribunals have invoked the doctrine with respect to individual criminal liability in circumstances where individuals, with the requisite intent, made a contribution to a common criminal purpose where they were not a direct perpetrator and were removed from the commission of the crime.[139] Nuon Chea argued that he did not have the requisite intent grounding the form of JCE accepted by the ECCC as applicable under international customary law in 1975.[140] He submitted that this form of JCE, known as JCE 1, applied to 'joint contributions to specific criminal conduct with shared criminal intent.'[141] On reviewing relevant post-World War II case authorities afresh the SCC found that criminal liability arises from 'a meeting of minds' in respect of the commission of crime encompassed by the criminal purpose even if the commission is neither 'desired nor certain.'[142] What matters is the acceptance by the members of the JCE of the commission of crime/s 'either as a goal, as an inevitable consequence of the primary purpose or as an eventuality treated with indifference.'[143] While the Trial Chamber erred in referring to crimes that merely 'resulted' from implementation of the common purpose, this had not invalidated the Chamber's judgment. Nor had the Trial Chamber erred in applying the standard of 'significant' contribution to the implementation of the common purpose with respect to the totality of the activities of each of the accused.[144] An accused need not hold a position of authority in order to make a significant contribution. Furthermore, where titles are held merely for symbolic purposes as Khieu Samphân claimed, this will not absolve the accused because they may serve the important purpose of endorsing the criminal policies and 'creating façades' which deceive the community.[145]

As summarised in Chapter 4, section 4.5.4, the Appeal Judgment confirmed the convictions of Nuon Chea and Khieu Samphân on multiple counts and upheld the life sentences imposed by the Trial Chamber. ECCC jurisprudence has contributed to the refinement of international norms and brought further investigation of case authorities cited in support of JCE liability. Yanev's analysis of the ECCC decisions prior to the Appeal Judgment for instance, suggests that

---

139 Ibid. 773 citing Decision on the Appeals Against the Co-Investigating Judges Order on Joint Criminal Enterprise 002/19-09-2007-ECCC/OCIJ/PTC (20 May 2010) para. 53; See also *Tadic* (Appeal Judgment) ICTY It-94-1-A, para. 185 *et seq*; *Brdanin* (Appeal Judgment) ICTY-IT-96-36-A, para. 393 *et seq*; *Brima* (Appeal Judgment) SCSL-2004-16-A, para. 75 *et seq*.

140 Ibid Pre-Trial Chamber Decision on JCE para. 69.

141 Nuon Chea Appeal Brief para. 485.

142 Case 002/01 Appeal Judgment para. 808.

143 Ibid. para 809.

144 Ibid. para. 980.

145 Ibid. para. 1029.

the few cases relied upon 'in support of the existence of JCE III, do not present potent evidence for its formation as international custom.'[146]

The Court's recognition of the significance of the historico-legal record as a medium of both communication and norm development within Cambodia and beyond enhances the institution's legitimacy. Furthermore, the findings of a growing number of ECCC impact studies point to other constructive effects of the ECCC proceedings.[147] Some of the studies take account of procedural justice considerations of concern to all participants of trial proceedings including the victims of crimes. Killean's study of civil party perceptions of the ECCC, for instance, showed that respondents evaluated the Court not only on substantive justice grounds: accountability, reparations and truth, but also on the basis of procedural justice. This encompasses quality of decision-making, and the quality of their interpersonal treatment incorporating respect, voice, representation and the provision of information. Those interviewed 'highlighted their approval at being involved in the Court's work, prized being treated well by the other actors in the proceedings and receiving representation.'[148] While they felt they were not always kept abreast of developments in cases they expressed a strong desire to be kept informed of the Court's progress.[149] Killean found that procedural justice within the internationalised court could both increase victim support for the institution and ensure sufficient representation of victim interests.[150] As discussed in Chapter Seven, a broader notion of justice is appropriate in the transitional context and fairness need not be diminished by the Court's efforts to include representative voices in trial proceedings. Respecting the interests of victims and other participants in transitional trials through procedural justice aligns with the goals of international tribunals and is a factor in assessments of the legitimacy of, and trust in court decisions.[151]

146 Lachezar Yanev, 'The Theory of Joint Criminal Enterprise at the ECCC: A Difficult Relationship' in Simon M. Meisenberg and Ignaz Stegmiller (eds.) *The Extraordinary Chambers in the Courts of Cambodia: Assessing their Contribution to International Criminal Law* (The Hague, Asser Press, 2016) 203 at 253; And see Katrina Gustafson, 'ECCC Tackles JCE' (2010) 8 *Journal of International Criminal Justice* 1324.

147 Pham above n. 87; Pham above n. 93; Nadine Kirchenbauer, Mychelle Balthazard et al, *Victim Participation before the Extraordinary Chambers in the Courts of Cambodia: Baseline Study of the Cambodian Human Rights and Development Association's Civil Party Scheme for Case 002* (ADHOC, January 2013); Ryan above n. 45, pp. 31–72; Rachel Killean, 'Procedural Justice in International Criminal Courts: Assessing Civil Parties' Perceptions of Justice at the Extraordinary Chambers in the Courts of Cambodia' (2016) 16 *International Criminal Law Review* 1–38.

148 Ibid. (Killean) p. 24.

149 Ibid.

150 Ibid. p. 4.

151 Eric Stover, Mychelle Balthazard and K. Alexa Koenig, 'Confronting Duch: Civil Party Participation in Case 001 at the Extraordinary Chambers in the Courts of Cambodia' (2011) 93 *International Review of the Red Cross* 503, 532; Ray Nickson and John Braithwaite, 'Deeper, Broader, Longer Transitional Justice' (2013) 11 *European Journal of Criminology* 445, 454.

Other surveys point to the significance of the historical record produced by the Court for the two trials held to date. An elderly Buddhist monk interviewed for the Ryan study noted that the ECCC had 'contributed a lot to truth and history … because there are a lot of witnesses, and a lot of documents that people can use to write history for survivors, their children and for humanity.'[152] Another interviewee commented on the importance to the public of the wealth of documents that have been made available by the Court to investigate Cambodia's past.[153] Both respondents highlight the importance of the historical record created by the Court to Cambodia's future.

9.7. ECCC LEGACY AND COMMUNICATION

Through the lens of communication at the ECCC a multi-faceted conception of the transitional trial emerges which is not limited to the retributive goal of trials or the expressivism of international criminal justice. Carefully mediated communicative proceedings are more representative and may accommodate a degree of discussion of serious contemporary matters connected with the crimes before the Court. Despite shortcomings in ECCC planning and resourcing, the Court accommodated socially significant dialogue within the framework of prosecution. This has special significance for Cambodia in light of the societal rupture caused by the regime and the national government's policy of 'reconciliation by forgetting'. The extent of post-traumatic stress disorder resulting from the Khmer Rouge regime, for instance, and the complex nature of perpetration had both local and universal resonance.

While the ECCC is a *sui generis* court by virtue of the particular historical and political imperatives affecting its formation, in the Duch trial, with judges attuned to the Court's reconciliatory purpose, the largely inquisitorial trial procedure expanded the trial dialogue beyond limits normally imposed by adversarial procedure. Yet, the magnitude and complexity of international crimes suggest the need for fluidity in procedural approaches in view of the varying potential for threats to fairness and expeditious proceedings. Analysis of the major procedural frameworks as they operate in international courts suggests that there is no ideal model, and that a one-size-fits-all approach may neither yield the necessary efficiencies nor approximate the goals of international criminal justice.[154] Rather, the 'best procedure is the one that is tailored to the court's legal-cultural environment, institutional setting and operational realities.'[155]

152 Ryan, above n. 45, p. 89.
153 Ibid.
154 Vasiliev, above n. 100, p. 431.
155 Ibid. p. 432.

The complexity of the Case 002 indictment and the operational realities faced by the ECCC saw the inquisitorial trial mode modified to a more adversarial form in Case 002/01. However, the scope for hearing the victim voice within the trial, not only as witness, but also as civil claimant, and with those claims heard during the trial proceedings brought more communicative proceedings. Even in the circumstances of a poorly designed admission procedure in Case 001 and modifications to procedure in Case 002, the civil party voice at the ECCC produced more representative proceedings than Mégret conceived, and catalysed broader trial discourse. The civil party presence contributed substantively to the trials and precipitated dialogue around appropriate reparations following in-trial discussion of the consequences of the crimes.

It was also the factor than shifted the proceedings towards restorative justice as the accused in both Case 001 and Case 002/01 were moved to engage directly with the civil parties who addressed them. This may seem unsurprising in Duch's case because he had assumed responsibility for his crimes and generally cooperated with the Court, but in Case 002/01, both Nuon Chea and Khieu Samphân also engaged respectfully with the civil parties. Furthermore, those exchanges occurred during proceedings which were less broadly dialogical following the changes to the examination procedure.

The scope for mediated interaction between victims and accused persons in trials as it operated in ECCC proceedings makes less stark the choice between instituting a truth-telling mechanism which may trade away prosecutions, and a transitional trial. Truth Commissions generally permit more comprehensive coverage of the context of the crimes than trials by their nature allow, and create space for dialogue between victims and perpetrators. However, it should be remembered that truth commissions may carry justice deficits where perpetrators do not come forward in response to offers of amnesty, and governments fail to prosecute those who refused amnesty in exchange for testimony at the relevant commission. Moreover, as we saw in the East Timor case, a truth and friendship commission may be more concerned with securing expressive outcomes than fostering genuine justice dialogue between victims and perpetrators. Trials admitting restorative justice processes may thus bridge what might be viewed as artificial divides in transitional justice theory through communicative trial proceedings.

The validity of a communicative theory of transitional trials finds support in the work of Habermas, Osiel and Mégret and in peace-building literature. The analysis herein suggests that the communicative view of the transitional trial is feasible within the hybrid or internationalised in-country tribunal engaging modified inquisitorial procedure. While the ICC gives voice to the victim of crimes in principle, in reality their voice in adversarial proceedings is constrained by the requirements of factual testimony, and this in turn limits dialogue around their testimony to that which is evidentiary, pursuant to retributory objectives. In addition, the remoteness of ICC proceedings from the subject community limits the immediate communicative impact of the proceedings witnessed *in situ* by the affected victim constituencies. Victims of crimes may also be removed from the direct support of local civil society groups who are invested in ongoing reconciliatory actions. The ICC Victims' Trust Fund provides scope for engagement with issues affecting victims' interests in a broad sense and reparations awards may bring relief to certain communities. However, the separation of reparations hearings from trial proceedings restricts the representative contribution that victims may make to the substantive proceedings and the resultant historical record. Nevertheless, given the breadth of the goals of international tribunals as discussed in Chapter one there is no reason why communicative rationality ought not to operate at the ICC to a greater extent, rather than singular reliance on the expressivism of the Court.

Certainly, the expressive value of accountability subsists at the ECCC, but the Court's communicative legacy may be more enduring. Youk Chhang, director of the Documentation Center of Cambodia, in a newspaper interview, observed that the ECCC had precipitated nationwide reflection on the Khmer Rouge era and 'encouraged a culture of dialogue' within Cambodian society as never before.[156] Others have noted the impact of the ECCC in creating space for unprecedented public debate on the Khmer Rouge regime.[157] Further outcomes include the dilution of generalised guilt assigned to those associated at lower levels with the Khmer Rouge. Faintly echoing the rationale of the Nuremburg tribunal, a Cambodian teacher working in a former Khmer Rouge stronghold interviewed for the Ryan study noted that the Court had

> opened a space for talking, a general political space which wouldn't have existed if it were not for the ECCC. People used to be ashamed, especially the former Khmer Rouge, but now they can speak in public … before it was quietly at night in the dark but now people speak openly in the daytime.[158]

This confirms the importance of the timing of trials and their location in the context of the crimes. The long durée of recovery from mass atrocity will include the acts, conversations and ongoing participation of survivors of past conflict in rebuilding their society. The Cambodian government's policy of co-optation and re-integration of former Khmer Rouge cadres without action to help people in

---

156 K Hodal, 'Khmer Rouge Survivor's Tale Helps Cambodia Confront its Brutal Past', *The Guardian*, 24 January 2012, http://www.the guardian.com/world/2012/jan/24/khmer-rouge-survivor-film-cambodia.

157 Ryan, above n. 45, pp. 76–77.

158 Ibid. p. 77.

communities reconcile means that many victims continue to live in close contact with their former tormentors, and that social relations are often constrained by fear and suspicion. As observed by expert witnesses Chhim Sotheara and Sironi-Guilbaud in the Duch trial, the ECCC trials represent an important step towards justice and reconciliation within Cambodian communities. It is reasonable to conclude that trials that facilitate constructive exchanges within proceedings between victims and perpetrators may foster further processes of social repair. In this, the ECCC has fared well. Viewing the unorthodox ECCC proceedings from the perspective of social dividends through communication strikes a less dissonant note than the often politically riven ambiguities of expressivism.

BIBLIOGRAPHY

BOOKS/ARTICLES/REPORTS

ACQUAVIVA, GUIDO, 'New Paths in International Criminal Justice: The Internal Rules of the Cambodia Extraordinary Chambers' (2008) 6 *Journal of International Criminal Justice* 129.

ADLER, MATTHEW D., 'Expressive Theories of Law: A Sceptical Overview' (2000) 148 *University of Pennsylvania Law Review* 1363.

AKHAVAN, PAYAM, 'Are International Tribunals a Disincentive to Peace? Reconciling Judicial Romanticism with Political Realism' (2009) 31 *Human Rights Quarterly* 62.

AKHAVAN, PAYAM, 'Beyond Impunity: Can International Justice Prevent Future Atrocities?' (2001) 95 *American Journal of International Law* 1.

AKHAVAN, PAYAM, 'Justice in the Hague, Peace in the Former Yugoslavia? A Commentary on the United Nations War Crimes Tribunal' (1998) 20 *Human Rights Quarterly* 737.

AKHAVAN, PAYAM, 'The Rise and Fall, and Rise, of International Criminal Justice' (2013) 11 *Journal of International Criminal Justice* 527.

AKHAVAN, PAYAM, 'The Yugoslav Tribunal at the Crossroads: The Dayton Peace Agreement and Beyond' (1996) 18 *Human Rights Quarterly* 259.

ALVAREZ, JOSÉ E., 'Crimes of States/Crimes of Hate: Lessons from Rwanda' (1999) 24 *Yale Journal of International Law* 365.

AMANN, DIANNE MARIE, 'Group Mentality, Expressivism and Genocide' (2002) 2 *International Criminal Law Review* 93.

AMER, RAMSES, *The General Assembly and the Kampuchean Issue: intervention, regime recognition and the world community 1979–1987*, Uppsala, Department of Peace and Conflict Research, Uppsala University, 1989.

AMNESTY INTERNATIONAL, *Position and Concerns Regarding the Proposed Khmer Rouge Tribunal* (25 April 2003): http://www.refworld.org/docid/3f12fb834.html.

AMOURY COMBS, NANCY, 'From Prosecutorial to Reparatory: A Valuable Post-Conflict Change of Focus' (2015) 36 *Michigan Journal of International Law* 219.

AMOURY COMBS, NANCY, *Guilty Pleas in International Criminal Law* (Stanford University Press, 2007).

ANDERSON, ELIZABETH and RICHARD H. PILDES, 'Expressive Theories of Law: A General Restatement' (1999–2000) 148 *University of Pennsylvania Law Review* 1503.

ANDERSON, KATRINA, 'Gender and Transitional Justice: Turning Reconciliation on its Head: Responding to Sexual Violence under the Khmer Rouge' (2005) 3 *Seattle Journal for Social Justice* 785.

APTEL, CECILE, 'Some Innovations in the Statute of the Special Tribunal for Lebanon' (2007) 5 *Journal of International Criminal Justice* 1107.

Arendt, Hannah, *Eichmann in Jerusalem: Report on the Banality of Evil* (Penguin Books, 1977).

Asian Human Rights Commission, *Cambodia: Civil Society Expresses Concern over Recent Developments in the Extraordinary Chambers in the Courts of Cambodia and Urges the International Community to Speak Out* (AHRC, 20 May 2011).

Asian International Justice Initiative, 'Hearing on Evidence', *KRT Trial Monitor* (Report No. 19, 30 August 2009).

Aukerman, Miriam J., 'Extraordinary Evil, Ordinary Crime: A Framework for Understanding Transitional Justice' (2002) 15 *Harvard Human Rights Journal* 39.

Bair, James P., 'From the Numbers who Died to those who Survived: Victim Participation in the Extraordinary Chambers in the Courts of Cambodia' (2009) 31 *University of Hawaii Law Review* 507.

Bass, Gary, *Stay the Hand of Vengeance: The Politics of War Crimes Tribunals* (Princeton University Press, 2000).

Bassiouni, M. Cherif, 'Accountability for Violations of International Humanitarian Law and Other Serious Violations of Human Rights' in M. Cherif Bassiouni (ed.), *Post-Conflict Justice* (Transnational Publishers, 2002).

Bassiouni, M. Cherif, '*International Recognition of Victims' Rights*' (2006) 6:2 *Human Rights Journal* 203.

Bassiouni, M. Cherif, *Introduction to International Criminal Law* (Transnational Publishers, 2003).

Bassiouni, M. Cherif, 'Post-Conflict Justice in Iraq: An Appraisal of the Iraq Special Tribunal' (2005) 38 *Cornell International Law Journal* 327.

Bassiouni, M. Cherif, 'Searching for Peace and Achieving Justice: The Need for Accountability' (1996) 59(4) *Law & Contemporary Problems* 9.

Bates, Alex, 'Transitional Justice in Cambodia: An Analytical Report' (Atlas Project, October 2010).

Becker, Elizabeth, *When the War was Over: the Voices of Cambodia's Revolution and its People* (Simon & Schuster, 1986).

Bertelman, Hanna, 'International Standards and National Ownership? Judicial Independence in Hybrid Courts: The Extraordinary Chambers in the Courts of Cambodia' (2010) 79 *Nordic Journal of International Law* 341.

Bibas, Stephanos, and William A. Burke-White, 'International Idealism Meets Domestic Criminal Procedure Realism' (2010) 59 *Duke Law Journal* 637.

Boister, Neil and Robert Cryer, *The Tokyo International Military Tribunal: A Reappraisal* (Oxford University Press, 2008).

Bonomy, Iain, 'The Reality of Conducting War Crimes Trial' (2007) 5 *Journal of International Criminal Justice* 348.

Bourdieu, Pierre, 'The Force of Law: Towards a Sociology of the Juridical Field' (1987) 38 *Hastings Law Journal* 805.

Boyle, David, 'The Rights of Victims: Participation, Representation, Protection, Reparation' (2006) 4 *Journal of International Criminal Justice* 307.

Braithwaite John and Ray Nickson, 'Timing, Truth, Reconciliation, and Justice after War' (2012) 27 *Ohio Journal of Dispute Resolution* 443.

Braithwaite, Valerie, 'Collective Hope' in Valerie Braithwaite (ed.), *Hope, Power, and Governance* (2004) 592 *The Annals of the American Academy of Political and Social Science* 6.

BRONITT, SIMON and BERNADETTE MCSHERRY, *The Principles of International Criminal Law*, 3rd ed. (Lawbook Co., 2008).

BROOKS, DUNCAN, 'Cambodia: Year Zero on Trial', *New Internationalist* (21–24 September 2008).

BROOKS, ROSA EHRENREICH, 'The New Imperialism: Violence, Norms, and the "Rule of Law"' (2003) 101 *Michigan Law Review* 2275.

BROOMHALL, BRUCE, *International Justice and the International Criminal Court: Between Sovereignty and the Rule of Law* (Oxford University Press, 2003).

BROWN, MACALISTER and JOSEPH ZASLOFF, Cambodia Confounds the Peacemakers 1979–1998 (Cornell University Press, 1998).

BROWNLIE, IAN, *Principles of Public International Law*, 6th ed. (Oxford University Press, 2003).

BUCKLEY, AARON J., 'The Conflict in Cambodia and Post-Conflict Justice' in M. CHERIF BASSIOUNI (ed.), *Post-Conflict Justice* (Transnational Publishers, 2002) p. 635.

BURCHARD, CHRISTOPH, 'The Nuremburg Trial and its Impact on Germany' (2006) 4 *Journal of International Criminal Justice* 800.

BURDACH, ANDREA and LOUISE CHAPPELL, 'Leaving Behind the Age of Impunity' (2014) 16 *International Feminist Journal of Politics* 543.

BURKE-WHITE, WILLIAM, 'The Domestic Influence of International Criminal Tribunals: The International Criminal Tribunal for the Former Yugoslavia and the Creation of the State Court of Bosnia & Herzegovina' (2008) 46 *Columbia Journal of Transnational Law* 289.

BURKE-WHITE, WILLIAM, 'Preferences Matter: Conversations with Cambodian People on the Prosecution of the Khmer Rouge Leadership' in JAYA RAMJI and BETH VAN SCHAAK (eds.), *Bringing the Khmer Rouge to Justice: Prosecuting Mass Violence before the Cambodian Courts* (Edwin Mellen Press, 2005) p. 97.

BURKE-WHITE, WILLIAM, 'Proactive Complementarity: The International Criminal Court and National Courts in the Rome System of International Justice' (2008) 49 *Harvard International Law Journal* 53.

CADY, JEAN-CHRISTIAN and NICHOLAS BOOTH, 'Internationalized Courts in Kosovo: An UNMIK Perspective' in C. ROMANO, A. NOLLKAEMPER and J. KLEFFNER (eds.), *Internationalized Criminal: Sierra Leone, East Timor and Cambodia* (Oxford University Press, 2004) p. 59.

CARLOS, NINO, *Radical Evil on Trial* (Yale University Press, 1996).

CAMBODIAN CENTER FOR HUMAN RIGHTS, *Severence of Proceedings in Case 002 at the Extraordinary Chambers in the Courts of Cambodia* (CCH, October 2013).

CARNEY, TIMOTHY, 'The Organisation of Power' in KARL D. JACKSON (ed.), *Cambodia 1975–1978: Rendezvous with Death* (Princeton University Press, 1989) p. 79.

CARNEY, TIMOTHY, 'The Unexpected Victory' in KARL D. JACKSON (ed.), *Cambodia 1975–1978: Rendezvous with Death* (Princeton University Press, 1989) p. 13.

CARTWRIGHT, SILVIA, 'International Criminal Trials: A Promise Fulfilled?', *2011 Annual Hawke Lecture*, Adelaide, 9 June 2011. Available at: http://w3.unisa.edu.au/hawkecentre/ahl/2011AHL_Cartwright.pdf.

CARTWRIGHT, SILVIA, 'Opening Speech to the Extraordinary Chambers in the Courts of Cambodia, 7th Plenary Session' (2 February 2010).

CASSESE, ANTONIO, *International Criminal Law*, 2nd ed. (Oxford University Press, 2008).

CASSESE, ANTONIO, *International Criminal Law* (Oxford University Press, 2001).

CASSESE, ANTONIO, 'Reflections on International Criminal Justice' (1998) 61 *Modern Law Review* 1.

CAYLEY, ANDREW T., 'Prosecuting Mass Atrocities at the Extraordinary Chambers in the Courts of Cambodia' (2012) 11 *Washington University Global Studies Law Review* 445.

CENTER FOR SOCIAL DEVELOPMENT, '*Voice of Justice:* Statement of Theary Seng to Pre-Trial Chamber: Nuon Chea's Appeal of Provisional Detention' (8 February 2008).

CHANDA, NAYAN, *Brother Enemy: The War after the War* (Harcourt Brace Jovanovich, 1986).

CHANDLER, DAVID P., *A History of Cambodia* (Westview Press, 2008).

CHANDLER, DAVID P., *Brother Number One: A Political Biography of Pol Pot* (Silkworm Books, 1999).

CHANDLER, DAVID P., *Voices from S-21: Terror and History in Pol Pot's Secret Prison* (University of California Press, 1999).

CHARLESWORTH, HILARY, 'Swimming to Cambodia: Justice and Ritual in Human Rights after Conflict' (2010) 29 *Australian Yearbook of International Law* 1.

CHUNG, CHRISTINE H., 'Victims' Participation at the International Criminal Court: Are Concessions of the Court Clouding the Promise?' (2008) 6 *Northwestern Journal of International Human Rights* 459.

CIORCIARI, JOHN D. and ANNE HEINDEL, *Hybrid Justice: The Extraordinary Chambers in the Courts of Cambodia* (University of Michigan Press, 2014).

CIORCIARI, JOHN D., 'China and the Pol Pot Regime' (2014) 14 *Cold War History* 215.

CIORCIARI, JOHN D. and ANNE HEINDEL, 'Victim Testimony in International and Hybrid Criminal Courts: Narrative Opportunities, Challenges and Fair trial Demands' (2016) 56 *Virginia Journal of International Law* (forthcoming).

CLADIS, MARK S., *A Communitarian Defence of Liberalism: Emile Durkheim and Contemporary Social Theory* (Stanford University Press, 1992).

COALITION ON WOMEN'S HUMAN RIGHTS IN CONFLICT SITUATIONS RWANDA: 'Akayesu Sentencing Victory for Women's Rights': http://www.essex.ac.uk/armedcon/story_id/000054.pdf.

COHEN, DAVID, HYDE, MELANIE, VAN TUYL, PENELOPE and FUNG, STEPHANIE, 'A Well-Reasoned Opinion? Analysis of the First Case against the Alleged Senior Leaders of the Khmer Rouge (Case 002/01)' (East-West Center, 2015).

COHEN, DAVID, 'Hybrid Justice in East Timor, Sierra Leone, and Cambodia: "Lessons Learned" and Prospects for the Future' (2007) 43 *Stanford Journal of International Law* 1.

COHEN, DAVID, 'Indifference and Accountability: the United Nations and the Politics of International Justice in East Timor' *East-West Center Reports No. 9* (East-West Center, Honolulu, 2006).

COHEN, DAVID, 'Intended to Fail: The Trials before the Ad Hoc Human Rights Court in Jakarta' (Occasional Paper, International Center for Transitional Justice, August 2003).

COLITTI, MARIA CARMEN, 'Geographical and Jurisdictional Reach of the International Criminal Court: Gaps in the International Criminal Justice System and A Role for Internationalized Bodies' in CESARE P.R. ROMANO, ANDRE NOLLKAEMPER and JANN K. KLEFFNER (eds.), *Internationalized Criminal Courts and Tribunals: Sierra Leone, East Timor, Kosovo, and Cambodia* (Oxford University Press, 2004) p. 417.

COMMISSION OF TRUTH AND FRIENDSHIP (CTF), *Final Report of the Commission of Truth and Friendship* (7 July 2010).

COOTER, ROBERT D. 'The Theory of Market Modernisation of Law' (1996) 16 *International Review of Law and Economics* 141.

CORMACK, DON, *Killing Fields, Living Fields: An Unfinished Portrait of the Cambodian Church* (OMF International, 2009).

CRUVELLIER, THIERRY, *The Master of Confessions: The Making of a Khmer Rouge Torturer* (Harper Collins, 2014).

CRYER, ROBERT, HÅKAN FRIMAN, DARRYL ROBINSON and ELIZABETH WILMHURST, *An Introduction to International Criminal Law and Procedure* (Cambridge University Press, 2010).

CRYER, ROBERT, *Prosecuting International Crimes: Selectivity and the International Criminal Law Regime* (Cambridge University Press, 2005).

DAMASKA, MIRJAN, *The Faces of Justice and State Authority: A Comparative Approach to Legal Process* (Yale University Press, 1986).

DAMASKA, MIRJAN, 'What is the Point of International Criminal Justice?' (2008) 83 *Chicago-Kent Law Review* 329.

DANIELI, YAEL, 'Reappraising the Nuremburg Trials and Their Legacy: The Role of Victims in International Law' (2005–05) 27 *Cardoza Law Review* 1633.

DANNER, ALISON MARSTEN, and JENNY S. MARTINEZ, 'Guilty Associations: Joint Criminal Enterprise, Command Responsibility and the Development of International Criminal Law' (2005) 93 *California Law Review* 75.

DE BERTODANO, SYLVIA, 'Current Developments in Internationalized Courts' (2003) 1 *Journal of International Criminal Justice* 1.

DE BERTODANO, SYLVIA, 'Current Developments in Internationalized Courts: East Timor Justice Denied' (2004) 2 *Journal of International Criminal Justice* 910.

DECAIGNY, TOM and PAUL DE HERT, 'You Can Change Your Hair Colour, But Not Your Hair: Convergence in Inquisitorial and Adversarial Systems' in C. KELK, F. KOENRAADT and D. SIEGEL (eds.), *Veelzijdige gedachten. Liber amicorum Prof. Chrisje Brants*, Vol 75 Willem Pompe Series (Willem Pompe Institute for Criminal Law, 2013) p. 235.

DEFALCO, RANDLE, 'Case 001 Appeal Judgment: Duch Sentenced to Life', *Cambodia Tribunal Monitor* (February 2012).

DEGUZMAN, MARGARET M., 'Choosing to Prosecute: Expressive Selection at the International Criminal Court' (2011–2012) 33 *Michigan Journal of International Law* 265.

DEGUZMAN, MARGARET M., 'Giving Priority to Sex Crime Prosecutions: The Philosophical Foundations of a Feminist Agenda' (2011) 11 *International Criminal Law Review* 515.

DE HEMPTINNE, JÉRÔME, 'Challenges Raised by Victims' Particaption in the Proceedings of the Special Tribunal for Lebanon' (2010) 8 *Journal of International Criminal Justice* 165.

DE HEMPTINNE, JÉRÔME, 'Victims' Participation in International Criminal Proceedings' in Antonio Cassese, *The Oxford Companion to International Criminal Justice* (2009) 562.

DE LANGIS, THERESA, STRASSER, JUDITH THIDA KIM and SOPHEAP TAING, Like Ghost Changes Body: A Study on the Imnpact of Forced Marriage under the Khmer Rouge Regime (Phnom Penh, Transcultural Psychosocial Organisation, 2014).

DEMBOUR, MARIE-BENEDICTE and EMILY HASLAM, 'Silencing Witnesses? Victim-Witnesses at War Crimes trials (2004) 15 *European Journal International Law* 151.

De Nike, Howard J., John Quigley and Kenneth Robinson, (eds.), *Genocide in Cambodia: Documents from the Trial of Pol Pot and Ieng Sary* (University of Philadelphia Press, 2000).

De Nike, Howard J. 'Reflections of an Anthropologist on the Trial of Pol Pot and Ieng Sary' in Howard J. De Nike, John Quigley and Kenneth J. Robinson (eds.), *Genocide in Cambodia: Documents of the Trial of Pol Pot and Ieng Sary* (2000) p. 19.

Des Forges, Alison and Timothy Longman, 'Legal Responses to Genocide in Rwanda' in Eric Stover and Harvey M. Weinstein (eds.) *My Neighbour, Myself: Justice and Community in the Aftermath of Mass Atrocity* (Cambridge, Cambridge University Press 2004) pp. 49–68.

de Wet, Erika, 'The Governance of Kosovo: Security Council Resolution 1244 and the Establishment and Functioning of EULEX' (2009) 103 *American Journal of International Law* 83.

Dickinson, Laura, 'The Promise of Hybrid Courts' (2003) 97 *American Journal of International Law* 295.

Doak, Jonathan, 'Victims' Rights in Criminal Trials: Prospects for Participation' (2005) 32 *Journal of Law and Society* 294.

Donovan, Daniel Kemper, 'Joint U.N.-Cambodia Efforts to Establish a Khmer Rouge Tribunal' (2003) 44 *Harvard International Law Journal* 551.

Douglas, Mary, *Natural Symbols: Exploration in Cosmology* (Barrie & Rockliff, 1970).

Douglas, Lawrence, *The Memory of Judgment: Making Law and History in the Trials of the Holocaust* (Yale University Press, 2001).

Drumbl, Mark A., *Atrocity Punishment and International Law* (Cambridge University Press, 2007).

Drumbl, Mark A., 'Collective Violence and Individual Punishment: The Criminality of Mass Atrocity' (2004–05) 99 *Northwestern University Law Review* 539.

Duff, Antony, 'Punishment, Communication and Community' in Matt Matravers (ed.), *Punishment and Political Theory* (Hart Publishing, 1999) p. 48.

Duff, Antony, 'Authority and Responsibility in International Law' in Samantha Beeson and John Tasioulas (eds.), *The Philosophy of International Law* (Oxford University Press, 2010) p. 589.

Dugard, John, 'Reconciliation and Justice: the South African Experience' (1998) 9 *Transnational Law & Contemporary Problems* 277.

Dunlop, Nic, *The Lost Executioner: A Story of the Khmer Rouge* (Bloomsbury Publishing, 2005).

Durbach, Andrea and Louise Chappell, 'Leaving Behind the Age of Impunity' (2014) 16 *International Feminist Journal of Politics* 543.

Durkheim, Emile, *The Division of Labor in Society*, George Simpson transl. (Free Press, 1933) p. 80 [transl. of *De la division du travail social* (first published 1893)].

Durkheim, Emile, *Suicide: A Study in Sociology* (Routledge & Kegan, 1897).

Elander, Maria 'The Victim's Address at the Extraordinary Chambers in the Courts of Cambodia' (2013) 7 *International Journal of Transitional Justice* 95.

Ellis, Mark, 'The ECCC – A Failure of Credibility' (International Bar Association, February 2012).

Ellis, Mark, 'Safeguarding Judicial Independence in Mixed Tribunals: Lessons from the ECCC and Best Practices for the Future' (International Bar Association, September 2011).

Etcheson, Craig, *After the Killing Fields: Lessons from the Cambodian Genocide* (Praeger Publishers, 2005).

Etcheson, Craig, 'Fair and Public Trial: A Political History of the Extraordinary Chambers', *Justice Initiatives* (Spring 2006) p. 7.

European Commission for Democracy Through Law (Venice Commission), *Report on the Effectiveness of National Remedies in Respect of Excessive Length of Proceedings* Study No. 316/2004, adopted by the European Commission for Democracy Through Law, 69th Plenary Session, 3 April 2007.

European Parliament, Report on the Proposal for a Council Framework Decision on Combating Certain Forms and Expressions of Racism and Xenophobia by Means of Criminal Law A6-0444/2007 (14 November 2005).

Extraordinary Chambers in the Courts of Cambodia, *ECCC Guide to the First Trial in Case 002* (ECCC, April 2014).

Extraordinary Chambers in the Courts of Cambodia, 'Statement by the Co-Investigating Judges Regarding Case 003' (28 February 2013): http://www.eccc.gov.kh/en/articles/statement-co-investigating-judges-regarding-case-003.

Fawthrop, Tom and Helen Jarvis, *Getting Away with Genocide? Elusive Justice and the Khmer Rouge Tribunal* (UNSW Press, 2005).

Feeley, Malcolm M., *The Process is the Punishment* (Russell Sage Foundation, 1979).

Feinberg, Joel, 'The Expressive Function of Punishment' (1965) 49 *The Monist* 397.

Findlay, Trevor, *The Legacy and Lessons of UNTAC* (Oxford University Press, 1995).

Fletcher, Laurel E., 'Violence and Social Repair: Rethinking the Contribution of Justice to Reconciliation' (2002) 24 *Human Rights Quarterly* 573.

Fletcher, Maria, Robin Lööf and Bill Gilmore, *EU Criminal Law and Justice* (Edward Elgar Publishing, 2008).

Galbraith, Jean, 'The Pace of International Criminal Justice' (2009) 31 *Michigan Journal of International Law* 79.

Garland, David, 'Punishment and Social Solidarity' in J. Simon and R. Sparks, *The Sage Handbook of Punishment and Society* (Sage Publishers, 2013).

Garland, David, *Punishment in Modern Society* (University of Chicago Press, 1990).

Gee, Stephanie, 'What about the Duty to Say the Truth? Duch Lectures his former Subordinate KaSet.com (16 July 2009): http://www.KaSet.com

Geisinger, Alex and Ashley Stein, Michael, 'A Theory of Expressive International Law' (2007) 60 *Vanderbilt Law Review* 77.

Gottesman, Evan, *Cambodia after the Khmer Rouge: Inside the Politics of Nation Building* (Yale University Press, 2003).

Gouri, Haim, 'Facing the Glass Booth' in Geoffrey H. Hartman (ed.), *Holocaust Remembrance: The Shapes of Memory* (Wiley, 1993).

Gustafson, Katrina, 'ECCC Tackles JCE' (2010) 8 *Journal of International Criminal Justice* 1324.

Habermas, Jürgen, *Between Facts and Norms: Contributions to a Discourse Theory of Law and Democracy* (Polity Press, 1996).

Habermas, Jürgen, *The Theory of Communicative Action: Volume 2 Lifeworld and System: A Critique of Functionalist Reason* (Beacon Press, 1987).

HAFNER D, and E. KING, 'Beyond Traditional Notions of Transitional Justice: How Trials, Truth Commissions and other Tools for Accountability Can and Should Work Together' (2007) 30 *Boston College of International & Comparative Law Review* 91.

HALL, JOHN, 'In the Shadow of the Khmer Rouge: The Domestic Trials of Nuon Paet, Chhouk Rin and Sam Bith, and the Search for Judicial Legitimacy in Cambodia' (2006) 20 *Columbia Journal of Asian Law* 235.

HARHOFF, FREDERIK, 'Sense and Sensibility in Sentencing: Taking Stock of International Criminal Punishment' in OLA ENGDAHL and PAL WRANGE (eds.), *Law at war: The Law as it Was and the Law as it Should Be* (Martinus Nijoff Publishers, 2008) p. 121.

HART, HENRY M. JR., 'The Aims of the Criminal Law (1958) 23 *Law and Contemporary Problems* 401.

HEDER, STEVE, 'Hun Sen and Genocide Trials in Cambodia: international impacts, impunity and justice' in JUDY LEDGERWOOD (ed.), *Cambodia Emerges from the Past: Eight Essays* (Southeast Asia Publications, Northern Illinois University, 2002).

HEDER, STEVE, 'Review of the Negotiations Leading to the Establishment of the Personal Jurisdiction of the Extraordinary Chambers in the Courts of Cambodia', *Cambodian Tribunal Monitor* (1 August 2011).

HEDER STEVE, and BRIAN TITTEMORE, *Seven Candidates for Prosecution : Accountability for the Crimes of the Khmer Rouge* (War Crimes Research Office, Washington College of Law, American University, 2001): http://www.wcl.american.edu/warcrimes/KhmerRouge.html.

HIGGONET, ESTELLE R., 'Restructuring Hybrid Courts: Local Empowerment and National Criminal Justice Reform' (2006) 23 *Arizona Journal of International & Comparative Law* 347.

HIMM, SOKREAKSA S., *The Tears of My Soul* (Monarch Books, 2003).

HINTON, ALEXANDER, 'Songs at the Edge of Democratic Kampuchea' in ANNE HANSEN and JUDY LEDGERWOOD, (eds.), *At The Edge of the Forest: Essays on Cambodia, History and Narrative in Honor of David Chandler* (Southeast Asia Program Publications, Cornell University, 2008) p. 71.

HIRST, MEGAN and HOWARD VARNEY, 'Justice Abandoned: an Assessment of the Serious Crimes Process in East Timor' (Occasional Paper Series, International Center for Transitional Justice June, 2005).

HORSINGTON, HELEN, 'The Cambodian Khmer Rouge Tribunal: the Promise of a Hybrid Tribunal' (2004) 5 *Melbourne Journal of International Law* 462.

HOVEN, ELISA, 'Civil Party Participation in Trials of Mass Crimes: A Qualitative Study at the Extraordinary Chambers in the Courts of Cambodia' (2014) 14 *Journal of international Criminal Justice* 81.

HITCHENS, CHRISTOPHER, *The Trial of Henry Kissinger* (Verso, 2001).

HUMAN RIGHTS WATCH, 'Not on the Agenda: the Continuing Failure to Address Accountability in Kosovo Post-March 2004' (May 2006): http://www.hrw.org/reports/2006/05/29/not-agenda.

HUMAN RIGHTS WATCH, *Serious Flaws: Why the UN Should Require Changes to the Draft Khmer Rouge Tribunal Agreement* (April 2003): http://www.hrw.org/reports/2003/04/30/serious-flaws-why-un-general-assembly-should-require-changes-draft-khmer-rouge-tr.

HUMAN RIGHTS WATCH, *Government Interferes in Khmer Rouge Tribunal – Donors Should Recognize How Government Tactics Threaten Entire Process* (5 December 2006): http://hrw.org/english/docs/2006/12/05/cambod14752.html.

HUMPHREY, MICHAEL, 'International Intervention, Justice and national reconciliation: the role of the ICTY, and ICTR in Bosnia and Rwanda' (2003) 2 *Journal of Human Rights* 495.

INTERNATIONAL CENTER FOR THE TRANSITIONAL JUSTICE, *Handbook on the Special Tribunal for Lebanon* (International Center for the Transitional Justice Prosecutions Program): http://www.ictj.org/images/contentt/9/1/914.pdf.

INTERNATIONAL FEDERATION FOR HUMAN RIGHTS (FIDH) 'Cambodia Tribunal Allows Victims of the Khmer Rouge to Participate in Proceedings' (28 March 2008): http://www.fidh.org/spip/php?/article5386.

INTERNATIONAL FEDERATION FOR HUMAN RIGHTS (FIDH), *Five Myths about Victim Participation in ICC Proceedings* (FIDH, December 2014).

IVISON, DUNCAN, 'Justifying Punishment in Intercultural Contexts: Whose Norms?' in MATT MATRAVERS (ed.), *Punishment and Political Theory* (Hart Publishing, 1999) p. 88.

JACKSON, KARL D., 'The Ideology of Total Revolution' in KARL D. JACKSON (ed.), *Cambodia 1975–1978: Rendezvous with Death* (Princeton University Press, 1989) p. 37.

JACKSON, KARL D., 'Intellectual Origins of the Khmer Rouge' in KARL D. JACKSON (ed.), *Cambodia 1975–1978: Rendezvous with Death* (Princeton University Press, 1989) p. 241.

JACKSON, KARL D., 'Introduction: The Khmer Rouge in Context' in KARL D. JACKSON (ed.), *Cambodia 1975–1978: Rendezvous with Death* (Princeton University Press, 1989) p. 3.

JASINI, RUDINA, *Victim Participation and Transitional Justice in Cambodia: The Case of the Extraordinary Chambers in the Courts Cambodia* (Impunity Watch, Research Report, April 2016).

JORDA, CLAUDE and JÉRÔME DE HEMPTINNE, 'The Status and Role of the Victim' in ANTONIO CASSESE, PAOLA GAETA and JOHN R.W.D. JONES (eds.), *The Rome Statute of the International Criminal Court: A Commentary* (Oxford University Press, 2002).

KAHAN, DAN M., 'The Secret Ambition of Deterrence' (1999) 113 *Harvard Law Review* 413.

KAHAN, DAN M., 'What do Alternative Sanctions Mean?' (1996) 63 *University of Chicago Law Review* 635.

KAHAN, DAN M., 'What's Really Wrong with Shaming Sanctions?' (2006) 84 *Texas Law Review* 2075.

KARSTEDT, SUSANNE, 'The Nuremburg Trial and German Society: International Justice and Local Judgement in Post-Conflict Reconstruction' in DAVID A. BLUMENTHAL and TIMOTHY L.H. MCCORMACK (eds.), *The Legacy of Nuremburg: Civilising Influence or Institutionalised Vengeance?* (Martinus Nijhoff Publishers, 2008) p. 13.

KHMER INSTITUTE FOR DEMOCRACY, 'Survey on the Khmer Rouge Regime and the Khmer Rouge Tribunal 2004': http://www.bigpond.com.kh/users/kid/KRG-Tribunal.htm.

KENT, LIA, *The Dynamics of Transitional Justice: International Models and Local Realities in East Timor* (Routledge, 2012).

KIERNAN, BEN, *How Pol Pot Came to Power: Colonialism, Nationalism, and Communism in Cambodia*, 1930–1975, 2nd ed. (Yale University Press, 2004).

KIERNAN, BEN, *The Pol Pot Regime: Race Power and Genocide in Cambodia under the Khmer Rouge* (Yale University Press, 1996).

KILLEAN, RACHEL, 'Procedural Justice in International Criminal Courts: Assessing Civil Parties' Perceptions of Justice at the Extraordinary Chambers in the Courts of Cambodia' (2016) 16 *International Criminal Law Review* 1.

KILPATRICK, RICHARD L., '*Prosecutor v Kaing Guek Eav alias Duch*: In First Round of Proceedings, The Extraordinary Chambers in the Courts of Cambodia Convicts Former Chairman of Khmer Rouge Interrogation Center of Atrocity Crimes' (2011) 19 *Tulane Journal of International & Comparative Law* 669.

KIRCHENBAUER, NADINE ET AL., *Victim Participation before the Extraordinary Chambers in the Courts of Cambodia: Baseline Study of the Cambodian Human Rights and Development Association's Civil Party Scheme for Case 002* (ADHOC, January 2013).

KLEIN, KATHERYN M., 'Bringing the Khmer Rouge to Justice: The Challenges and Risks Facing the Joint Tribunal in Cambodia' (2006) 4 *Northwestern University Journal of International Human Rights* 549.

JULIE KORNFIELD, "ECCC Case 002/01: The Effect off the Hybrid Court in Cambodia' MJIL Online: http://mjilonline.org/eccc-case-002-01-the-effect-of-the-hybrid-court-in-cambodia/ (26 September 2014).

KOSKENNIEMI, MARTTI, 'Between Impunity and Show Trials' (2002) 6 *Max Planck Yearbook of United Nations Law* 1.

KREVOR, TOR, 'International Criminal Law: An Ideology Critique' (2013) 26 *Leiden Journal of International Law* 701.

KWON, O., 'The Challenge of an International Criminal Trial as seen from the Bench' (2007) 5 *Journal of International Criminal Justice* 360.

LAPIE, PIERRE-OLIVIER, 'The Partie Civile in the Criminal Law of France' (1928) 10:1 *Journal of Comparative Legislation and International Law* 33.

LAPLANTE, LISA, 'Outlawing Amnesty: The Return of Criminal Justice in Transitional Justice Schemes' (2009) 49 *Virginia journal of International Law* 915.

LEDERACH, JOHN PAUL, *The Moral Imagination: the Art and Soul of Building Peace* (Oxford University Press, 2005).

LEDGERWOOD, JUDY and JOHN VIJGHEN, 'Decision-Making in Rural Villages' in JUDY LEDGERWOOD (ed.), *Cambodia Emerges from the Past: Eight Essays* (Center for Southeast Asian Studies, Northern Illinois University, 2002) p. 109.

LEDGERWOOD, JUDY, 'Ritual in 1990 Cambodian Political Theatre: New Songs at the Edge of the Forest' in ANNE RUTH HANSEN and JUDY LEDGERWOOD (eds.), *At the Edge of the Forest: Essays on Cambodia, History and Narrative in Honor of David Chandler* (SEAP, Cornell University, 2008) p. 195.

LESSIG, LAWRENCE, 'The Regulation of Social Meaning' (1995) 62 *University of Chicago Law Review* 943.

LIEBERMAN, MICHAEL, 'Salvaging the Remains: The Khmer Rouge Tribunal on Trial' (2005) 186 *Military Law Review* 164.

LINTON, SUZANNAH, 'Cambodia, East Timor and Sierra Leone: Experiments in International Justice' (2001) 12 *Criminal Law Reform* 185.

LINTON, SUZANNAH, 'Putting Things into Perspective: The Realities of Accountability in East Timor, Indonesia and Cambodia' (2005) 3 *Maryland Series in Contemporary Asian Studies* 1.

LINTON, SUZANNAH, *Reconciliation in Cambodia* (Documentation Center of Cambodia, 2004).

LINTON, SUZANNAH, 'Rising From the Ashes: The Creation of a Viable Justice System in East Timor' (2001) 25 *Melbourne Journal of International Law* 122.

LINTON, SUZANNAH, 'Unravelling the First Three Trials at Indonesia's Ad Hoc Court for Human Rights Violations in East Timor' (2004) 17 *Leiden Journal of International Law* 303.

LINTON, SUZANNAH, 'Safeguarding the Independence and Impartiality of the Cambodian Extraordinary Chambers in the Courts of Cambodia' (2006) 4 *Journal of International Criminal Justice* 327.

LINTON, SUZANNAH, 'Unravelling the First Three Trials at Indonesia's Ad Hoc Court for Human Rights Violations in East Timor' (2004) 17 *Leiden Journal of International Law* 303.

LINTON, SUZANNAH and CAITLIN REIGER, 'The Evolving Jurisprudence and Practice of East Timor's Special Panels for Serious Crimes on Admissions of Guilt, Duress and Superior Orders' (2001) 4 *Yearbook of International Humanitarian Law* 16.

LY, SOK KHEANG, *DC-Cam's Education Tours: How do Participants Feel about the ECCC, Justice and Reconciliation*: http://dccam.org/Projects/Living_Documents.htm.

LUBAN, DAVID, 'After the Honeymoon: Reflections on the Current State of International Criminal Justice' (2013) 11 *Journal of International Criminal Justice* 505.

LUBAN, DAVID, *Lawyers and Justice: An Ethical Study* (Princeton University Press, 1988).

LUFTGLASS, SCOTT, 'Crossroads in Cambodia: The United Nation's Responsibility to Withdraw Involvement from the Establishment of a Cambodian Tribunal to Prosecute the Khmer Rouge' (2004) 90 *Virginia Law Review* 893.

LUKES, STEPHEN and ANDREW SCULL (eds.), *Durkheim and the Law* (Robertson, 1983).

MCCARTHY, CONOR, 'Victim Redress and International Criminal Justice: Competing Paradigms or Compatible Forms of Justice' (2012) 10 *Journal of International Criminal Justice* 351.

MACDONALD, LAURA, 'After Two Days of Questionable Witness Testimony, Duch Lectured His Former Subordinate: "Just Tell the Truth"', *Cambodia Tribunal Monitor* (15 July 2009).

MACDONALD, LAURA, 'Duch and Expert Disagree on Khmer Rouge Communication Structure, But Disagree Regarding Responsibility', *Cambodia Tribunal Monitor* (27 May 2009).

MCEVOY, KIERAN, 'Beyond Legalism: Towards a Thicker Understanding of Transitional Justice' (2007) 34 *Journal of Law and Society* 411.

MCEVOY, KIERAN and KIRSTEN MCCONNACHIE, 'Victims and Transitional Justice: Voice, Agency and Blame' (2013) *Social and Legal Studies* 1.

MCGONIGLE LEYH, BRIANNE, *Procedural Justice? Victim Participation in International Criminal Proceedings* (Intersentia, 2011).

MCGREGOR, LORNA, 'International Law as a 'Tiered Process': Transitional Justice at the Local, National and International Level' in KIERAN MCEVOY and LORNA MCGREGOR (eds.), Transitional Justice from Below: Grassroots Activism and the Struggle for Change (Hart Publishing, 2008) p. 3.

MARKS, STEPHEN P., 'Forgetting 'The Policies and Practices of the Past': Impunity in Cambodia' (1994) 18 *Fletcher Forum of World Affairs* 17.

MATRAVERS, MATT, 'Introduction' in MATT MATRAVERS (ed.), *Punishment and Political Theory* (Hart Publishing, 1999) p. 1.

MAY, GERALD V. III , 'An Unlikely Culprit: Examining the U.N.'s Counterproductive Role in the Negotiations over a Khmer Rouge Tribunal' (2004) 27 *Boston College International and Comparative Law Review* 147.

MÉGRET, FRÉDÉRIC, 'Beyond Fairness: Understanding the Determinants of International Criminal Procedure' (2009) 14 *UCLA Journal of International Law and Foreign Affairs* 37.

MÉGRET, FRÉDÉRIC, 'The Case for Collective Reparations before the ICC', Paper presented at McGill University Faculty of Law, 15 November 2012, p. 9. SSRN2176911.

MÉGRET, FRÉDÉRIC, 'In Defence of Hybridity: Towards a Representational Theory of International Criminal Justice' (2005) 38 *Cornell International Law Journal* 725.

MÉGRET, FRÉDÉRIC, 'Practices of Stigmatisation' (2014) 76 *Law and Contemporary Problems* 287.

MÉGRET, FRÉDÉRIC, 'A Special Tribunal for Lebanon: The Council and the Emancipation of International Criminal Justice' (2008) 21 *Leiden Journal of International Law* 485.

MEIJER, ERNESTINE E., 'The Extraordinary Chambers in the Courts of Cambodia for Prosecuting Crimes Committed by the Khmer Rouge: Jurisdiction, Organization, and Procedure of an Internationalized National Tribunal' in CESARE P.R. ROMANO, ANDRE NOLLKAEMPER and JANN KLEFFNER (eds.), *Internationalized Criminal Courts and Tribunals: Sierra Leone, East Timor, Kosovo and Cambodia* (Oxford University Press, 2003) p. 209.

MEISENBERG, SIMON M. and STEGMILLER, IGNAZ (eds.) *The Extraordnary Chambers in the Courts of Cambodia: Assessing their Contribution to International Criminal Law* (Asser Press, 2016).

MINEAR, RICHARD H., *Victors' Justice: The Tokyo War Crimes Trial* (Princeton University Press, 1971).

MINNOW, M., *Between Vengeance and Forgiveness: Facing History after Genocide* (Beacon Press, 1998).

MOFFETT, LUKE, *Justice for Victims before the International Criminal Court* (Routledge, 2014).

MOHAN, MAHDEV, 'The Paradox of Victim-Centrism: Victim participation at the Khmer Rouge Tribunal' (2009) 9 *International Criminal Law Review* 733.

MORRISON, SEAN, 'Extraordinary Language in the Courts of Cambodia: Interpreting the Limiting Language and Personal Jurisdiction of the Cambodian Tribunal' (2008–2009) 37 *Capital University Law Review* 583.

MYDANS, SETH, 'Khmer Rouge Victims Given a Voice in Cambodia Trials', *International Herald Tribune* (16 June 2008).

NEILSON, KATHRYN E., 'They Killed all the Lawyers: Rebuilding the Judicial System in Cambodia' (Occasional Paper No. 16, Centre for Asia Pacific Initiatives, University of Victoria, British Columbia, 1996).

NEWTON, MICHAEL, 'East-West Center's "Well-Reasoned Opinion?" Professor Michael A. Newton Offers Expert Analysis', *Cambodia Tribunal Monitor* (18 February 2016).

NGUYEN, LYMA and SPERFELDT, CHRISTOPH, 'Victim Participation in International Criminal Trials: Ethnic Vietnamese Civil Parties at the Extraordinary Chambers in the Courts of Cambodia' (2014) 14 *Macquarie Law Journal* 97.

NICKSON, RAY and BRAITHWAITE, JOHN, 'Deeper, Broader, Longer Transitional Justice' (2013) 11 *European Journal of Criminology* 445.

O'Connell, Jamie, 'Gambling with the Psyche: Does Prosecuting Human Violators Console their Victims?' (2005) 46 *Harvard International Law Journal* 295.

Office of the United Nations High Commissioner for Human Rights, *Rule-of-Law Tools for Post-Conflict States: Maximising the Legacy of Hybrid Courts* (Office of the United Nations High Commissioner for Human Rights, 2008).

Olsen, Tricia D., Leigh A. Payne and Andrew G. Reiter, 'The Justice Balance: When Transitional Justice Improves Human rights and Democracy' (2010) 32 *Human Rights Quarterly* 980.

O'Neill, Lily and Göran Sluiter, 'The Right to Appeal a Judgment of the Extraordinary Chambers in the Courts of Cambodia' (2009) 10 *Melbourne Journal of International Law* 596.

Open Society Justice Initiative, *The Future of Cases 003/004 at the Extraordinary Chambers in the Courts of Cambodia* (OSJI, October 2012).

Open Society Justice Initiative, *Political Interference at the Extraordinary Chambers in the Courts of Cambodia* (OSJI, July 2010).

Open Society Justice Initiative, Recent Developments at the Extraordinary Chambers in the Courts of Cambodia Update 16 (OSJI, August 2009).

Open Society Justice Initiative, *Recent Developments at the Extraordinary Chambers in the Courts of Cambodia* (OSJI, March 2010).

Open Society Justice Initiative, *Recent Developments at the Extraordinary Chambers in the Courts of Cambodia* (OSJI, June 2011).

Open Society Justice Initiative, *Recent Developments at the Extraordinary Chambers in the Courts of Cambodia* (OSJI, November 2011).

Open Society Justice Initiative, *Recent Developments at the Extraordinary Chambers in the Courts of Cambodia* (OSJI, February 2012).

Open Society Justice Initiative, *Recent Developments at the Extraordinary Chambers in the Courts of Cambodia* (OSJI, March 2015).

Open Society Justice Initiative, *Recent Developments at the Extraordinary Chambers in the Courts of Cambodia* (OSJI, October 2015).

Open Society Justice Initiative, *Recent Developments at the Extraordinary Chambers in the Courts of Cambodia* (OSJI, December 2015).

Orentlicher, Dianne, 'Settling Accounts' (1991) 100 *Yale Law Journal* 2538.

Orentlicher, Dianne, 'Settling Accounts Revisited: Reconciling Global Norms with Local Agency' (2007) 1 *International Journal of Transitional Justice* 10.

Osiel, Mark, *Mass Atrocity, Collective Memory and the Law* (Transnational Publishers, 1997).

Osiel, Mark, 'Why Prosecute? Critics of Punishment of Mass Atrocity' (2000) 22 *Human Rights Quarterly* 118.

Parmentier, Stephan, 'Dealing with International Crimes in Post-war Bosnia: A look through the lens of the affected population' (2012) 9 *European Journal of Criminology* 553.

Parmentier, Stephan and Elmar G.M. Weitekamp, 'Political Crimes and Serious Violations of Human Rights: Towards a Criminology of International Crimes' in Elmar G.M. Weitekamp and Stephan Parmentier (eds.), *Crime and Human Rights* (Elsevier Ltd, 2007).

Pena, Mariana, and Gaelle Carayon, 'Is the ICC Making the Most of Victim Participation?'(2013) 10 *International Journal of International Criminal Justice* 1.

PETIT, ROBERT and AHMED ANEES, 'A Review of the Jurisprudence of the Khmer Rouge Tribunal' (2010) 8 *Northwestern Journal of International Human Rights* 165.

PHAM, J. PETER, 'A Viable Model for International Criminal Justice: The Special Court for Sierra Leone' (2006) 19 *New York International Law Review* 37.

PHAM, PHUONG N., PATRICK VINCK, MYCHELLE BALTHAZARD, HEAN SOKHOM, *After the First Trial: A Population-Based Survey on Knowledge and Perception of Justice and the Extraordinary Chambers in the Courts of Cambodia* (University of California, Berkeley, 2011).

PHAM, PHUONG N., PATRICK VINCK, MYCHELLE BALTHAZARD, HEAN SOKHOM and ERIC STOVER, *So We Will Never Forget: A Population-Based Survey on Attitudes about Social Reconstruction and the Extraordinary Chambers in the Courts of Cambodia* (University of California, Berkeley, 2008).

PHAM, PHUONG N., PATRICK VINCK, MYCHELLE BALTHAZARD, JUDITH STRASSER and CHARIYA OM, 'Victim Participation and the Trial of Duch at the Extraordinary Chambers in the Courts of Cambodia' (2011) 3 *Journal of Human Rights Practice* 264.

PHIM, NAVY, *Reflections of a Khmer Soul* (Wheatmark, 2007).

PONCHAUD, FRANCOIS, *Cambodia: Year Zero* (Holt, Reinhart and Winston of Canada Ltd., 1978).

QUINN, KENNETH, 'Explaining the Terror' in KARL D. JACKSON (ed.), *Cambodia 1975–1978: Rendezvous with Death* (Princeton University Press, 1989) p. 215.

QUINN, KENNETH, The Pattern and Scope of Violence' in KARL D. JACKSON (ed.), *Cambodia 1975–1978: Rendezvous with Death* (Princeton University, 1989) p. 179.

RAAB, DOMINIC, 'Evaluating the ICTY and Its Completion Strategy' (2005) 3 *International Criminal Law* 92.

RAMJI, JAYA, 'Reclaiming Cambodian History: The Case for a Truth Commission' (2000) 24 *Fletcher Forum of World Affairs* 137.

RAMJI-NOGALES, JAYA, 'Designing Bespoke Transitional Justice' (2010–2011) 32 *Michigan Journal of International Law* 26.

RATNER, STEVEN R., JASON ABRAMS and JAMES L. BISCHOFF, *Accountability for Human Rights Atrocities in International Law*, 3rd ed. (Oxford University Press, 2009).

RATNER, STEVEN R., 'Justice for the Khmer Rouge? Sir Ninian Stephen and the United Nations Group of Experts for Cambodia' in TIMOTHY L.H. MCCORMACK and CHERYL SAUNDERS (eds.), *Sir Ninian Stephen: A Tribute* (Melbourne University Publishing, 2007) p. 206.

RATNER, STEVEN R., 'The Cambodian Settlement Agreements' (1993) 87 *American Journal of International Law* 1.

RATNER, STEVEN R., 'New Democracies, Old Atrocities: An Inquiry in International Law' (1999) 87 *Georgetown Law Journal* 707.

RATNER, STEVEN R., 'The Schizophrenias of International Criminal Law' (1998) 33 *Texas International Law Journal* 237.

RATNER, STEVEN R., 'The United Nations Group of Experts for Cambodia' (1999) 93 *American Journal of International Law* 948.

RAUB, LINDSEY, 'Positioning Hybrid tribunals in International Criminal Justice' (2009) 41 *International Law and Politics* 1013.

REDRESS TRUST, *The Participation of Victims in International Criminal Court Proceedings: A Review of the Practice and Consideration of Options for the Future* (London, Redress Trust, October 2012).

Ritzer, George and Douglas J. Goodman, *Sociological Theory*, 6th ed. (McGraw Hill, 2003).

Roht-Arriaza, Naomi, *Impunity and Human Rights in International Law and Practice* (Oxford University Press, 1995).

Roht-Arriaza, Naomi, 'The New Landscape of Transitional Justice' in Naomi Roht-Arriaza and Javier Mariezcurrena (eds.), *Transitional Justice in the Twenty-First Century: Beyond Truth Versus Justice* (Cambridge University Press, 2006) p. 4.

Roht-Arriaza, Naomi, 'Overview' in Naomi Roht-Arriaza (ed.), *Impunity and Human Rights in International Law and Practice* (Oxford University Press,1995) p. 73.

Romano, Cesare P.R., André Nollkaemper and Jann K. Kleffner, (eds.), *Internationalized Criminal Courts and Tribunals: Sierra Leone, East Timor, Kosovo and Cambodia* (Oxford University Press, 2003).

Ryan, Heather and Laura McGrew, *Performance and Perception: the Impact of the Extraordinary Chambers in the Courts of Cambodia* (Open Society Justice Initiative, 2016).

Sadat, Leila Nadya, 'The Nuremburg Paradox' (2010) 58 *American Journal of Comparative Law* 151.

Safferling, Christoph, *International Criminal Procedure* (Oxford University Press, 2012).

Saliba, Michael, 'Civil Parties Boycott Start of Character Witness Testimony while Experts Offer Psychological Assessment of Duch', *Cambodia Tribunal Monitor* (31 August 2009).

Saliba, Michael, 'Civil Party Participation at the ECCC: Overview', *Cambodia Tribunal Monitor* (6 November 2009).

Saliba, Michael, 'Court Allows Challenge to Civil Party Applications', *Cambodia Tribunal Monitor* (26 August 2009).

Sarkin, Jeremy, 'Enhancing the Legitimacy, Status, and Role of the International Criminal Court Globally by Using Transitional Justice or Restorative Justice Strategies' (2012) *Interdisciplinary Journal of Human Rights Law* 84.

Scarf, Michael P., 'Tools for Enforcing International Criminal Justice in the New Millennium: Lessons from the Yugoslavia Tribunal' (1999–2000) 49 *DePaul Law Review* 925.

Schabas, William, 'Cambodia: Was it Really Genocide?' (2001) 23 *Human Rights Quarterly* 470.

Schabas, William, 'The Contribution of the Eichmann Trial' (2013) 26 *Leiden Journal of International Law* 667.

Schabas, William, *An Introduction to the International Criminal Court*, 3rd ed, (Cambridge University Press, 2007).

Schabas, William, 'Should the Khmer Rouge Leaders be Prosecuted for Genocide or Crimes against Humanity?' (2001) 22 *Searching for Truth* (Magazine of the Documentation Center of Cambodia): http://www.dccam.org/Tribunal/Anlaysis/Debate_Genocide.htm.

Schabas, William, *The UN International Tribunals: The Former Yugoslavia, Rwanda and Sierra Leone* (Cambridge University Press, 2006).

Schabas, William A. 'Problems of International Codification: Were the Atrocities in Cambodia and Kosovo Genocide?' (2001) 35 *New England Law Review* 287, 289–293.

Scheffer, David, *All the Missing Souls: A Personal History of the War Crimes Tribunals* (Princeton University Press, 2012).

SCHEFFER, DAVID, 'The Crime of Obedience', *Cambodia Tribunal Monitor* (26 November 2009).

SCHEFFER, DAVID, The Extraordinary Chamber in the Courts of Cambodia' in M. CHERIF BASSIOUNI (ed.), *Introduction to International Criminal Law*, 3rd ed. (Martinus Nijhoff Publishers, 2008).

SCHEFFER, DAVID, 'Genocide and Atrocity Crimes' (2006) 1 *Genocide Studies and Prevention* 229.

SCHEFFER, DAVID, *Memorandum on the Application of International Standards of Due Process by the Extraordinary Chambers in the Courts of Cambodia* (Open Society Justice Initiative, 2006).

SCHEFFER, DAVID, 'Negotiating History of the ECCC's Personal Jurisdiction', *Cambodia Tribunal Monitor* (22 May 2011).

SENG, THEARY, *Daughter of the Killing Fields: Asrei's Story* (Fusion Press, 2005).

SHAWCROSS, WILLIAM, *Sideshow: Kissinger, Nixon and the Destruction of Cambodia* (Andre Deutsch, 1979).

SHAWCROSS, WILLIAM, *The Quality of Mercy: Cambodia, Holocaust and Modern Conscience* (Simon & Schuster, 1984).

SHERMAN, LAWRENCE and HEATHER STRANG, *Restorative Justice: The Evidence* (London Smith Institute, 2007).

SHKLAR, JUDITH, *Legalism: Law, Morals, and Political Trials* (Harvard University Press, 1964).

SHRAGA, DAPHNE, 'The Second Generation UN-Based Tribunals: A Diversity of Mixed Jurisdictions' in CESARE P.R. ROMANO (ed.) *Internationalized Criminal Courts and Tribunals: Sierra Leone, East Timor, Kosovo, and Cambodia* (Oxford University Press, 2004) p. 16.

SIEGEL, RICHARD L., 'Transitional Justice: A Decade of Debate and Experience' (1998) 20 *Human Rights Quarterly* 433.

SHORT, PHILIP, *Pol Pot: the History of a Nightmare* (John Murray, 2004).

SIKKINK, KATHRYN, *The Justice Cascade: How Human Rights Prosecutions are Changing World Politics* (W.W. Norton Co., 2011).

SLOAN, ROBERT D., 'The Expressive Capacity of International Punishment: The Limits of the National Law Analogy and the Potential of International Criminal Law' (2007) 43 *Stanford Journal of International Law* 39.

SLUITHER, GÖRAN, 'Due Process and Criminal Procedure in the Cambodian Extraordinary Chambers' (2006) 4 *Journal of International Criminal Justice* 314.

SLUITHER, GÖRAN ET AL., *International Criminal Procedure: Principles and Rules* (Oxford University Press, 2013).

SLYE, RONALD C., 'The Cambodian Amnesties: Beneficiaries and Temporal Reach of Amnesties for Gross Violation of Human Rights' (2004) 22 *Wisconsin International Law Journal* 1.

SOSNOV, MAYA, 'The Adjudication of Genocide: Gacaca and the Road to Reconciliation in Rwanda' (2008) 36 *Denver Journal of International Law and Policy* 125.

SPERFELDT, CHRISTOPH, 'Broadcasting Justice: Media Outreach at the Khmer Rouge Trials' (June 2014) 15 *Asia Pacific Issues* 6.

SPERFELDT, CHRISTOPH, 'Cambodian Civil Society and the Khmer Rouge Tribunal' (2012) 6 *International Journal of Transitional Justice* 150.

SPERFELDT, CHRISTOPH, 'From the Margins of Internationalised Criminal Justice: Lessons Learned at the Extraordinary Chambers in the Courts of Cambodia' (2013) 11 *Journal of International Criminal Justice* 1111.

SPIGA, VALENTINA, 'No Redress without Justice: Victims and International Criminal Law' (2012) 10 *Journal of International Criminal Justice* 1377.

STAGGS KELSALL, MICHELLE ET AL., *Lessons Learned from the 'Duch' Trial: A Comprehensive Review of the First Case before the Extraordinary Chambers in the Courts of Cambodia* (Asian International Justice Initiative, December 2009).

STAHN, CARSTEN, 'Between Faith and Facts: By What Standards Should We Assess International Criminal Justice?' (2012) 25 *Leiden Journal of International Criminal Justice* 252.

STANTON, GREGORY, 'The Cambodian Genocide and International Law' (Monograph 41, Yale University of South East Asian Studies, 1993).

STANTON, GREGORY, 'The Khmer Rouge did Commit Genocide' (2001) 23 *Searching for Truth* (Magazine of the Documentation Center of Cambodia): http://www.dccam.org/Tribunal/Anlaysis/Debate_Genocide.htm.

STANTON, GREGORY, 'Perfection is the Enemy of Justice: A Response to Amnesty International's Critique of the Draft Agreement between the UN and Cambodia 2003: http://www.genocidewatch.org/images/AboutGenPerfectionIsTheEnemyofJustice.pdf.

STARYGIN, STAN, 'Internal Rules of the Extraordinary Chambers in the Courts of Cambodia: Setting an Example of the Rule of Law by Breaking the Law' (2011) 3 *Journal of Law and Conflict Resolution* 20.

STEINBERG, RICHARD H., *Assessing the Legacy of the ICTY* (Martinus Nijhoff Publishers, 2011).

STEPHEN, CHRISTOPHER, 'International Criminal Law: Wielding the Sword of International Criminal Justice' (2012) 61 *International Criminal Law Quarterly* 55.

STOVER, ERIC, MYCHELLE BALTHAZARD and K. ALEXA KOENIG, 'Confronting Duch: Civil Party Participation in Case 001 at the Extraordinary Chambers in the Courts of Cambodia' (2011) 93 *International Review of the Red Cross* 503.

STOVER, ERIC, *The Witnesses: War Crimes and the Promise of Justice in The Hague* (University of Pennsylvania Press, 2005).

STOVER, ERIC, 'Witnesses and the Promise of Justice in the Hague' in ERIC STOVER and HARVEY M. WEINSTEIN (eds.), *My Neighbour, My Enemy: Justice and Community in the Aftermath of Mass Atrocity* (Cambridge University Press, 2004) p. 104.

SUNSTEIN, CASS R., 'On the Expressive Function of Law' (1995–1996) 144 *University of Pennsylvania Law Review* 2021.

TALLGREN, IMMI, 'The Sense and Sensibility of International Criminal Law' (2002) 13 *European Journal of International Law* 561.

TAYLOR, TELFORD, *Nuremburg and Vietnam: An American Tragedy* (Random House, 1970).

TEITEL, RUTI G., *Transitional Justice* (Oxford University Press, 2000).

TEITEL, RUTI G., 'Transitional Jurisprudence: The Role of the Law in Political Transformation' (1997) 106 *Yale Law Journal* 69.

THAYER, NATE and NIC DUNLOP, 'Duch Confesses', *Far Eastern Economic Review 6 May 1999*: http:natethayer.typepad.com/blog/1999/.

THOMAS, SARAH, 'Civil Party's Repeated Attempts to Address Bench and Poor Management of Proceedings Force Worrying Precedent for Victim Participation', DC-Cam Release (3 July 2008).

TRANSCULTURAL PSYCHOSOCIAL ORGANISATION and UN TRUST FUND TO END VIOLENCE AGAINST WOMEN, *A Study about Victim Participation at the Extraordinary Chambers in the Courts of Cambodia and Gender-Based Violence under the Khmer Rouge Regime* (September 2015).

TRUMBULL, CHARLES P. IV, 'Giving Amnesties a Second Chance' (2007) 25 *Berkeley Journal. International Law* 283.

TRUMBULL, CHARLES P. IV, 'The Victims in Victim Participation in International Criminal Proceedings' (2008) 29 *Michigan Journal of International Law* 778.

TRUTH AND RECONCILIATION COMMISSION, *Report of the Truth and Reconciliation Commission of South Africa* (October 1998) Volume 1.

TURNER, JENIA IONTCHEVA, 'The Expressive Dimension of EU Criminal Law' (2012) 60 *American Journal of Comparative Law* 555.

UNIVERSITY OF CALIFORNIA, BERKELEY, Human Rights Center and International Human Rights Clinic, and Center for Human Rights, UNIVERSITY OF SARAJEVO, 'Justice Accountability and Social Reconstruction: An Interview Study of Bosnian Judges and Prosecutors'(2000) 18 *Berkeley Journal of International Law* 102.

UNIVERSITY OF CALIFORNIA, BERKELEY, Human Rights Center, *The Victims' Court: A Study of 622 Victim Participants at the International Criminal Court* (UC Berkeley, 2015).

VAN DEN WYNGAERT, CHRISTINE, 'Victims before International Criminal Courts: Some Views and Concerns of an ICC Trial Judge' (2011) 44 *Case Western Reserve University Law Review* 475.

VAN SCHAAK, BETH, 'Closing Arguments Part II: Duch Addresses the Court': http://www.intllawgrrls.com/2010/01/closing-arguments-part-ii-duch.html.

VASILIEV, SERGEY, 'Trial Process at the ECCC: the Rise and Fall of the Inquisitorial Paradigm in International Criminal Law?' in SIMON M. MEISENBERG, and IGNAZ STEGMILLER (eds.), *The Extraordinary Chambers in the Courts of Cambodia: Assessing their Contribution to International Criminal Law* (Asser Press, 2016).

VERDIROME, GUGLIELMO, *The UN and Human Rights: Who Guards the Guardian* (Cambridge University Press, 2011).

VICKERY, MICHAEL, *Cambodia 1975–1982* (Allen & Unwin/South End Press, 1984).

VICKERY, MICHAEL, *Kampuchea: Politics, Economy and Society* (Allen & Unwin, 1986).

VOGLER, RICHARD, *A World View of Criminal Justice* (Ashgate, 2005).

VOGLER, RICHARD, 'Making International Criminal Procedure Work: From Theory to Practice' in RALPH HENHAM and MARK FINDLAY (eds.), *Exploring the Boundaries of International Criminal Justice* (Ashgate, 2011).

WALD, PATRICIA, 'Iraq, Cambodia and International Justice' (2006) 21 *American University International Law Review* 541.

WHITING, ALEX, 'International Criminal Prosecutions, Justice Delayed can be Justice Delivered' (2009) 50 *Harvard International Law Journal* 323.

WILDAVSKY, AARON, 'Choosing Preferences by Constructing Institutions: A Cultural Theory of Preference Formation' (1987) 81 *American Political Science Review* 1.

WILLIAMS, SARAH, 'The Cambodian Extraordinary Chambers: A Dangerous Precedent for International Justice? (2004) 53 *International and Comparative Law Quarterly* 227.

WILLIAMS, SARAH, *Hybrid and Internationalised Criminal Tribunals: Selected Jurisdictional Issues* (Hart Publishing, 2012).

Williams, Sarah and Emma Palmer, 'Transformative Reparations for Women and Girls at the Extraordinary Chambers in the Courts of Cambodia' (2016) 10 *International Journal of Transitional Justice* 1.

Yanev, Lachezar, 'The Theory of Joint Criminal Enterprise at the ECCC: A Difficult Relationship' in Simon M. Meisenberg and Ignaz Stegmiller (eds.), *The Extraordinary Chambers in the Courts of Cambodia: Assessing their Contribution to International Criminal Law* (Asser Press, 2016) p. 203.

Zappalà, Salvatore, 'The Rights of Victims v the Rights of the Accused' (2010) 8 *Journal of International Criminal Justice* 137.

Zegveld, Liesbeth, 'Victims' Reparations Claims and International Criminal Courts' (2010) 8 *Journal of International Criminal Justice* 79.

UN RESOLUTIONS AND SELECTED DOCUMENTS

UN RESOLUTIONS

UNGA Resolution affirming the principles of international criminal law recognised by the IMT Charter. UN Doc. A/RES/1/9 (11 December 1946).

UNSC Resolution 827 (1993) establishing the ICTY and approving its Statute. UN Doc. S/RES/827 (25 May 1993).

UNSC Resolution 955 (1994) establishing the ICTR and approving its Statute. UN Doc. S/RES/955 (8 November 1994).

UNGA Resolution 54/171 (1999) recommending Cambodia's acceptance of international justice standards in tribunal negotiation. UN Doc. A/RES/54/171 (17 December 1999).

UNSC Res 1244 (1999) providing a mandate for a transitional administration in Kosovo. UN Doc. S/RES/1244 (10 June 1999).

UNGA Resolution 57/228 (2003) 'Khmer Rouge Trials'. UN Doc. A/RES/57/228 (27 February 2003).

UNGA Resolution 57/228B (2003) adopting the draft ECCC Agreement between the UN and the Cambodian government. UN Doc. A/RES57/228B (22 May 2003).

UNSC Resolution 1315 (2000) requesting the negotiation of an agreement with the Government of Sierra Leone for a special court. UN Doc. S/Res/1315 (14 August 2000).

UNSC Resolution 1644 (2005) requesting negotiations with Government of Lebanon to create a hybrid tribunal. UN Doc. S/2006/176 (21 March 2006).

UNSC Res 1757 (2007) recalling the negotiated STL agreement and deciding that the STL Agreement would enter into force on 10 June 2007 unless prior to that date the Government of Lebanon ratified the Agreement UN Doc S/RES/1757 (30 May 2007).

SELECTED DOCUMENTS

Advisory Services and Technical Cooperation in the Field of Human Rights: Report of the Special Representative of the Secretary-General for Human Rights in Cambodia, Yash Ghai, UN Doc. E/CN.4/2006/110 (24 January 2006).

Basic Principles and Guidelines on the Right to a Remedy and Reparation for Victims of Gross Violations of International Human Rights Law and Serious Violations of International Humanitarian Law (adopted by UN General Assembly Resolution 60/147, 16 December 2005); (2006) 13 IHRR 907.

The Declaration of Basic Principles of Justice for Victims of Crime and Abuse of Power, UN Doc.A/Res/40/34/Annex (29 November 1985).

Ninth Annual Report of the International Tribunal for the Former Yugoslavia for prosecution of Persons Responsible for Serious Violations of International Humanitarian Law Committed in the Territory of the Former Yugoslavia since 1991, UN Doc. S/2002/985 94 (September 2002).

'Principles of International Law Recognised in the Charter of the Nurnberg Tribunal and in the Judgment of the Tribunal, with Commentaries' [Nuremburg Principles] *Yearbook of the International Law Commission* (1950) Volume II.

Report of the Group of Experts for Cambodia established pursuant to General Assembly Resolution 52/135, 18 February 1999, UN Doc. A/53/850-S1999/231 (15 March 1999).

Report of the Secretary-General on the Khmer Rouge Trials. UN Doc. A/57/769 (31 March 2003).

Report of the Secretary-General on the Khmer Rouge Trials, UN Doc. A/59/432 (12 October 2004).

Report of the Special Rapporteur on the Situation of Human Rights in Cambodia, Surya P. Subedi, UN Doc. A/HRC/15/46 (16 September 2010).

Role and Achievements of the Office of the United Nations High Commissioner for Human Rights in Assisting the Government and People of Cambodia in the Promotion and Protection of Human Rights: Report of the Secretary General, UN Doc. A/HRC/4/95 (18 January 2007).

Role and Achievements of the Office of the United Nations High Commissioner for Human Rights in Assisting the Government and People of Cambodia in the Promotion and Protection of Human Rights: Report of the Secretary General, UN Doc. A/HRC/30/30 (22 September 2015).

The Rule of Law and Transitional Justice in Conflict and Post-conflict Societies: Report of the Secretary General, UN Doc. S/2004/616 (23 August 2004).

Situation of Human Rights in Cambodia, Report of the Special Representative of the Secretary-General on Human Rights in Cambodia, Mr. Michael Kirby, UN Doc. E/CN.4/1995/73 (21 February 1994) and Doc. E/CN.4/1995/73 Add.1. (24 February 1994).

Situation on Human Rights in Cambodia: Recommendations of the Special Representative for human rights in Cambodia and the Role of the United Nations Centre for Human Rights in assisting the Government of Cambodia and People of Cambodia in the Promotion of Human Rights, UN Doc. A/49/535 (3 November 1994).

Situation of Human Rights in Cambodia: Report of the Special Representative of the Secretary-General on Human Rights in Cambodia, Mr. Michael Kirby, UN Doc. A/CN.4/1995/87 (24 January 1995).

Situation of Human Rights in Cambodia: Report of the Special Representative of the Secretary-General on Human Rights in Cambodia, Mr. Michael Kirby, Addendum A/CN.4/1995/87 Add.1 (13 February1995).

Situation of Human Rights in Cambodia: Recommendations made by the Special Representative of the Secretary-General for Human Rights in Cambodia on Matters within his Mandate, UN Doc. A/50/681 (26 October 1995).

Situation of Human Rights in Cambodia: Report of the Special Representative, UN Doc. E/CN.4/1996/93 (26 February 1996).

Situation of Human Rights in Rwanda, UN Doc. A/49/508, S/1994/1157 (1994).

Technical Assistance and Capacity-Building: Report of the Special Representative of the Secretary-General for Human Rights in Cambodia, Yash Ghai, UN Doc. A/HRC/7/42 (29 February 2008).

United Nations Development Program. Special Audit of Human resources Management at the Extraordinary Chambers in the Courts of Cambodia, Report No. RCM 0172, (4 June 2007).

MEDIA RELEASES

'As judge resigns UN reiterates need for non-interference in Cambodian Tribunal', *UN News*: http://www.un.org/apps/news/story.asp?NewsID+39997&Cr+Cambodia&Cr1=.

Elizabeth Becker, 'Cambodia Spurns U.N. Plan for Khmer Rouge Tribunal', *New York Times*, 14 March 1998, p. 4.

'Cambodia: Civil Society Expresses Concern over Recent developments in the Extraordinary Chambers in the Courts of Cambodia and Urges the International Community to Speak Out', *Asian Human Rights Commission* (20 May 2011): http://humanrights.asia/new/forwarded-news/AHRC-FPR-025-2011.

Di Certo, 'Judge Decries 003, 004 "Sabotage"', *Phnom Penh Post* (22 March 2012).

Chhang, Youk, 'Sad Situation for Civil Parties', *Phnom Penh Post* (1 October 2009): http://www.phnompenhpost.com/national/sad-situation-civil-parties.

'Compensation to Five Kosovar Albanians for Torture and Unlawful Detention', *Humanitarian Law Center* (30 April 2013): http://hlc-rd.org/?=22889&lang=de.

'Deployment of International Co-investigating Judge', *Extraordinary Chambers in the Courts of Cambodia*: http://www.eccc.gov.kh/sites/default/files/media/ECCC%20PR%2030%20Jul%202012%20En.pdf.

'Decrease of DK tribunal registration fee for foreign layers welcome': http://www.people.com.cn/200705/01/eng20070501_371114.html.

'Dispute Over Lawyers' Fees is Latest Threat to Long-Delayed Khmer Rouge Trial', *VOANews.com* (7 April 2007): http://www.voanews.com/english/news/a-13-2007-03–19-voa19.html.

'The ECCC is Processing Hundreds of Complaints from Khmer Rouge Victims' (11 February 2008), *Khmernews*: http://www.khmernews.wordpress.com/2008/02/11/eccc-release.

'ECCC Review Committee on Internal Rules Concludes Meeting', *Extraordinary Chambers in the Courts of Cambodia* (26 January 2007).

'ECCC Ruling Risks Unrest: PM', *Phnom Penh Post* (8 September 2009): http://phnompenpost.com/index.php/2009090828258/National.

'Ex-Khmer Rouge Leader Weeps at Killing Field', *CBC News* (26 February 2008): http://www.cbc.ca/world/story/2008/02/26/duch-khmer-rouge.html.

'Government Interferes in Khmer Rouge Tribunal – Donors Should Recognize How Government Tactics Threaten Entire Process', *Human Rights Watch* (5 December 2006): http:///hrw.org/english/docs/2006/12/05/cambod14752.html.

'Internal Rules Governing Khmer Rouge Tribunal Reached', *Voice of America* (19 March 2007): http://www.voanews.com/english/news/a-13-2007-04-07-voa11-66547937.html.

'Just a Series of Ghastly Screw-ups', *Phnom Penh Post* (10 August 2009): http://phnompenpost.com/national/just_a_series_of_ghastly_screw_ups.

'Khmer Defense Teams a no Show at Meeting to End Boycott', *Cambodia Daily* (22 October 2014).

Loy, Irwin, 'Resignation Raises Doubts Over the Khmer Rouge Tribunal' (October 2011): http://ipsnews.net/news.asp?idnews+105431.

MacKinnon, Ian, 'Khmer Leader Leads Judges to Killing Fields', *The Guardian* (27 February 2008): http://www.the guardian.com/world/2008/feb/27cambodia.warcrimes.

Mydans, Seth, 'Cambodian Denies He Opposed Trial for Khmer Rouge', *New York Times* (2 January 1999): http://www.nytimes.com/1999/01/02/world/cambodian_denies_he_opposed_trial_for_khmer_rouge.

O'Toole, James, 'Outgoing Consultant Blasts Tribunal Judges', *Phnom Penh Post* (14 June 2011): http:kimedia.wordpress.com/2011/06/14/ki-media-outgoing-consultant-blasts-tribunl-judges-blunk-and-you-benlong.

Neth, Pheaktra and George Wilkins, 'Judges Should Focus on Current KR Suspects: Gov't', *Phnom Penh Post* (12 March 2008): http://www.phnompenhpost.com/national/jusdges_should_focus_on_current__KR_suspects_govt.

Ryan, Rosalind, 'Torture Victims meet Top Khmer Rouge Inquisitor', *The Guardian* (28 February 2008): http://www.theguardian.com/world/2008/feb27/cambodia.

'Secretary-General, United Nations Rejects "Media Speculation" that Judges Received Instructions to Dismiss Case before the Extraordinary Chambers in Courts of Cambodia', *UN News* (14 June 2011): www.un.org/News/Press/docs/2011/sgsm13642.doc.htm.

'32633 Persons Visit the ECCC in 2010', *ECCC*: http://www.eccc.gov.kh/em/articles/32633-person-visited-ECCC-2010.

'UN-Backed Tribunal Processing over 500' Complaints', *UN News Centre* (7 February 2008): http://www.un.org/apps/news/story.asp?NewsID=25544&Cr+cambodia&Cr1.

Wallace, Julia, and Kuch Naren, 'Judge Details "Dysfunction" at Tribunal: Kasper Ansermet describes stonewalling that led to his resignation', *Cambodia Daily* (22 March 2012).

'Wide Ranging Support Secured for the Reparations for Victims of the Khmer Rouge Regime', *Extraordinary Chambers in the Courts of Cambodia, Victim Support Section, Press Release* (21 April 2014).

Wilkins, Georgia, 'Indifference? Impossible' (Interview with ECCC Co-Investigating Judge Marcel Lemonde), *Phnom Penh Post* (19 September 2008): http://www.phnompenhpost.com/index.php/2008091921747/National-news/Indifference-Impossible.html.

INDEX

ABOUT THE AUTHOR

Cheryl White is currently a visiting scholar at the School of Regulation and Global Governance (RegNet) at the Australian National University. She was awarded a PhD in Law from the ANU in 2015 and also holds a Bachelor of Arts and a Bachelor of Laws from the University of New South Wales, as well as a Graduate Diploma in Legal Practice from the University of Technology, Sydney.

She was Director of Continuing Legal Education at the University of New South Wales, Faculty of Law from 1993–1998 where her work included developing culturally sensitive education programmes for professional groups from the Asia Pacific region. She lectured subsequently at the University of Newcastle, School of Law in subjects including contract, consumer protection, international law and the law of employment. Her experience in innovative, cross-cultural education and concern for justice and human rights in peacebuilding processes underpins her interdisciplinary research and teaching.